DEVON RA

THE AREA MANAGER'S DIARY

1986 to 1987

A diary of how the nationalised railway was operated in the 1980s

To the railway staff in the Exeter Area of British Rail from 1983 to 1990 for their professionalism

and Linda for her encouragement.

With thanks to David Hunt, Colin Marsden, David Mitchell, and Roger Penny for their generous photographic contributions.

PREFACE

It is April 1986 and I have been British Rail's area manager at Exeter for three years. It is the longest time I have ever spent in any job so far. Some might think that being sandwiched between unionised staff and unreasonable Headquarters is an uncomfortable position, but it is generally recognised to be a plum posting.

My appointment, aged 32, to a job with almost 1,000 staff and in such a traditional industry, surprised me. Initially, it was necessary to learn my craft, sometimes painfully, but now I feel that there is time to keep a diary of events, with the aim of eventual publication.

There have been many accounts of life with locomotives and careers in the signal box but few of supervision and management. Exceptions include the writings of Gerard Fiennes and R.H.N. Hardy, whose works inspired me as a teenager and led me down the probably erroneous path of joining the railway, following the premature death of my father, instead of following a more fashionable profession.

In preparing the manuscript I have concentrated on faithfully reproducing what my handwritten notes said, even when they cause me embarrassment. A few names have been tactfully edited out, although many (tactlessly?) remain. A few routine events have also been removed, but again many have been retained in an attempt to show the daily management process. Where subsequent experiences have prompted me to comment, additions to the text have been made in italics.

CHAPTER 1: DISASTER AVOIDED

Monday 28th April 1986

Clairvoyance or operator's instinct? As I went to bed the previous night our long haired chinchilla cat was already asleep on the telephone table with his head on the receiver. "It will make him jump if the phone rings at three o'clock," I remarked to my wife, Linda. In the event the call came at 07.00, from my operating assistant Bernard Price. It had been his phone that had rung at 3 a.m.

At 02.45 the Ince & Elton to Truro block fertiliser train had been running along the sea wall between Dawlish and Teignmouth. As it leaned into the bend approaching Teignmouth station, its driver was horrified to see a road coach standing on its nose and blocking the up main line.

Teignmouth box was switched out on night shift so the driver had an anxious journey, showing red headlights, to report the incident at Newton Abbot East. "Obstruction Danger" emergency regulations were applied and the Exeter St. David's duty manager, Howard Davies instituted the call out arrangements. Bernard Price was first and he immediately rang his trusty team of operators. He started with area signalling inspector Derek Old as single line working responsible officer, relief signalman Brian Warren as his pilotman and Matthew Kinsella to open Teignmouth box earlier than scheduled. Matthew was new from the Youth Opportunities Scheme and receiving an early blooding in real railway work. Perhaps a good few cats had been startled in the early hours.

There is a council car park high on the cliff above the railway to the landward side of the track. The coach carrying the Perros-Guirec twin-town visit to Teignmouth had run away and crashed through the fence. At such times railwaymen pause, but briefly, to contemplate the timing of these events. We had been lucky. The first train had been on the down line.

Bernard assessed the situation quickly. Single line working over the down line between Dawlish Warren and Teignmouth was not a major obstacle. Most of the traffic early on a Monday morning was flighted, with down trains until around 05.00 and then a string of up ones, so there were few conflicts. Capacity was perhaps six trains an hour with smart working at each crossover. *(This now seems optimistic. Five would probably be the maximum and probably two in the current age.)* The greatest problem was the limited length of the head-shunt at Teignmouth where trains needed to draw ahead of the trailing crossover road in order to reverse to the down line. The location of the coach made the positioning of the detonators protecting the obstruction a little tighter than was comfortable.

The backlog of down trains was cleared before single line working was implemented from 05.00. This was a basic but elegant piece of operating. If all the trains are on the down line there is no need to provide single line working until an up train arrives. Bernard liaised with control to thin out the service to meet the line capacity available. The first two up local trains were cancelled and Inter City 125s, which were given priority, paid the price of their preferential treatment with additional calls at local stations.

In the meantime steps were being made to clear the line and ensure safe working conditions existed to do so. Howard Davies had been letting his fingers do the walking through his Yellow Pages. "P" was for "Plant Hire", 24 hour plant hire to narrow down the search. Here was the benefit of on call staff who knew the area intimately. Howard described the site and the task. Yes, they could tackle the job. Yes, they could start straight away. And yes, here was the piece of luck all successful operations need. They had a suitable crane standing on Teignmouth Docks.

At 06.15 it was in position. Unbelievably, at 06.30 the line was clear! A 5mph temporary speed restriction was in force until the civil engineer could iron out the kink in the rail that had resulted from the crash landing.

So that is when my telephone rang at 07.00. Many operating teams felt it was their duty to protect their area manager and some area managers even felt a little guilty that they were looked after so well. Bernard was wide awake. I was less so. He thought he had better ring me so that I did not find out about it when I arrived at Dawlish station for my normal train. My bleary mind sorted the unlikely narrative. One thing was clear. This had been a superb piece of railway work carried out by staff with a fierce pride and sense of independence.

A hasty breakfast and a car trip to Teignmouth found me talking to the police at the side of the coach. Then it was time to thank the staff for coming out and the train register book then had to be signed. Neither were routine tasks. Although the first was sincerely meant, it had to be expressed carefully, hoping to avoid sounding glib. Signing the book meant that I had given approval for the correct application of the safety regulations. The engineers arrived in the signal box to remove the temporary speed restriction and my normal train was offered from Newton Abbot East. There is no time in front line railway work to sit and contemplate past events. This incident was over, except for discussions with the council on how to prevent a recurrence. It was still only 07.55 as I joined the driver on my way to the office.

The Western Morning News has been left open on the desk with a letter from Barnstaple M.P. Tony Speller highlighted. His train had been 20minutes late and "it is high time railway operators stopped using 'cows on the line' as an excuse". Populist vote catching will always come before any concern for the morale of the people targeted.

It is too long since I looked in at Exeter Central so I nip up on the 09.38 Exeter-Waterloo. After a quick chat with two members of staff I call in at a nearby jewellery shop. Taunton drivers' depot is to close on 11th May and I intend to present a commemorative plaque to the last driver to sign on duty. It will be the last gasp of a long and proud tradition. There have been rumblings that managers in the past have been so keen to pocket their budgeted savings that they have ignored the passage of history. The danger is that it might be seen as celebrating a funeral but I shall risk it. The cost is £4.50 plus engraving.

Back to St. David's at 10.15 with Richard Westlake, ASLEF branch secretary and county councillor. After a few years here I feel there is some trust on both sides. Richard has opinions on everything in general and railways in particular. *(Was this sentiment indeed reciprocated?)*

10.48 and the third dmu footplate trip of the day, down to Teignmouth with talkative driver Les Stevens. I have to get the family car back. We are on time and all is well. I have some paperwork in the bag to do over a lunchbreak at home. This is most unusual but I have an evening meeting scheduled. In the middle of my meal, my secretary Karin rings. Can I ring the deputy general manager (dgm), Brian Scott, urgently? We are due to meet at 15.15 so I anticipate a change of plan. I cover my tracks by phoning from Dawlish station on the internal system. It is a routine matter about sponsoring Mid-Devon Enterprise to stimulate local industry. We already sponsor Exeter and there are few tangible benefits so the answer is "no". I return home to do the paperwork and then catch the Paignton-Newcastle HST to Exeter in time to meet the dgm and Swindon Provincial Services manager, John Pearse.

Brian Scott is a dour Mancunian who gives little away, his mouth corners twitching slightly at only the more sarcastic jokes. John is able and earnest but we see eye to eye less than anytime in my three years here. I despise the clawback of responsibility from area level to headquarters. His organisation has ceased to consult us and he has put off seeing me four times now. (*Brian Scott was destined to become general manager and then fat cat when he sold out Great Western to FirstGroup. After John Pearse had retired he won the Rail Brain of the Year quiz in 1998)*

We are bound for Barnstaple to meet the Transport Users' Consultative Committee (TUCC), travelling on one of the new

Class 142 "Skippers" briefing Mr Scott on the issues as we go along. *Appendix 1 shows a hand-drawn diagram of the lines of the Exeter Area.* At the Imperial Hotel, John and I attend a special meeting with the TUCC and the North Devon Line Development Group. Unlike many such bodies, the North Devon Group is very positive and supportive. We get on well. They suggest more tourist exploitation of the line, through trains to London and more Sunday trains when resignalling reduces the branch opening costs in the near future. "No Signalman Key Token" is scheduled for introduction which will abolish Eggesford signalbox. The loop will remain, using self restoring points and releasing single line tokens direct to drivers after a telephone call. I reply that the stock for through trains is available only early morning and late evening. In the middle of the day more remunerative work is available. Harsh but true. Robert Wall, the TUCC chairman welcomes the reassurance that the matter is regularly reviewed. He is a Tory Bristol councillor and a very fair minded individual.

The Group is reminded that it promised an expert would provide us with information on walks that could be completed from Barnstaple line stations. There are red faces as they admit they had forgotten. Our plans for a better service after resignalling are unveiled to a row of surprised expressions. Then it is off to a sherry reception at the Civic Centre. Councillor Wall is kind enough to commend me to the council as "progressive". Mr Scott, whom I am now getting to know, fails to hide a sceptical look. Back to the Imperial for a fine dinner. Conversation ranges from feminist politics to the disastrous West Indies cricket tour, and only rarely strays into the realms of the consumer's relationship with the railway.

My policy is to catch the train wherever possible. I enjoy the journey which is always productive, either in paperwork or staff relationships. It also prevents cheap jibes. I am the only passenger on the last up train. Frank Derbyshire is the guard. Last year I gave him an award for extinguishing a fire on a locomotive. He has had 3½ years in Northern Ireland during a nine year stint in the Marines. The squaddies on the late night

Exmouth trains do not worry him. "Get some service in, I tell 'em," he says.

At Exeter I chat to the supervisors, stop for a word on the platform, and generally take care to be seen "out of hours". I turn down the offer of a special Dawlish stop in the empty Waterloo stock which is on the way to Laira. It is important that there should not be separate rules for management. I take the railway car home arriving 00.30. Linda is not interested in what I had to eat.

<u>Tuesday 29th April 1986</u>

After stealing half an hour's lie-in, I drive into Exeter to return the "area manager's" car. Not that I see much of it. The first job is in Yeovil at 10.45 so I take the 09.38 Exeter-Waterloo and arrive precisely on time. The former Southern Railway West of England main line between Sherborne and Axminster has been under my control for only two months having previously, and perversely, been administered by the Westbury area. It had clearly been under-managed. Given the geography and the pressures of the stone traffic at Westbury this was entirely understandable; but I wanted to correct that. There is also a drive to improve performance and I chair a line-of-route committee of Area Managers which reports directly to Gavin Scott the London and the South East Sector "South Western service group manager". Whereas Provincial is clawing back power Gavin Scott is trusting us with advertising budgets as well. All the staff are responding well.

Today's purpose is to walk the triangle of land from Yeovil Jct to a point on the former Great Western line in the Weymouth direction where a supervisor has suggested a spur could be extended from the "Junction". Then we intend to walk along the up line to Yeovil Pen Mill and back to Yeovil Jct. The idea would involve the abandonment of the direct line at the cost of extended journey times by reversing at Yeovil Jct. The benefits would include a range of improved connections across southern England, the possibilities of through trains to and from the South West to Dorchester and Weymouth - and reduced costs to please the accountants. The technical departments are interested in promoting this business-led initiative as there are expensive renewals due, especially at Yeovil Jct.

At the furthest point from shelter, it rains torrentially. Just as it reaches unbearable intensity, it starts to hail. As we begin to dry out the Signal and Telecommunications department opens a discussion on costs. They are talking hundreds of thousands. As for the Pen Mill signalling costs Sid King attacks our potential scheme cost savings by saying Pen Mill signalbox could be closed by installing No Signalman Key Token without diversion of trains to Yeovil Jct. We arrive back from our stroll with dampened spirits in all respects. (*Pen Mill box remains open at the time of writing 27 years later and extensive work at Yeovil Jct has only recently been completed but South West Trains has started to run trains between Yeovil Jct ad Pen Mill*)

I catch the 11.10 Waterloo-Exeter back to the office. As I climb up onto the loco I am greeted by Exeter traction inspector Graham Smith. Graham is a former Exmouth Jct driver and is at home on this road. He is supervising a young traction trainee. Leaving Yeovil 11½min late with four minutes recovery time I judge that an on time arrival is impossible. The run is impressive - spirited acceleration, sharp braking, good station work. One minute late St. David's! As I alight I turn to congratulate the driver, who turns his head in embarrassment.

Brian Scott arrives to discuss the devolution of headquarters' work to area level, with Plymouth area manager Jim Collins, area civil engineer Peter Warren, H.Q. operations officer Ken Shingleton and deputy regional civil engineer David Harris. The scope of the discussion covers train planning, the inspectorate, engineering infrastructure, finance and personnel.

The dgm floats the idea of no headquarters influence beyond Cogload Jct. Surprisingly; no-one thinks that will work. It is possible we were all aware that our jobs would go in such a set up and that anyone of us could have finished up working for one of the others. I genuinely feel that regional headquarters has a role. It should convert policy into action plans and audit the areas' achievement. At present they want to keep hold of the detail as well. That is the job of the area. Four hours later Mr. Scott wants a drink. There is just time to gulp it down before he catches the 19.35 to Bristol. I get home at 20.40.

Wednesday 30th April 1986

There are many important jobs today. Bernard Norman is coming to do the safety audit, there is a Sectional Council meeting *(i.e. with regional staff representatives)* to discuss summer staffing levels, and a parcels presentation to a major customer. Bernard Price has his safety audit information at his fingertips so I am reluctant to steal any of his thunder. John Beer, area customer services manager, is easily capable of handling the second item and Parcels manager Tony Crabtree will be better than me at the third.

So I treat myself to a trip to Barnstaple and Meldon on the civil engineer's inspection saloon. My job is to give the engineers the business perspective to the problems they encounter. One of the first we find is Copplestone platform face. It is a most unattractive station, unfavourably located in the village with the mournful lowing of cows awaiting slaughter in the adjacent abattoir to entertain prospective passengers. Regular users number six per day. Safety work costing £18,000 is necessary. It is the economics of the rural railway. Options include station relocation with County Council help, and the politically unsound possibility of closure. Shortening the platform, possible in this era of Class 142s, would be a major expense in itself. This is one I do need to discuss with John Pearse to get a policy steer. *(The abattoir perished, houses were built and the station now enjoys a much better service.)*

At home I do 1½ hours of paperwork covering tenancies to taxi bills, public complaints and public commendations, level crossings to budgets. 45 items in all.

Thursday 1st May 1986

I catch the early train to ensure a visit the panel signalbox this week. It seemed unlikely that there would be another opportunity and I consider once in a week is below the acceptable minimum for the area manager to be seen there. *(I still awake from recurrent nightmares of being unable to perform sufficient visits)*

Back in the office at 08.30 a former personnel management trainee wants to see me. He has being doing a senior clerical job at the end of his training and he is anxious to take his first management post. There is peer group pressure from contemporaries who have been promoted. His duties require him to relate to the staff and make innovations. There has been no evidence of either so far. When other area managers have contacted me about his applications I have told them this. Today he tells me he wants to make a lateral move to Old Oak Common. I tell him he would be eaten alive. He counters that he would like an interview with the regional personnel manager (rpm) about his prospects. I respond that he will be seeing the rpm - about his performance. Karin tells me that he muttered, "I've blown it now!" as he passed her on the way out.

Accelerated promotional schemes should be rigorous. Only in that way can the industry thrive. To be the best, it is necessary to apply ones-self to the tasks in hand, even if they seem too menial for your talents. David Thear, the deputy rpm, will see my ex-trainee on Friday. He will probably sympathise with him about the ogre he works for, but give him some guidance as well.

At 10.00 Roy Slack, railwayman mayor of Exeter, and still under 40 years of age, arrives with other invited guests for a demonstration Class 142 Skipper run to Kingswear via the Torbay Steam railway. I have also opened the trip to the public but we have sold only ten tickets. It is enough to deflect accusations of joy riding though. A few official guests fail to turn up so I manage to have the fare paying passengers invited to the buffet on the River Dart cruise that has been arranged. Their profuse thanks makes it well worthwhile.

Photo: The Skipper special at Kingswear.
Credit: R. W. Penny

Unfortunately the boat is late back which means our Skipper special will clash with the 15.15 service train from Paignton. I am not pleased and ensure a message is relayed that the 15.15 is to be given priority. This means the staff know it is more important to ensure connections for customers than to get a few VIPs home on time. Arrival back at Exeter is 30min late.

Peter Brown, the new human resources manager in Provincial Services at Swindon, is on the phone. There has been a meeting in Swindon about deployment of the Skippers, even though one was held only two weeks ago in my office. The plans have been altered again. The dgm does not need to look far to find his administrative savings.

Friday 2nd May 1986

It was the intention to have today off and travel back to Yorkshire, where both Linda and I were raised and where our parents live, for the Bank Holiday weekend but it is the only date available to discuss my scheme for reducing the Exmouth branch guards' cover from two to one per train. Up until now an assistant has been employed to issue tickets through the three car trains. The staff are arguing that there is a lot of short distance travel between stations that are close together. In a three car unit they feel one guard cannot do it efficiently. Although tickets are still examined at Exmouth, despite the "open station concept", there is still some evasion. The figures I have obtained show that the only exceptions to one guard on the new two car Skippers should be the two heaviest peak hour trains and the unruly last train, which has staff safety implications.

The weakness of my case is that I am using last October's figures for the new summer timetable. Sunny summer figures might disprove the proposition. Rainy summer ones would be of no use. My personnel assistant, Bernard Brown, says that Swindon H.Q. feels we will not be successful. More admin savings to be had there? The strengths of our case are that some trains are now semi-fast, they are shorter and the increased Skipper frequency will cause peak loads to be spread.

Chairman of the staff side is the formidable Chester Long; prominent in local politics he is both feared and respected by the people he represents. He has contacts everywhere and Swindon H.Q. officers bend over backwards to accommodate him. He asks how many guards we were thinking of saving. This is not the opening we anticipated. He says the guards' LDC (Local Departmental Committee), appointed from the staff and released as representatives as required) has prepared suitable rosters that save seven turns. This is more than hopeful. Next they accept that the semi-fasts do not need assistance so we have at least created a precedent there. They accept the scheme for immediate implementation with a review in October. In addition, an awkward Wednesday and

Friday Only freight job has been accommodated in the links the staff have worked out. (*Sectorisation and privatisation stopped this kind of economy being achieved.*) It is money in the bank and a huge chunk of my budget savings for 1986/7 achieved. What is more it has been achieved through truly constructive consultation.

There is time to clear the desk before setting off to Yorkshire where I have Best Man duties to perform for Bryan Wilkinson, my best friend since childhood. There is a choice of how to get there: 14.17 to Waterloo, 14.04 to Paddington, (both Class 50s) or the 14.40 HST to Paddington. All are worked by Exeter drivers and all mean cab rides. I could go direct via Bristol but that would be a bit tame. I select the 14.04 with driver Albert Watts who does a nice line in sugared almonds. He has 12 vacuum braked Mark 1s and No.50037 Illustrious. We are 6½min late away with a load that exceeds the timing allowance. Albert says the loco is not very responsive but we are still in with a chance as we approach Reading. As usual the station is congested and we are held for the Ultrasonic test train to run into the yard. 3½min late away, 4 minutes recovery time to come and no temporary speed restrictions in force; Albert has the target in his sights. Having taken 6min 3sec to pass Twyford we have the lumbering load on the move and run the 24½mile stretch from Maidenhead to Ealing Broadway at an average speed of 90.3mph. The Paddington arrival is ½min early. As we glide to a stand Albert turns and gives me a grin.

I collect my belongings and head for St. Pancras. It is years since I managed to travel this line. It's an executive service via Nottingham and all is well until a delay at Bradway tunnel that causes a 6min late arrival in Sheffield. No. 45103 is on the 17.09 relief to Leeds where we arrive 8½min early. There is another Class 45 on the Scarborough Holyhead. The rumour is that they are being removed from passenger diagrams in May, so I'm not doing badly. The 21.56 arrival in Huddersfield on this roundabout trip has cost me 1hr 45min.

*Photo: While the area manager was away for the weekend No. 31406 became involved in this derailment at Aller Jct., Newton Abbot.
Credit: R. W. Penny*

CHAPTER 2: A REFUSAL MAY CAUSE OFFENCE

Monday 5th May 1986

My mother's 63rd birthday today but I've had the Bank Holiday off so need to get back to Exeter to see what has been happening. The journey via Manchester and an HST is punctual except for the final leg with a Plymouth guard on the 'Skipper' *(Class 142).* The doors prove too much for him at Exeter and on arrival at Dawlish, one was unnecessarily isolated.

Tuesday 6th May 1986

Just missed the early train to work which had been delayed by brake trouble. The subsequent pathing problems cause my train to arrive 4min late at Exeter. The phone was ringing as I opened the office door. It was Ken Shingleton, former divisional manager at Reading and now Operations Officer at H.Q. He wanted to know if I'd heard that the 05.48 Exeter-Waterloo, powered by a Class 33, had failed at Chard where it had been overtaken by the 06.43 from Exeter. *(Ken had been brought up on a farm at Milborne Port and had a special interest in the old 'Southern'.)* The week had started badly but there was worse to come.

A ballast train had derailed at Newton Abbot on Sunday. The subsequent single line working had not been to Bernard Price's satisfaction and it had not been cleared up until 11.00 yesterday. *(Reading my notes now I feel guilty at not having been told about this, but Bernard would not have wanted to have spoilt my weekend.)* The cause was clear. The train was passing over unclipped trailing points in the wrong direction, and they had moved. A derailment was predictable but it was unusual to see Bernard scratching his head over a rules question as no one could find a clause in the Rule Book that said they should have been clipped in these special circumstances.

At 10.30, the phone rang. It was David Thear, employee relations manager at Swindon to say he had appointed my personnel assistant on a lateral move to Plymouth. Was this the first step in the disintegration of the area in favour of Plymouth? I was very annoyed, but mainly with myself. If I'd made Bernard Brown move home from Plymouth when I appointed him, he would not have been moving back now. It was all very civilised. I wished Bernard well and he said how much he had enjoyed working at Exeter. The arrangement was that Bernard could stay as long as I needed him. I phoned Plymouth Area Manager Jim Collins and told him he could have Bernard a week on Monday. Bernard Brown was surprised; Jim, too. I wanted to make it a clean break and send out the message that no one was indispensable. It was probable that Clarence Woodbury, Bernard's deputy and head of paybills & rosters would either get the job or sit in for a while. He might as well start straight away.

11.00 saw me in the cab of the 08.45 from Paddington with Exeter Driver Ireland *(probably Colin and not Dennis, but my notes do not specify)* on my way to a Royal Train planning meeting at Plymouth. We caught up the preceding local at Dawlish Warren and Teignmouth, then there was a relaying slack at Marley so a late arrival was inevitable. I was surprised how quickly speed rose from 55mph to 75mph on Hemerdon bank before the brakes were applied.

I had been told that the royal visit of Prince Charles was an official one and so I was prepared to come in during my booked holiday, but it transpired that it was a private 'Duchy' visit, alighting at Totnes on the third day of his trip so it began to look like an uninterrupted holiday.

Back to Exeter on the 15.08 Plymouth-York, 2min early and into our weekly informal management meeting. It was routine stuff but binds the team together. Some areas have a meeting every day but that inhibits the ability to get out on the patch. The main point of interest to me was area customer services manager John Beer's comments on steps being taken to improve uniform standards in travel centres.

Linda had been shopping in Exeter and arrived in the office at 17.00 so we took the opportunity of a trip out, catching the 17.11 HST to Totnes for a walk round the narrow streets and a quick drink at the Seven Stars. The main news at the station was that there was a vacancy. Sally the station cat of four years' standing had fallen victim to a road accident and had been buried in the station garden. The good news was that this opportunity had been taken to re-stock the pond with goldfish. A few more out-of-hours visits while changing at Newton Abbot and back into Dawlish at 20.15.

Wednesday 7th May 1986

One of those days that seem to consist of a lot of paperwork but, at the end of the day, there seems to be more than when I started. Much of the time was involved with the arrangements for the visit by the BRB director of operations tomorrow and the opening of Tiverton Parkway station. I have insisted that a Class 118 dmu is used for the special as the new Class 142s are still not passed to use Hele level crossing without being hand-signalled due to doubts about their tripping the treadles for the auto-half barriers. That might be hard to explain to the Minister of Transport on board; others would not like him to get the impression we had 'Skippers' to spare. There has been some backlash from H.Q. but they have been told I will alter my decision only if instructed by the general manager personally.

Regional operating manager Bob Poynter *(my immediate line manager)* is back from Crete . Recently we have had two trains pass signals at danger with drivers who were either learning the road or refreshing the road in the driving seat. I thought I might get away with written warnings for the Exeter drivers who had allowed them to take charge. The over-runs were quite small but there is a million miles between being one yard in rear of a stop signal and one yard in advance of it. The boss is pushing for 'Form 1' formal discipline and recordable punishments. The supervising drivers will probably be reprimanded and the 'learners' given a written warning. The logic is that the booked driver is in charge of his train –

regardless. A point of principle is involved but the corollary might be longer route learning times and a reluctance of drivers to allow their colleagues to learn from handling the train.

At 15.00, I experienced a 'first'. Two ladies from Lympstone handed in a 200-signature petition saying that the 'Skippers' are difficult to board with prams and that the gaps between the platform and the train are too large. Guards are unhelpful, trap people in the new automatic doors and charge inconsistent fares. On top of this, drivers are over-running platforms. All this is pretty desperate. *(I was relieved to read this last sentence in the original manuscript as it was what I was beginning to think now.)* Perhaps the guards are playing difficult when supervisors are not around? My plans to reduce coverage will not help. I will need to mount a campaign to achieve an improvement. All-in-all the presenters of the petition are quite reasonable and agree to my proposition that they should contact me in three months if the situation remains unsatisfactory.

I note that my personnel trainee has still not been to see me, or withdrawn his application for Old Oak Common, but decide to let it ride for a while.

At home, I spend an hour amending my working timetable, which I pride on keeping up-to-date *(probably the only one on the area)*.

Thursday 8th May 1986

In to work on the 07.08 train to clear the paperwork. The local staff at Dawlish are starting to play awkward about chasing people for their parking fee *(very few are rail users)*. The new senior railman started to get the bit between his teeth during our discussion, playing up to an audience of two permanent rail staff. It is time to appear tough. I told him that I refused to take evasion as an accepted fact. No, it was not a matter for the LDC (local staff representative meetings) because it was an existing duty. If they did not co-operate, I would put in Pay & Display and review the remaining staff workload as a result.

Unusually, we hold a local management meeting about the two VIP specials today and one on Monday, the Royal Train, re-signalling at Taunton, closure of Taunton drivers' depot and a host of minor problems. Just as I said something would go wrong, I found out that it already had done. The night turn shunters had flattened the wheels on the Inspection Saloon due to be attached to the 09.38 to Waterloo and return with the BRB director of operations, Bob Poynter and his Southern Region opposite number, Alec Bath on the 15.10 down. On top of this, the night turn supervisor, a management trainee in his first appointment, had failed to have the train properly marshalled. The train made a 22min late start through mismanagement and it was reported that the official party would be riding in a normal coach.

Home for a bite of lunch on the 09.05 HST from Paddington with driver Mick Lockyer with whom I have now ridden many times. This was my fourth fastest run to Dawlish with speeds no more than 2mph over the top, achieved by fast acceleration and hard braking. He had been the driver who had discovered the bus on the line a week last Monday. When he had first seen it, he thought that someone must know about it but when he saw no lights around, he realised it was a real emergency and reacted appropriately.

Back at work. It had been miraculously divined that Class 142s could now work over Hele level crossing with perfect safety, Ken Shingleton saying he would send out a new authority. So it was all change again but at least the special's timings would be more realistic.

The paperwork is now mounting up but I have to catch the 14.17 to Salisbury to meet the special party on the 15.10. I decide to ride on the loco with the Exeter driver.

"No, you can't come on the footplate," is the response to my routine and almost casual courtesy request while showing my pass. And he's not joking. I have to think quickly. I have the right to insist, in line of promotion, with the proper pass, but this is probably the time for a little discretion.

"What's the problem?" I ask.

The driver dismounts his Class 50.

"Did you apologise to an invalid at Teignmouth?"

My memory stirs up an incident last year. I don't think I did apologise but a lot has happened since then. I do remember that the incident was not handled well and I remember being quoted in the press that an assistant fare collector had been provoked into swearing at the man. On the tip of my tongue is a remark that it is none of his business but before I decide whether to say it, he continues.

"Because if you did I don't want anything to do with you."

Now, this is a red rag being waved at a bull. He cannot decide who he wants to manage him and I will decide what he has to do with me. But I need to restrain my natural inclination to lower my horns and charge. Think hard. There are only 3min to the departure time of an important train. One word out of place and he might claim he is too upset to drive. Might he even consider doing something deliberately stupid and blaming our discussion? If I relieve him of his duties, will the train crew supervisor have a replacement? Is it worth disrupting the line for the rest of the day? Has he been drinking? Is he fit to drive?

"I'm not going to say anything here and now, just before you drive a train. We'll have a chat at Salisbury if you like?" I offer. This is a risk strategy as the driver might still be affected for his back working.

The 'too upset to listen syndrome' is evidenced in his reply.

"Tell you what, I've time at Salisbury if you have." The driver says.

"Yes," I accept, and we part.

I've been refused access to the cab only once before, on the reasonable grounds of road learners being there. Was it the same driver? I don't think so. If it was, is there some reason he dislikes having management accompany him?

Sitting in the train, I feel to have had my feathers ruffled and settle to writing a couple of memos to the Area Manager's Conference. The first is one about Inquiry and disciplinary procedures that Ken Shingleton has asked me to write and the other is a bee in my bonnet about re-gradings granted by HQ officers without reference to the budget.

The incident with the driver is typical of managing in the South West. Something like this in Yorkshire would have been aired immediately and forgotten within a couple of days. The driver and I meet half way along the platform at Salisbury and the reason for his reaction is soon apparent. The assistant fare collector in question was the driver's brother, although he insists he would have felt the same whoever was involved. Strictly speaking, I shouldn't discuss the disciplinary matter, even with the brother of the person involved, but if I refuse we will get nowhere.

I make two immediate points. I am not answerable to him for my policy and it is part of my duty to ride in the cab, on my area, or with my drivers. I am not 'asking' to ride with him but I did not wish to insist in the circumstances.

It is somewhat surprising when the driver says he agrees with me. I explain that a passenger who is sworn at deserves an apology, he received no refund, as an invalid there was no question of prosecuting him on public relations grounds, and that the last sentence of the reply to him was a warning that he must always be in possession of a valid ticket when travelling by train. The driver admits he must have been wrongly informed and seems satisfied. Still, it is worrying that this has been 'bubbling under' for such a long time.

I subsequently made a point to ride with this driver from Exeter to Taunton, ensuring the supervisor could cover the turn if I met with a similar reaction but the driver made me feel welcome even dusting down the secondman's seat with a flap of his newspaper.

I board the 15.10 and join the special party, Maurice Holmes, director of operations at the BRB, Bob Poynter, Alec Bath, who has just been appointed deputy to Mr Holmes, and Bob Poynter's safety assistant Bernard Norman. My first job is to apologise for the ineptitude of the shunters *(and their managers perhaps?)* who have robbed them of their inspection saloon. From that point until after dinner in their hotel at 23.00 I feel to be grilled from all sides. What is the role of an area manager, now and in the future? To whom should area managers report? How are audits conducted? Interspersed with this, come tracts of H.Q. politics, it seems. Messrs Holmes and Bath are very sharp and Bob Poynter appears to have designs on Mr Bath's old job. I'm home for 23.30.

Friday 9th May 1986

At 08.00 I'm in Teignmouth signal box doing a routine visit, followed by two more at Newton Abbot. I have discovered that the two signalmen whom I consider are the most difficult on the Area are on duty. George Dennis is at the East box. He is in a good mood today, very chirpy despite his poached egg having emerged too hard. Brian Warren *(the pilotman from the Teignmouth coach incident)* is not on duty, as believed, at the West. Instead it is John Haycock, destined for Exeter Panel signal box and an ideal person for a pleasant and relaxing visit.

Yesterday's special party arrives. Alec Bath used to be area manager at Newton Abbot from 1966 to 1970. It is clear that he was both respected and well liked, an impressive combination. Back at Exeter, I make a short presentation on the imminent re-signalling, tour the box and the stabling point and enjoy a surprisingly good Travellers-Fare buffet lunch. Things have greatly improved under the two new young women managers.

To compensate for the missing saloon ride, train crew assistant Alan Bell has arranged a special dmu to Taunton with stops at Tiverton Jct and Tiverton Parkway, followed by visits to Taunton East and West signal boxes. At 15.06 they depart for Reading with handshakes and thanks. Alec Bath knows I will be glad to see them go and says as much. His parting words are, "Well done. It's a good area." I walk away wondering whether he means good to live in, work in, or well run?

On the platform, I stop for a word with the senior railman to tell him what a pleasure it is to see someone so well turned-out in the right place for the arrival of the train without being asked.

I return to Exeter behind No. 47403 'The Geordie' which evokes recollections of my days at Newcastle. On the train, I have a chat with the station catering manager based at Bristol, giving the opportunity to commend today's buffet arrangements to him.

The paperwork on the desk is 18in high but I leave it behind and go home where Linda has been busy organising Mike Hodson's visit this weekend *(my colleague during management training who was to hold three train operating company managing director jobs before retiring).*

Saturday 10th May 1986

I looked in at Taunton on my way to Minehead with Mike and Linda. Everything was relatively peaceful with signal testing going on for the Taunton stage of the multiple aspect signalling scheme (MAS). The occupation was from 21.00 Friday to 06.00 Monday. Two items were causing concern but Bernard Price was firmly in control of both. Most immediately, 1,300 Butlin's passengers were descending on Bridgwater for buses to Minehead. Normally they transfer at Taunton so we had a proprietorial interest. Bernard and trains' inspector Ray Thorn were venturing onto the Bristol patch to ensure smooth arrangements there. As Bernard watched the pushing and shoving, he was heard to murmur, "I wouldn't like to think I was sharing a knife and fork with that lot."

The second item was the more serious. The 00.05 Paddington-Penzance, known colloquially as 'The Owl' *(This was one of the Western ways I made the mistake of not clarifying when I moved here, but believed to be applied to this train and a relic of Broad Gauge days.)* had been retimed to run via Yeovil and had arrived there with a door open. The line had been examined but nothing had been found. Daylight had revealed the body of a man in a ditch and a lady had arrived at Exeter looking for her husband who had not arrived overnight. On the bright side, there was no question of the police stopping the line, which was fortunate in the light of the intensively planned use during the weekend's diversions.

CHAPTER 3: A NEW INTERCITY STATION OPENS

Sunday 11th May 1986

A walk from Starcross to Exminster indicates that trains were running well. After lunch, I go to Exeter St. David's and a visit to the Panel Box which reveals everything is in order. The only problem is a delay to the test train single power car at Taunton. Bristol had not booked anyone to the job so we were having to cover. I drive to Taunton for 17.30 for the closure of the depot. Alan Bell is already there and driver Dingle completes the formalities by signing on and accepting his commemorative plaque in a low-key event. Home for 19.30.

Monday 12th May 1986

The morning is alternately wet and drizzly. The bowler hat and brolly are in the back of the car on their way to Tiverton Parkway for the opening ceremony. At 06.30, the first passengers are already arriving to take advantage of the '50% off Savers' opening offer but the small print says, 'subject to normal Saver conditions' which meant the first train was barred. There were three people involved, one of whom wanted to take his bike with him. The problem is solved by endorsing their tickets for travel on the early train and ensuring the guard had no objection to the bike. *(Public relations own goal avoided.)*

There are interviews with Devonair radio and local BBC TV. The Transport Minister David Mitchell duly arrives, cuts the ribbon unveils the mandatory plaque, inspects the premises and catches the special Skipper to Exeter Central for lunch at the Rougemont Hotel.

By 15.36 the Minister, InterCity director and general manager are all on their way east again. Tony Harrington and Peter Pitt from Europcar are in the office. We had managed to wring some sense out of regional InterCity manager John Bourne who had been objecting to a Europcar office at Tiverton Parkway but we could now go ahead. The opposition had seemed obstructive and illogical but common sense had prevailed. *Even at this distance, the only conceivable problem could have been abstraction of revenue from the Exeter-Barnstaple line, but it had been decided to build the station in the light of that danger on the basis that the overall market would expand. Branch line revenue was not his concern and, if it was, surely the existing Exeter Europcar office could be seen as putting Exmouth line revenue at risk.*

A quick chat with Clarence Woodbury over his cover for Bernard Brown and a discussion with drivers' LDC Secretary Len Purse, then home on the 17.25.

Photo: Opening party at Tiverton Parkway including (from left) 1st Tony Speller M.P, 2nd General Manager Sidney Newey, 3rd Inter City director Dr John Prideaux, 5th Author (bowler hat!), 6th Minister of State for Transport David Mitchell M.P., 7th Inter City sub-sector manager John Bourne, 10th Mayor of Exeter Roy Slack. 4th, 8th 9th civic dignitaries - apologies for names not having been recorded.

Tuesday 13th May 1986

The aftermath of the last few days was showing in the growing amount of paperwork and it would have been easy to stay in the office and do it *(sensible but less enjoyable?)* but I choose to get out and about instead. I catch the 09.19 to Topsham and do a box visit. The new half-hourly interval service we have introduced *(a local initiative)* is causing the signalmen to do a lot more running around. Then it's down to Exmouth for ten minutes and back to Exeter for No. 50024 'Vanguard' with Driver Ray Slack *(mayor Roy's uncle)* to Taunton. This was my first view, from the cab, of the newly installed flashing yellow signal aspects *(newly authorised nationally to provide a smoother run through turnouts than conventional approach control)*. Ray took them cautiously, and therefore wisely, but still arrived on time.

In the East box, Ken Marney was getting used to his new temporary mini-panel with Signalling Inspector Bill Marden training him.

In the cab of the 14.42 to Tiverton Parkway the 'B' driver *(This was the time of two drivers on trains running in excess of 100mph)* said that his first experience of flashing yellows had been to meet with a red instead of the expected green. This is not designed to breed confidence. *(This now worries me. Where, when? Did the driver understand the new system properly? In the light of the subsequent head-on crash at Colwich I suspect the latter might have applied)*

At Tiverton Parkway the Senior Railman is extremely busy so there is no time to chat before I catch the 10.39 Manchester-Plymouth back to Exeter. Guard Perks is working this train, specifically announcing the on time arrival *(when such initiatives were unusual)*.

Alan Bell is a little concerned about the local National Union of Railwayman (NUR) secretary John Pearman who is suggesting a guard should not be issued with a Form 1 for failing to collect £14.40 from a passenger on the Golden Hind. Another guard, who is far less popular with both management and the Union, has been issued with a Form 1 in similar circumstances recently. John claims the context was totally different, but there is no question of withdrawing the Form 1. John Beer and I make a note of the marketing issues we want to raise with Colin Leach at Swindon on Thursday.

My train home fails to depart on time and I suspect slackness. The senior railman says it is waiting to connect out of the delayed Exmouth *(17.00-finishing office workers from Central to Paignton)* which has been held at Topsham waiting to cross a Skipper that had experienced door trouble. As we roll out of the station, the Exmouth Skipper emerges from the tunnel. This was a manifestation of the problems of running the new intensive Exmouth service that need precise operating. The next Paignton service was then late and the contingency plan to run an extra in such circumstances, was unable to work as the next Exmouth was 18min late. I was not sure that this was the best solution so it will need reviewing tomorrow *(in an era before comprehensive computerised information was available)*.

At Dawlish, the leading railman, on a new middle turn, is nowhere to be seen. The senior railman claims he has mistaken the new times but it will be interesting to see what the signing-on sheet shows has been claimed.

Wednesday 14th May 1986

In to work at 07.30 on the early train. By 09.35 I was heading west again on the stopper with No. 50010 'Monarch'. At Torquay, I had a quick talk with travel centre manager John Hedge over his summer staffing issues. A lot of part time jobs have been agreed and we will have to recruit quickly.

The 'party travel' Clerk Lionel Watts has asked for a personal interview. Lionel had been at the sharp end of some exchanges with me a couple of months ago when he had intervened in a private conversation I was having with John. This time he wanted to know if his son could transfer from the traffic Youth Training Scheme (YTS) to the clerical one. He does not know his son's qualifications, what subjects they are in, at what level and what grade, but I undertake to check it out for him. *(This strikes me as a good example of a matter that I should perhaps have allowed to go from the Travel Centre Manager to the Customer Services Manager to sort out with the Personnel Manager but if I had the time again I would still opt for accessibility.)*

I ride down to Paignton in the cab of a Skipper with drivers' LDC chairman Colin Harrison *(a genial man)*. The distant is on and the home unusually remains on. With unfamiliar traction on a steep downgrade, Colin does not hesitate, putting the brake into emergency and halting with a loud screech ten seconds after the signal is cleared. *(There is no further comment in the manuscript about the incident. Of course, I could not query the decision to use 'emergency' for a number of reasons, nor could I suggest the signal should have come off earlier as a caution signal means be prepared to stop at the next signal. If Colin had got it wrong he would be embarrassed enough to have ensured he got it right next time.)*

There is a preliminary meeting to discuss the future of the station buildings. Investment, Provincial Services, the Property Board and engineers are present. Dry rot has a hold but temporary measures will stave off the problem for only three years. It seems to me that a property development scheme will be the answer but it must be self-financing and there are complications concerning road alterations. The next step will be to involve the architect, who seems to be about the only person not represented. *(Very little has since been done, just a bit of tidying up with the removal of the most decrepit remains of the 1950s railway. Paignton has not enjoyed the most prosperous of eras so property development was probably impractical. The booking hall is unaltered.)*

Back to Newton Abbot with Colin Harrison on his next trip, sharing his 'Twix' *(which probably demonstrates the quality of Exeter Drivers' LDC)*. Over the bridge for the train to Totnes where Colin Harmes, the staff representative, is on duty. I tip him off about the Royal Train on the 28th, in the knowledge he will ensure that cleanliness is correct. After a box visit and chat to booking clerk Mike Chard, I return to Newton Abbot. Ex-Neville Hill drivers Caslin and Smith are learning the road so I ride in the train recording a cautious run.

At Newton, I have a long chat with clerk Roy Watts in the booking office. The Skipper to Teignmouth has John Madge as guard. *(Guards' LDC Secretary)*. He is complaining about the staff at Torquay having given him a parcel on the down trip to save them carrying over the footbridge. John often makes a mountain out of a molehill although quite often he is basically correct. Linda picks me up at Teignmouth at 17.00. There is a briefcase-full of paperwork to process this evening.

Thursday 15th May 1986

Two meetings at Swindon today. The first is at 10.00 and can be reached only via Reading *(what a contrast from nowadays)*. So it's the 06.37 to Exeter where I can dump some of the paperwork. When I reach the platform for the Reading train, it is already in so I elect to ride in the train instead of the cab and continue with the admin. There are only three people waiting to join at Tiverton Parkway but twenty vehicles in the car park, which means there must be a number of overnight customers. Arrival at Reading is 2min late, mainly as a result of a signal check outside Taunton which I must follow up. There is 3min to cross over the bridge at Reading before catching the 08.35 from Paddington.

The first meeting is about the level of assistant ticket examiner (ATE) diagrams. My view is that the current level of checks is too comprehensive, often duplicate each other and are not sufficiently random. A headquarters inspector decides the level of coverage and the train planning office issues diagrams to which there is slavish adherence. Two area managers are not represented at the meeting and I'm the only one who has deemed it sufficiently important to attend so it's up to me to make the running. The Traction and Traincrew Officer David Hounsell is in the chair. Once we get to the purpose of the meeting he soon capitulates saying, "If that's the way you want it then you can have it all *(the specification and administration)* but don't come to my organisation for any help because I'll have cut the *(train planning)* jobs out."

We are already responsible for achieving the laid down percentages of ticket checks which are 90% of long distance journeys and 60% of local journeys. My figures from the surveys are 98% of both, achieved by random barrier checks, ensuring guards do their jobs and by using the ATEs. The only thing is that the ATEs are not deployed as we want them to be. *(In the current climate of reintroducing barrier checks to prevent fraud, I was surprised at my attitude to ticket checks at this meeting but the figures seem to justify my stance, even allowing for possible inaccuracy.)*

The other seven areas agree we can do the work at no extra cost. Two minutes later, David gathers up his papers, and issues his parting shot, "Of course I haven't the authority to agree this. I'll put the facts to Bob Poynter to decide, but I'm against it." Hmmm. I am confident we have got the actual agreement minuted and I also think Bob Poynter will back the areas but we shall see. *(I think to myself, is it any surprise that I sometimes had a jaundiced view of H.Q.?)*

John Beer arrives at 13.35. I'm already talking to Colin Leach about local service publicity. John and I think Colin has been unhelpful to our local plans so we are aiming to remove any obstructions, but perhaps we have been wrong. Yes, he agrees that our Yeovil-Bath/Bristol promotion can continue. Yes, he agrees that capacity problems mean no special promotions to Weymouth this summer. *(Sounds negative but there was no point in discounting a product where we have no current hope of meeting demand.)* There's money for local newspaper advertising, he might push for more next year, and there is no truth in the rumour that he's not going to cancel out previously-agreed local timetable mail-drop. *(The privatised railway does not seem to think it is worthwhile to mail-drop a local timetable using the firms dropping off the local Co-op leaflet.)* We are also empowered to negotiate local radio advertising rates. Devon Ranger availability can be extended to Yeovil and Salisbury areas. Totally positive, totally successful. John reckons Colin has changed his stance on all these points so recently that he will be rushing out to order extra timetables for the mail-drop right now.

The journey back is via Bristol Temple Meads where the Newcastle-Plymouth is 30min late following a hot box at Gloucester. I use the journey to discuss points with John and ask him to decide what he would do with various items in my pile of paper. The Exeter supervisor has correctly severed the connections with the 17.25 to Paignton and 17.20 to Barnstaple. I use the Glasgow relief to get home, No. 50033 'Glorious' on 11, 6min late.

Mike Hodson rings at 21.45. Someone is criticising him over the management of Calder Valley services, my home territory. He wants some ammunition. What is the method of control of sets at Neville Hill? Is a 3-car 720h.p.three car that much better than a 300h.p. twin and how do they compare to a 600h.p. Metro-Camm twin. I hope my train timing records and experience at Neville Hill as senior operating supervisor give him some answers and leads.

Friday 16th May 1986

The alarm is set for the early train again and by the time the office kicks into life at 08.30, I can see some space on the desk.

There is some desperately bad news. British Rail has lost the Parcels Post traffic. Keith Joint, Regional Parcels Manager, thinks we will cut out five jobs and three relief posts. It looks more like three and no relief to me but we will review the continuation of the night turn pilot as a result.

At 10.30 Taunton drivers Dodd, Blew and Hubbard arrive for their retirement interviews with an average of 47 years of service each. I have ridden with two of them *(Taunton drivers were hard to track down, doing a lot of work on nights with newspaper trains).* Driver Hubbard was travelling passenger on the 12.45 HST from Paddington a couple of years ago *(having worked the up newspaper empties)* when it was stuck on the B&H behind a failed freight. I was on the 13.40 from

Paddington with an Exeter driver who did not know the road via Bath. We dropped down to Reading West Jct as the HST came back from the B&H. Driver Hubbard alighted and took our Class 50 non-stop back to Taunton via Bath. I was travelling with Taunton driver Dodd on the 13.40 from Paddington in the last timetable when we arrived at Exeter St. David's 29½min early, a 30min early arrival having been prevented by the Silk Mill distant being against us.

The rest of the morning is taken up by Bernard Brown handing over, prior to his transfer to Plymouth. I take him for lunch at the Great Western. Might as well do things with a good grace.

One of the items in Bernard's basket is a form to re-advertise a TOPS *(computerised freight vehicle control system)* clerk vacancy for which there was only one applicant, Nigel Gooding. Nigel is a relief leading railman who, I think, has the potential to enter the Advanced Management Training Scheme. He should start a guard's training course on Monday but he is coming to see me to say whether he prefers the TOPS job.

Nigel was from a solid railway family, his father being one of the most dependable members of staff. When I first encountered Nigel, he was a rather embittered university drop-out and was in danger of turning inwards on the organisation. I also think that he had the capability of becoming the next Chester Long and was anxious to claim him for management. In the meantime he had declined a Union invitation to join the LDC and looks set on his career. *(Nigel did subsequently make the Training Scheme.)*

John Beer has gone to the Devon Show on professional duties for half a day. There is a letter needing urgent attention from a solicitor claiming £200 for a couple from Crediton for a lost holiday to Amsterdam, claiming they were not told of a retiming in London. They had allowed only 38min from their original Paddington arrival time to the booked departure from Liverpool Street. They had then returned home and made their first contact with British Rail a month later, via a solicitor's letter threatening County Court action. There are two choices;

an ex-gratia payment and risk getting stung for the lot, or denying liability.

I seek advice from a totally unhelpful solicitor at the British Railways Board H.Q. Reviewing the papers, there are claims for £11 in fares from Crediton to Exeter, £17 commission for changing currency into guilders, £25 hotel cancellation fee. It would have been cheaper to hire a taxi from Paddington to Harwich and anyone could claim to have been given wrong information. Perhaps they had been misinformed by a travel agent and tried them out for a refund first? Exeter travel centre manager Frank Lethbridge admits his staff might have missed the retiming but there is uncertainty about where they have booked their tickets and there has been no other complaint. In any case the original 38min is the main issue so I plump to deny liability.

Saturday 17th May 1986

Shopping in Newton Abbot with Linda, I take a look in at the station to see what is happening. The Milton Keynes Central to Paignton rolls in, formed of a Liverpool Pullman Mark 3 set and the 08.45 from Penzance arrives with a Class 47 assisting a defective HST.

This evening we are supposed to be going to Oldway Mansion, the splendid former home of the Singer family and with associations to Isadora Duncan, as guests of the NUR for a civic reception being held by Torbay Council on the occasion of the Union's annual conference. We have been to a few of these but there is only a certain amount of things to say to the latest batch of local politicians and NUR executive members. I have said only that we 'hope to attend' and neither Linda nor I can muster the energy to get out of the starting blocks. *(Oh dear. So many of my colleagues love these events but I am useless at small talk. I feel embarrassed now to have ducked this.)*

CHAPTER 4; READY FOR HOLIDAY

Sunday 18th May 1986

A walk along the sea wall on a beautiful day. There is a new lead being installed at Dawlish Warren, from the down loop to the down main, prior to the installation of a main-to-main facing crossover earlier than previously scheduled to help with future single line, and subsequently reversible, working.

Monday 19th May 1986

The 07.08 is formed of an HST this morning following the failure of No. 50050 'Fearless' *(I am tempted to quip 'Useless' but the former D400 has many dedicated preservationists to whom we owe a debt of gratitude)* at Laira. The HST should work the 06.24 from Newton Abbot but this has been covered with the special stops in the 06.00 Plymouth-Paddington and the HST has formed the Class 50 duty, the 06.40 from Totnes. The morning peak has otherwise gone quite well. *(Sounds complacent to me. Couldn't Laira have produced another Class 50 though?)*

Ken Shingleton is on the telephone quite early. There were two loco failures on trains in Cornwall late on Saturday afternoon which had met with single line working between Dawlish Warren and Exeter, after their eventual rescue. Ken says that the engineering work and single line working should have been subjected to a late start, after allowing them to pass. *(I can see his point, but can he be sure the work would have been given back on time or that the work would have been incomplete and have needed another possession?)*

Bernard Price is out at Taunton. There has been a total failure of telephones between Stoke Canon and Taunton so trains are being cautioned. If there is a signal failure in these circumstances it will be a major safety and delay problem. A search is being made for an appropriate spare part at the GEC factory.

There is a 10.30 meeting with St. David's station LDC. It is a long and tedious agenda with the most controversial items being rosters, hours of duty, towelmaster machines and locations of keys, seventeen items in all. There are few bright spots, largely due to the overwhelming lack of humour being displayed by staff-side chairman Ray (Spider) Long, Chester's brother, ex-mayor, Chairman of Exeter Council housing. We finish at 13.15.

I go to collect my railway issue made-to-measure overcoat from Collier's and ask a few travel agents about air tickets to Switzerland. Three enquiries, three entirely different answers *(unbeknown to me, a situation that would beset the railway within a decade or so)*.

Back at Exeter Central, Driver Lear comes up the bank with 2xClass 142s for the 14.22 to Paignton, six minutes late. He thinks it was due to the signalman not letting him out of the yard on time. Guard Paul Stannard *(well known for his amateur dramatics, including the King in The King and I)* thinks it was due to his '21' standard key breaking in the unit's lock. Not much communication there between the driver and guard then.

Alan Bell, Bernard Price and I discuss a serious incident that occurred last week. All the reports are now in. The booked guard of the 20.15 Paddington-Plymouth was not available so a freight guard was used who insisted in taking all his time allowances in full before setting off. The station supervisor, an ex-management trainee in his first job, entered into an intense argument with him and decided to send the guard home. In the meantime, the train crew supervisor had intercepted the freight guard and put him on an empty stock working *(From memory, the run to Plymouth was outside the agreed criteria for Driver Only Operation then)* with the empty stock guard being switched to the HST. In a situation like this, the supervisor must be given backing, even if he could perhaps have done better.

It is decided to give a ticking off to the incoming guard who left his train before relief appeared and to the train crew supervisor who undercut the station manager. The young station shift supervisor will be 'counselled' by Bernard. The freight guard, known to be a bit of a hothead, is to have a

Form 1 *(the guard subsequently became a pillar of the railway community and a friend in my retirement).* The charge will show serious subordination and a failure to make 'every effort to avoid delay' as per the Rule Book wording. *(This seems a bit tough on the train crew supervisor in the light of experience. True, he could have stepped up the empty stock guard and looked for further cover to the less sensitively timed train but late presentation at Laira would have been a maintenance issue.)*

Next follows the weekly meeting of the management team. The budget is looking healthy which is just as well because there is a finance audit on Thursday.

Tuesday 20th May 1986

This morning I think I had better take a look to see how Tiverton Parkway is doing. There are 38 vehicles in the car park by 10.45 and 20 people waiting for the 10.48 to Paddington. One passenger is travelling from South Molton to London and says she normally uses the coach. She looks well-heeled, the rail price does not seem to worry her and she is amazed that the return journey time is just 2hrs 9min. *(Now 1hr 57min.)* A middle-aged couple say they normally use Tiverton Jct but Parkway is much more convenient. Yesterday's takings amounted to only £1,000 but the signs today of new business and a better service give cause for hope. *(The car park is now regularly full to overflowing despite being no longer free.)*

My first Chamber of Commerce meeting takes place at 17.30. I have avoided membership in the past but have now been press-ganged, partly through the interest of general manager Brian Scott. I am elected to the Central Policy and Transport committees. *(I cannot recall ever attending either committee though.)*

Looking through the Exeter Express and Echo, I see they have printed my letter refuting their inaccurate suggestion that our A-Z departure posters have not been displayed on time. The only changes by editor John Budworth concern the missing last paragraph demanding a retraction. It seems that they are quick to criticise perceived railway mistakes but less keen to admit their own. *(It seems unrealistic to have expected any more.)*

Another letter to the Western Morning News in response to unfounded comments by one of their columnists has been copied to Ken Shingleton at his request and has re-appeared marked 'Good!' from the General Manager so I suppose that's worth a gold star.

Back at St. David's at 18.45, I have a long talk with a driver about the potential Yeovil Pen Mill/Yeovil Jct scheme. I have just heard that the earthworks are only £95,000 so there might be some chance. The driver had expressed his interest in the idea during a cab ride some months ago.

Wednesday 21st May 1986

Today, I have to attend a funeral at Newton Abbot. Brian Worth, one of the Newton Abbot platform staff has died suddenly, aged 58. He was also an occasional occupant of jobs at Dawlish. I decide to go box visiting beforehand. The weather is torrential rain with blustery gales *(arguably the sort of weather that brings the railway to a stand nowadays?)*.

At Dawlish Warren, Roy Pearce is on duty. I'm supposed to be playing in his son's cricket team at Starcross in the evenings but he has been unable to contact me. Roy was at Dawlish Warren when I was doing my signalling training at Easter 1975 and I managed to tag a few days extra onto my bank holiday break in Dawlish, unofficially seconded to the Western Region.

Aller Jct is next on the list. John Congdon there has recovered from a heart attack of two years ago. He is 58 and has elected not to take a job in the Panel box. He wants to know his redundancy figures but hopes he might be accommodated in another job. *(The key to the resignalling is to make sure there is no compulsory redundancy. I think I am right in claiming that the Exeter scheme made no one redundant who was not happy to leave.)* Six weeks ago this looked doubtful but all the

Taunton men have now been placed and Newton Abbot is looking manageable. Two signalmen send 'train out of section' without call attention, a 'normal irregularity' usually prevented by the signalman who is being visited tipping off his colleagues. It is a worry that John has not been on the ball enough to do this as I do not creep up to a box I am inspecting. Two sharp exchanges on the telephone are called for.

I am drenched on my way to Dainton box, scrambling down the embankment and walking along the cess to the box. Signalman Kemp is a quiet, studious individual but I had imparted some information on my last visit about his options when the box closes and he seems to have warmed up a bit as a result. *(The personnel people seem to have a desire to keep the seniority lists and redundancy arrangements as some sort of state secret. It is possible to inform people without necessarily having promised them anything.)*

There is time for a quick coffee at Newton Abbot before the funeral. I have a bit of a phobia about funerals *(who doesn't?)*. Bernard and I tend to share the attendance depending on who knew the deceased the better. *That also went for staff who die soon after retirement but the problem is people who die a long time after leaving. Families quite rightly often expect representation from the railway but it is not much of an exaggeration to say that it would be a full time occupation to cover them all. It is a failure to meet the staff's not unreasonable expectations though.* Alan Bell usually attends traincrew funerals. I am convinced that funerals break down barriers between management and the staff who attend, more so than social events for instance.

Later in the afternoon, Paul Silvestri arrives to check out his thoughts against mine on local service train planning. It will be 'status quo' on the improved Exmouth timetable, and Barnstaple. There is a complicated resource problem affecting the evening peak Paignton service in the summer and Paul wants to know if there will be any signalling cost implications in running an 06.20 from Exmouth and a 21.48 to Barnstaple.

Thursday 22nd May 1986

An early start is called for to clear the correspondence backlog. *My first secretary, Bunty, claimed I had doubled the paperwork through the office since my arrival which I considered to be criticism not praise!* One of the elements is that I insist on signing all replies to public complaints. Tony Hill ensures that replies are accurate, the English is good and that sound judgment is exercised but I turn the odd one or two back and it gives me the key to knowing what needs to be improved.

The finance audit starts at 08.45 with David Warne in the chair. There are also two finance men, Colin Leach from Provincial Services and Peter Griggs, the newly appointed InterCity Route Manager *(who used to be freight salesman with an office near the St. David's parcels office. Peter would be the first to admit he was a cocky young man but he was likeable, despite being an aspiring football league referee).*

On the Exeter team there is budget clerk Ken Boobyer and me. We go through the budget schemes one by one. Train Planning has failed to deliver an altered train plan necessary to allow me to cut out the Riverside Train Preparers jobs. Swindon H.Q has also prevaricated over arranging Sectional Council regional consultation meetings. Most of our schemes have been over-achieved or are on course. *I used to try and backload the budget reduction measures and then prepare them for delivery early in the year. A cost reduction measure for say Period 9 introduced in say Period 3 would achieve nine months of budget savings instead of three, i.e. triple.*

The H.Q. representatives adjourn for the luxury of a 30min lunch break. I join John Pearse and his new local services route manager, former Oxford area manager David Mather to brief them for the forthcoming visit of the sector director Provincial Services. It has not been long before the sectors have started to re-centralise and build their own empires but I suspect they are scared they will not know enough detail to survive questioning. I suppose the BRB thinks Swindon is somewhere near Devon and Cornwall.

In the afternoon session, the central financial problems are travel centre staffing levels, small station policy and InterCity terminal staffing levels. I have been through a long and painful process with Management Services at Swindon to establish this budget but the assembled company is talking of back-tracking. They are lost for detail to support their argument though.

We then come to a key moment when it is announced that the Regional Operating Manager has an unsupported £1.3m budget cut as yet not underwritten by schemes. I take the business on at their own game, pointing out the effect the ideas being suggested will have on the new buzz word 'quality'. They back off for 'further investigation' and the meeting concludes with a net increase in my budget and easing of what pressures might have been emerging.

This afternoon's session has been attended by Stephen Barnes, a teacher from Taunton who has been seconded to British Rail in "Industry Year". He teaches economics and demonstrates a sound grasp of the debate when we discuss events after the Swindon contingent has departed. He will be undertaking an eight-day area visit in a fortnight's time so we run through the details.

Friday 23rd May 1986

There is quite a collection of us in the office by 08.00. Parcels Manager Tony Crabtree *(who recently retired as ERTMS Project Manager on the Cambrian)* had been out to watch the newspaper train operation at 02.30. John Beer is in and Clarence Woodbury who says he will not be applying for the Personnel Manager's job as he intends to retire at 60 in eighteen months time. I appreciate his candour as at least I know where I stand and can plan accordingly.

At 09.38 I take a bundle of paperwork on the train to Yeovil Jct. Visiting Yeovil Jct signal box I meet, for the first time, the signalman on duty there. He had a motorbike accident a year ago in which his wife was killed and he has been back at work for only the last two months. He is obviously living on his nerves and has a terrible limp but he is hoping to re-marry this summer and go to St. Lucia for his honeymoon. A cup of tea and back to Exeter. *There is nothing in the diary about any worries on the health score but Yeovil Jct, in those days was stressful only during block failures and diversions.*

I drop off at Central for travellers' cheques and holiday insurance cover. Then it's the 14.53 York relief to Taunton with No. 45134. Class 45s are rare west of Bristol nowadays. I visit the travel centre and supervisor's office before returning to Exeter just 28min later on the Liverpool HST.

I have a session with a promising and well-qualified travel centre clerk who has failed to be selected for a new Marketing Management Training Scheme. The results show that he was not in serious consideration for selection so there is no easy let down. Next year he feels he might have a go for the Operations Scheme.

I'm taking the car home tonight for an early departure on holiday on Tuesday so I drop off Bernard Price at home and finish for two weeks.

Saturday 24th May to Sunday June 8th June 1986

I usually take some holiday at this time of year now that Linda is involved with language school teaching from mid-June to the end of August. This year, Linda is reluctant to go abroad, partly due to the weather which seems out-of-sorts all over Europe and partly due to Libyan bomb threats to cross-Channel ships and hovercraft. One on a hovercraft and the whole vessel would disintegrate.

The alarm rang at 04.45 and I caught the 05.48 to Waterloo with an ample 45min to reach Waterloo East for the Charing Cross to Dover train to meet the hovercraft. At Salisbury there was a worrying announcement that the preceding train had failed and delay should be expected. Fortunately this was limited to a 12min late arrival.

The crossing was rough, taking 52min instead of the booked 35 and the turbo-train to Paris left 21min late leaving a potential 34min to cross to Gare de l'Est. We gained 8min to Amiens but encountered a succession of delays to Gare du Nord leaving me just 10min to catch the 17.06 to Zurich (L'Arbalète) from Gare de l'Est to the first stop at Belfort with powerful diesel loco No. 72036 on nine. A pleasant meal in the restaurant car revived my spirits.

The following day I made my way to Lucerne to visit the impressive transport museum and then across the narrow gauge Brunig line to Interlaken. The aim was a trip on the Jungfrau railway but it was evident that the weather had set in and visibility would be negligible. I had a meal, made for the station and caught the couchette train to Paris, making for Huddersfield for a couple of days with relatives. I subsequently found out that my original itinerary would have landed me for a 24hr French rail strike.

It was on my way home that I had my first taste of a holiday on my own patch and the pitfalls that are involved. Leading railman Terry Blackburn wanted to eject the National Express party rail courier from first class. The courier was arguing that a letter had been sent allowing him to travel first class but his pass clearly showed 'second'. *Terry had been made redundant as a welder at Exmouth Jct wagon repair shops and been accommodated as an ATE. He was regularly in trouble for being rude but he always comprehensively beat his colleagues when revenue per diagram was assessed. He did not know the meaning of discretion though, and passengers sometimes ....well..... exaggerated. I always felt I would be like Terry if I was doing his job.* The 'offender' decided to move without a fuss.

Holiday in Torquay on Tuesday, Shanklin on the Thursday, Penzance on the Friday....and a succession of "I know you're on holiday but..." conversations. Then there was driver Carpenter taking his deckchair to the beach during his

Penzance turnround and a St. Blazey guard entering our compartment and asking if I minded his asking a question. Suspecting the motives I was cagey and asked why.

"Are you Mr Heaton?"

"Yes, why?"

"Because I've never seen you before on trains."

"Well you mustn't travel much then!"

"No I don't."

He then alights at Teignmouth behind us. Unsettling.

CHAPTER 5: OPERATIONS UNDER PRESSURE

Monday 9th June 1986

Not much of a holiday and I return to a litany of minor derailments, disciplinary hearings and loco failures. No. 50028 'Tiger' has failed three times on the Waterloo route. Operating clerk Karen is keen on Class 50s and almost intuitive so far as they are concerned. She says she knew 'Victorious' would fail because it was ex-Works and 'Fearless' was obviously unwell and leaking something. She says she will compose a letter to the regional operating manager summarising the problems.

There is some good news though. The sector director Provincial Services visit has been cancelled as has my course at the end of the month. My struggling personnel trainee has been moved laterally to an Old Oak Common job. He'll need to sharpen up. Clarence Woodbury has changed his mind and will now apply for the personnel assistant's job having resolved some domestic matters. I arrange with the regional personnel manager Ken Beresford to keep James until the new Personnel Manager is in place now that Bernard Brown has been released. This time a macho response to the move would not be appropriate.

Work is absolutely non-stop from 07.30 to 17.15. At the top of the stairs to my train home, with five minutes to spare, a driver is coming the other way. "Can I have a railcard for the Church Fete like last year please?" he asks. The cost to B.R. is notional if someone wins it who would not have bought one. "Last year the winner spent £90 with us," he adds as if reading my mind. "Yes, let me know the winner's name after the draw and I'll fix it up," I reply. As I ride home I reflect that I have got more satisfaction from that one moment in the day than he could ever guess. *The driver's name is not in the diary but I guess it was Charlie Clyst who was a keen churchman and went to school with Bob Poynter.*

Tuesday 10th June 1986

Yesterday's Western Morning news is put in front of me by John Beer. "Count to ten before you read it," he says. Railway publisher David St. John Thomas of 'David and Charles' has returned from holiday and seen a letter I have written, in response to an article of his, which says he was 'factually incorrect.' His reply denies this and he patronisingly says I am doing 'some good things' but I shouldn't slavishly follow the party line. *I was easily patronised in those days and it looks like praise and good advice at this distance.* His letter says B.R. sometimes insists it is right when clearly it is not, quoting the locking of sleeping car doors before the Taunton train fire some years ago. I decide to stand and fight. I tell him he is wrong again and speaking on second-hand information, finishing with, "It is with great sorrow that one so eminent in West Country circles is prepared to score points out of the Taunton fire tragedy by tenuously linking it to the matter under discussion." I drop a copy to the General Manager, who had approved of my first reply, but I expect fireworks. Head of the Traffic Section, Tony Hill tells me no one has taken St. John Thomas on before. *Tony had family connections to landed gentry and I sometimes felt like Mainwaring to his Sergeant Wilson. Not that Tony has any of the latter's failings. As for David St. John Thomas, we seemed to maintain a healthy respect for each other during my tenure and he was personally very kind to me when I contacted him about writing fiction in later years. I also succeeded him as president of the Friends of the Newton Abbot Library Railway Studies Collection and went to his Nairn home to help organise his kind bequeathal of many railway books to the Library.*

At 11.15 Joe McEntee, former Area Manager at Westbury until its recent abolition comes to see me about a project he is doing on train running information and duplication with Control. Joe is going to take redundancy but I think he is only around 54 years old, a thinking railwayman with his feet firmly fixed on the ground and someone whom the railway cannot afford to lose. He speaks frankly. Bob Poynter is fed up of the low quality of decision making by sector managers at Swindon and he feels the post of general manager is quickly becoming marginalised. Two hours later and Joe is on his way to see his next area manager.

In comes John Curley, the newly appointed route manager for Cardiff-to Portsmouth and Weymouth. Joe McEntee has just given him a good testimonial and he seems to have the right idea. He is prepared to consider promotions and even cut ordinary fares but he agrees we should not exacerbate the capacity problems to Weymouth in the summer school holidays. But we will promote normal fares and railcard discounts.

It is 15.15 and after a tough twelve hours yesterday, including two hours at home, and eight unbroken hours today I take an early finish and go to Starcross to play cricket. I start to clear my diary of Tuesday evening commitments this summer.

Wednesday 11th June 1986

Despite the pressures of administration, today is going to be spent on the area. *Gerry Fiennes's two books convinced me of the need to make days out on 'the patch' safeguarded in the diary in the same way as a meeting.* The 08.00 to Tiverton Parkway has the general manager on board on his way back from Plymouth to Swindon. He's supposed to be on the 09.31! Business is brisk at Tiverton Parkway. There are 40 vehicles in the car park and weekly takings are standing at £5,500. Still slightly below expectations but heading in the right direction.

The main snag to growth is the return service from London which has a 12.45 to 16.45 gap, or 19.00 if you want to use a Saver. This has been brought to the notice of route manager Peter Griggs three weeks ago but there has been no response. I suppose I will have to gee him up and take the brickbats in the evening press, replying, a weak, "It will be considered." *Tiverton Parkway's custom, discounting new business, should have come from those who have been driving to Taunton or Exeter. I reasoned that those who have been using the Barnstaple branch who did not have access to a car would continue to do so. The construction of the North Devon Link Road to join the M5 caused us to locate our new station at the road junction. It was felt that once on the M5 drivers would be disinclined to leave the motorway and park at Taunton, or counter-intuitively to turn right to find an improved*

Tiverton Jct. The gap in the down service was unlikely to support a change in travel habits or to dissuade passengers from using the motorway.

A quick cup of coffee and up to Taunton in the cab of the 07.30 Plymouth-Paddington. Then once round the travel centre, announcer and supervisor before returning on the 07.25 Paddington-Penzance. In the travel centre lounge *(since closed, passengers queue in a draughty booking hall)* the June page of the French Travel Service/B. R. European calendar displays a topless model paddling on the Riviera. I decide to censor it, partly as I feel it is more appropriate to a garage messroom and partly because we are rightly being encouraged to make the work place more female friendly.

I catch the 10.28 to Exmouth, encountering recently retired travel centre manager Deryck Rawle who is busily working as the part-time summer clerk. *It is my recollection that Deryck refused an upgrading to management staff in order to be able to retain his Sunday overtime slot on the roster.*

I tackle some paperwork on the journey through to Barnstaple before again doing a trip round the station. We still maintain a travel centre here, despite it being unjustifiable in theory. It is always very busy when I'm there and I cannot readily see where the business would transfer if we closed it. *In the electronic age I can of course.*

The Class 50 cab ride back to Exeter with Driver Jack Davy is a pleasure, the Class 142 having been replaced by the Exeter Secret Set of loco plus coaches we have pilfered from passing Cardiff-Plymouth trains to prevent cancellations. No. 50017 'Royal Oak' is in the new Network South East 'ice cream van' livery. Earlier in the day I had studied No. 50023 'Howe' on the newspaper van empties and given it a thumbs down. *Harsh.* What with No, 33008 'Eastleigh' on the Taunton-Bristol stopper in supposedly malachite green and No. 50007 'Sir Edward Elgar' in the Brunswick shade of the same colour on the 11.10 Paddington –Penzance, there can be no complaint about a lack of variety.

Jack reminisces about former area managers. He wonders where Alec Bath is now and confirms he was well respected.

"Where's the Doctor now," he asks meaning Dr. John Prideaux who was onetime area manager at Newton Abbot.

"Director InterCity," I reply. This news is less well received. *It also showed the irrelevance of the BRB's upper echelons to a driver.*

Jack continued. "The first LDC meeting I went to with him he started by telling us that for our future reference we should call him 'doctor'. I told him I'd call him either sir or guv'nor," and then added, "After that I called him guv'nor because he didn't merit calling sir". I try to hide my amusement because I think Jack has already called me guv'nor a couple of times today. In fact I'm quite often addressed in that way and I had never realised there could be a West Country nuance. I wonder whether he is laughing at this same point but who cares if he is, I think it's funny. *I preferred guv'nor to sir anyway although, in my mid-30s, I quite relished occasionally overhearing 'the 'old man's about' when I was approaching.* On arrival at Exeter I cross the bridge to catch the down 'Torbay Express' which is waiting to take me to Newton Abbot.

There is an opportunity to visit the travel centre (and censor the clearly popular calendar) then visit Newton Abbot East signal box where Gordon Tincombe is coming towards the end of a twelve-hour shift, demanding both physically and mentally. Gordon is an excellent signalman who looks much younger than his sixty years. To watch someone like him working a large and busy signalbox is to observe a fast-dying art form. I make the most of watching it while I can. Recently, I gave Gordon some information about his potential golden handshake after he had asked me. I then remembered to follow it up when circumstances altered and his previous slightly prickly attitude seems to have altered.

The train to Exeter is ten minutes late and this time it is Mr. Speller's cow on the line to blame, at Ivybridge. We make up a couple of minutes but it could have been three had it not been for a signal check approaching St. David's.

Next it is the TOPS Office and the Panel Box. Dennis Davy, a former Taunton manual box signalman and current NUR branch secretary, is learning the middle of the three positions (St. David's station) and enjoying it. *I suspect Dennis always wanted to influence matters further afield than the box he was working.* The 14.35 Plymouth to Paddington fails to stop at Tiverton Parkway and five people are over-carried to Taunton. The two waiting London passengers are picked up by the following York train. Taunton supervisor Bob Johnson asks Exeter Driver Copp for his explanation. He's 'forgotten'. There had to be a first, I suppose. The normal level of punishment for this that Alan Bell and I exert is a written warning for a first offence and formal discipline with a reprimand for a second instance. Reports are requested and Control informed. *Such disciplinary action would be considered extremely soft in the modern era.*

The train crew supervisor confirms we are still short of Class 142s and a single power car we have purloined is in use once again. I suggest he uses the twin power car Class 118 we have on hand and the single power car on the Exmouth vice the two Class 142s booked but I wonder if he has taken it in.

Back in the office there's a pile of paperwork and I set off home in the new 'area manager's car'; a Maestro. England play Poland in the World Cup tonight so it will be an 01.00 bed-time before setting off early to Swindon, the car saving me 25min in getting to Exeter. *It was officially my car but I did not use it much, as can be seen from the day's activity. You could not meet traincrew while in the car and you could not do paperwork while travelling. On top of that, the day would have been exhausting if I had driven the equivalent distance that had been done by rail.*

Thursday 12th June 1986

The Class 142 position is relatively O.K. this morning. I team up with Plymouth area manager Jim Collins *(who eventually went into consultancy via Managing Director of Thameslink)* on the 08.00 to Bristol Parkway and a change for Swindon. It is a surprise to find No. 50038 'Formidable' on a vacuum braked relief from South Wales to Paddington.

The subject of the meeting is the Travel Centre Staffing Review. There is a problem because the consultation document supplied to the Union does not reflect what was agreed with Area Managers and that much of the additional cost involved is not supported by InterCity. There is a full discussion with the regional ops manager's representative David Warne who threatens at one stage to abandon tomorrow's meeting with the union. Three hours later an agreement is reached with David's cards duly marked. Jim and I are glad we are not in his shoes tomorrow as he does not have a strong position to maintain.

The 14.58 from Swindon to Bristol is 15min late with loco and coaches vice an HST. At Bristol Temple Meads, the Newcastle train is 20min late and incurs 17min overtime because the crew will not take their defective loco to the shed. Then Taunton turns out the cement train in front and we are stopped at Cowley Bridge Jct for the Barnstaple to run in front of us. The Newton Abbot connection has gone so the Newcastle will call there additionally and a 50min late Plymouth arrival can be expected.

Meanwhile the next connection for other Torbay stations is the Glasgow, running 58min late. The supervisor has earmarked a Class 118 to form a special to Paignton to accommodate the Saga passengers who will have alighted from the Newcastle at Newton Abbot. The arrangement has been diagrammed to cover commuters being inconvenienced by a missing Glasgow train. It is a 'contingency working' at local level, using a crew which is finishing peak hour work on the Exmouth line who have spare time on their diagram, but their inbound train is 10min late.

The Panel box has blocked Platform 1 with the cement train which is waiting to attach a banker and the Class 118 is blocking Platform 3, the only other one accessible by the

Exmouth train. Train crew supervisor Ben Griffiths works some magic and provides another crew for the Paignton special which gets away 8min late on the Glasgow timings. Tough Terry Blackburn is the fare collector and touchingly *(and unnecessarily of course)* thanks me for helping out at Taunton last week.

On arrival home, I decide to ring Bernard Price. What with all the operating problems today, some trip working problems, Class 142 availability and the new cleaning arrangements going badly, positive action is needed. I tell Bernard to withdraw from a meeting at Swindon tomorrow about the Yeovil layout. The Area will not be represented. Bernard can put his considerable energies into getting the cleaning right and I want traction, guards' and signalling inspectors out on the ground and visible on two shifts tomorrow and we will discuss a high profile campaign for next week. *On reading this account it strikes me that the problems were exacerbated by staff being unused to Panel Box working, for instance the pitfalls of platforming at St. David's and margining down freights from Taunton.*

Friday 13th June 1986

The 'purge' starts well with the best operating morning for a while. Guards' inspector Ray Thorn was on the platform at St. David's and averted a serious delay to the 08.00 to Exmouth which would have had a knock-on effect for most of the morning. Station Supervisor Gordon Hooper *(a legend amongst train timers at the end of Southern steam, I subsequently discovered)* wanted to take No. 142019 out of the working because it was known to multiple badly with other sets. No. 142022 was available in West Yard but it needed preparing. He told me his plan at 07.47.

"If it's not off the yard by 08.00, the train goes on two cars." I tell him, taking in a gulp of air at the prospect of severe overcrowding. The unit came off at 08.00½ and coupled to the unit waiting in the platform but the guard could not make the doors work in unison. Ray, who is an expert on Class 142s, intervenes effectively and gets the train away 8min late, a delay which will work itself out relatively quickly with sharp turnrounds at Exmouth. *Ray was a huge man both in size and character, an old 'green badge' Southern man through and through. I attended his funeral in 2013.*

Ray, Bernard and Signalling Inspector Derek Old meet me in my office. Bernard is going to see to the cleaning and the two inspectors know what is needed, There is a problem with the new trap points from the down loop at Dawlish Warren. There seems to be some disagreement between the Signalling and Telecommunications (S&T) department and the civil engineers. I phone area civil engineer Peter Warren who assures me a gang is on its way to site and he expects the problem to be solved.

11.30 sees Jim Collins and me in the Devonair radio studios for a live phone in. I have done many interviews, but the phone-in is my first. I feel a bit trapped into it, as does Jim because his assistant David Langton *(now Train Planning Manager with TransPennine Express and a good friend)* had agreed to their request on our behalf. We both think it is likely to be negative but we were wrong *(and David Langton had been right to concur).*

With the exception of one trivial question about a second-hand alleged conversation at Newton Abbot, the questions are of a high standard and interesting; Motorail economics, punctuality of the Glasgow trains, disabled railcards, facilities for nursing mothers, and a couple of unsolicited glowing testimonials.

At 14.00 I meet a representative of the freight business to check his allocation of work between sub-sectors within freight. Decisions do not seem to be his strongest point. I describe what happens on each diagram and what the pilots do and tell him he can allocate the costs however he wants, it makes no difference to me. 32 minutes later and he is on his way back to H.Q.

Tony Crabtree wants to talk about a long list of parcel business matters. He certainly has many good ideas, perhaps needing some re-direction, but he is certainly developing quickly and I tell him how well he is doing. He wants to adjust hours at Paignton to give better parcels' coverage and create a dedicated parcels clerk and accounts clerk in his office from three existing posts. I'm going to save one anyway but his proposals give a better end result.

Next is the personnel trainee, soon bound for Old Oak Common. One of his management objectives has been to introduce team briefing sessions. He has discussed it with everyone but it will fall short of implementation at signalman/traincrew level simply due to the logistics involved. He is going to make a presentation to the local management meeting next Monday afternoon.

Saturday 14th June 1986

Linda is tied up with her language school teaching today so I'm going to take the opportunity of looking at the summer Saturday working. I intend to catch the 07.55 from Dawlish to Paignton which has begun life last night in Glasgow Central at 22.50. It turns up 16min late, pulls back 3min to Teignmouth and should be well under 10min late by Paignton *(not that 'under 10' featured in our thinking in those days)* if Torquay improves on its generous 5min station allowance. We make up 20sec at Teignmouth but it should have been at least a minute. The Bristol guard has wandered off down the platform and eventually returns and illegally gives the right-away without using his flag.

I introduce myself to him, essential to prevent the initial response of, "And who are you?"

"Why were we longer than we needed to be at Teignmouth?" I ask.

"Someone bought some cigarettes from the kiosk," he replies.

"Someone, or you?" I growl, beginning to see red.

"Me," he says, unconcernedly.

"Well, I'm not having that."

"The train's running a quarter on an hour late anyway," he counters. Although West Country rail staff are nearly always reliable, this outlook to punctuality is not unusual.

"That's even more reason for hurrying, but if that's going to be your attitude...." I begin to counter.

"No, it's not." He has seen trouble looming.

"Right, let's get things straight. When you are on my area you try to make up time and you <u>always</u> use a green flag to give the right-away."

"O.K." he shrugs.

The green flag is out at Newton Abbot but he takes his pound of flesh at Torre, making doubly sure, quite rightly, that all doors are secure on his ten coach train at this unmanned station. 30sec overtime. 9min late at Paignton.

Typing up this passage I experience a strange mixture of embarrassment and admiration. In the context of working with staff that had twice as much experience as I had then, both emotions are probably accurate. There can be no doubt that I had intervened to prevent some slack working and that was my job. I ask myself whether I should not have challenged the driver why he accepted a right-away without the flag.

There are fair amounts of passengers about *(and the summer Saturday service was more intensive then than now of course)* but there are too many staff on duty despite recent cuts. There is no need for a traction inspector to be there either. There are still some ticket examiners on train and Dawlish and Teignmouth stations are still open despite my recent intentions to have barriers on summer Saturdays. *I was a strong advocate of 'open stations' and 'on train' examination but only in fairly sparse traffic areas. Having seen Terry Blackburn fail to get to grips with inspecting a crowded Cardiff-Paignton compartment train with standing passengers a year earlier, I changed my views on summer Saturdays in the Exeter area. Now, most main stations have had their barriers re-instated but there are substantial inspection gaps between closely-*

spaced small stations, especially if being served by HSTs and Voyagers.

John Beer is on call and has followed me down from Exeter. Definitely too many managers now! I return to Exeter via 15min at Torquay, arriving at Exeter St. David's 5min late behind the late running Penzance-Glasgow and 10.15 from Paignton. There is just time to stride over the footbridge for the 07.15 Milton Keynes-Penzance, fortunately for me, 5min late. No. 47435 of Gateshead is in charge.

This train was an example of the Cross Country route manager's innovatory attitude. Brian Johnson was a management trainee in my year and had decided to use the Liverpool Pullman set tapping a new market from a new town, populated to some extent by people from London who have traditionally been inclined to holiday in the West Country. Brian used to come down to check on the operation every summer and used to go through every coach, including toilets, with a notepad. He remains a valued friend and is one of those rare individuals about which no one has a bad word, including former Paignton summer Saturday train turnround staff.

There is a track circuit failure at Ivybridge *(just off my area)* causing 15min delay to up trains. On visiting the signal box, I find that the emergency block bell to Plymouth has been out of order since 10.00 yesterday morning. I ring the Duty Manager in Swindon Control for him to track down the S&T staff and raise a fuss. It is back to Exeter behind No. 47456 for half an hour, where John Beer has made a cup of tea.

I was going to go back to Paignton but my willpower is beginning to ebb away in the heat of a Devon summer mid-day. There are also occasions when management can get in the way and this might be one of them. On the platform the 08.20 from Liverpool, another West Coast Mark 3 set, is late with Nos. 31467 and 31404 in multiple on the front. Interesting enough for a trip to Torquay and the 15.15 Paignton-Nottingham back to Dawlish.

The buffet car crew on the Liverpool is still giving an at seat coffee service leaving Exeter. We have been given 'customer service award' vouchers *(£10 I think)* to hand out in cases of exceptional service. I decide to issue my second example, much to the stewardess's surprise, as she comes round again between Newton Abbot and Torquay.

A 4min delay is encountered at Aller Jct on the return trip. The Newton Abbot supervisor tells me there is a points' failure. Once again the S&T is looking like a 9-5 Mon-Fri organisation. Signalman John Congdon is clipping the points himself, with his history of heart trouble. The station supervisor says he is short-handed already but I insist that he must send someone and ring Exeter supervisor Paul Silvestri to ensure John Beer knows so that it gets proper attention. If nothing else, on-call Signalling Inspector Bill Marden can go. *It strikes me now that I could have gone or replaced someone on the station.*

Back home there is a chance to read the paper and have something to eat before looking through the paperwork in my briefcase. Teignmouth Harbour Commission minutes and an invitation to a Firefighting Through the Ages display at Taunton are a couple of topics less central to performance.

In terms of the Exeter area's rivalry with Plymouth there is some good news. Bob Poynter is going to experiment with 'depot management' at Cardiff, adopting the Eastern Region system of integrated maintenance, shunting and cleaning under which I worked at Neville Hill. This would rob Jim Collins of large staff numbers, possibly 75 at a guess, if Laira were to change. *75 seems high, possibly 75 shifts?*

CHAPTER 6: THE FIRST "NETWORK SOUTH EAST DAY"

Sunday 15th June 1986

Today I spend a couple of hours knocking together a consultation document to alter the platform staffing at St. David's and station supervision throughout the area. I opt to go for complete withdrawal of shift supervision at Newton Abbot and Taunton. The re-signalling makes both jobs simpler. If I retain some supervision in the document it will be hard to defend different reporting lines at different times of day. Full withdrawal is not in the budget and there will be scope to concede some posts if pressed at consultation, thereby satisfying both sides of the table.

Recent re-grading of the Exeter Supervisors to Grade E gives some headroom for adding responsibilities to their post in the confidence they will not apply for the next grade, MS1 with reduced earnings from losing overtime payments.

Monday 16th June 1986

A routine day in the office. I discuss the new consultation documents with Tony Crabtree and Clarence Woodbury before going home for lunch and returning for the local management meeting. I take some time to visit the station and Panel Box. The service from the North and Paddington is once again in tatters with 'multiple track circuit failures' according to the Control wire. It is a typical hot and humid South West summer's day but hardly extreme weather conditions.

I am giving a talk to the Exeter University Railway Society on the subject of "A week in the Life of an Area Manager". Not enough to keep the students from the bar on an evening like this though. The attendance amounts to just four but they aren't inclined to alter the structure to an informal chat in the bar. I talk for 50min and they ask questions for 80min. As I walk to the car one of the students catches me up and asks if I would like to go for a drink in the bar. A little late perhaps, and I make a note not to waste my energy next year. I get home at 22.30. *Perhaps a little unkind with the perspective of age. I believe that one or two of the audience joined British Rail, which probably justifies the visit in itself.*

Tuesday 17th June 1986

Having driven home, I have to drive back in the morning of course. Passing Exminster, I see the tail-lamps of the 07.00 Plymouth-Newcastle disappearing but as I drive into St. David's it is only just arriving. I phone the Panel Box where an experienced relief signalman tries to spin me some yarn about the freight trip working to serve the yard being in the way and the Newcastle driver being slow getting to and from the phone.

"Was it the driver's fault or a signalling error?" I ask.

"I'd rather not say," he replies. I'm getting rather exasperated with this prevarication.

"Well put someone on who would then," I bark.

Frank McDonough comes on. He thought it was a loco for the shed but it was the trip for the yard. Untangling the mess has caused the delay and, yes, it was his fault.

Shortly afterwards, I speak to Derek Old who is at Taunton to ensure he hears the official version of events, adding that I did not appreciate the first signalman trying to pull the wool over my eyes.

Derek goes straight back to the Panel and repeats exactly what I have said instead of taking more suitable action. This signalman and I have had our differences in the past, once concerning the illegal operation of signals at City Basin with the distant on, home off and starter on with no train closely approaching the home signal. He took umbrage then, until it was proved a driver could not see the home signal when the berth track showed occupied so the driver was entitled to think all City Basin stop signals had been cleared. Later in the morning he phones to speak to me but I am tied up and Karin refuses to put him through. Instead, he asks her to give me the message that he was not trying to pull the wool over my eyes and he does not like to be accused of it. I start to rise to the bait but this type of thing is better disregarded unless and until a direct opportunity arises to deal with it face to face. *Hmm. Not sure about this. I think I might have been better to call him to my office for an interview.*

The morning is fully occupied with a series of retirements. Endless coffee and biscuits. "Thanks for 45 years ; a lifetime of dedicated service," is how it goes. It is not that I am in any way cynical about it; more that it feels inadequate. I think I'll just collect my cheque and go when it is my turn. Same goes for a Long Service award. *Ironic in the turn of events when I did not really get the opportunity to put my words into action.*

First to leave is guard Johann Jacob Vincenz Makosch, a steely grey-eyed man with a self-deprecating sense of humour but one whom I have noticed always went about his job with an aura of calm detachment. I read his service history. *In those days there was always a military history line or two for staff with approaching 50years service.* Guard Makosch's service card says "German Air Force 1939-1945". Perhaps not a good idea to mention the War this time. Today he is very chatty. His wife has just retired as a teacher and had broken her ankle. She intends to study for a degree and he is contemplating living with his son in Switzerland. Filling in the 45min allowed is not a problem.

Next we have four Taunton guards including one retiring at only 49 who has another job lined up and a young signalman from Newton Abbot who is taking redundancy and using the money to start his own business. Both examples are very unusual and perhaps are an indication of an improving economy.

Next we have eight drivers in two batches of four. I am happy to do individual retirement interviews but Personnel assures me a lot of them prefer to be in a group, especially when they have worked together for so long. Sometimes I feel left out of their lively conversation. I know only one in the first group of drivers well, but it goes smoothly. I know three of the second batch but it is sticky. Perhaps it is my fault and I've gone off the boil and stopped trying enough.

More positively, there are four transferred drivers from Leeds arriving today and they are seeing the former personnel trainee first. I ask him to ensure they come to see me when he is finished with them. I always feel this does a lot of good and most are pleased to find a Yorkshireman in charge. Some say they have never spoken to their area manager, but of course present areas in the North tend to be a lot larger. One is from Huddersfield and has not even been given a free ticket with which to make his journey to Exeter. Driver Walker's wife is coming down house-hunting and is using a ticket from her own allocation. I tell him this is not good enough and he appreciates it being put right.

I'm still running on time at 13.30. An Exeter driver has passed a signal at danger at Topsham entering the single line to Exmouth. The guard has led him into a trap by buzzing the train away without observing the signal still being on *(before it became a prime responsibility of the guard after a number of similar incidents elsewhere).* The driver was in possession of the token and was watching two people on the foot crossing, forgetting to observe the signal. He is represented by L.D.C Secretary Len Purse.

The driver sits contritely in front of me, best suit, 45 years unblemished service, and 12 weeks from retirement, pride dented. I have had a few cab rides with him and know he is extremely conscientious, which is in any case obvious from the evidence. But signals passed at danger are grave matters and the message cannot be given that you are allowed a free one in your last three months of course. There is no argument about the facts, so I issue a lenient reprimand. We shake hands and Len says there will be no appeal. *I remember being subsequently ticked off by H.Q. that the normal punishment for a first disregard of a signal, as opposed to a minor misjudgment, is more severe. The possession of the token had been a mitigating factor though and it has to be the decision of the disciplinary officer after all.*

Bill Marden is waiting outside. There is a buckled rail at Wellington between the pair of crossover roads. If it is the up line we could work through the two crossovers but it is not, so it looks like crippling single line working between Silk Mill and Tiverton Jct. *Easier nowadays, just turn trains round at Taunton and Exeter or Tiverton Parkway and try to hire a few buses?* The civil engineering staff rise to the occasion by permitting passage with a 5mph speed restriction. I go to the Panel Box to see what is happening and, when Bernard Price returns from his meeting at Bristol, go box visiting by car.

Wednesday 18th June 1986

Today, I am having a day with Stephen Barnes, the Taunton teacher on secondment for Industry Year. He is sharp and incisive. I leave the car at Teignmouth signal box with Fred Rooke who has bought a copy of Modern Railways with a generous account by Michael Harris of the work we did when the sea wall collapsed last winter in which Fred has been pleased to see his name in print (see Modern Railways June 1986).

I have forgotten to tell the senior railman about the new car so I expect to find a ticket on it when I return to the station this evening. There is an Exeter driver on the down stopper HST school train, a Cross Country set on its way to form the Devonian and offering extra capacity in the peak, so I ride with him.

When Stephen arrives, I take him to the booking office and Newton Abbot West box where John Haycock, destined for the Panel, is on duty. There is a meeting at Plymouth this morning chaired by the rather explosive regional mechanical & electrical engineer John Butt concerning the parlous Class 142 position. Ian Cusworth, former area maintenance engineer at Laira is there, current occupant of the post Tony Coles, Jim Collins, and John Savage from Cornwall.

John Butt and I are rather wary of each other but we exchange pleasantries in the pre-meeting discussion. The engineering situation was discussed at length and the problem defined. Whether we have defined the solutions is a different matter. *Even now.* It appears that we will be drafting back more Class

118s to provide cover for an otherwise impossible task. *One imposed by an unrealistic BRB Provincial Services target and unopposed right through the system in an environment ruled by fear.*

Back at Exeter I run through a few final points with Stephen and catch the 17.25 to Teignmouth. The inspectorate is still out in force. Guards' inspector John Phare *(another giant of a man who had great ability and presence, very similar to Ray Thorn although by nature less ebullient)* thinks the exercise has been worthwhile, which is good news. At least it demonstrates that there is not just blind acceptance of deteriorating standards or, worse, a lack of awareness of what problems need to be tackled. Local punctuality figures have improved, at least.

Bill Midson is in charge of the middle platforms, one of the keenest members of staff but not an opinion universally shared by other managers.

"Do you need two inspectors to help you get the train away?" I joke.

"No they've come to watch the star senior railman in action," he rejoins, raising his arm to the guard and pressing the right-away button spot on time.

There is no ticket on my car at Teignmouth so my suspicions about the lack of car parking checks by the station staff are confirmed. Relief man Bob Baker is on duty so I leave a request for reports from the early and middle turn men. And at the same time, can they remove some fly-posted bills that have been on the back of the pay-and-display information boards for the past couple of weeks? He'll do it tonight, he says.

<u>Thursday 19th June 1986</u>

There should be a special exercise today on the Exeter-Waterloo line but a fire in Clapham Jct signal box has caused postponement so I have the benefit of a clear diary.

I start at Tiverton Parkway again. Takings were only just over £5000 again last week and we should be recording progressive increases at this time of year. Ken Murray, a former relief signalman is training in the booking office with Steve Woodbury (son of acting Personnel manager Clarence). Ken Price is the senior railman.

After half an hour I catch the 08.48 to Taunton, encountering Chester Long on the train. A couple of years ago I would have sought to avoid him *(and he, me)* especially if I was going further than the next stop, Still, we have a helpful and reasonable conversation, both putting out some markers for our forthcoming meeting next week.

Conversation turns to my staffing problems, holding vacancies until the closure of the signal boxes so there are slots for displaced staff. My most pressing problem is Riverside Yard where we are holding vacancies for shunters that signalmen will probably not want. It obviously suits Chester not to go to a London meeting tomorrow *(probably City Council business in the afternoon?)* so he says he will send another Sectional Council representative and go himself to discuss Exeter staffing with Clarence Woodbury.

At Taunton, I take the railway van, which is stationed there to get staff to points' failures at Cogload Jct etc, and visit Silk Mill signal box. John Manley is learning a temporary mini-panel from Derek Locke, a loquacious and pro-management L.D.C member. The atmosphere would otherwise be a bit sterile between John and me. He has never forgiven me for insisting, on our first encounter, that a shunting disc at Taunton West must be maintained in the on position. I suspect he thought I would not notice and he could tell the tale on the box-to-box circuit phone. *I was later to have published in The Railway Magazine a review of the circumstances of the 1940 Norton Fitzwarren crash. I now wish I had tried harder to create a more positive tone with the remaining Taunton signalmen who had been on the railway back then, not that they would have divulged much to me I suspect.*

The residual shunting at Taunton has lately been transferred to Fairwater Yard. It is an engineering yard rather than a marshalling yard so shunting is difficult with long moves between roads, but it is ideal for long-welded rail trains and long trains from the concrete factory. *It is now much busier than back in the 1980s being the main supply point for track panels and relaying trains for much of the former Western Region. It is not unusual to see six Class 66s there at once.*

I take a long walk round with the Chargeman, who is critical of his new accommodation and forthcoming proposed staff reductions. He has calculated that if he ceases to get overtime his pay will be just £6 more than if he went on the dole. All I feel able to say is that to surrender his employment is a very big step.

It is swelteringly hot and I have a splitting headache. On returning to the station I visit Gerald Manning at Taunton West Station *(as opposed to the defunct Taunton West Junction, the locals, and with a certain delight used to inform me if I simply called it Taunton West).* He made a regulating error last week and kindly but unnecessarily says he still feels guilty about it.

I catch the 12.04 back to Exeter with EX1 driver's diagram and L.D.C secretary Fred Butler in the co-driver's seat. The HST is six minutes late with a bogie isolated, therefore restricted to 10mph below normal speed restrictions. The front power car had also failed en route but regained power along the way. We reach Bradford-on-Tone automatic half barrier crossing before meeting a track circuit failure.

"Pass the signal at danger and obey all other signals," is the instruction from the signalman. The next one is green so we get into our stride but, as we touch 60mph there is a sudden silence in the cab. The gradient starts to rise from Wellington, steepening at 1-in-80 to Whiteball Tunnel and an HST doing 90mph (10mph below line speed) at the bottom in Notch 4 of 5 will probably manage 90mph at the top. *Full power Notch 5 I would have said now or perhaps a 2+7 in Notch 4?* We are in Notch 5 but the amps are showing zero. The front power car, No. 43127, has failed. As we enter the tunnel, the speedometer shows just 47mph and we have then to brake for a 20mph temporary speed restriction (tsr) caused by the removal of the points at the west end of the old Whiteball loop. At Tiverton Parkway, we are 15½min late. I pass a message to senior railman Ken Price to tell Exeter the situation and that fitter's attention is required. We have a 2+8 formation which is booked to stop at Totnes and standing instructions state that such trains must not make the station call if running on one power car.

As we set off again, power returns. Fred Butler goes into the power car to check the coolant. He should not do this but it will pay us to know the situation. With 2min recovery time we are 13min late at Exeter.

We are in luck. Three fitters are travelling back to Laira as some form of insurance and the new Exeter driver is keen to go but Maintenance Control insists on withdrawing the Totnes call. Totnes passengers will have to be de-trained at Newton Abbot and the 06.57 Newcastle-Plymouth (non-stop Exeter-Totnes) will call additionally to pick them up. With a coolant top-up and both cars working I feel this is over-cautious. The Controller attempts to justify his decision by claiming the 10mph below line speed restriction is relevant. Of course it is not. The only way it would have to be limited to 50mph between Taunton and Rattery is if it was fully functional on two power cars. He still insists and I tell him he had better prepare his justification for Mr Poynter as I will not let this unnecessary disruption rest. *I think the Controller was probably right and I felt committed to my preference, having told my drivers I thought it would be alright.*

I opt for coffee, pilchard sandwiches and aspirin instead of a trip up the Waterloo line then clue-in Alan Bell on traincrew developments while he has been holiday. John Beer is understandably annoyed about fire precautions duties I have allocated to him. He has some justification but the majority of the work features station premises and he is the natural recipient of the responsibilities. We agree to discuss it at the local management meeting on Monday.

The Network South East special travel day on Saturday is approaching with a cheap flat fare anywhere on their system. It is obvious many passengers will be heading to Whimple, our particular margin of the NSE. John and I are expecting hordes to join and alight at trains that call there plus those heading for Exeter who do not want to re-book en route. John anticipates we will receive many complaints, but only from barrack-room railway enthusiasts, and most other passengers will concentrate simply on enjoying themselves. *From memory I seem to recall that everyone had a good time and complaints were negligible.* Extra trains have been planned, maximising track occupation and we will have a lot of supervision around, bearing in mind that it is a normal summer Saturday on the Western.

Friday 20th June 1986

Today involves a trip to Paddington for a meeting with Travellers-fare and InterCity, the latter now having taken charge of on-train catering. I have been complaining about standards of catering announcements, dress, staff lounging in first class and stock shortages. You name it. *It is no better now. The last Paddington-Penzance HST I used had virtually no food, no order either having been made on the up journey or furnished at Paddington and Coach K remains the best place to overhear all about the rosters of customer service hosts.*

The 06.37 from Dawlish arrives 2min early and I am still 200yds from the station. Shall I run and risk missing it or walk directly on to it. I hurry up but the guard says he had seen me anyway.

At St. David's, Ray Thorn is on 'punctuality' duty. The empty stock for the 06.40 from Totnes has divided on its way up from Laira. The guard has recoupled with the originals rather than using the emergency coupling, so that looks like formal discipline. *Seems like a decent example of initiative in difficult circumstances, especially if the guard has an inkling Laira has not tested the buck-eye properly, if it has been recoupled while there.*

The 06.00 from Plymouth rolls in. Don Jemmett is driving, a huge man with a long grey beard – the epitome of a Gooch 'Single' Victorian driver. He is usually very quiet but always has a twinkle in his eye. The 'B' driver *(in the days of two drivers for 100+mph running)* is Bill Harris *(probably the very best of an excellent body of Exeter drivers, a Great Western man but more like the Exmouth Jct drivers than the 'green badge' drivers themselves).* We are on time but we have not reached Tiverton Parkway before Bill Harris starts to air what is on his mind.

He was 'B' driver when his colleague passed a signal at danger near Midgham with a Bristol road learner in the driving seat. He backs the resultant local ASLEF branch action not to allow learner drivers to take charge. We have a very constructive conversation. Bill is 'old school'; if he passes a signal at danger he expects a Form 1 but he thinks the disciplinary action against his colleague was unfair. *This is a complicated issue. Clearly the driver should intervene opportunely to prevent an incident but management relies on goodwill to ensure practical training is completed. No disciplinary action sends a message to less conscientious drivers that they do not need to bother, automatic discipline offends the constructive drivers and the exercise of discretion encourages allegations of favouritism.*

We suffer a track circuit failure after Witham. Then, as we wait in Westbury station, a Bristol-Paddington HST runs across the far leg of the triangle, diverted from the Chippenham route due to a derailed Foster Yeoman train at Didcot. General Motors No. 59003 is waiting to follow us.

A little more time is lost to Reading where we sit at the junction for another up HST to precede. Bill Harris goes to the 'Admiral's Hat' signal (*so nick-named because it looks like Nelson's headgear)* to phone the signalman but, as he returns to the train, he summons me down to the track.

"What's the matter? I ask.

"What do you make of this?" he counters, pointing to the near front wheel of the power car. The steel tyre is partially missing, cracking and peeling.

"It's not fit to go over facing points at 125mph", he says, definitively.

I tell the box that we are going to go forward at 80-90mph which should also mean a full-service brake application should be unnecessary. In any case we are checked by the train in front with a Slough stop, then halted outside Paddington for an HST to depart. Arrival is 22min late but I am thankful to be there at all. A fitter is waiting and says he thinks the set will have to be taken out of service, not a problem at this time of day. I'll see what the Control log says tomorrow. Bill Harris has stood all the way and refused my offer of his seat at every station en route. *I do not think I would have allowed the set to have gone further than Reading station in these circumstances today and I suspect I shouldn't have done so then either, but I probably reacted to Bill Harris's '125mph' verdict as I was aware that he knew a lot more about it than I would ever know.*

The meeting is underway and has to finish at 11.00 so I make a brief presentation. The Travellers-Fare chief is leaving under early retirement so there is not much chance of making headway there. John Bourne is in typically smooth, if ineffective, mode and will not talk about bringing Travellers-Fare staff under area management control just yet. *That would be 'just yet' as in 'never'. The sector objective seems to have been to remove everyone from area control and assimilate directly into their own respective empires.*

After the meeting I phone the deputy general manager. We decide that I should chair the Sectional Council meeting next Tuesday and not send a representative to Swindon for the Dart Valley meeting with its chairman, Ian Allan. This suits me admirably. I can play cricket on Tuesday evening without any trouble.

I have a chat with Peter Griggs about a few InterCity issues and we wander down to catch the 11.45. Booked 11, load 12, 18min late start with a Class 50. Still 18min late from Reading, we have a spirited run down the B&H making back some time. Passing Bruton down the initial 1-in-98 the pace begins to quicken. 104/107/107.4/106.8/106.8 says my stopwatch before the brakes are applied for the 90mph restriction at Castle Cary. The Bruton-Castle Cary average has been 103.4. Arrival at Exeter St. David's is 6min late.

Peter is receptive to InterCity changes in the West of England. He feels that the Golden Hind could run non-stop from Exeter and reach Paddington not much after the 06.00 Plymouth, say about 09.40. This sounds very ambitious. *It has actually been given an extra stop and decelerated since this discussion.* Also, the Taunton business is needed for a viable load factor. He seems to agree that the Torbay Express should run all winter. What about promotional fares between Exeter, Totnes and Plymouth where most trains have spare capacity? And a revised fares structure to and from Barnstaple where current prices reflect the fact it is 40miles 'beyond' Exeter, rather than a similar distance by road from Taunton? He has made referee in the Western League and jokes that the World Cup 1994 is within range. *I think he ran the line in the Football League and did reserve matches, which is a huge achievement in itself. Peter left the railway early for consultancy and a bridal wear business in West Yorkshire with his wife from Mirfield.*

Back in the office there is a problem in the next timetable at Dawlish Warren where two Waterloo sets coming up from Laira on Sundays need to be overtaken by HSTs, not possible with a nine-vehicle load. I suggest that the impasse can be avoided if we detach a coach here on Saturday evenings and reattach it on Sunday afternoons. *Not sure how I intended to either shunt or service this arrangement.*

Saturday 21st June 1986

The first Network South East Day. At short notice, Chris Green has decided to promote his new business sector by offering journeys between any two NSE stations for a fare of £3. The NSE border on my area lies at Whimple which could cause complications. The 05.48 Exeter-Waterloo sets the standard for the day, full and standing from Honiton. In all, we sold 2,500 tickets at my NSE stations, Whimple to Sherborne inclusive. *This was typical of the excitement engendered by working for Chris Green, with whom I had the good fortune to do some management training when he was Area Manager at Hull in the mid-1970s. Despite the impulsive nature of the arrangement, it was of course fully supported by all kinds of merchandising; carrier bags, badges etc.*

My day begins with a toasted bacon sandwich at Dawlish station café. The Newcastle train calls here on summer Saturdays at 07.35 so I travel into Exeter on it. No. 50017 'Royal Oak', appropriately bedecked in NSE livery has backed down onto the 08.11 to Waterloo. Andy Snowdon is the driver, first of the Yorkshire emigrants two years ago, via Cricklewood and redundancy under the Bedford electrification programme.

At departure time, guard John Madge finds he has no reservoir brake pressure on his gauge. It is necessary to react quickly and I decide to go single-piped, getting away 7min late. This is less than ideal on a densely occupied single-track railway, but it could have been worse. As usual, Andy drives the train with apparently great concentration while discussing railway economics and transport politics. We have 'load 10' instead of 9 and incur some station overtime dealing with the crowds. After a 20mph tsr, we arrive at Yeovil Jct 12min late. I chat with supervisor Ken Davey before returning on the 07.00 from Waterloo which is running 8min late.

I alight at Axminster to see what is going on and, needless to say, I have never seen the station so busy. The up train is 8min late, having crossed the 07.00 down at Honiton. No. 47258 is on the front with the set again made up to ten. It feels very sluggish compared to No. 50017, which is the acknowledged best Class 50, and is 15min late at Yeovil Jct. *I rarely believe stories about one diesel being better than another and certainly not over long periods of time, but if there were exceptions they were 'Royal Oak' and No. 50003 'Temeraire'.* I go through to Sherborne where the staff are obviously experiencing a morale boost from so many full trains.

No. 47258 loses more time through to Gillingham and the 09.10 from Waterloo arrives 27min late. The 7min delay to the 08.11 set off much, if not all, this delay but there is no way back now short of manufacturing cancellations. With the Brighton trains running in both directions and a Control special on the run from Salisbury without a path, the scene is set for cumulative time losses all afternoon.

I return to Yeovil Jct to pick up the down Brighton. It has been reported 27½min late passing Wilton but rolls in 21min late with Nos. 33040 and 33201 in multiple on ten bogies. A young Exeter driver is in charge *(still driving and still as motivated as modern management permits).*

"I might have known this would be an Exeter driver going home, making up so much time from Wilton," I greet him.

"Oh you've noticed" he replies.

We are quickly underway, the driver pointing out that the AWS is isolated, which is legal (as opposed to the driver's safety device) if it has not come off a depot like that and there will be undue delay remedying it. *Shades of the Southall crash after privatisation.* The Class 33s are very noisy and bounce around, finding out the roughest spots on the track. The driver points out the 70mph psr board approaching Axminster which, he correctly says, is to allow a safe signal stop in poor visibility, but the signal is green so he disregards it. This is common sense but wrong. I, probably wrongly, keep quiet. We take it at 80mph, brake slightly. We are already upon Axminster level crossing and it is immediately clear that we are likely to overshoot Axminster platform.

"Oh. No!" the driver gasps as we shoot through the station with the locomotives and seven coaches off the platform and three remaining at it. The female Salisbury guard and senior railman wave for us to reverse. Strictly speaking with a level crossing in rear we need the permission of the signalman at Chard but we are not going to go near it. Back we go and off again after 1½min overtime. *I am not happy with how this was handled overall.*

"First time I've ever done that," says the driver

"Settle down," I reply.

As we go through Seaton Jct, I ask him why it happened.

"It's a very poor brake," he says. "You should be able to stop from 60mph at the crossing." However, I think we were doing more than 60mph there.

"If anyone asks you for a report, tell them I've dealt with it." I explain further. "If it's misjudgement, that is! If it's the brakes we'll need to have the stock examined."

"No we don't want that," he replies.

"Right. If anyone pushes me I'll send you a letter but I don't think it will come to that. It's bound to happen if you're trying hard to make up time." He looks genuinely relieved.

The conversation turns to the ban on route learning drivers being allowed to take charge. I had forgotten he was an ASLEF local official. Then it is thoughts about the incident between the guard and supervisor the other night at Exeter and the severity of two days suspension. This is not a subject I can discuss but I say there was no excuse for what the guard did and he basically accepts that. *I should not have been discussing anything at all in the circumstances but I think I was trying to take his mind off the incident.* As we approach Exmouth Jct, the down distant remains firmly 'on' and, with no AWS, the driver does not immediately respond. I point at the board and he slams on the brake. I fervently hope that they operate better than at Axminster, but the home comes off in plenty of time. *On reflection, I am satisfied that the second mistake stemmed from the first. My presence has not helped the driver either.*

I intend to return from Exeter Central on the 13.35 from St. David's but, while I am waiting, news comes of the loco on the

08.40 Liverpool Paignton being on fire at Cowley Bridge Jct, so I catch the first unit down the bank. *A taxi to Cowley Bridge might have been better advised.* The customer information screens have been hit by lightning and are showing trains two hours earlier than it should. The level crossing barriers are on manual control and five main line trains in each direction are building up, with local trains in disarray.

When I reach the Panel Box, I discover that driver Dave Whittle has detached the 2xClass 31s from the train and taken them to Riverside Yard where the defective one has been detached. The Fire Brigade has attended and left hoses all over the track and at 14.30 the line is still not clear. I jump into the Panel railway van and head for the site, *perhaps an hour later than I should have but it would arguably have been difficult to take an overview if I had done so. Not sure where the on call inspector was either. Probably on the Southern, quite properly.* Typically, I arrive just as the line is given back to traffic, and matters slowly return to normal.

The Penzance-Brighton is dealt with commendably quickly and then the Liverpool is brought in by its remaining Class 31. Apparently the driver with whom I had ridden from Sherborne volunteered to help with the fire incident and went straight out to Cowley Bridge after he arrived at St. David's. *So perhaps the questionable rules' management had been motivational, but he is the type to have gone anyway.* I am told that we are going to re-engine the Liverpool but we find another Class 31 and drop it onto the good one, multiple them up and send them away to Paignton. *I suspect this epitomises the professionalism of the Exeter staff under pressure.*

Amidst the chaos, there is a chance to thank driver Whittle before he goes to hospital to have a badly split knuckle repaired. The ex-Longsight man passes it off as nothing. I will ask the Regional Operating Manager to authorise a special award. *Surely I could have done it?*

Driver Davy *(the one who was involved in the 'call me doctor story' on the Barnstaple line)* has been coming to work on a train delayed at City Basin. He has alighted and walked to the station, arriving rather hot and bothered. We were within a hairsbreadth of having the platforms blocked with trains waiting driver relief by trains delayed by the blocked platforms. No. 31306 takes the Barnstaple away from Platform 6 to break the stalemate.

I head home at 17.22. Newton Abbot West Jct signalman Charlie Beatson is on the train. He is hoping to secure a supervisory job in Scotland and comes to have a chat about it.

CHAPTER 7: THE SECTORS START TO MEDDLE

Monday 23rd June 1986

The railway is in good shape this morning and I arrive at Exeter 1sec early. My first appointment is at 10.00 for the retirement of guard Bowerman. The discussion does not flow easily and we talk about his canary-breeding hobby much of the time. Next it is chargeman Miller, then senior railman Blackmore who seems to have had a burden lifted from his shoulders by being offered early retirement. It was mutual consent really. He said he wanted to go and I cut his job out. *One of the best bits of advice I was given by my boss was by Arnold Wain, the area manager at Middlesbrough, who told me I could cut out as many jobs as I wanted as long as I was seen to be looking after the displaced people. As with most good advice there were exceptions, but not this time.*

Next comes a 'representative of the freight business'. They mostly look the same, in their dapper suits and matching shirts and ties. He outlines the changes proposed for the Westbury to Exeter Central cement traffic. It will use 51tonne air braked wagons and be converted from trainload operation to a new Westbury to Exeter Riverside Speedlink service. *Sounds like a backward step even now*. Getting 15/51tonne wagons up the 1-in 36 or so gradient from St. David's to Exeter Central is not the easiest task but provides a rousing fanfare of horn exchanges and diesel engine noise from train engine and banker.

Meanwhile the news arrives that the City Basin trip has had a derailment due to a signalling error. The down line is clear but only just. Bernard Price has sent for a locomotive to push the derailed wagon clear of the up line. I don't ask why when Bernard makes arrangements like this. Proof of this wisdom comes in the total delay attributable to the incident - 2min to the down Bradford.

John Beer has organised a meeting with the City tourist officer and a Dutch travel company chief. He wants to know what he can offer them in the way of additions to the package, such as a Devon Ranger. And what about including a rail trip to Cornwall? And the trip to and from the London Airport? It is easy to be positive about the first two but it gets difficult speaking for InterCity who are likely to contradict common sense. *I think it is fair to say that there are few such local initiatives in the privatised railway, but that is partly a function of the high calibre of assistant local managers who had either a lifetime experience in signalling or driving like Bernard and Alan Bell or were highly qualified with creative young minds like John, Tony Crabtree and Paul Silvestri.*

We have a routine local management meeting. John and Bernard are not too keen on the new fire precautions document that has been circulated. Neither am I, so it is withdrawn and it is back to the drawing board.

Tuesday 24th June 1986

I was supposed to be going to Swindon today for a meeting with the deputy general manager and Ian Allan about Dart Valley Railway payments to British Rail. The dgm rings with a couple of queries, quickly followed by John Pearse with a few more.

At 10.15 the management team for the Sectional Council meeting concerning local freight trip working starts to assemble. In my opinion, and Bob Poynter's as he admits in retrospect, the meeting should not need to have been held. Basically, the freight business made a mess of the trip arrangements in January and we have kept the job going in the meantime, primarily with the cooperation of the drivers' LDC who have run single manned if necessary if the trips were needed on a day they were not booked.

We have also played a risky game by allowing St. Blazey crews to pick up the export clay from the Heathfield branch once. Sectional Council B (drivers' representatives) say it is a serious issue to let men in who do not know the road. *It would be a disciplinary offence for their members to go too.* I know all about this and can vouch that the men who were used did know the road and the working was actually in the St. Blazey trip book so they had a right to retain the knowledge they had.

The man from Speedlink admits the Tuesday/Thursday Only arrangement was a mess and there is now a loco available off an extra Speedlink all week. After a little token argument the meeting breaks up. It is significant that Sectional Council C (station/guards/shunting/signalmen representatives) chairman Chester Long has attended the staff side meeting but then disappeared to a City council appointment in Bournemouth.

The meeting finishes just in time for me to meet Peter Semmens, writer of train performance articles in The Railway Magazine, off the down Cornish Riviera. His train is 4min late and has apparently been stopped twice on my area unnecessarily. If so, this is embarrassing as the last time he complained about unjustified delay I told him it was due to manual signalling. *Doubly embarrassing if I had known that Keith Farr and I would take over the column in due course. At least I did not tell him it was due to multiple aspect centralised signalling this time.*

I ask for the signalling reports on one of them. On the other, signalling inspector Derek Old was training a signalman on the St. David's station 'middle panel' area and was showing his trainee how he could not clear the signal without lowering the level crossing barriers first. I don't think that a delay to the 'Limited' to encourage the signalman to learn his lesson was worth it. Later in the day Peter calls in the office for a cup of tea and I take him over to the Panel Box. I don't suppose it will prevent an adverse comment or two in the Magazine. *I certainly don't think it would have deterred me.*

The plans for Matford Marshes out-of-town shopping centre have arrived. Contrary to our discussions, the proposed new station shows up and down loops which are unnecessary and likely to sink the scheme on cost grounds. Letters will have to be sent seeking an amendment. It would also cost line capacity by taking longer to stop and start. *The shopping complex never materialised but the trading estate expanded considerably. The station is now in the planning stage but I fear it will simply erode line capacity and journey times with no compensating benefit.*

There is also a proposal for a bridge to replace Red Cow Crossing at the east end of the platforms at St. David's. The plans impinge on our precious car parking space and prevent access to the former National Carriers yard area and are unacceptable. *Another scheme that has never come to fruition. The practice of escorting passengers across with an attendant while the barriers were down, partly financed by the City Council continued. Although it looked dangerous it was less so than alternatives such as keeping the barriers down for long periods, thereby risking passengers leaping over them. There would also have been a major difficulty of lowering the barriers as a succession of pedestrians used the wide crossing. Even so, I would not have bet on the same system being in place in a 'Health and Safety' dominated 2016.*

Before leaving, I have a chat with Alan Bell about an appeal by an Exeter driver being adjourned at headquarters. A Bristol driver has had a statement taken by a traction inspector alleging that the Exeter driver was not paying attention when the Bristol road learner passed the signal. The driver concerned is so much like a mother hen that it is more likely that he would have interfered, even to an annoying extent. The driver has been in to say how much he is worrying about it and that he still expects to be reprimanded.

Alan and I then sort out a problem about signage and a special notice I have drafted concerning Exeter signal 558 out of the loco sidings. This has been passed at danger three times, twice by Laira drivers and once by a Gloucester man. Neither depot has much cause to go onto the depot. They have rung out to the box saying they were at 560 signal whereas they were at 558. There being no track circuits there, the signalman duly clears 560. The driver sees the aspect, proceeds and passes 558, running through and damaging the points. I have erected a small sign saying which signal applies to which siding, which I have been told by safety staff at Swindon is not permissible. Let them remove it and take the consequence of a collision. *It is still there and I have not heard of any further incidents. The measure presaged the current anti-signal passed at danger precautions often involving extra information and signage.*

Wednesday 25th June 1986

There are just three Class 142s fit for service in Devon today with the shortfall made up of Class 118s, including two twin sets to try and keep the sharper Pacer timings. I drive in to Exeter to catch the 08.11 to Salisbury, formed of 8 Mark 1s out of circuit. The only first class is a Brake Composite Compartment coach (BCK) with just twelve first class seats. We must try to get this set out of its diagram before tomorrow evening when it would work the 17.38 from Waterloo. Salisbury is reached just 1min late. The driver has been Bob Harris whose family come from Devon. He has transferred in from Tunbridge Wells and was originally considered to be a left-wing hothead by the Exeter LDC. They now say he has settled down and he has certainly completed his traction and route learning exceptionally quickly.

The Salisbury meeting is to consider marketing plans for Salisbury to Exeter. John Beer, Salisbury area manager Gerry Daniels and Alec McNab, marketing manager for Network South East South West (if that is not too much of mouthful) are there, It is a long-winded affair but productive as we pave the way for spending our area NSE marketing budget. NSE is devolving responsibility, whereas Provincial has clawed it back. *This probably best illustrates the different characters of Chris Green and Edmonds.*

There is some nonsense from Gerry Daniels about running steam from Salisbury to Yeovil Jct on three weekends which I see as being peripheral and even counter-productive so far as reliability of the core service is concerned. There is a turntable at Yeovil Jct but it looks a bit delicate for large steam engines. For devilment *(obstructionism?)* I mention that the Western Region mechanical engineer has eyes on taking it to St. Blazey for turning Class 142s to even up flange wear. The plan was actually suggested last week but quickly dropped but it will give Gerry something to think about.

The return journey is in the same set of Mark 1s as the outward one, minus one vehicle detached at Waterloo, but on time at Exeter. Bernard Price has been busy with failures of both up and down trains plus Department of Transport Inspector Major Olver in connection with the re-signalling scheme.

And the award for sector silliness today concerns a proposal that displaying publicity for local services on B.R.'s own poster sites should be debited against our local budgets at the full commercial rate.

Thursday 26th June 1986

Colin Leach of Swindon Provincial Services raises the bar in the silliness competition. Having centralised local publicity, and having made a mess of it, it was decided he would issue an errata slip. Now he is going to organise the household mail drop but he is not going to include the errata slip much less re-print the information. The leaflet shows the Dawlish to Paignton fare as £2.00 whereas it is £2.40. We have been handing out the errata slip with the leaflet. Now we will get a queue of people demanding a £2 fare. If we reduce the price accordingly then the errata slip that has been issued will be wrong.

There is a lot of work to be done this morning so my plans for going round the area are shelved. Much of the time is spent discussing personnel issues with Ken Boobyer and Clarence Woodbury. Tony Crabtree arrives and we agree how to alter the station staffing, moving a step nearer to consultation.

Ken Shingleton comes in at lunchtime. He is not happy about how a BRUTE (B.R. Universal Trolley Equipment- a parcel cage) has become stuck in the door of a brake van and then bounced out onto the platform. The 'train ready to start' had then been pressed even though the crew to work the train away was delayed on an up train. In the meantime the middle platform senior railman, Bill Midson, has left duty so that will be one for tomorrow. Ken leaves towards Waterloo on the 14.17, on time. Still, I reflect we are faring better than Cornwall where a passenger on the 09.33 from Penzance has died of a heart attack and another has jumped off the 10.00 from Penzance while it was moving and fractured his skull.

Bernard Price has been escorting Major Olver around the area along with engineers etc. He has also been pumping points during a failure. The DoT Inspector pronounces himself impressed before departing.

Tomorrow sees the Travel Centre Review taken a step further in a meeting at Bristol. I slip the Transport Salaried Staff Association (TSSA) circular in my bag to read on the way home. David Warne (rom's office at Swindon) has said it has the backing of Area Managers. It certainly has not.

Friday 27th June 1986

I thought I would have a lie-in and catch the 08.49 to work with No. 50047 'Swiftsure' on ten and a cab ride on a steaming hot morning. Smack on time at Exeter St. David's. Mail is light so there is no trouble catching the 09.31 to Bristol and a few words with the Exeter guard who seems to think it was too much to expect ticket checks, with 14,14 and 39 minutes between stations, without assistance.

The other area managers are assembled to discuss the travel centre review. The mechanics of getting the consultation document out are simple enough but the tactics are more complicated. I enjoy the cut and thrust, especially with the two senior area managers, Frank Markham from Bristol and Conrad Clark from Paddington and we have some success. *I am not sure what level Frank had achieved before taking the job at Bristol but I think it was divisional manager. I suspect he had taken the Bristol job after being in charge of many of these Swindon H.Q. managers and he was not afraid to show it. Conrad on the other hand was my idea of a South-East manager. Lots of edge, bluster and a dose of bluff to go with it. No doubt all necessary to manage Paddington and something*

I doubt I would have been sufficiently flexible to manage successfully.

There is agreement that we will have our hands tied at consultation and be landed with the job of defending a wholly inconsistent InterCity approach. It is not that I think more resources should necessarily be invested in travel centres, and I certainly do not think there should be a wholly uniform approach. For instance, InterCity is insisting that 95% of inward telephone enquiries should be answered within 30sec, a target that reflects reasonable customer expectations. The business will support three extra staff at Exeter but none elsewhere on the area which fail the standard. The business managers do not have to chair the Sectional Council meetings so do not concern themselves too much with this kind of irksome detail.

As we break up today's sector silliness award goes to InterCity. They have asked for a feasibility study into the effect of concentrating staffing at one platform with all trains using it. *This looks even sillier in view of the growth in services and expansion of this station. Foresight was not a talent with which the business seems to have been imbued.*

No. 50010 'Monarch' is in good form on the way home with a 5min early arrival in Exeter, although it is one coach short of the timing load and should have a little in hand.

ASLEF organiser Ross Goff and LDC secretary Len Purse are in discussion with Alan Bell. They have been lobbying their own drivers not to enforce their ban on traction and road learning from the driver's seat. Perhaps this approach would work only on the Exeter area. *It possibly shows the wisdom of not tackling this problem head-on as it was in the best interests of most drivers to allow it to continue. It is also the first appearance in this diary of Ross Goff who was an extremely able adversary but one who always acted honourably and fairly. As for Len Purse, he was a gentleman but a wily one who would always act in the best interests of the depot and did this by befriending management rather than taking them on. His members might have occasionally suggested that the best work always landed in Len's own link but, if so, it was a further example of his abilities.* Alan is satisfied the problem will evaporate now and Alan's instinct in footplate matters has never needed any questioning.

I have been writing many consultation documents for items as diverse as introducing pay & display car parking, withdrawal of some supervisory jobs and the platform staffing. *This could be an example of failure to delegate. I am not sure how many area managers wrote their own documents but, since I was going to be the one chairing the meeting, I could be confident it said what I wanted it to say and it was probably as quick a process as revising someone else's efforts – and less demoralising for them too.* Clarence Woodbury is going on holiday for two weeks, the personnel ex-trainee will be going to Old Oak soon and with Bernard Brown's vacancy the personnel department will be under pressure without the workload of preparing consultation documents.

Exeter Station Supervisor Paul Silvestri, who is occasionally seconded to do local train service planning, comes in to discuss his latest ideas. They have the benefit of his local business knowledge, operational expertise and his intellect. He demonstrates his ingenuity with slender resources once again.

On the train home, the Bristol guard is late to the train, so we exchange a few sharp words. He says he has been a long time obtaining change from the Travel Centre. I tell him that he should be using the Cash Office and where it can be found. He tries to re-open the argument about the queue in the Travel Centre.

"Look, you'll not get change easily at the Travel Centre, especially at this time of day. I've told you where the cash office is, and so next time I hope you'll be at your train on time," I say. The guard does not respond.

When I got home last night the Dawlish Senior Railman was washing his car at 20.00, despite the fact it was parked next to mine and I might turn up anytime to collect it. I tell him I don't think much to it and if he has some spare time he can brush up some of the shingle thrown up by the sea onto the down platform. *It seems as though I was in a bad mood, but the car washing issue was more that the staff member had been caught out so easily, rather than the act itself.*

The weather is still stiflingly hot so Linda and I unwind with an evening walk along the sea wall. The Glasgow relief and Aberdeen train are embarrassingly late again and the manual signalling is incapable of alleviating the resultant bunching. Well, it is the last summer it will be a problem and capacity will be doubled next year.

Saturday 28th June 1986

A mixture of work and pleasure today. I have decided to go to Bristol on the 09.52 Liverpool train from Dawlish with No. 50027 'Lion' on eight coaches. Mike Stone is the driver and 85mph is about par for the course but we are only a couple of minutes late at Temple Meads despite signal checks outside the station. I then catch the 11.10 Weston-super-Mare to Birmingham which is formed of two West Midlands suburban units.

The 20min at Bristol Parkway give the opportunity for a cooling orange juice and a sandwich before the 08.40 from Liverpool rolls in with Nos. 31407 and 31427 in multiple on the Pullman set. Although it is an incongruous combination, it represents an excellent standard of summer Saturday accommodation. *Much better than a Voyager in every respect except speed.* Mike Stone is the driver on the return and speeds remain in the low 80s but at least there is no fire this week, unlike last Saturday. Arrival at St. David's is on time and Paignton is reached 2min early.

There is just time for a quick tour of Paignton before catching No. 45140 on the Nottingham back to Dawlish. There is time to kick a few Class 45 enthusiasts out of first class and get them down off the tables.

CHAPTER 8: ESTABLISHING THE CAUSE OF A DERAILMENT

Sunday 29th June 1986

At lunchtime we have a family gathering with visitors from Yorkshire. I am on my third glass of wine when the phone rings. It is Bernard Price, who is supposed to be coming off call at 09.00 for his holidays. He has been called out at 05.35 to a ballast train derailment at Newton Abbot West. It seems that a ground disc signal has been passed at danger but the three members of the train crew swear it was off. The locos are re-railed at 02.00

Monday 30th June 1986

I catch the 07.20 to Newton Abbot to reconstruct the accident. Although I am convinced in my own mind that it was a signal passed at danger, I think an Inquiry is required. I could do without chairing it if Bernard is on holiday but having an H.Q. officer is a far worse alternative. I speak to Bob Poynter about it and arrange the Inquiry for Wednesday.

I start interviewing for a new Personnel Manager at 10.15. There are twelve interviews but I do not identify a suitable applicant. Clarence did not have a good interview and seems nervous, not coming up with any imaginative ideas. Ken Boobyer has designs on the job as well. An applicant from Scotland has the presence but not the substance and two younger applicants are promising but nowhere near experienced enough. There is one more applicant on leave but it is not hopeful. I contemplate re-advertising in the hope that it attracts people who might have thought they had no chance. For instance, Chris Dickinson, area manager at Middlesbrough, has someone ready for promotion. *Area manager's old boys network I suppose. Chris had followed me into the first supervisory job I had, at Bradford.*

At 17.30 I go to the Chamber of Commerce Council meeting with a reception afterwards and manage to get away at 21.00. Most of my conversation is with Harry Blundred who is waiting to hear from the Secretary of State for Transport whether his management buy-out of Devon General bus company will be accepted. It's certainly a huge step. *And one that would affect many a railway manager in the years to come.*

Tuesday 1st July 1986

The diary has been filled up at the last minute. David Warne, chief controller Ray Spackman and Mike Winstock, a senior manager in the Regional Mechanical and Electrical Engineer's department, arrive to discuss my proposals for improving reliability of Class 50 locomotives on the Waterloo line. Winstock is pretty aggressive and I have to match him or withdraw. After about half an hour, we start to converse normally. There is little comes out of it but it seems to have got under their skin. *I would be intrigued to know what I had suggested as I do not recall it at all.*

Ken Shingleton phones at least three times during the morning over delays that have come to his notice and lunchtime is spent investigating them. At 14.00, I have a demonstration of a portable telephone from a man representing British Telecom. I undertake to have a twelve-day trial to test it but, at £30 per week on a two-year lease that includes maintenance and calls, it sounds useful. I suppose we could save the annual rental with one call in an emergency.

At 15.00, I meet assistant area civil engineer Colin Carr and two people from the Torbay local authority. The proposal is for a new station at Torbay Hospital on the Paignton line. There's a new retail development taking place at the opposite side of the line to the hospital and the traffic potential looks good. The deal on offer is a payment of £150,000 from the Council for a good station in a difficult location, on a gradient and curve. Colin says the price is £200,000 to include design fees, This is a private party rate, whereas work for British Rail would have been £150,000. I offer the difference between the two as the British Rail contribution to the scheme. I suppose I should have asked Provincial Services Route Manager David Mather but the process will be interminable and he might say 'No'. *Someone somewhere must have eventually said no as nothing was ever done. The absence of a railway station at the increasingly important hospital and the expansion of the retail park provide an endorsement for the stance taken at the meeting. However, it has re-emerged as a serious proposition since the first draft of these 'italics'. I await the final cost with interest.*

Wednesday 2nd July 1986

The 07.08 from Dawlish is formed of a set on its way from Laira to Exeter to work the 08.11 to Waterloo but it is late off maintenance this morning. I take four passengers to Exeter in the B.R. car. Regional operating manager Bob Poynter is at Newton Abbot and in a rage but, thankfully, it is directed at Plymouth and not us. We have time only for a perfunctory talk about delegation and objectives before I have to start the Joint Inquiry. *'Joint' refers to the inquiry's inter-departmental nature, always chaired by an operator. They are to be held if the cause is in doubt or if the incident is serious, including anything that might require a Department of Transport Inspectorate investigation. Clearly, they should be arranged as soon as possible after the event.* I am supported by managers from the signalling, mechanical and civil engineering departments and interview the driver, secondman and guard of the derailed ballast train, the signalman, permanent way supervisor, the engineering 'person in charge of the possession', the signalling maintenance supervisor and operations signalling supervisor Bill Mardon.

The witnesses are questioned by the panel and the evidence is then presented in the report. I have been brought up to do the summary to prevent endless repetition and 'Are you sure' questions. The witnesses are free to suggest alterations and there are union representatives as 'observers' Unlike some chairmen I never let the observers stray towards the duty of the panel but I do try to involve them and periodically ask them for their observations.

On hearing the evidence it is clear that I should have called the civil engineer's handsignalman who might have seen what went on. It will be necessary to re-convene tomorrow but the issue seems simple. All three traincrew are insistent that the disc signal was 'off'. It was one of three such signals grouped together. The technical evidence suggests the signal was on and at least we have been able to eliminate loco faults, permanent way faults and the signalman moving the points underneath the train.

As we break up, Peter Griggs arrives with Nigel Pennington, the marketing manager from InterCity Cross Country. Barnstaple travel centre manager Richard Burningham and John Beer also attend. *Richard was a young appointment to the job and eventually became the South West community rail officer.* The attitude is constructive and we get the price reduction we have been seeking on Barnstaple to London Savers, an experiment on Plymouth-Exeter fares and improvements to Tiverton Parkway services – a good package. We then have half an hour on InterCity staffing before the train home.

Thursday 3rd July 1986

I am not happy about the Inquiry so I decide to go to Newton Abbot West for 07.00. Charlie Beatson is on duty. Have I heard whether the rumour he has got the supervisory job at Perth is correct? I'll ring the area manager there later this morning. *Poor Charlie, he must have thought I was coming to bring him the good news when he saw me climbing the box steps at that early hour.*

There is no new direct evidence available. However, Charlie and I set up a combination of lever movements which results in the lever being over in the frame with the appropriate disc 'on' with the points ever-so-slightly open. And when the lever is released it flies back into the frame. Charlie Beatson is quite candid about events. He is certain that the signalman concerned knew the box so well he would have known the signal had not come off. Did the crew see the lever being pulled and assumed it had come off? It is all very interesting but not central to the direct cause.

Back at Exeter by 08.30, the new witness does not wish to tell us much. Yes, he was there. No, he did not notice anything. No, he did not talk to anyone. "The Panel concludes that disc signal 123 was passed at danger by Driver ….." This is a bit rough and will cause resentment but there is no real alternative from the evidence presented. I'm suspicious that neither the driver nor secondman could recall a ballast train move ten minutes before their derailment so it suggests they might have been dozing.

I cannot find my copy of the Inquiry report but from this distance three points emerge. It is likely that Charlie Beatson was telling me something directly this morning. Did the signalman pull the lever but not observe the signal clear and, with the points 'slightly' open (enough to cause the derailment) and then give the driver the tip to set off?. Why did I not question the signalling inspectors more closely? I suspect I was missing Bernard's guidance with him being on holiday. The more I think about it the more questions emerge.

ASLEF observer Richard Westlake might cause some trouble about the verdict but he stays on an hour after the inquiry to talk about some of his County Council issues as an elected representative of the people.

I go back to Dawlish for lunch using an HST with Andy Snowdon driving. This afternoon there is a meeting of the Teignmouth Harbour Commissioners, an ex-officio appointment for the area manager. The amount I know about dredging the navigation channel is minimal. Gribble worm is attacking the Harbour Master's boat and No. 2 Salty Buoy has had to be replaced. The function of this representation nowadays is to mix with the community. The commercial port operators value my voting power as they think it will counterbalance an influx of wind-surfers and other leisure users of the harbour but the origin of the seat on the Board comes from the Great Western Railway's interests in the Stover Canal that brought the china clay to the quay.

It is my intention to get home early, attack the paperwork and start writing up the Inquiry Report. On arrival at Teignmouth station I find a buckle in the down main line with a 5mph tsr in force. Within thirty minutes assistant area civil engineer Dave Doggett has arrived, eased the restriction to 20mph and posted handsignalmen. Signalling Inspector Bill Mardon and Control both seem impressed but it has been a matter of good luck and Dave being prepared to back his judgement. *I honestly suspect we would have had a 5mph tsr in force all evening nowadays, if not a complete stop on down line trains.* Bill is taking steps to have the box opened tonight to deal with the 04.15 'between trains' possession that has been granted. By 20.30 the paperwork is finished, barring that of the Inquiry which has yet to be started. *It is really important to do the report quickly otherwise details can be inadvertently omitted.*

Friday 4th July 1986

This morning I am straight into three retirements. John Beer is away sick with a strained back ligament and Tony Crabtree kindly agrees to step into John's on call slot. My portable phone arrives for testing and Long Service Awards follow at 14.00 before I go across to the Panel Box. At 16.00 an M.A. student arrives to ask some questions for a dissertation and it is time to go home. Tony Crabtree is negotiating radio advertising rates with Steve Snell from commercial station Devonair. By 22.30 the Joint Inquiry report draft is complete.

CHAPTER 9: PADDY ASHDOWN TAKES AN INTEREST

Monday 7th July 1986

Today is spent mainly producing the Report, checking and cross checking it before it is sent to the other members of the inquiry team for perusal, amendment and signature. It then has to be sent off to the Regional Operating Manager who either accepts it or, heaven forefend, rejects it.

Regional personnel manager Ken Beresford rings up about the area personnel manager interviews. What do I suggest we should do if the remaining applicant to be interviewed is unsuitable? "Re-advertise," I suggest, realising the time loss will be significant. He asks if I would be amenable to trawling for suitable Personnel Management Trainees, similar to the one I have released to Old Oak Common. I agree. He is aware of the one I have identified at Middlesbrough and there is another one in Glasgow who is on the point of resigning – and does so before the end of the day. There are two women possibilities at Old Oak and Woking which will be a shock to the West Country traditions but I realise they will probably be far better than their male equivalents in getting to the position they have reached already.

Bernard is back from a week's so-called holiday. It started with working all day on the Sunday from the 05.30 time of the Newton Abbot derailment and finished with taking up on-call again last night. In the meantime he went to Derby for a day to look at some new signalling equipment and had come out this morning at 02.30 to ensure the new cement working went without a hitch.

Tuesday 8th July 1986

The desk is clearer today. All the consultation documents are either being typed or processed in the personnel office – issuing to staff representatives, arranging meeting dates etc. Tony Crabtree has submitted one that gives more coverage to Paignton parcels office counter. He reckons it will get more business with more consistent staffing. I can remember taking permanent staffing out because of under-utilisation but I accept that 'ring the bell' and wait for, perhaps reluctant, service is not attractive to customers. *This is an example of where the Parcels Sector's focus on what was considered a marginal activity is positive. However they ceased to operate on a marginal cost basis and eventually lost all their traffic in what was eventually a booming market.*

I also remember conceding an extra job to handle newspaper traffic at 04.40 and the early morning summer trains. With a few strokes of the pen, Tony gets his extra coverage and I can still claim 'minus one railman' whom I think can be accommodated in a Newton Abbot vacancy if nothing materialises at Paignton in the meantime.

Phil Shepherd, plant engineer at Laira wants to discuss rolling stock technician (RST) flexibility for a joint report we have been charged with writing. After October there should be six RSTs on the area, pre-inspecting wagons for traffic and trains en route. In quiet locations, traffic staff could be trained to do this. We reckon minus three posts is achievable, probably minus four but we had better leave some elbow room in case a budget meeting demands we should achieve it.

Tim Davies, from Devon County Council, and an assistant arrive to meet David Mather and me about support for a package of improvements on the Exmouth line. *I really did not require David. If the Provincial Services need to reduce costs why did they introduce this level of management? Tim, on the other hand was to prove one of the great survivors and was still doing his Transport Co-ordination job when I last saw him in 2013.* There has to be some hard talking in the first place about what we have achieved. Some local bus services are now back in the interchange bus/rail station after an absence. We have invested in the new half-hourly service in terms of stock, wages and fuel and Council Planning and Transportation Committee wants a further £40,000 of expenditure from us to justify £20,000 from their budget. *My indignation seems a bit misplaced in the privatised railway context but we were used to going round with the B.R. begging bowl in those days.*

Eventually, we decide to ditch the £20,000 plan to raise Topsham up platform and suggest we contribute £20,000 towards a £48,000 package of customer information systems, station improvements and a free car park for rail users at Exmouth. In addition, there is talk of reviving the Digby & Sowton station project to serve park and ride and a retail development planned for the site of the Digby hospital with a £40-50, 000 contribution and some support for keeping Copplestone station open, where revenue was less than £1,000 a year and the bill for repairing the platform face was going to be £15,000. A productive morning's work.

David wants to take a trip out to Barnstaple so I accompany him, bending his ear about the complete mess that has been made of the Provincial local advertising. He confides that a direct order from his boss, John Pearse, has been internally ignored and suitable steps are being taken to prevent a repetition. Both trips are on time.

At 13.45 I have to meet the office clerical staff LDC. More chaos has emerged from Bernard Brown's arrangements for computer equipment in the Paybills section and Clarence Woodbury's version of the same events. I talk for about 15min, explaining the problem, why it is in a muddle, what the objectives are, the priorities in tackling them and the new proposals. I think this has taken most of their ammunition away as I have not tried to deny or defend the mismanagement. After a quick inspection of the rooms affected, implementation is agreed for next Monday.

Wednesday 9th July 1986

The day starts at Newton Abbot at 07.30. Complimentary coffee served at my seat on the HST adds a touch of luxury. *Complimentary refreshments in first class were not an invention of the privatised railway, although there are those who believe it was.* Business was good at Tiverton Parkway last week, takings having risen to £6,500. Next comes a visit to Taunton where much of the available time is occupied by sorting out a pensioner who has missed the 10.10 to Bristol. She wants to go to Worcester which is in the 'obscure' category of B.R. destinations. *It is different now.* The 11.11 involves a mere 3½hrs wait at Cheltenham. If we endorse her ticket 'via Birmingham' she will get there a little more quickly and hang around a lot less. Free coffee and sandwiches, plus use of the phone overcome her distress.

I catch my fourth train of the day back to Exeter, all four being on time. After a few hurried phone calls I go home in the cab of an HST for a break. Most of the time is spent on paperwork, but in a relaxed atmosphere. Back at Dawlish station the down Manchester is 65min late but Paul Silvestri has found a Class 142 to run to Paignton and back as a substitute.

This evening I have to attend the Yeovil and District Rail Action Group (YADRAG) meeting so I catch the 17.33 to Yeovil Jct. I get the impression that the assistant ticket examiner, one Mrs Pretty, wife of a retired Exeter station supervisor, has told her regulars that they can't sit in first class tonight because her 'boss is on board'. I make a note to tell Ray Thorn that this is not on, and to check the train at Pinhoe one night. *Sounds like overkill at this distance.*

Yeovil Supervisor Terry Gale has drafted a timetable plan, on his spare days, for the Weymouth line. I'm picked up by the Group's secretary. It is a committee meeting of around ten people and we exhaustively cover most aspects of railways in the area. Salisbury are going to run their steam specials to Yeovil Jct in October and John Beer wants to organise a 'Steam Extravaganza' using YADRAG stewards. I doubt John has the capacity to manage the huge workload but he obviously knows best and it is necessary to take a positive line. After a constructive meeting, the secretary drives me back to the station.

"Oh, by the way," he says, "we have to report how it went to Paddy Ashdown (the high profile Liberal M.P.). There's nothing you don't want us to tell him is there?" I don't think this is on but I have to accept it and I certainly cannot sit there and give him a list.

On the way back I ride with Andy Snowdon again. It is light at 21.30 leaving Yeovil Jct but twilight drifts into darkness as we head west. We are ten minutes late at Crewkerne after a tsr but fortune is on our side. We do not need to go into Chard loop, as booked, because the 21.00 up service from Exeter has reached there first so we make up 5min as a result. With 4min recovery time and No. 50009 'Conqueror', rumoured to be fitted with experimental loco DP2's engine, in good condition we arrive 2min early at Central and on time at St. David's.

Thursday 10th July 1986

I intend to visit Paignton, Torquay and Totnes but Newton Abbot is in turmoil and I get the impression that the experienced and normally competent supervisor is letting events run away with him. Late empty stock arrivals and problems with the west end ladder points again have contributed to the problem. A few hasty alterations to the train plan start to pull things round and Paignton chargeman Ernie Bittlestone (normally very negative because he feels the railway does not match the one with which he was brought up, I think) manages to run round the Glasgow stock and get it away just 21min after it had left Newton Abbot.

Totnes is busy with Dart Valley traffic and 59 computers for Dartmouth Naval College which have arrived by Night Star and amount to ten round trips for the Night Star delivery taxi. Something for Tony Crabtree to consider to improve efficiency for large volumes. *Computers were bigger in those days. A special stop in the Nottingham parcels to unload the five BRUTE loads of computers had shown commendable initiative.*

After a signalbox visit, I return to Exeter. Bernard Price has been taking a consultation meeting at Taunton, removing one job on the station and two in the yard. Instead of two chargemen and two leading railmen in the yard, we have proposed two senior railmen covering 07.00 to 19.00 with a midday overlap. The staff side has made a counter-submission resulting in one senior railman and one leading railman covering 07.00-15.30. Things aren't like that in the North or at Paddington.

While at Newton Abbot, I thought the up through line's signals cleared too soon after the Manchester. I ask Supervisor Vernon Baseley at Exeter to question the driver of the following Laira-Waterloo empty stock about the signal sequence he had received. I'm right! The empty stock driver had encountered the home off and the starter on. The signalman is the experienced relief man who was on duty at Newton Abbot West during the ballast train derailment. I ponder the conclusion of the Joint Inquiry. Have I missed a trick?

Guard Cocks has submitted a very good complaint about the behaviour of a Salisbury guard. We cannot ignore it, but I cannot just send it off to the area manager at Salisbury because Brian's life could be made very difficult.

Friday 11th July 1986

There was some incentive to get out of the office today. I reject an invitation from the television company to defend British Rail's punctuality record before making arrangements concerning anti-rail Totnes M.P. Anthony Steen's cab ride on the 08.50 from Paddington. I clear the desk and ensure everyone knows to give the 08.50 special attention. The cab ride has been offered to show him the efforts being made to run a punctual train service. I ensure a discreet profile presence on platforms and visit the signal box to make sure the message is received.

I catch the 09.35 to Paignton for a 20min walkabout before getting the 10.45 to Torquay with driver Carpenter. The last time I saw him he was sitting on the beach in Penzance. There has been some trouble about the so called 'pigeon menace' at Paignton. I have refused to allow the pigeons to be forcibly ejected from the premises. My check reveals two specimens and no mess yet an estimate for £400 had been put in front of me for signature to keep them out.

On arrival at Torquay, a middle-aged lady with a Spanish accent, an Irish name and a Scottish destination is talking to the platform senior railman. She starts to cry and wants to speak to the Station Master. I suppose that would be me today then. She has four reservations for Edinburgh tomorrow for her family but she has lost her travel ticket. She thinks she must have thrown it away last Saturday when she arrived on holiday. I ask why she still has the other tickets. She says she travelled down separately from her husband and children. I explain that she has to pay the single fare because someone else could be using the ticket she has lost and be avoiding payment. The tears flow again. She says she would not be here crying if she had given the ticket to someone else, perhaps a shade too readily and picking up on what I may have unintentionally implied very quickly. Can she pay? No. Can someone pay the money in at Edinburgh perhaps? No. But she has a cheque book and a £50 bank card. The fare is £47 so that will do nicely. That just about takes care of the 20min I have allocated at Torquay.

The 11.05 Paignton-Paddington is in the hands of another young and capable Exeter driver, Tony Boston *(who went to drive Eurostars eventually)*. The loco is No. 50023 'Howe' in NSE livery. Despite a 20mph tsr between Aller Jct and Newton Abbot and a 1min late start we are three minutes early at Exeter after a 2min recovery allowance. A respectable-looking middle-aged gent compliments driver Boston on the run and he looks embarrassed at such praise. 11min 35 sec is reasonable for an HST from Dawlish to Exeter. *11min is more like 'reasonable' now but the already soft net HST schedule has been extended to 11½min.*

Passing Teignmouth I see Mr Steen's train being checked by the down local in front to Newton Abbot, but 'as booked'. I remember that I had not specifically told anyone to make sure the 11.07 empty stock from Exeter was to be kept out of the way of the 08.50 Paddington but it had been done anyway.

At Exeter, there was some confusion concerning whether to split the 2xClass 142s on the Exmouth line before working the

12.12 departure, resulting in a 4min late start. On reaching Exeter Central, a passenger was allowed to keep his foot in the door for an extra minute while his friend joined. This is insufficient discipline to keep the half-hourly service operations up to standard, with a cross in the passing loop at Topsham to be made on every train.

Visiting Topsham, I found signalman Ray Brackley was his usual relaxed self before I caught the next train, which was on time, down to Exmouth. There was a chance to ask questions about how the business was developing under the new service. Reliability is seen as a major factor but some days have shown an extra 120 or so day returns above average. That's not a lot of cash but a good initial figure. In summer, it is impossible to monitor this on a daily, or even weekly, basis as the weather is all important. But revenue is about 12% up in comparison with 5% elsewhere. And the unit is on time going back. I alight at Central for a quick visit to the bank before returning for the 14.22 to Paignton. No. 142019 and its crew have returned straight up the hill on the Down Waterloo reversible line and, with John Madge as guard, we are quickly away again.

On return to the office there is the surprising news that the personnel trainee has decided not to go to Old Oak Common but is to resign and go to Selfridges. He hastens to ensure I have got the message; he is not going to sell fridges. Despite his forthcoming move, he had started to show signs of settling down but presumably his 'outside' applications explain a lot. I'll have to look round a few corners, with the personnel job unfilled and the head of section now vacant without a readily available understudy.

Saturday 12th July 1986

A weekend trip to Yorkshire on the 08.58 from Dawlish via Stockport. Pullman Car 'George Stubbs' provides an excellent atmosphere for the run. The only sour note was a 2½min <u>early</u> start from Dawlish. *This could happen on summer Saturdays with extra station dwell time and staff being accustomed to running late and making up time.* The guard is smoking a cigarette at the Dawlish Warren stop when I approach him to ensure he stands time there. The fact that he received 'the tip' from the Dawlish staff is irrelevant. *That just meant station duties were complete, the guard is the custodian of time-keeping.* And I am sure he can manage without a cigarette. The journey is punctual throughout with No. 47443 just touching 100mph down Whitmore bank to Crewe after a definite 98mph. Arrival at Huddersfield is 1min early with No. 45123.

CHAPTER 10: SNAKE ON A TRAIN

Sunday 13th July 1986

The return trip is with No. 45136 non-stop Huddersfield to Manchester Victoria with a cross-city taxi to connect with a through train to Dawlish, a stop inserted this timetable I'm pleased to say. With ten minutes before departure, there is only one power car working but two fitters get the second one going just in time. *Would this have happened under privatisation? It was also a good effort considering HSTs were by no means the staple power at Manchester.*

Monday 14th July 1986

The day started badly when the 2xClass 142s on my train to work failed at Exeter St. David's with a string of faults. Fortunately they are back in service by 09.00. It is a frustrating day with just a limited measure of success. I have to leave the Exeter-Waterloo punctuality report until this evening but I manage to set up some useful meetings. The Dutch inclusive package is a problem. Richard Jenkins at Bristol says to speak to Richard Willis at Swindon, who says I need to consult the inclusive tour at Board H.Q. They say I need to speak to Richard Jenkins at Bristol. It really is too stupid to be funny. Anyway, I am seeing Richard Jenkins tomorrow and Richard Willis has agreed that it is an area he wants to enter and to keep him in touch with any obstructionism. *And the sectors were looking to reduce costs?*

Even the regional operating manager's team are getting in on the silly act with a David Hounsell letter signed by Bob Poynter concerning train crew working extended hours, which is both illogical and out-of-touch with reality. *This was very unlike the Boss and I presumed it must have been a biased briefing or one at the bottom of his signature pile.* I draft a strong reply suggesting that the instruction should be withdrawn.

At the local management meeting we review the progress on the staff reduction schemes which are moving on apace and the budget out-turn is looking reasonably good.

Tuesday 15th July 1986

Experienced drivers Vowden and Watts are in charge of the Golden Hind this morning as I board the cab for a run to Taunton. 3½min early will do nicely. I transfer to the Bristol-bound HST and write part of my analysis of the special monitoring day Exeter-Waterloo punctuality figures *(average minutes gained and lost per station etc)*.

At Bristol, I have 45min with Richard Jenkins who is the new 'field sales officer InterCity West of England'. First on the agenda is the nonsense over the Dutch travel firm. Today he wants to be involved and takes the project on board, promising to Telex Holland straight-away. *Telex?!* He explains his new organisation and we straighten out our wires over the sales function which he has taken on and servicing that we are supposed to provide. *Whatever way it is put, it seemed like extra overheads and two people to do one job.*

I meet regional personnel manager Ken Beresford ready for the area interviews. The first applicant had rung up yesterday to say that, if he was appointed, he would want his 19yr old son to be accommodated on welfare grounds to prevent splitting up his family. Had he not considered this before applying? Did he not realise that this could not be guaranteed? He withdrew. The Middlesbrough applicant is next but interviews poorly with little knowledge of budgets or new technology. Too much reliance on 'systems of control' and less on actually doing anything. He is a young 26 and Ken reckons I could take the risk. I don't.

Next is a 27yr old woman from Woking. She is confident and fluffs only one area of questioning but almost overdoes the 'question' section by interviewing the two of us but she gets the job. This seems to surprise her. Her long-term boyfriend has a job at Aldermaston and she thinks she might have trouble finding somewhere to live 'half way'. I insist she must live on the Exeter Area and that means no further than Sherborne. I give her until Friday to decide but I suspect she will be the second female personnel trainee to have been offered a job in the organisation and declined. Equal opportunities need to be taken up.

Back at Temple Meads at 15.25, the 15.20 (12.00 Liverpool-Plymouth) is still there. On closer inspection it is an HST set off maintenance waiting to replace the loco-hauled set running 18min late. I open the door but am intercepted by a senior railman who says the set is going to Paddington now. *Not an option under sectorisation.* There has been a blockage at Bathampton Jct and the down Paddington is late. The 15.32 up service is now going to be formed by this empty HST and the loco-hauled Liverpool scratch set is going through to Plymouth.

The Liverpool runs in with No. 47501 on five Mark 1s, no buffet, all windows open in the stifling heat. All the passengers get off as the guard has instructed them to do so and have to get back on. It is a complete mess, but one that has begun with the best of intentions. Departure from Bristol Temple Meads is 24½min late, not unreasonable after the unfortunate chain of events. It is soon clear that the Bristol driver is not going to waste any time. He needs to brake for the crossings at Huish and Puxton but we are up to 98mph before Uphill Jct, speed gradually climbing to 105mph before easing for Bridgwater. There is a 20mph tsr approaching Taunton that costs 2min but our combined running time from Bristol to Exeter is 58min 28sec, beating the HST booked time *and the current Voyager gross schedule.*

Wednesday 16th July 1986

The time between 08.00 and 10.00 is mainly spent getting ready for an important meeting tomorrow. Cardiff-Portsmouth/Weymouth route manager John Curley has come to meet Yeovil supervisor Terry Gale at admirably short notice to discuss the draft Weymouth line timetable. We make good progress with some long running items such as starting the 06.55 Yeovil Pen Mill to Bristol Temple Meads from Yeovil Jct which he incorporates in the 1987 timetable specification. I have to put out some markers when I think John is starting to trespass on some of my responsibilities but he is very helpful on marketing, our town centre office proposition and the diversion into Yeovil Jct. Providing someone will pay for the north to west existing curve to be re-signalled it looks as though we have a good chance of getting the south to west curve. *This never happened and at this distance I am not sure it was ever going to be worth the hassle. However, it was predicated on extensive renewals being due and improvements being available at only marginal cost. It was nearly 25yrs before the renewals were done and it was January 2014 before I had a run on a diverted Paddington HST non-stop through Yeovil Jct and Pen Mill with no token exchange necessary.*

The afternoon is spent on a couple of domestic issues, including the difficulties that is likely to result in my secretary, Karin, moving back to London whence she came on marriage.

Thursday 17th July 1986

The Exeter-Waterloo line of route performance meeting is at Waterloo this time. *I was chairman and rotated the quarterly meetings at Exeter, Salisbury, Woking and Waterloo.* I travel up on the 09.38 with Vernon Baseley, a young Exeter duty manager, who is acting as secretary. I have written a report on the monitoring day we undertook when the average late arrival at destination was a deplorable 15min late. We arrive at Waterloo a typical 13min late, having been 12min late from Honiton after crossing the late 07.00 Waterloo-Exeter.

Efforts to regain time have been frustrated by 7min of engineering work, overtime at Gillingham and Salisbury and stopping in the slow line platform at Woking for a fast up Bournemouth to precede. It would have been interesting to see what would have happened had we been stopped in the up fast platform and the Bournemouth run through the up slow. *Or whether we would have been given priority if we had been working under the modern 'within 10min' regime?*

The meeting itself is routine, the main aim being to focus attention on the service group for everyone to improve efforts on what is within their span of control. David McKeown, the Exeter area signalling & telecommunications engineer, has strong views on what everyone else needs to do but has few initiatives regarding his own department, which is responsible for a large slice of delay when the tokenless block signalling system fails. However, David is extremely able and forceful and I would tip him for BRB signalling director in due course. At present, he seems constrained by the bureaucracy above him.

I hope for an unaccompanied run home. Vernon has disappeared to Paddington to get back for his night shift. *Really? That's a bit much.* But David comes with me on the 16.38, a Mark 1 Class 33 diagram train. I was hoping to ride with the Exeter driver from Salisbury, LDC member Rodney French. This job requires all-out effort for the Type 3 loco. We pass the 19.40 Exeter-Waterloo running right time, partly because of a re-platforming exercise at Exeter to give it a better chance of a right-time start which, in turn, means that the 16.38 stands a chance of getting in on time at 20.25. This is an example of attention to detail.

At St. David's, duty manager Gordon Hooper wants a planned change of re-platforming at 16.00 to accommodate a crew change on the Meldon-bound ballast. It involves putting the 16.12 Exeter-Exmouth on top of the 16.18 Exeter-Waterloo so I'm against it on the grounds of the punctuality risk. The alternative means the ballast empties need to be booked to stand for 15min at Exmouth Jct which endangers the punctuality of the approaching 13.10 Waterloo-Exeter. *The Exmouth departure a few minutes in front of the standard xx.26 Waterloo departures is the customary arrangement at present.*

Friday 18th July 1986

I am supposed to meet Peter Griggs and InterCity Cross Country manager Brian Johnson at Taunton today. I can't get away from the office until 11.30. Colin Pulleyblank is driving the Paignton-Manchester so it is a pleasant cab ride to Taunton. Colin is the agent for the Engineman's Assurance Fund and takes a big interest in welfare. He keeps us informed of problems and we try to reciprocate.

At Taunton, I show Brian round the station and Travel Centre before a bite of lunch. Peter turns up at 14.08 on the 11.45 from Paddington, spot on time. There are long queues in the Travel Centre and telephone answering is not meeting the required standard. The InterCity staffing review is prepared to support only half an extra post but perhaps they will be more generous after today's demonstration.

We call off at Tiverton Parkway before a session in the office. Peter is growing over-confident. We talk about the new system for 'signing off' contracts between businesses and area managers. "Oh, so you are familiar with the system then?" Peter asks. "Yes, I venture to suggest I know a good deal more about it than you," I reply, having been involved with just such an example with NSE.

We cover such subjects as turnround times at Paignton on summer Saturdays next year. We want 75min to allow for some degree of late arrival, disembarkation, shunting to the yard, labelling, watering, running round and shunting back to the station 10min before departure. This does not suit InterCity. They are going to have a look around tomorrow and I ought to accompany them, both to keep them away from anything I do not want them so see and correct any false impressions they hatch. I am also embarrassed about three people looking at what one person could decide. *Sectorisation has had a good press over the years but it involved nonsense and extra costs such as this.* It will probably cause me more trouble to dig in my heels though.

Tony Crabtree comes in to tell me that the Press has got hold of a story about a parcel consigned from Newton Abbot on the 14.20 Paignton-Newcastle. Inside the box was a royal python which has escaped at Birmingham New Street. The thoughts of encountering that are unspeakable.

There is also a crisis about covering ballast turns with guards. There is a big sea wall job involving outside contractors and we are very short of cover. At 17.15 Alan Bell, Bernard Price and roster clerk Graham Freestone are still grappling with the problem. Clearly, I cannot walk away from this and go home on the 17.25. Bernard is talking about moving a train with an Inspector and I try to steer him away from this action of last resort. There must be another way out. I go to the phone to tell Linda I will be late and, when I get back, the problem is solved.

Eddie Ardern, an import from Blackpool, will work 01.00 to 09.00 on Sunday and double back from 21.00 to 06.00. I have time to visit the Panel Box before catching the Glasgow-Paignton which is mercifully 3min early with a senior L.M. manager in the cab. Perhaps that is why it has negotiated the Crewe-Birmingham maze successfully today. At Dawlish, Joe Cockram wants to discuss the Pay & Display car park proposals before I go home for dinner.

Saturday 19th July 1986

It is a beautiful day and far too nice for work so Linda and I head for the beach with a picnic from 09.50 to 16.00. 53 trains pass. One is 23min late, four are 10-13min late 16 are in single figures and 32 are precisely on time or early. There is a preponderance of Class 50s, as well as a large number of HSTs and Class 47/4s. No. 45122 works the Nottingham down and back. The Liverpool has 2xClass 31s on the Pullmans as booked. No. 47372 has charge of the 10.10 Penzance-Leeds and an up special empty stock has No. 47202 in Railfreight livery. No. 47093 is on the Leeds mail but otherwise there are no major surprises, other than the fact that all the HSTs seem to have both power cars working.

CHAPTER 11: FAREWELL TO A HERO

Monday 21st July 1986

Today is one of those days where working continuously seems to make very little progress. John Beer is back from holiday. The Woking applicant has declined the Personnel move and Ken Beresford has agreed to it being re-advertised. Bob Poynter has agreed to most of my points in the letter about extended hours of train crews. Sue Carroll, newly appointed regional customer care manager arrives to discuss what she hopes to achieve and how she might do it, although at a purely formulative stage apparently. I am not sure how the post fits in with the new sector power struggle.

The local meeting is unproductive. John Beer is against the production of the October A-Z departure sheets using the new software since he thinks the deadlines will not be met if we do. I contemplate Paul Silvestri or Tony Crabtree for the personnel job but Paul likes his shift job and both would be a loss to operations.

Tuesday 22nd July 1986

A bright and early start to clear the paperwork, again without success. The five former Leeds drivers join the train at St. Thomas. They are perturbed to have read in the newspaper that Boycott's cricketing career might be in jeopardy with a broken wrist. He scored 137 not out, with it broken, last Saturday.

The Class 142s are performing reasonably for a change. John Beer reports that Devon General has withdrawn from the through-ticketing arrangements we have introduced on bus/train because their new ticket machines cannot cope. To think they had once voiced aspirations to issue London rail tickets from Acacia Avenue or wherever!

My second attempt at getting a portable phone takes place with a representative who is scarcely literate and can't add up. I presume he must be a brilliant engineer. I sign up for three years providing battery life and coverage is adequate.

From 12.30 to 15.30 Bernard Price and I interview for a relief Grade E supervisor traffic assistant. It would suit me to appoint one of the Grade Ds I am cutting out at Taunton. Fortunately Wally Pipe is the best but we still have to see the senior applicant who is absent with flu. It never ceases to amaze me how many people fail to come across at interviews. It really is not a good way of selection in isolation. One applicant, aged 34 whom I knew at Skipton, could scarcely formulate an answer and he seemed so tired.

I am preparing to replace the personnel trainee at interviews next week so I ring Charles Nicholls, my opposite number at Feltham who moved there from Plymouth, concerning a candidate who worked on his new area until recently. He tells me that I am strongly tipped for area manager Victoria. It is news to me that it is even vacant. I have heard I will be replacing Frank Markham at Bristol when he retires at the end of the year but neither prospect interests me. In the meantime the move to Selfridges has migrated to the inevitable selling fridges and then on to a move to Sainsbury's. Such is the nature of British Rail's rumour machine. Charles Nicholls is from a family that held senior Western Region positions right back to the era of Sir Felix Pole

Wednesday 23rd July 1986

I took the car home last night to get a good start on some signal box visiting today. I have been neglecting this area a little recently. Aller Jct is first and then Dainton where Peter Davies is occupying a post that is well below his substantial capabilities while he recuperates from illness. Back to Teignmouth then home for coffee before Dawlish Warren, Exminster and City Basin. At Pinhoe, signalman Slater seems as if he wants to chat a while, perhaps to help pass on the shift at a location that sees around one train an hour.

At Exmouth Jct, Ray Conium is on, a peppery but very pleasant character who has worked the busy boxes in the past. Jack Warren, who has recently retired, comes to the box ostensibly to make a waste paper collection but more likely to share a cup of tea. He seems a little unsure about stopping with me there and I detect he does not want to embarrass me, so I put his mind at rest as I leave. It is difficult to balance rule enforcement and discretion. I believe neither of these signalmen will abuse my 'blind eye' and, talking of blind eyes, either of them could work Exmouth Jct 1986 with their eyes firmly closed.

Back in the office, mayhem has broken out in the clerical operating section. Tony Hill is on leave without cover for the next two weeks. Clarence and Tony believe that his normal understudy, Karen Graeme, has declined to be paid to cover and that junior Richard Utting has agreed to do it. *Richard used to delight in his status as the most senior grade 1 clerk on the railway.* Karen says she has not been asked, and Richard says neither has he. In between, Karen has threatened to resign. The matter is resolved by Karen agreeing to do the higher grade work and Richard doing any unavoidable overtime.

Mr Poynter arrives in the office prior to catching the 17.35 train to Bristol, so that's my train home missed.

Thursday 24th July 1986

After a quick look round the station I ride in the cab of No. 50013 'Agincourt' to Yeovil Jct on the 08.11 Exeter-Waterloo arriving 3min late due to a tsr, having passed No. 33119 on a down ballast empties at Honiton. I have arranged for Yeovil Supervisor Vic Hull to give me a lift to Maiden Newton so that I can do a box visit before covering the line to Weymouth and back to Pen Mill.

Typically, it is a Yeovil relief signalman and not a resident signalman when I can manage to visit the box so rarely. The Weymouth train is loco-hauled for the school summer holidays with No. 47490 on ten, returning from the seaside on the 11.10, allowing me 15min relaxation on a sunny sea front bench.

The run back on dmu timings is unenthusiastic. At Pen Mill we pass a six-car dmu on its way down. I am introduced to a person who seems to have a problem with his staff travel card that is difficult to comprehend. I am suffering from a sore throat and can hardly speak so I put this down as an apology for my failure to communicate effectively with him.

On visiting Pen Mill signal box, I raise what has just happened at the station and am relieved to hear that the person is a local eccentric. He has allegedly been prosecuted for putting some sleepers on the line but the local staff think he just took the blame for some local vandals.

John Dubbin, the chief clerk, is perturbed by the number of rest days his staff are being expected to work but I explain that the only reason we are not recruiting is to keep posts available for staff that might be displaced by some reduction schemes afoot.

After visiting Yeovil Jct box, where the signalman is having some difficulty with the Property Board over moving into the station house at Chard Jct, I ride back with the same driver I had on the up run. Driver Bradbrook, ex-King's Cross, is learning the road and seems a bit suspicious of an area manager. By Crewkerne I think he has thawed a little bit and kindly offers me his seat.

Visiting Honiton box I find Stuart Street on duty. Stuart is far from being the best signalman on the line but he has his single-line crosses worked out perfectly. For instance, he talks confidently about empty ballast trains taking 23min from Chard Jct. He also explains an unofficial practice the signalmen apply. If it is thundery they do not clear the block after the previous train until the last possible minute before the next train so that lightning does not cause the needle to flutter to train in section and cause a block failure. *Not the kind of thing that could be passed on to the S&T without risking more block failures by cracking down on the unofficial working.*

Back on the station the senior railman Jerry O'Brien, a genial Irishman, has the kettle on and has made me a coffee with some local Honiton honey in it for my throat. Then it is up to Crewkerne in the cab of No. 50045 'Achilles'; a poor loco struggling to get within 5mph of normal speeds. Still, we arrive on time. The relief senior railman displays a bit of attitude when I ask him if he has run out of timetables. I tell him not to use that tone of voice. Then the shift leader at Exeter St. David's sounds a bit that way out when I phone him about supplies. I tell him to report to my office at 16.45.

The down train is reported 20min late and arrives 17min late despite a 3min tsr. No. 33037 is working in multiple with No. 50004 'St. Vincent'. Presumably the ballast empties have been cancelled and the Class 33 has been attached to reduce line occupation. Albert Reid is the guard, and he assures me that the initial delay has been waiting a connection and not attaching the loco.

We are off like a shot, making up 2min to Axminster and another 1min to Honiton whereas this morning No. 50020 'Revenge' lost a minute with 48mph at the top of Seaton bank. With the aid of good station work we arrive at St. David's 7min late. Not too bad considering.

The travel centre shift leader is sorry for his attitude. He has had an hour to reflect, and possibly take advice. Coming to the office is a useful weapon which often has a salutary effect. It is, however, one that always amazes me.

Charlie Beatson calls in to say thanks for helping him get out of the signalbox and into supervision. He goes to Perth a week on Monday. With a middle name of Fraser he is heading home.

Friday 25th July 1986

Most of the day is spent saying goodbye to five people who are retiring plus the former personnel trainee on his way to Selfridges. Driver Guerin, with his stories about lodging jobs to Shrewsbury with Newton Abbot Castles, is first. Then driver Wright, whose solicitor son-in-law had rung one evening to say he was going to ring the Sun newspaper that B.R. had drivers aged over 60 driving high-speed trains to London. He then rang up the following day to say the calls had been made by a dinner guest whom he had discovered had made a number of hoax calls. Driver Thomas has been travelling from

Taunton to Exeter since the depot closed but has decided he cannot face doing it over winter. He is followed by senior railman Binder from Axminster and then signalman Les Tarr. Les has been signalman at Dawlish Warren for 38years since 1948 and, lest anyone might be tempted into a superficial judgement that this has been an unadventurous career, they should look at his war service as a rear gunner. Quite enough adventure for anyone.

Alex Stuart from public relations wants to clear some details about the award to driver Whittle for dealing with his loco fire. I tell Alex that I do not see what Dave's age and address have to do with anything and ask him to omit these details from the press release.

Photo: Newton Abbot East Jct signal box in July 1986, due for closure in May 1987 and clearly not deemed worthy of a final, if expensive, coat of paint. Credit: R. W. Penny

CHAPTER 12: LEVEL CROSSING PROBLEMS

Monday 28th July 1986

This morning I am in the car to Totnes, calling off at Newton Abbot to visit the station and West signal box. At Totnes, I am meeting the lord mayor of London off the 07.25 from Paddington which is making a special stop. The official party from South Hams Council arrives as the train pulls in and they are soon on their way.

I stay to watch the Dart Valley steam train that uses the up platform at 11.25 and then drive to Torquay. It is a wet day and the roads are congested with holidaymakers who cannot use the beach. There is a 3mile queue into Totnes from Torquay and also into Torquay from Totnes. I have a chat with travel centre manager John Hedge about the disappointing receipts at Newton Abbot before Ken Shingleton catches up with me on the phone.

After calling in home for lunch I return to the office. When everyone has gone home there is time to make a leisurely visit to the Panel Box. At 19.00 we have the Pensioners' Committee meeting. Only six committee members turn up. Active staff arrange a tea party in Exeter for retired staff who have worked in the Exeter area. The main business is to fix the venue for the dinner where the helpers are thanked for volunteering. Someone asks if we can afford it but there is no question of not holding the dinner after people have volunteered. We settle on the Cowick Barton where we have had good meals in the past but poor service. Last year we went to the Lazy Landlord which had matched what it said over the door.

Tuesday 29th July 1986

When I arrive at work I find that Driver Whittle's age and address has already been published, along with the amount of the award. I am furious and tell public relations so. Dave Whittle will have read about it before he has been officially informed. A journalist from the Dawlish Post has already tried to ring him at home. He is on rest day today and on at 07.16 tomorrow so I will try to catch him then.

The senior applicant for the Grade E supervisor post is available for interview today, having recovered from last week's 'flu. He has a very good interview and is excellent on his rules. However, he is on a potential lateral move so he should be better than the others and, of course, I do not want to be bringing supervisors into an area where supervisors are about to be displaced. If I promote one of the two Taunton supervisors, that will be one of them looked after. The senior applicant says that his reason for applying is that he wants to get out of the Watford Area Operations Centre, which is located in the Panel Box, and back out onto the ground. I explain that the Exeter job will develop in terms of an area operations centre and be less involved with being outside. I ask what other jobs he has applied for. The answer is none. What are his geographical limits?

"Western Region outside London," he replies

"Would you apply for an outside job at Euston?"

"No."

What about an MS1 assistant station manager job at Temple Meads?" *(One grade higher than this job)*

"Yes."

That should just about constitute enough justification for passing him over. He has not been forthright on his application form. It is clear that geography is more important than job content. He would be a strong applicant for the Bristol job I mentioned so there would be a waste to the industry by paying for his house move to Exeter and then potentially to the promotion for which he is ready. There is also potential waste moving him from a job he can do in the same grade.

I appoint supervisor Pipe from Taunton, aged 60. Sometimes he does not seem too effective but he has an extremely pleasant personality. The train crews and station staff have the utmost respect for him so he does not have to work on being 'effective' because staff rarely challenge him.

In the afternoon, I go through a pile of items with John Beer, including the content of a new "announcers' guide". There is a knock on the door and Len Purse, the drivers' LDC secretary is there. He comes in and waits to be asked before sitting down. He gets out an envelope containing a letter. This could be trouble. Then he tells me that he has come to thank me for the way driver Ousley has been dealt with under his ill health resettlement. Mr Bell has been to see him and Len thinks the letter I have signed is perfect. He is going to read it out at the next ASLEF branch meeting, because he says he would be the first to complain if we are wrong. We have a pleasant five minutes before he goes and I thank my lucky stars for this job. *There was a lesson here for industrial relations. By their not adopting an adversarial stance the drivers were more effective at ensuring the welfare of the depot than if they had been unpleasant.*

Wednesday 30th July 1986

As I arrive at work driver Whittle is sitting at the controls of No. 50047 'Swiftsure' at the head of the 08.11 Exeter-Waterloo. I go and apologise for him finding out about the award in the newspaper. He's quite affable about it. Someone did contact him at work and then on the phone at home. In a typical Northern fashion he says he has made a lot of it for the railway's benefit, realising the public relations value. "For instance," he says, "I told them I only did what anyone else would have done and things like that." *This was the Northern way of making a lot of it!*

I travel to the Area Manager's Conference on the 08.00 with Plymouth area manager Jim Collins. He has many of the same problems as we have at Exeter. There are a few large issues at the meeting, not the least being the long working hours problem. For all my shortage of guards, caused by work being allocated on a shorter timescale than recruitment and training takes, I have incurred only seven instances last week of guards working in excess of 12hrs. *Sounds a lot to me now but some of the excess time is often spent travelling back to home depot 'on the cushions'. There were no instances of Exeter footplate staff incurring over 12hrs.* A reasonable and practical compromise is eventually reached.

I catch the 15.20 HST back to Exeter, leaving Temple Meads to the east and describing an arc via St. Phillip's Marsh to Bedminster in order to turn the set due to a defective windscreen wiper. This unfortunately results in following No. 33011 on a stopper between Yatton and Worle and also the 14.15 Paddington-Plymouth through Taunton. It is running on one power car and both trains have to stop for a caution at Bradford –on-Tone automatic half-barriers. *Yet again?* We drop into platform 3 at Exeter with the London-Plymouth in Platform 4. It has already had a Class 47 attached to the front and is ready for off; very smart work.

In the office, I discover that Bernard Price has been called out to Bradford-on-Tone because a horse-woman has reported a train passing over the crossing without operating the barriers. Ken Shingleton has rung to say Bernard must speak only to the Police and not directly to the woman. No doubt he is motivated by some idea of legal liability or press relations but I am doubtful that the police will ask the woman the right question and Bernard has a lot of natural credibility with the public as it is clear to them that he knows what he is talking about.

On Saturday last there was a disaster at Lockington, on the Bridlington-Hull line at a level crossing, which has killed seven people. This has sparked a public reaction and I have just had a letter saying Umberleigh crossing did not seem to be working a fortnight ago. I have already ordered extra checks just to be sure all is well. People can genuinely think they have seen something they have not.

All seems set for a good run on the 17.25 home but we are delayed at Exminster with no tail lamp on the train. The Bristol guard seems to doubt it is his responsibility.

We are supposed to be going to Huddersfield this evening for a family visit and to see Mike Hodson but my throat is still playing up and I do not suppose it is a good idea to go and infect three households and come back for a full week's work worse than I am now. So I will have my two days leave at home and a clear weekend.

CHAPTER 13: MARINES GO ON LEAVE

Monday 4th August 1986

I am not feeling much better today, and Linda is worse than me now. Most of the morning is spent interviewing for the post vacated by Selfridges's new recruit. The most likely applicant is Michael Stacey who was area personnel manager at Worksop until he reduced himself to the lowest clerical grade to move to Devon for domestic reasons. In two years he has hauled himself up from CO1 to CO4 and if he is appointed to this job he will be just one grade short of his original one.

Regional H.Q. has sent a 28yr-old woman who did not apply for the job originally. She is well qualified and wants some area experience. Some of her responses reflect H.Q. attitudes but that is not a surprise. A man from Waterloo wants to come on a lateral move. He would manage the job well but has been described by the former occupant as a non-decision maker.

At 15.30 I depart for Newton Abbot on the 12.47 Paddington-Plymouth relief with a Class 47/4 in charge. Gordon Tincombe is working the East box. The 12.00 from Liverpool has had a chequered history recently and today is no different. It is to be terminated at Newton Abbot because the down Manchester has been similarly terminated at Bristol with a vandalised windscreen and there is no stock for its 17.18 return from Plymouth. The Liverpool stock has no further booked work today after arriving at Plymouth at 17.20 so it will cover for the missing Manchester from Newton Abbot. My 12.47 relief is booked back to Paddington empty stock at 17.25 so it will form the 17.18 between Plymouth and Newton Abbot with passengers transferring to the Cross Country stock at Newton Abbot. The Manchester stock will come west to form tomorrow's first leg of the Liverpool diagram.

The solution is neat. Perhaps it would have been better just to turn the Liverpool round as quickly as possible at Plymouth rather than trans-shipping the passengers on both the down and up trains with less than 15min delay. I ask the announcer to do the virtually impossible and ensure passengers know what is happening and why. The abandoned Liverpool train passengers have 15min to wait for their onward connection to Plymouth on a Paddington starter.

My train back to Dawlish is delayed for a line examination because of stone throwing at Teignmouth. *Presumably this was an examination of the line rather than a caution. I tend to be precise about the difference and I assume we were checking for children on the line rather than dodging the bricks.* Inner-city Teignmouth strikes again. The assistant ticket examiner starts at one end of the train and I start at the other explaining what is happening to passengers who are starting to become restless. We are 13min late at Dawlish.

Tuesday 5th August 1986

After an early start, I catch the 09.31 to Taunton arriving spot on time. I talk to travel centre manager Mervyn Berryman about a disciplinary hearing that is pending for one of his clerks. The telephone answering standards are also low with only 40% or so being answered within 30sec. I have a chat with supervisory staff rep Bob Johnson about the forthcoming staff reduction and he is happy that Supervisor Pipe has got the Exeter job.

At 11.00 I am supposed to meet Mr Waley Cohen, a local notable and former lord mayor of London. His family should be given a lifetime achievement award for complaints to British Rail and its former component parts, probably not without good cause. He is bad on his feet and partially deaf. I suggest we have a coffee and he subjects me to stories of memorable correspondence with Great Western chairman Sir James Milne. His chief idea today is to charge premium rates to disabled train users. That should go down a bomb. His favourite complaint is the lack of left luggage trolleys opposite the first class coaches on down Paddington trains. He has a good point and it is a disgrace that we cannot organise to work empties back to the appropriate place when we collect them from the car park etc. I should make it a priority for the Taunton staff, despite reducing their workload as much as I can in order to achieve budget cuts.

At 12.02 I travel to Tiverton Parkway in the cab. Traction Inspector Graham Smith is training drivers Bruford and Edwards on HST handling. *I met driver Bruford in the cab of a Class 37 at Buckfastleigh recently and Nick Edwards is now ops standards manager with DB Schenker and a Royal Train operations manager. He was a signatory to the Bittern 90mph run certificates in 2013.* Tiverton Parkway's takings have stabilised around £5,500 per week which is not bad for the holiday period when business traffic for meetings is reduced. We are 2min early back at Exeter with the 06.57 from Newcastle and it is back to the paper on the desk.

I have asked the local management team to gather at 15.00 to prepare for the visit of the general manager on Thursday. *My natural instinct is not to make special preparations but my Middlesbrough Area Manager Arnold Wain showed me how important it was not to make simple mistakes in front of visiting bosses.*

There is a letter from a senior Yeovil clerk objecting to a letter from John Beer that says one of the Yeovil man's statements was 'untrue'. There is a copy to the Transport Salaried Staffs' Association so any sympathy, that I might have had, has evaporated. I doubted the commitment and ability of this member of staff from the moment we took over the Yeovil area. I think John disagreed with me but I doubt that he does now. I had seen the letter before it went out and John had successfully justified the use of the word 'untrue' so I now ask John to draft the reply he would like to see sent, reserving the right to alter it as I think fit. John's original letter amounted to no more than a slight rap of the knuckles so the clerk had better be prepared for worse than this if he antagonises his managers in this way.

At 17.30 I go across to the Panel Box. Everything is going smoothly except for the Glasgow-Paignton running 25min late behind the Aberdeen-Penzance. We have devised the contingency plan to run a dmu in the booked path of the Glasgow as it is an important commuter train home so I ride down to Dawlish with the dmu driver arriving on time.

Wednesday 6th August 1986

The day starts on the down school train to Paignton which is a Cross Country HST that forms the up Devonian but provides sufficient capacity for the packs of schoolchildren and their County Council season tickets. Traction Inspector Graham Smith is on board with driver Bruford again. Arriving at Torquay there is time to look round before going to Paignton. In the meantime I phone Ken Beresford to ensure he agrees to my advertising Secretary Karin's job outside the industry and before she leaves. He accepts but when I tell him his junior staff have said it cannot be done, he says he will 'let me know'.

Paignton booking office staff have claimed they are rushed off their feet between 09.30 and 11.00 in the school holidays but my observations from 10.00 reveals a steady workload for the two permanent and one summer temporary members of staff.

Changing at Newton Abbot for Totnes, I ring Karen in the operating section to investigate why the 11.07 Exeter-Laira empty stock has been allowed to delay the 08.50 Paddington-Plymouth HST by 6min. Totnes is quite busy with Dart Valley traffic. Colin Harmes and Alf Turnbull are their usual chatty selves. There is a Youth Training Scheme young man on duty, the son of a Plymouth guard who has tackled me to see if there is any chance of his son being given the Totnes vacancy. I spend ten minutes explaining that the vacancies are being held for redundant signalman but we will be recruiting within twelve months. Two Exeter trainees are taking booking lad jobs at Waterloo, a pretty certain path to well paid signalling jobs in the capital, so there is no reason why his perseverance should not result in a full time job.

No 50015 'Valiant' is on the up Liverpool, on time at Exeter where I take No. 50049 'Defiance' on the 14.17 to Axminster. More coffee and discussion, then back on the 15.57, 1½min early. The 17.25 stopper is full again, mainly with language school students whose business has been secured by John Hedge at Torquay.

Thursday 7th August 1986

Mr. Scott, deputy general manager, is arriving at 11.15 today so I start the day at 07.30 swatting up on the Class 142 position. We are supposed to have nine Class 142s per day in the Exeter working. Today, we have five and a Class 118 traditional set on three engines instead of four. That means no standby for failures, no strengthening set on the 10.10 from Barnstaple, only one unit on the Exmouth double-set working, and the Class 118 underpowered for Class 142 timings.

At 10.30 I interview an applicant for the former personnel trainee's job, on a lateral move. He has been to Syria on holiday because he has a particular interest in Crusader castles. The interview is a bit sticky and there is little rapport. I make the decision to appoint Michael Stacey from the concrete works and set about a rather needlessly difficult process of finding someone who can agree the transfer date, as the manager of the concrete works is off sick at present.

Mr. Scott has a session with Bernard Price and me about the Class 142s and a trip to the Panel Box before a buffet lunch. Then it is down to Exmouth and back with the dgm and John Beer on the ailing and tatty Class 118. We have a coffee before going to Newton Abbot on the down Manchester and changing onto an even tattier Mark 1 loco-hauled set to Paignton. Coming back, we change at Newton Abbot into the London. Bernard Price has rejoined us and escorts the dgm to Newton Abbot West signal box.

In the meantime I discuss an incident with supervisor Harry Perrett. Harry is an experienced and steady railwayman with all the best aspects of an old school outlook. He has been reported by a rail enthusiast. Karen Graeme was somehow involved, but I tell him that his report has been accepted in full and the enthusiast has been informed to that effect and there is no stain on Harry's record.

It has been a long day's grilling by Brian Scott. I think that Newton Abbot is in pristine condition but he spots some cobwebs and asks if I have considered having specialised cleaning gangs. Not really. Most platform staff have lots of marginal unused time, the key is to ensure they use it productively. I leave Mr. Scott at Exeter and have just enough time to catch the down Glasgow home, 5min early at Exeter with No. 50013 'Agincourt'.

Friday 8th August 1986

At 07.30 today we have six Class 142s and no 118. It has lost another engine overnight. Laira Depot manager Tony Coles and Plant Engineer Phil Shepherd have asked for a meeting about the difficulty of lifting freight wagons for repair on the stabling point. Alan Bell is taking a hard line, but not one that is easy to defend as it is not entirely logical. Some compromise is necessary, while bearing in mind our chief job is getting the train service out of the depot. *I might have added that the maintenance engineers' chief job was the same and perhaps their efforts might have been applied to the Class 142s today.* We end up giving them the use of No. 5 road on Wednesdays for a four-week trial. That's not giving much away.

Today is the breaking-up day for the summer holidays of the Marines at Topsham. We have secured, after substantial brinkmanship, a 12-coach train. The aim is to run with a Class 47 on each end to Lympstone Commando, load 850 Marines and return to Central. There is a small gap in the Exmouth service where we rotate the regular interval pattern to allow this tight path and ensure that ideal Exeter Central morning work arrival times alter to convenient evening peak departure times.

At Central we usually lose 200 passengers for South East and South West destinations as the relief train sets off for Newcastle, first stop Bristol Temple Meads. *This train was the result of direct liaison with the Camp by guards' supervisor Ray Thorn, and the co-operation of Cross Country route manager Brian Johnson who realised that the cost of running the train was well worth the £35,000 revenue that might be lost if coaches were used…and also that the invasion of ordinary service trains by Marines on leave was not ideal.*

This operation happens twice a year but this is the first time I have had an opportunity to experience it at close quarters. The empty stock is very late from Bristol after having detached a coach. No.47131 has to run round to the rear eventually to work the train away to Newcastle.

Duty manager Gordon Hooper estimates that the train will be here by 11.00. *I was not really aware that this was the legendary Bulleid Pacific driver of the 1960s. He was probably basing his expectations on his style of driving.* I think he is being optimistic. My guess is that we will not be underway until 11.20 and will not be back at Topsham with the troops until 11.50 at best. If the 11.12 Exmouth stopper goes first, our special will not be at Lympstone Commando until about 12.10 and the next Exmouth service train round trip will have to be cancelled.

We must go first which will mean the 11.12 stopper will be about 11.52 from Topsham and 12.02 at Exmouth, back from there at 12.05, 20min late. That means 12.16 at Topsham where the next Class 142 will be 15min late. This means missed connections all afternoon as we recoup time for the next three hours, assuming nothing else goes wrong.

It is still only 10.45 so I push a reluctant duty manager Hooper into a planned cancellation of the 11.45 from Exmouth and organising taxis to Exeter for long-distance passengers. That means the 11.12 stopper will arrive at Exmouth at 12.02 and coming back as the 12.15 'on time'. The cancellation of the next down train that should form the 12.15 puts the service back on time all afternoon. The train crew supervisor Wally Gee is supportive and can make any adjustments necessary rather than having to react to events.

The empty stock rolls in at 11.03 *(Good estimate, Gordon)* with the Bristol guard complaining that the rear sliding door will not shut properly, and the explosives experts ready to do the security check. Wally has his train crew forces marshalled as well. No. 47131 runs round and No. 47544 is attached to the front. The French pin is in the rear door so I tell the Bristol guard that I will be responsible for it. The brake test is done and the military personnel stand clear. I board the rear loco with driver Bartlett . The special instructions say we may not apply power until after Exeter Central but we blast out of St. David's in fine style up the steep bank where most trains in steam days were routinely assisted in rear, as are our current cement trains. The drivers are accustomed to the working and there is no risk involved in ensuring we do not stick.

As we pass Topsham station, I notice John Beer on the platform taking our photograph on his day off. In accordance with regulations, the single line staff is shown to the front driver and carried by the rear one, transferring it to No. 47544 on arrival at Lympstone Commando. Ray Thorn and two guards are issuing last-minute tickets. Just in case anyone should think this exercise not worth the disruption that has occurred, the takings at Exmouth booking office for the whole of July are equal to the revenue on this one train.

Lt. Col. Clough is on the platform with a sergeant-major. The 850 Marines file on board in an impressively disciplined manner as the train draws up three times. *I wonder why we did not make them march through but it might have been quicker than squeezing kitbags through the train.* The payload reduces to 849 as one Marine is marched back to Camp as Ray has spotted an altered ticket being used. Guard Jenkins has his list of calling points and connections for the destinations involved. This has been another extremely professional job from the Exeter Guards' inspectors.

Eleven minutes after the train's arrival, No. 47131 heads the cavalcade back to Exeter and we pass Topsham at 11.49 with the unit waiting for us. On balance the operational decisions have worked out as planned. At Central we lose about a hundred more Marines than planned as they head for the off-licence or trains with buffet cars. I drop down to St. David's in the cab of light diesel No. 47544 with driver Day.

Back in the office, Ken Shingleton wants to discuss how we cover open turns and the repair of telephone faults in the Panel. Permission has been received to advertise secretary Karin Martin's job before it becomes officially vacant and

Clarence Woodbury goes away to prepare the advertisement. It is a quiet afternoon, enabling me to catch up with paperwork, finishing with a paper on part-time staffing opportunities that regional operating and personnel managers Bob Poynter and Ken Beresford have both requested, albeit to slightly different remits and timescales.

Saturday 9th August 1986

It is a relatively sunny day so Linda and I decide to spend a few hours on the beach for me to watch the trains. There are 33 trains in 3hr 35min. Dawlish signal box is open and saves a lot of delay. *When it is not possible to open Dawlish, the block is Dawlish Warren to Teignmouth with trains being unable to proceed until the previous down services have passed Teignmouth box after whatever length of time has been spent in the platform there. The train service, and budget, is planned on Dawlish box not being staffed but we open it, whenever the tight pre-resignalling staffing allows us, to recover inevitable delays.* The latest of the 33 trains is 10min and most are precisely on time. H.Q. has been suggesting that Dawlish station is losing a lot of time but I collect enough data to demolish any such suggestion. The highlights are No. 47649 'Glasgow Chamber of Commerce' in Scotrail livery on a Newcastle train and Nos. 31416/31403 on the down Liverpool. No. 47242 has charge of a relief from the Midlands and noisiest performance from the day comes from No. 50041 'Bulwark' which at least sounds to have recovered from its crash on the up Sleepers, repair and subsequent chronic unreliability.

CHAPTER 14: HOW TO HANDLE A FATALITY?

Sunday 10th August 1986

Since it is a dull, drizzling travesty of a summer's afternoon, I think I'll take a train ride. The 14.03 from Dawlish to Exeter St. David's is a Waterloo set, reduced to eight coaches at Exeter on Saturday nights to allow it to be overtaken at Dawlish Warren without causing disruption. It is booked to arrive there at 14.07 and depart at 14.20 after being passed by a Penzance-Paddington HST which has to then clear Exminster. *This manoeuvre is still awkward but it is much slicker under multiple aspect signalling and with no practical constraints on passenger train length.* The Waterloo set arrives at Dawlish Warren 2min late. The HST is ½min late and the signal comes off to allow a right-time departure.

At Exeter, there is just time for a quick talk with duty manager Vernon Baseley before picking up the 12.00 Paddington-Penzance with No. 47646 on a completely first class set, heavily declassified. We are a few seconds late away, connecting out of a down Waterloo train. We grind to a halt at Exminster's home signal with nothing in front of us, costing a 4min late arrival at Newton Abbot. We are 5min late at Totnes and 6min late away. Very unsatisfactory. There is 4min recovery time as we skirt Dartmoor at a reasonable speed, arriving into Plymouth just 30sec late. I have time for coffee before catching the Penzance-Waterloo back to Dawlish.

Monday 11th August 1986

I get the week off to a good start with a visit to the panel box before 08.00. The half hour up to 08.30 is fascinating. As well as the usual train moves there is a shunt to Premier Transport *adjacent to Platform 6, access being via the depot entrance,* newspaper vans to be attached to the rear of the other empties in Platform 6 and an additional locomotive sent on my train to work the 09.38 to Waterloo. The chilly 06.09 from Salisbury, which forms the 09.38, is in the hands of a non-ETH Class 47.

The 06.35 mail from Bristol is 10min late, meaning it would still be in Platform 1 until 08.23 blocking the arrival of the Paignton-Exmouth unit which will delay the 07.30 Plymouth-Paddington that is hot on its heels. Today, there is also an empty stock for an 08.23 relief to Paddington running 35min late and sandwiched between the Exmouth-bound dmu and the Paddington express.

It is decided to switch the mail to Platform 4, arriving at 08.15. It used to convey a van of parcel post from Bletchley but that traffic has been lost so it can get away at 08.18 creating a slight conflict as the Class 142 has to wait for it to cross its path to the down main.

Most of the remaining morning is spent on routine matters, including preparation for a disciplinary hearing tomorrow. There is also a difficult complaint. One is from a C.B.E who has been charged the difference between the saver and ordinary fare for travelling on a restricted train. The customer's first attempt to claim a refund was based on not having been told about the restriction but my office had decided there were staple holes in the ticket, suggesting that the restrictions leaflet had been stapled to the ticket in line with our standard procedure. His follow-up reply has been declined because it was stated that the booking clerk involved has said that he clearly remembered the transaction and he had definitely attached the restrictions leaflet. The third letter now contains a number of dire threats. I look at the source documents and find the clerk has not specifically stated that he could recall that individual transaction and now there are four sets of staple marks in the original ticket from its passage back and forth within the organisation. To simply make a refund will look stupid but we now have no grounds for not doing so. There is also a requirement to support the staff that have had the authority to handle these matters delegated to them. But responsibility cannot be delegated so I have a chat with John Beer and I decide that the only recourse is a confessional on the telephone to the C.B.E. and then a refund. *Would the action have been different if the complainant had not been a C.B.E.? I would like to think not but I think it removed some of the grounds for suspicion. Quoting the staple marks as the basis for the decision is at best unconvincing to the customer.*

The other awkward issue is a bill for £975 for an advertisement we have placed in the Exeter Handbook, published by the City Council to promote Exeter throughout the country. We are supposed to participate in the community and several railwaymen are on the council whom we need to support. InterCity at Swindon has challenged the decision but John Beer has said that the InterCity route manager Peter Griggs, had agreed. Now Peter has allegedly "taken great exception" to my claim he had been consulted. Fortunately, I am able to make peace with Ian Body at InterCity Marketing who reasonably suggests we try to withdraw it but otherwise he will support the expenditure. The copy is at the publishers who claim it is too late to cancel it, despite as much arm-twisting as I can muster.

I make a couple of minutes to ask the Exminster signalman about yesterday's puzzling delay. He says it was a 'sticking lock button'. "So I was wrong, you weren't asleep then!" I reply. The line man had not been called though. This is followed by the derailment of a bitumen tank in the siding at City Basin, not for the first time; the layout is tight for 45tonne tanks. *No further comment seems to have been necessary about this event that would be put right locally but would probably have been headlines in, at least, the local paper now- if the traffic still existed of course.*

Tuesday 12th August 1986

After an early start I catch the 08.00 to Tiverton Parkway. Chester Long joins me and we have a useful conversation in which he suggests that three trained Gloucester guards might want to transfer to Exeter. Apparently there is an agreement that staff whose jobs are threatened by 'driver only operation' can move with the benefit of redundancy conditions. Business is a little slow today at Parkway and after half an hour I return to Exeter on the 06.45 Swindon-Penzance, 3min early into Exeter.

Bernard Price comes to see me to recount an incident that happened last night. He was out looking at carriage washing and was told that the 20.58 Exeter-Salisbury had hit a cow near Axminster. The damaged loco could not create a brake and there had been no delay in sending a loco to assist the disabled train from the rear. Eventually the train was pushed through to Chard Jct where the 19.10 Waterloo-Exeter was released after a two-hour wait. The up train is then delayed while the assistant loco ditched the train engine in the Creamery Sidings and returned to the front of the train. It was a massive 3hr 22min late. Mr Scott (*my notes do not say it was the NSE route manager rather than the Western general manager but I think it was*) has said that the 19.10 passengers should have been detrained at the closed Chard Jct up platform and taken by road. It seems to me that such a suggestion does not understand the difficulties on site and the time involved in getting road transport to and from such a remote location.

Next is a disciplinary hearing with Transport Salaried Staffs Association (TSSA) line secretary Ian Byiers defending a booking clerk who has been charged with five instances of sloppy work. There is history involved. When the TSSA last defended him, against a charge of driving for Godfrey Davies car hire when claiming to be sick, I gave three days' suspension in the face of all kinds of threats. The 'Form 1' disciplinary charge is uncontested and the emphasis is on mitigating circumstances: a maintenance claim from his estranged wife, the cot death of his 11-week-old son by his common-law wife and his enrolment with Alcoholics Anonymous. The punishment is a reprimand, which is all that was intended anyway. The charge was unrelated to the dishonesty of the suspension and, to my mind, is parallel to it rather than cumulative. In the event of future troubles, this reprimand keeps the pot boiling.

It is cricket tonight so I catch the Manchester home; just in time to have a row with a taxi driver and his two drunken customers for blocking the entrance and exit from a car park that is usually full over the summer school holidays.

Wednesday 13th August

The 08.13 to Paignton has a secondman driving and I cannot quite make out the driver, as I join the train. As I talk to the booking office staff at Newton Abbot, the secondman walks by. I break off to ask what job he is working. "Just going home," he replies. A long lecture follows, explaining that he must not take charge of a train while off duty. He understands. *Difficult one this- how to enforce rules without quashing enthusiasm. Unsure that this course of action did so either, but a blind eye was out of the question. If this train had been involved in a suicide then great play would have been made about the train being driven by someone who was not on duty.*

On the phone, John Beer says he has the chance of securing a charter train contract but needs the lure of some rare track to clinch it. What about Paignton to Goodrington and 'Happy Valley' sidings? Ian Johnson, the permanent way engineer, will play ball so John can go ahead. He has asked me to take note of the booking clerk workload when I am at Paignton. The temporary summer clerk has been permitted to work his rest day making three positions open. During my visit there are no more than seven people at the three windows. *Unsure whether I concluded this was correct or generous.*

After visiting the north and south boxes, I ride up to Torquay with driver Andy Snowdon, formerly of Leeds Holbeck. He has a lot to say about a brick being thrown at his cab last week and says he would have throttled them if he had been able to get his hands on them. Andy is a fit young man and the cretinous thugs can think themselves lucky he didn't. He is most upset by the fact that they had waved at him before throwing their missiles. Three other Leeds drivers are learning the road and overhear the conversation. "In Yorkshire they throw fridges at you not bricks," one shouts. This is the

Yorkshire way of showing their sympathy with Andy, not making light of it.

After 20min in the booking office I catch the Torbay Express up to Taunton with No. 47501 which achieved 105mph (maximum permissible 95mph) recently. Driver Jemmett is in charge with the Leeds drivers learning the road so I travel in the train to Exeter St. David's. Driver D. Rogers is climbing on the loco but driver Ellis is at the controls. There feels to be a bit of an atmosphere for some reason. Afterwards I ask driver manager George Reed about it but he says that driver Ellis is just reticent. *I subsequently heard that he has taken offence at my not having made a special effort to meet him on arrival because he is a prominent local politician. Three years on from my arrival, I could not have done much about it. As long as he does his job properly there is no need for him to be pleasant.*

Doing the rounds at Taunton, a senior railman says that his father, the last chief inspector at Taunton, has died and could I please inform the admin office. The down train is headed by No. 50002 'Superb' –far from that in terms of its external condition -but 4min early. Archie Beer is the driver with Charlie Clyst assisting. We are stopped at Victory with the half-barriers on local control. We had left Taunton 2min early (difference of advertised and working times) but we are now 3min late. I note the inspection saloon is in the siding at Wellington. I hope this has not caused the barrier failure one way or the other, not activating treadles perhaps. I will have to check. There are 3min recovery time approaching Exeter St. David's and we arrive 42sec early. *If the modern driver advisory system had been in operation this train would have been on time at Taunton, on time by working times (2min late by advertised times) late away and 1½min late at Exeter.*

At 14.00 we have a visit from a BRB representative to discuss relationships with the sectors so we run through familiar ground of reporting lines and devolution (or lack of it) for 1½hours. *Who could deny that reorganisation drains resources from running the railway? It seems from the current standpoint that the aim of the exercise was probably to abolish area management rather than knocking some sense into the sectors.*

John Beer comes in to discuss some tricky issues and I phone the C.B.E in Launceston. The conversation with his wife is prickly and it is arranged that I should phone tomorrow at 09.00.

Thursday 14th August 1986

The phone call goes well with a gentlemanly response from the plaintiff, who says he quite understands the problem. A written apology will follow.

An award to driver Whittle is scheduled for this afternoon to recognise his work in extinguishing the fire on the Class 31 at Cowley Bridge. Journalists are already interviewing him when I intervene to offer coffee and a chat. Headquarters has failed to send the cheque, probably intending to put it through his paybill and where it will lose any significance. The handover ceremony takes place on the steps of No. 50007 waiting to take the 14.17 to Waterloo. I present a large envelope and resist the reporters' entreaties to have it opened. A couple of quick radio interviews seal the event. Almost immediately, two journalists from Radio Leicester arrive to prepare for a programme on our 'Skippers' *(Class 142s),* in the form of a pleasant chat and a taped interview before a trip on one with Ray Thorn. *Radio Leicester?!*

The figures for the Lympstone Commando special have come through, the final total amounting to £37,000 plus 75 return halves of inbound tickets, with £28,000 of that going to InterCity Cross Country. There is the added advantage of potentially rowdy young men being separated from normal InterCity passengers. The camp officers are pleased with events (having been buttered up by Ray Thorn) and have ordered another train for 14th December. I phone Nigel Pennington at Birmingham to ensure there will be no slip-up. *This is another example where the modern sectorised and then privatised railway was no longer able to manage such peaks.*

Friday 15th August 1986

The phone rings at 07.30. It is John Beer on his way home having been called out for a fatality at Exminster. The Laira driver of the 04.25 Exeter Riverside to Tavistock Jct has hit someone at Exminster's down distant signal. John has asked the Exeter duty manager Gordon Hooper to get an engine ready to take him to the site and not to tell the Police until he is there. Gordon asks, "What if he is still alive?" Hmmm. Good point but hardly likely. John says to tell the police it is at Exminster. The distant is the best part of a mile away so John's engine, and driver Colin Ireland, get there first and prevent heavy delay. The worst is 24min to the 05.48 Exeter St. David's to Waterloo. *I believe they do things somewhat differently nowadays! A risky strategy but the end thoroughly justified the means.*

I have to attend a meeting at Yeovil Jct this morning concerning the plans of Salisbury area manager renowned steam enthusiast Gerry Daniels to run six days of steam specials using a Merchant Navy and King Arthur from Salisbury to Yeovil Jct. I am opposing the plans on the grounds of the more than likely delay this will have on regular services that barely have enough infrastructure or reliability to keep their own timetable promises. I find it unbelievable that he has Network South East sector backing. He has also broken protocol by sending literature direct to my Yeovil supervisors which I tell him is both unprofessional and unethical.

Mike Romans from Swindon Operations, Gerry Daniels, the Police, the Yeovil Jct supervisor and I manage to take two hours to discuss a simple run-round turning movement and crowd control. At 12.35, despite not being chairman, I ask if there are any further comments. As they draw breath, I say, "No? Good, Right. Thank you" and the meeting breaks up.

This is typical of the way BR could distract itself from its main task. If we had been providing a good service on the line then it would have been different. Nowadays, I defend the right to run steam specials as having equal running rights over a privatised network but this was not then the case.

I take the outbased Metro car to Pen Mill for a chat with the travel centre manager over the failure to investigate a complaint properly. He says he does not want to involve the TSSA or get anyone into trouble. I am puzzled by his response but I think he believes I might be in trouble. I leave him in no doubt who is responsible for the failure to investigate the problem properly, not anyone above him or below him in the hierarchy. He gives me the impression he had failed to grasp the point but at least we have cleared the air.

It is Friday so I can catch the 'Fridays Only' Brighton to Penzance back to Exeter with a Class 33. We are 20min late at Chard Jct but it would have been single figures at St. David's had it not been for an elderly lady with at least ten pieces of luggage, and two Swedish students with bikes, at Exeter Central. See Appendix D.

Saturday 16th August 1986

A late decision to go to Huddersfield results in our joining the up summer Saturday Pullman train again. Starting off with driver Andy Braund we are within 2min of right time all the way to Manchester. Leaving Taunton, Linda and I have our first experience of using an on-train telephone which is effective despite the price of 1p per second. *What a revolution in personal communications was to come that would quickly see this apparatus redundant through saturation ownership of mobile phones.*

Photo: An IC125 arrives at Tiverton Parkway on 17th August 1986 with the 09.30 Plymouth to Paddington.
Credit: R. W. Penny

CHAPTER 15: CEMENT TRAIN DERAILED AT COGLOAD JCT

Sunday 17th August 1986

The return journey entails a cross-Manchester run (*pre the use of Piccadilly via TransPennine trains and with no Sunday Stalybridge-Stockport service*). The Newcastle-Liverpool with No. 45106 is retimed 26min later and I start to get anxious as we encounter single line working at Greenfield. From passing the box to leaving on the 'wrong' line, having passed the crossover, reversed through it and picked up the pilotman takes only 4½min. We pass another Class 45 at Stalybridge waiting for the single line. At Dawlish Warren No. 97652 is out on the sea wall with a repairs train and more single line working is in force. This time it is a facing crossover and from passing the signal box to setting off on the single line is less than 1min. *Single line working and retiming is no longer fashionable. Complete blockades, and diversionary routes that take 30min but result in trains falling back into the next hour's slot are typical solutions.*

Monday 18th August 1986

Train crew manager Alan Bell is back from holiday. The new regional agreement with the guards on fare collection on 7th August has been a sell-out to the unions. If there are two sets and no inspection staff for the second unit it must be locked out of use! It could result in 2xClass 142s with fifty standing in the front set and the rear set locked off. With no corridor connection tickets cannot be collected in both sets but regional management has chosen not to seat its customers so that no fares are missed. If it is as full as that, the guard will not be able to get through the front set anyway. I put the papers in my bag to write a document to get us out of this position. Chester Long is behind this and area managers feel many of the substratum of regional managers are in awe of him. We also have a meeting coming up about depot working under the negotiation arrangements (as opposed to consultation where management has more strength to implement what it thinks is necessary). I suspect the local representatives could well be instructed to ensure there is no agreement resulting in the issues being referred to regional Sectional Council, chaired by Chester Long. Any more hassle and I shall try to implement driver only operation on the branches.

Alan has also seen Chester about the transfer of the Gloucester guards. It appears that they cannot now transfer under the redundancy arrangements. So much for the discussion on the train last week.

We have had two derailments at City Basin bitumen sidings last week and a tank is off the road again. Bernard Price is sure the track is wrong but the engineers deny it. When Bernard arrives to deal with today's incident he discovers makeshift track repairs nevertheless underway.

I have an appointment at home with social services over the adoption we have been trying to progress for two years so I take an early finish. We are delighted to hear that we have been matched with a baby boy and we can go to see him at his foster parents' house in Saltash on Friday afternoon. As Linda and I eat our evening meal at 17.40 in a state of both excitement and apprehension, the telephone rings. Bernard Price is on the other end so I know this is urgent because he does not ring otherwise. The 16.10 Westbury to Exeter Central cement train formed of No. 47144 on 18x50tonne PCA cement tanks has derailed fouling both main lines at Cogload Jct. London trains are being diverted via Yeovil Jct and Waterloo-Exeter trains are being started/terminated there. Cross Country trains are being turned round at Bridgwater and Taunton with buses between the two. This level of organisation is outstanding in the half hour since it happened. Wally Pipe, the Taunton supervisor, is on site. After a few phone calls, gulping down dinner, adoption has to take a back seat and work has again to take precedence. I pack my bag and jump in the car in the gathering gloom of a grey drizzly evening.

Arriving on site, I discover an appalling scene. The locomotive is standing near Radford's Bridge. Behind it, are eighteen derailed 50tonne tanks up to four feet down in a deep hole the train has dug for itself. The down line has been completely destroyed and the up line badly damaged. Thank goodness there was no train on the up line as an HST could have ploughed into this lot at 90-100mph here.

The Bristol toolvans are already in position, having come via Westbury to get into position behind the derailment - but without their crane which is under repair. The Cardiff toolvans are on their way with a crane. The Plymouth crane will be too light for this job and we really need a crane to start working at the Taunton end. Bernard is on site and area civil engineer Peter Warren arrives about an hour after me. The only mechanical engineer there is the breakdown van supervisor who is disinclined to speculate about the cause until some of the wreckage has been cleared.

It is debatable whether this is to be classified as a 'plain line' derailment which has caused consternation for many years and usually involves calling Derby Research. It is too early to do that, especially if the cause becomes clear overnight.

The guard was in the front cab *(at this time the rules required him to be in the rear one)* and the driver says he was travelling at 55mph. Liaising with my boss regional operating manager Bob Poynter, he says he will not be sending out one of the regional team and it is my lead. *I suppose this was a compliment and it also meant I would be taking the Inquiry.*

Darkness is falling. Being satisfied everything is in order with protection and management of the site, that the diversion and bus replacements are in position, I head home, make a couple of phone calls and go to bed by midnight. *Bernard and his team of inspectors need no guidance or interference in these situations. They staff the points necessary and do twelve hours days or nights as appropriate. Buses would have operated from Bristol not Bridgwater if this happened nowadays. Class 159s would run from Yeovil Jct and Exeter and the odd London train would be diverted that way with long delays on the single line.*

Photo: Clearing up the mayhem at Cogload Jct

Tuesday 19th August 1986

At 06.30, St. David's seems ready to deal with the forthcoming disruption. Train plans are in existence – one aspect at which the Region excels – and Tony Crabtree is going to look after the station. The 06.00 Plymouth- Paddington pulls away up the bank towards Exeter Central, having reversed, just 6min late. The essential task is now to discover the cause of the derailment so I head for Cogload Jct feeling apprehensive. I have been told that the Eastleigh crane is in position at the Taunton end so site clearance can be expedited.

The senior mechanical engineer on site is regional officer Mike Winstock. He is an extremely capable manager but hard-headed and sarcastic. If you don't stand up to him he will steamroller you. There is a representative from Blue Circle cement present. He is not a happy man as the firm has not been properly notified of the crash. Control asked my TOPS office to tell Blue Circle at Central but they had gone home and did not find out until 06.00 today. Blue Circle Westbury was not informed until midnight and they did not tell anyone else in their organisation.

Mike asks if I have seen the flats on the front wagon. It was not visible last night but this morning it is clear that the hand brake has been left screwed on and dragged along at 60mph for 35 miles. In this time it has developed a secondary flange on the outside of the rail and when this has encountered the trailing points at Cogload Jct it has burst them open. The secondary flange has hit the V of the crossing as it approached the facing points and run along the outside of the point blade and then been squeezed back over the rail to the left-hand side of the running rail. A 5ft 2in shape was now being forced through a 4ft 8½in space with inevitable results. The rails have then splayed and wheels have fallen onto the fishplates and web of the rail and a weld has burst. I am a little puzzled about how the first two wagons are upright. To be sure I call John Weaver from Derby research who says he will come and take a look. I mentally note that absolute block manual signalling would have spotted this situation developing by Clink Road Jct.

There are many sightseers and photographers around, including local television cameras. I am chatting to the television reporter as we wait for the camera crew to set up when a Westbury guard says, "I've been saying for years now that these trains are too heavy." I grin and try to freeze him out. I can hardly tell him to keep quiet in front of the reporter. It is clearly a stupid comment as we run trains four times heavier than this one, and from Westbury too. What the guard means is that if there were lighter trains and more of them there would be more jobs for guards. More likely, there would be no trains at all as the costs would be too high.

Earlier, a driver had said that whoever re-routed this train via Taunton instead of Honiton was responsible. Since Regional operations officer Ken Shingleton and I were the ones who arranged this to increase Exeter-Waterloo train reliability I am not likely to agree with this. I tell him that if the cause was a track fault another train would have been affected and if it is a wagon fault it would have derailed elsewhere, which he accepts. Two other train crew agree with me. I think Exeter crews would have been both more astute in their observations and more discreet in their approach with the press around.

Inevitably, the second question in the interview is, "There have been suggestions that the train was too heavy, are they correct?" I have no trouble in denying the suggestion. When asked about the cause I say that we have found a problem with the front wagon that seems to be responsible subject to formal enquiry. The standard response is to say we do not know until after the enquiry but I am conscious of the images being shown of cement wagons all over both tracks and I want to assuage any fears that it could happen any time again as we do not know what had caused the derailment.

Around lunchtime I return to Taunton where the traffic arrangements are going quite well. After half an hour back at the site, I go to Bridgwater to pick up John Weaver and find the Bristol inspectors there do not know which train is approaching and I have to tell them. When John arrives on site he explains the process in impressive detail. A similar accident has occurred at Witham on the Norwich main line where PCAs have developed a secondary flange and derailed. Subject to running the facts through the Derby Research computer, analysis of the weld plus the Inquiry itself, the cause has established.

At 18.00 I leave the site in the hands of Alan Bell and go home where Linda tells me the TV item came over well.

Wednesday 20th August 1986

I have been promising 16.00 for single line working and midnight for both lines being reopened to traffic, despite some pessimism at times from the engineers. I am going to be on site at 06.30 and the state of play on arrival will be crucial.

Both lines are clear, all wagons having been removed by 05.30. The breakdown vans are ready to leave. The up line has been replaced length by length as each wagon has been removed, although it will need new rails in due course and four welds need replacing. A breather switch for the down line has been moved in and the diggers have arrived. One lucky break has been that the down relief trackwork that was made redundant under resignalling and remodelling is still in situ and can simply be moved across to replace the down main. The five wagons rerailed on the down side are not too badly damaged and are pushed away towards Taunton so the diggers can then get behind a 15-length stretch of the down relief and wrench it across to the down main formation ten yards at a time. Next comes the 'Jackapacka', a small tractor-like machine which somehow digs itself into the trackbed and lifts both itself and the track. A ballast train is standing by to fill in the gaps.

The up line is back in traffic at 17.00 with the Leeds Mail and the first train planned over the single line working is the down Glasgow. Two hours later the down line is given back and single line working is taken out with the Golden Hind that has come via Bristol. Normal Working resumed within 50 hours with just the cement to be reclaimed from the wagons and the empties removed in due course.

The incident recovery demonstrated some of the strengths of the centralised national railway. The separate departments all did their own job, coordination seeming to happen naturally. No contracts were involved. Resources were available when required, but the operators and engineers were under the single management of the region if any quarrels had broken out. I would venture that the privatised railway would have taken longer.

Thursday 21st August 1986

The need to be convincing on television is very important to ground level staff just as much as for the public or senior management and the feedback is positive. My desk is quite full and a few priorities need to be sorted out. The most annoying of these is a Heritage Trust special train next week with Hon. William McAlpine and the Western Region general manager. We do not have much to do other than organise a few minibuses and turn up but I will be tied up with it for much of the Wednesday after the bank holiday.

There is a complaint from Sherborne School about having been unable to secure group reservations for their girls returning in September before they broke up. They are entirely justified. After I have been given the run around by various Network South East London numbers, I know how they feel. Mind you, Sherborne School is not much better. Their headed notepaper shows an old phone number and directory enquiries lists only a boys school. Eventually I reach the bursar who says the letter-writer is on a different number again, on which there is no answer. Eventually I find the right person and discuss the difficulties, asking her to contact me personally if the situation is unsatisfactory for the Christmas break and I will authorise the travel centre to make individual reservations if necessary. It is no exaggeration to say I felt more stress from this bureaucratic nonsense than the whole of the main line blockage and the interface with the public, engineers and operating staff.

I am being pestered by local media concerning a press release about guard Jeyes who discovered a kitbag with a ticking alarm clock in it on his Paddington-Plymouth express and has shown great presence of mind in disposing of it without any fuss. They want to interview him but he is on leave and I refuse to divulge his home phone number. The reporters are, to say the least, displeased but I do an interview for Devonair Radio about it.

On top of this, the Exeter Express & Echo rings to ask if they can interview driver Reg Lankester who is working his final turn today. It transpires that the driver has asked to take two days of his outstanding leave on Friday and Saturday so he can retire at the end of a London job. Saturday has been granted but Friday refused. This has upset him, ruined his last day and led him to say he will not be coming to work on Friday. What terrible circumstances with which to end a 46-year career. Reg is someone who can appear naturally grumpy but he has a strong and devilish sense of humour which I always enjoy. I certainly do not want him interviewing on the radio as soon as he gets back. I palm them off with some feeble excuse and ask Alan Bell to contact Reg while he is having his break in London to tell him his Friday off has been granted once the full nature of the problem has come to light.

Friday 22nd August 1986

We are starting to get back on an even keel this morning and I start by chatting with one of the Leeds drivers in the lobby at 07.45. We even have all nine 'Skippers' available. A long-promised Exeter & Echo report about the units has been published and it is surprisingly fair to us, despite a long session with the reporter who seemed to think trains from Dawlish to Exeter travelled via Exmouth. I phone him up to tell him that his report is appreciated.

Today is the big day in Saltash so I leave work on the 12.34 to Dawlish with Rodney French, an LDC representative. When we reach Plymouth the social worker hands the baby to Linda, tells her his name and then says there is a bit of a problem and he will come back in ten minutes. The baby's birth mother has changed her mind. We are stunned and retire to a car park overlooking the railway at Saltash before going home. *Journeys into Cornwall were never to be the same again when we see the car park and re-live the trauma.*

Saturday 23rd August 1986

Matters to discuss. Linda and I walk to Dawlish Warren. The trains are running well.

Photo: Nos. 31439 and 31402 head a train of London Midland Mark 3 Pullman stock forming 16.25 Paignton to Liverpool through Dawlish Warren on 23rd August 1986.
Credit: Colin J. Marsden

CHAPTER 16: A ROW WITH INTERCITY AND A BUFFET WITH CHRIS GREEN

Sunday 24th August 1986

An unexpectedly fine day and a need to relax results in a trip to Dartmouth for the day making use of a complimentary pass kindly provided by manager Barry Cogar. No. 50039 'Implacable' takes us to Paignton 4min late and 2-8-0 No. 5239 is working on the Torbay Steam Railway. A deck chair on the promenade is about all we are fit for, before returning with the same motive power throughout. I nearly commit the cardinal sin of taking the wrong train home from Paignton. No. 47600 on a string of Mark Is looks more like an Oxford or Bristol train rather than a Paddington service but I catch an announcement before joining which states that it is a Llanelli excursion. Apparently the 17.35 to Paddington does not run on bank holiday weekends. The excursion probably picks up at Teignmouth and Dawlish but with our luck it would probably be first stop Bristol for crew relief only. *I think this is called taking your eyes off the football and probably demonstrated my state of mind more clearly than words can describe.*

There is just time to have a few words with Sid Oak who is the guard of the 18.30. He knows Linda as they both help at the Pensioners' dinner. He has found a copy of Woman's Own on the train and gives it to her.

Monday 25th August 1986

Linda has fortunately been given an extra week's language school teaching this week which will keep her mind off the adoption. There is no point in my going in to work for the two days British Rail generously allows for the bank holiday because I will never be able to get them back. I have a briefcase full of paperwork so I write a few letters including a general one to all staff thanking them for their efforts during the Cogload derailment. There are consultation documents to write for getting out of the multiple Class 142 manning arrangements and the conductors at Totnes for Dart Valley trains entering the main line station.

Tuesday 26th August 1986

After taking the cat to the vet's I write the Travel Centre Review consultation document. It takes about two hours but is complete except for an appendix of present and proposed duty lists.

Wednesday 27th August 1986

The general manager is getting twitchy that only one area has submitted its consultation document (*presumably on the Travel Centre Review but not stated*). Clarence Woodbury is away sick and Ken Boobyer is covering his job and three others. Filling the personnel job has been frozen as there is a ban on advertising jobs (*a false economy in other than very short term cash flow*) so compiling consultation documents is not as easy as it seems. We have also been somewhat preoccupied recently of course but there is no point complaining.

Apparently Mr Poynter had been trying to get hold of me yesterday. He was at work on Saturday and Tuesday and I am in danger of having a black mark by spending the bank holiday doing paperwork it seems. InterCity route manager Peter Griggs has apparently been criticising the handling of the Cogload mishap (*not sure how many major derailments he had masterminded but I suspect none*). He rings to arrange a meeting but there appears to be no space in my diary for some time to come. Instead, he telephones for 1hr 15min which settles nothing. Trust is an important issue. I don't know how he feels but mine is at a low ebb. *This is an example of working for two bosses; line management from the G.M. and R.O.M. and direct to the Sector. What we have on the privatised railway of today is very little local management and no one putting right faults that recur day after day.*

Peter now wants me to justify the InterCity-allocated staffing on the area, through which hoop we have only recently jumped before his appointment and which we are consulting upon next week. He has been given until mid-September to complete his task across the Region. Tough. He should have mentioned it earlier. It will have to wait until the end of September when I get back from holiday. He counters by saying he has not been allowed to take his holiday and I get under his skin by saying back room staff don't need holidays but front line troops do. Peter moans that ex-management trainee duty manager Vernon Baseley responded to one of his complaints by saying, "You'd better speak to Mr. Heaton about that" and walking away. I will have to remember to congratulate Vernon. The business managers want instant access to meddle but none of the man management consequentials of doing so. *'Face-to-face management' is the phrase I normally employed instead of this old-fashioned 'man management'.*

The businesses were convinced they owned their section of the railway and saw the strengthened area management regimes as a negative influence on their plans. The results of their having their own way led to the privatisation problems of this century. They might say it led to the doubling of business but perhaps neither claim is valid. At one point I suggested privatising the areas. We would bid for the right to operate the railway to certain standards for a fixed tender. Engineers would then bid for the maintenance contract from us. I accept this had many snags but any form of fragmentation creates problems. On the other hand I would probably agree that British Rail is too large to manage efficiently as a single entity. John Major's template for privatisation on a regional basis was probably more sound than most as the criticisms about the effect that such an arrangement would have on competition have proved to be of only marginal importance.

I have to be in Taunton by 12.00 and I just manage to get away on the 10.45 Paignton-Manchester driven by driver Dingle, the last driver to sign on at Taunton and now an Exeter man. I cannot spare the time to ride in the cab today. When I arrive at Taunton there is just time to phone the Taunton East Station signalman to report a missing red aspect in ground position signal 611 (strangely there is no alarm in the box for bulb failures at these signals perhaps because one red remains visible if one of the two fails). I then look in at the travel centre before the arrival of the Heritage Fund charter train conveying Hon. William McAlpine, the general manager, various ex-general managers, the editor of Country Life and others who feel they can justify the squandering of resources and time.

The loco is No. 37430 'Cwmbran' in immaculate condition hauling the open-ended former Great Eastern inspection saloon. We pause to take a look at Stoke Canon signal box, which has rather ridiculously recently been listed. Then we stop at Exeter St. Thomas for a quick look round before taking a minibus to the Brunel pumping house at Starcross and rejoining the train at Dawlish Warren. I travel on the train to Totnes where we meet Barry Cogar to discuss South Devon Railway issues. The Plymouth area manager joins the train and I return to Exeter on the 15.10 Plymouth-Paignton to Newton Abbot and the 15.48 Plymouth-York.

Photo: No. 37430 'Cwmbran' hauls the GE1 inspection saloon eastbound through Ivybridge on its return journey the following day, 28th August 1986. Credit: R. W. Penny

Thursday 28th August 1986

Since I have a late night in the offing I start the day in the cab of the 08.49 local to Exeter which is today a Paddington relief with No. 47568 on 11 coaches. Clarence is back so I have a chat with him about the Travel Centre Review. Fortunately my opinion on the figures, which might be controversial at consultation, is in line with his thinking. Time runs away with me and there is enough time only to grab a sandwich before boarding the 13.12 to Paddington. Paperwork or cab ride? Cab ride, I think. No. 50031 'Hood' is working ten bogies and we are in front of time all the way, arriving 5½min early, just in time for me to have a brunch in the Tournament Bar before finding my way to the J. Walter Thomson advertising agency in Berkeley Square for a presentation by the agency and Chris Green about the Network Card and the next Network Day.

The euphoria of an expanding business carries the meeting along. The boundary of the fares will be at Whimple which is rather artificial and might cause a threshold that will result in a wasteful and annoying mass re-booking. As ever with Chris Green, such problems are details to be overcome while pursuing the main goal. *There have been very few managers in whom I have felt I might have been prepared to follow over the top if transported back to the World War 1 trenches but Chris Green is one of them.* He has clearly done his homework as he knows every area manager on first name terms, a wonderful gift that he has nurtured and which goes right through to ground level. Colin Hall and Graham Eccles, area managers at Liverpool Street and London Bridge respectively, pause for a chat and give me the impression that the issue of whether to accept such a job is whether you are prepared to take the aggravation to get the money. *Both were managers whom I respected and who enjoyed operating but I never felt aggravated like that about the Exeter job even when suffering at the hands of my headquarters colleagues. Clearly Exeter is a totally different proposition to a London terminal.*

Charles Nichols, former Plymouth area manager and now area manager Feltham is as irrepressible as ever, interrupting his general manager and Chris Green alternately. NSE route manager Gavin Scott says he has put his contract with me in the post and would like me to sign it as soon as possible. *This was on the lines of the privatisation model discussed above.*

Back at Paddington, it is a temptation to ride back in the cab but the paperwork needs doing. Guard Roach brings me an Evening Standard but I resist the temptation to read it. We are 5min late at Reading but back on time at Westbury, arriving at Dawlish at 23.00

Friday 29th August 1986

This morning is tied up with retirements. On the 'Skipper' to work I write a letter to the regional operating manager about the repair book on No. 50031 yesterday. The windscreen wiper would not work despite it having been entered in the repair book and having received attention with the fitter's entry reading, "Bodged for now." No one should be surprised if this causes a delay in heavy rain. *Although it might be thought that this should have been taken up with the loco's home depot, it was a specific example of a far more widespread disease.*

First to retire is Ron Sprague who was a fireman on the Bulleid Pacific that derailed with a broken axle at Crewkerne in 1953, causing them to be withdrawn for inspection. Next is Reg Lankester, who had experienced trouble with his 'final turn' last week. A real gentleman, he makes no mention of it. He tells a tale of when he was partnering Ern Pope on a 'two driver' HST turn accompanied by an inspector. Ern told the inspector that Reg would not be saying a word after taking over at Westbury because he needed to concentrate. Reg liked to tell a good yarn but took up the joke and said nothing all the way to Paddington. The inspector then went to train crew manager Vic Bragg and told him that Reg needed watching because he was not confident with the London road. Nothing could have been further from the truth of course.

Syd Ousley came in next taking ill health retirement. Having lost one kidney he was waiting the call to hospital for an operation on the remaining one, yet he was still the most cheerful driver of the day. His papers were on the table in front of me with a medical report that stated, "His G.P. does not predict a bright future."

Les Gurney followed, blooming with health and with a part time gardening and fencing job lined up and looking as though he could give the railway another 45 years. Finally comes driver Guerin retiring on ill health with bronchitis and emphysema and unable to walk very far. It has been a sobering morning.

We have lost four Exmouth Jct drivers and a Newton Abbot man, to be replaced by drivers from depots such as Southall on Monday morning. The make-up and character of the depot is changing radically.

At 12.00 we gather the management team together to meet the regional fire officer. He is from Leeds so he talks some sense but we will have a lot of work to do in order to comply with both the letter and spirit of the enhanced regulations.

After talking to Provincial Services route manager David Mather at some length, there is just enough time to visit the panel box. Red Cow level crossing barriers have failed and the road system is snarled up. This is the least of our problems though. The up traffic has to make its way over the crossing but the main problems are on the down. The loco-hauled Liverpool Plymouth is expected at 16.50 and the 14.15 Paddington-Plymouth is on its tail. There should be time to push out the 16.47 stopper behind these and in front of the following Newcastle-Plymouth and 14.35 Fridays only from Paddington. It takes a long time to get the Liverpool over the level crossing and then the guard is missing and it does not leave until 17.00 followed by the 14.15 Paddington at 17.07. The barriers are now back in action but the 16.47 does not get away until 17.10 with the down Newcastle in the platform. The stopper will not get into Newton Abbot until 17.46 with the Newcastle at 17.53 and the Paddington relief at 18.00. The 17.25 stopper will be badly hit as well. In retrospect the 16.47 stopper should have been sent away on time. *We often see similar situations to this developing on the modern railway with strict Public Performance Measure guidelines governing the order of trains. Sometimes the method works, sometimes it does not.*

CHAPTER 17: SAD NEWS

Sunday 31st August 1986

I take the newspaper to the beach. It is evident that there is a special train around judging from the cameras and it turns out to be English Electric Type 1s Nos. 20124 and 20094 in multiple, on an enthusiasts' special, with a lot of arm waving out of the windows.

Photo: The Class 20 special passes Dawlish Warren. Credit: R. W. Penny

Mike Hodson, with whom I did my management training at Doncaster and who is now area manager at Leeds, telephones to announce his forthcoming marriage and does me the honour of requesting that I should be Best Man. I am flattered to be asked and mark the January date in the diary.

Monday 1st September 1986

The main aim this week is to ensure the desk is clear of any admin issues so Bernard Price does not have to waste time on it while I am away next week. The afternoon management meeting is light with Bernard and Alan Bell on holiday and Ken

Boobyer away on a course. We go through a tedious list of locations, fire evacuation arrangements and inspection systems. Then we review lessons learnt from the Cogload incident. Tony Crabtree focuses on aspects of receiving and transmission of information *(in the days before mobile phones)*. His scientific training shows in the precision of his response on matters like this. Improvements need to be made in the duty manager having a 'runner' to transmit information on his behalf, to double up on announcing/customer information systems and to open the cash office for 24hrs a day, which will ensure dissemination of information at night and keep guards out of the duty manager's hair. It transpires that the duty manager does not hold a key to the photocopier or the stores so this is immediately remedied…. to the horror of the admin office.

Tuesday 2nd September 1986

I'm determined to visit Barnstaple this week as my last two visits have amounted to only ten minutes on each occasion. First I visit Tiverton Parkway by car where Ken Murray is on duty. He says he would welcome the opportunity to operate vending machines and even a shop under his own management, provided he did not have the outlay of £1,500 on fitting out the retail area. He would also consider a small newsagency. Both Ken and today's senior railman are former signalmen who have been successfully redeployed here. *The success is a tribute to their adaptability and proves that accommodating redundant staff does not necessarily mean square pegs placed in round holes.*

There are 48 cars in the car park which is about the number projected at this stage. *The car park and its extension are now always full with perhaps nearer 200 cars.* My drive to Barnstaple shows the lack of threat to the Barnstaple line. Despite driving at the maximum permissible speed where possible, a cement lorry trundles in front of me over the last 15 miles and the journey from Parkway takes 76min. This is long enough to catch a train to Exeter, wait for a connection and be half way from Exeter St. David's to Tiverton Parkway.

At Barnstaple, chargeman George Facey has experienced problems with the lack of a strengthening unit on the 10.10 departure when we have been short of sets. Bikes have also caused a problem. It must be remembered many of the staff worked here pre-Beeching and it is hardly surprising that they see current developments as yet another downward spiral. At least we are well placed today with ten units available but long term solutions are not obvious.

I have a chat with Richard Burningham, a young man whom I have recently appointed from London to travel centre manager. It looks as though the Travel Centre Review will displace him and he will slot into a shift supervisor job at Exeter travel centre. He was told this might happen when he was appointed so he has no regrets - and being his own boss 40 miles away from any supervision with a traditionally minded staff will have been good for him. I resolve to ensure that people like Bristol area manager Frank Markham and Richard Jenkins of the National Sales Force *(what a ridiculous set up - whereas marketing should indeed be national, sales should be local)* are aware of his potential. *Richard's eventual promotion as local government rail officer for Devon and Cornwall, has given him the opportunity to put initiatives back to local level.*

After a visit to the signalbox I drive to Eggesford and spend 20min with Harry Toulson and his wife in the station house. Harry is a signalman who has been away from work for two years with heart problems. He rents the house from the British Rail Property Board and has been negotiating to buy it, with some procrastination on the Board's part, but the deal has now been finalised. His wife is doing home piecework making gloves and also occupied by baking fruit cake for the area manager to consume. Their hospitality and friendliness is humbling.

After 15min visiting the signalbox I move on to Crediton where Cyril Blunt is the signalman. I am not the only one to find Cyril somewhat difficult and today he is in monosyllabic mode. Signalman Stone is training there and wants sponsoring for the Lions' Club raft race. He is a part-time smallholder/farmer in his spare time but has moved to Crediton.

It is 16.00 by the time I get back to the office and take a look at today's mail.

Wednesday 3rd September 1986

Today should involve paperwork and a long LDC meeting about staff reduction at Exeter St. David's. However, in the middle of a meeting with Ken Boobyer and Tony Crabtree (about the budget and this morning's consultation) there is a bombshell. A relief clerk is outside and shaking visibly so I take him to a spare office across the corridor. He feels I should know that Barry Thorn, chairman of clerical regional Sectional Council 'A', chief TOPS (freight vehicle tracking system) clerk at Exeter and brother of guard's inspector Ray Thorn has died at age 44. "How did it happen?" I ask incredulously and the clerk replies that he was found dead in his car on Woodbury Common this morning, before dissolving in tears. This is a real shaker and the implications are of immediate importance. A cup of coffee and a few words of consolation are necessary. I tell him to have a walk round the car park before returning to work. *I was obviously all heart.* In the meantime Bernard Price has sprung into action and taken Ray in hand, going round to Barry's wife and taking Ray's wife to his own house to sit with Bernard's wife, Jean. *We have recently lost Ray to cancer after he beat all the cancer specialists' estimations. The reasons for the suicide and the relief clerk's involvement cannot reasonably be discussed further.*

Eventually the LDC meeting starts with Ray (known as 'Spider' but I always called him Ray) Long, brother of Chester and councillor chairman of Exeter Housing, in the staff side chair. He and I never communicate well. I think he talks in riddles and he no doubt thinks even worse of me. Rumour has it he used to spend a lot of time in the area manager's office before I came, some versions embroidering his visits with tales of his having his feet on the desk. Fortunately he had a year's sabbatical as Mayor in my first year so the habit was able to be broken. His railway job is chief messenger which means he is able to read most of my mail before I do. Consultation is always undertaken in the knowledge that any failure to comply with procedure will result in brother Chester being all too willing to take the matter to Sectional Council, with all the delay and compromise that such an action will entail.

The plan is for a reduction of ten jobs and the budget reflects nine being taken out. Staff side replies with a more than reasonable counter-submission agreeing to the withdrawal of eight posts. Normally this would be good news but we really need that ninth job. We counter attack strongly and Ray threatens to have the matter as a failure to agree and be referred to Sectional Council under what he and others term the Guidelines. When I have, in the past, asked to read them they seem to be a Regional exercise in obfuscation. If we are going that way I need him to specify his grounds. First, he claims it is unsafe and we demonstrate that the proposals are not unsafe. Then he claims the staff cannot encompass the remaining workload. Under consultation rather than negotiation, I am entitled to reserve the right to manage and implement the scheme, having answered the points made. This will need the regional personnel manager to agree with me that it is not a Sectional Council matter. If Swindon concedes to Chester Long that it contravenes 'Guidelines' we will have at least a three months' hole shot in the budget and Ray is well aware of this.

Then I become unstuck. Talking about staff flexibility, I say that the leading railman who deals with the *(old fashioned)* concourse destination boards could assist with train dispatch on Platform 1. This suggestion is not covered in the document and there are no present and proposed duty sheets for that post so Ray says he had not realised it was in the proposals and has been unable to consider the implications. He is clearly, and arguably correctly, sticking to the letter of the procedures but the point will muddy the water even further so I take the eight job offer rather than risk never getting the ninth. The staff proposals have two jobs at a lower grade than my proposals so perhaps I have saved 8.25 jobs. In the meantime we have more efficient working and have saved a number of Saturday enhanced pay rates. *On reflection it seems to me that Ray's proposals were more genuine than I believed at the time and I should have agreed immediately. On the other hand I always felt there was some hidden agenda being progressed and I was wary of staff representatives bearing gifts. Perhaps it was the budget that was too ambitious under pressure from above.*

We break up at 15.00. Bernard has some more information about the suicide. Barry has left four notes and it seems to involve the Staff Association. We had all been worried by his recent weight loss and I had just missed seeing him on Friday after reading a report he had sent me on Thursday about the working of St. Blazey TOPS office. *St. Blazey was not on my area but was a satellite of the Exeter office for operational matters.* The last time I had spoken to him was on Exeter High Street about four weeks ago when I had gained the impression that he had almost jumped out in front of me to stop and talk. He was about to go on a fortnight's holiday to Ibiza with his family. What torment he must have been suffering. Barry was well liked by both staff and management and when chairing Sectional Council staff side he was adept at cooling matters down with a genial sense of humour that I would have counted on getting him through most crises.

Thursday 4th September 1986

The Travel Centre Review document is finalised with Clarence by 08.30. The travel centre managers at Torquay, Barnstaple, Exeter and Taunton have been called in to see it before it is dispatched to Swindon. Ray Thorn is outside. He comes in and talks non-stop about his brother for over half an hour. I feel inadequate and simply nod or express agreement as he unwinds. Ray is tough and 'old school' but I can see the tears welling in his eyes. He is told he does not need to worry about work and he must do whatever needs doing. He is grateful but will be doing his usual stint at Paignton with the summer Saturday trains. I do not press him to do otherwise as it might be better for him to be occupied. I remember how I felt when my father died at a similar age to Barry and going to play football the following day in order to have something to think about. *Nowadays I would be worried about Ray working on or about the track in these circumstances.* If there is a hint of bitterness it concerns the relief clerk. "He took it almost worse than me guv'nor," says Ray. "He was almost collapsed on the stairs after telling you." Ray clearly had his own ideas on what had transpired and there were unstated implications for the railway. *Again, the full facts and allegations must be withheld but many times afterwards Ray would thank me for the time spent with him that day, much to my embarrassment as my response seemed woefully inadequate both then and now.*

At 10.00 I meet the Exeter City Planning and Transportation Committee plus officers. We go to the panel box with Bernard Price and then on a 'Skipper' to Exmouth and back. They are having a meeting that afternoon to consider a £20,000 package of improvements to passenger information systems and a car park for Exmouth rail users.

Exmouth line takings have risen in the new timetable by 15% in May, and 42% in the last period. The committee is impressed but I just hope they do not side-track themselves and spend the money on raising the height of the up platform at Topsham instead, which they seem keen to do.

Provincial Services engineer Peter Maunder asks if I want to go for a lunchtime sandwich. No, I want to work through lunch as usual. He then comes to my office and wastes 45min there. We had first met this morning and he touched a few raw nerves while on the Exmouth trip. On top of this he really does not believe in devolution to the areas. He would not have had this £20,000 if it had depended on HQ contacts.

Paul Silvestri comes in for an hour or so to go through the local train servicing plans he has been seconded to devise. As usual, the work is truly excellent and he has been to Swindon to finalise resourcing. In the middle of our conversation, Peter Fearnhead (with whom I worked at Newcastle having followed him into the area operations job at Middlesbrough) telephones from his current job at Marylebone. Did I know that David Jones, who was area terminals manager at Middlesbrough while I was there, had died at the age of 36 (my age)? He had suffered from arthritis and been given gold injections, having improved sufficiently to be placed on six-monthly check ups. He had moved to Shenfield, then back to Middlesbrough to my old job and recently to Norwich. He had suffered a suspected heart attack, been given tests but had died in hospital. David, another management trainee Peter Fazackerley and I all disliked Teesside. Peter died of a brain tumour at 34 *(so perhaps my decision to retire when I suffered ill health was sensible).* David was a pleasant young man, slow to anger and the last person you would have imagined to have suffered a heart attack. Suggestions from Peter Griggs that I should postpone my holiday to do his budget review had a hollow ring.

Friday 5th September 1986

In at 07.45 to write a dozen *(pre e-mail)* letters and tie up a few loose ends with Bernard and Paul. At 15.30 Bernard suggests I go home and get off on holiday and at 16.00 I put just two items in the pending tray and go.

Saturday 6th September 1986

I call in at Teignmouth signal box for 20min. Matthew Kinsella is on duty and is a bit upset. He has heard that someone in the signalling engineer's department is coming to see him about taking a job with them, for which he has not applied, and I have appointed him to a guard's job on imminent closure of his box. I phone Bernard who knows nothing about the signalling engineer's job either. *I seem to think Matthew remained in signalling, perhaps with just a short time out of the grade, and he eventually came back to the panel box.*

There have been problems with the standard of car park charge enforcement by the senior railmen at Teignmouth but I do not have the inclination to check. No need to, really because there is a ticket on the railway car. Not sure if this is incompetence (having not seen the permit) or deliberate cheek but I am not too concerned either way.

Sunday 7th September to Sunday 21st September 1986

I play cricket for Starcross at Kenn before setting off on the long railway trek to the South of France. We start on the 07.08 from Dawlish behind a Class 50 and take the Golden Hind to Paddington with complimentary teas *(when this was not the norm)* kindly provided by Guard Jenkins. Paris is reached by 19.20 and, after a noisy night in the hotel, we catch the 07.40 TGV from Gare de Lyon, arriving at Marseille at 12.35 after a smooth journey. The Corail connection to St. Raphael is 13min late and full. We spend the journey to Toulon standing in the vestibule before we find a seat. After no explanations and three extra stops we reach our destination in a downpour which develops into a thunderstorm. In those days we booked our hotel on arrival so we could inspect the premises before committing ourselves. *If we had been able to use the internet and, I must admit, cheap flights our holidays would have been so much easier.*

The weather improves by the end of the day and we settle in to a beach holiday with the only transport elements being a boat trip to St. Tropez and a rail trip via Marseille to Aix-en-Provence.

In the meantime there have been some bomb incidents in Paris so we consider a detour home via the Nice-Metz train but eventually decide to brave Paris. The TGV journey is unpleasant at a cramped middle table opposite some French girls who smoke incessantly. The atmosphere in Paris is tense and, after another noisy and smoky journey to Calais we are pleased to board the ship, amid strict security. The Paddington-Dawlish trip home is probably the best of the holiday for the balance of speed, comfort and smoke-free atmosphere.

CHAPTER 18: EXPLOSIVES AT HONITON

Monday 22nd September 1986

I am in the office for 07.00 to start on the backlog. There are no nasty surprises and the paper is sorted into piles by 08.30 leaving a reasonable workload for me. *With Bernard Price and Alan Bell in charge of the safety and staff relations aspects it was rare for there to be any practical problems on return from holiday.* The top priority is to familiarise myself with the arrangements for the special trains conveying the Duchess of Kent on Tuesday and Wednesday. The diary was already full before I went away and there are even more entries now so there is going to be insufficient time for local visits. Most of the day is spent in discussion with departmental heads followed by a combined meeting. I cannot get away to the local Institute of Transport meeting and drive home at 17.30.

I have caused a stir at home by informing Linda she is required to be in the presentation line-up to meet the Duchess at Honiton tomorrow. Fortunately she has an outfit and hat that are suitable.

Tuesday 23rd September 1986

All arrangements are well in hand so Linda and I take a leisurely car ride to Honiton for 10.00 in readiness for the booked 12.05 train arrival which is on time at Taunton. The station is alive with police searching all the buildings, the track, the drains, piles of grit...you name it, they've searched it. Sniffer dog Ben finds an unexploded signalling detonator. Apparently he hates railway guards because they carry these explosives in their bags.

At 11.30, the dignitaries arrive, the deputy Lord Lieutenant, the Sheriff, the Mayor of Honiton, the County Council Chairman and its Chief Executive. The five-coach train arrives on time hauled by No. 47484 'Isambard Kingdom Brunel' in immaculate green livery and formed of 2 x brake first compartment coaches (BFKs) and three royal saloons.

The Duchess alights and shakes hands with the line-up. "Nice to meet you", for those she does not recognise and "So nice to meet you again", for those whom she does. When she reaches Linda she says, "What a beautiful colour of dress," so her day, and mine, is made. Everyone goes to their cars and we go for lunch. The empty stock goes to Yeovil to run round prior to setting off for Heathfield.

Meantime there is an emergency to be handled. Although it was not mentioned in the programme, Linda is expected to be in the line-up at Torquay for the Duchess's departure tomorrow so there is a rush to buy a suitable hat to go with selected outfit No.2. I go to Newton Abbot to keep an eye on the arrangements there because the empty stock is not due to arrive on the branch until 16.45, with the Duchess scheduled to board her train at 17.00 and it would not do for her to get there first. All goes well and so I go down to Torquay where there is much tidying-up left undone.

Wednesday 24th September 1986

Back down to Torquay for 09.00 ready for the 10.06 arrival which is 2min late due to optimistic running times. The train then goes to Goodrington. Bernard Price and Bill Marden check the measurements for the 'stop board' and red carpet this afternoon and it is confirmed they are correct. The relentless security checks continue while I have a chat with the special train manager, David Warne, and nip back home to collect Linda.

The Duchess is back on time with the train awaiting her arrival. She has had a hectic programme and is by now presumably on auto-pilot, but still able to frame the odd question and spend some time with the Chief Constable to thank him for the security checks.

The train leaves my patch and I pick up 3hrs of paperwork. Well known rail critic and adviser Barry Doe has been appointed to the Southern Transport Users' Consultative Committee, a lady from South Molton has a page of 'helpful' suggestions, senior railman Mitchell is to be commended for promptly stopping a train when a passenger had fallen between the train and the platform edge and the inter-sector wranglings continue in the mistaken belief that they are doing anything but obstruct the running of the railway.

Thursday 25th September 1986

Back in the office this morning I am almost up-to-date. I have a 10.15 meeting with Youth Training Scheme (YTS) local manager Roy Slack and the regional scheme manager. It is an interesting subject, and the scheme is going well locally, but I am disturbed to hear that we have a burglar and a football/train hooligan on the books this year. Roy knows as well but it is a moot point under the Youth Offenders' Act whether either of us should do so. This is the first two-year intake which should ensure a supply of young railway staff who can go into shift jobs at 18. The one-year scheme ended with the youngsters being 17 with very few jobs that are exempted from the shift-working legal restrictions available for them to take.

At 12.30 I have a non-meeting with Roger Lewis from Regional Finance and Tony Bird from Security over the closure of the Plymouth Cash Office. My suspicion is that they will expect my area staff to prepare wage packets in allegedly marginal time and distribute them in cash boxes chained up in dmu guards' vans. I think they sense my negativity and back off.

The only internal applicant for my secretary Karin's job has withdrawn so I arrange newspaper advertising for it, invite applications from speculative contacts whose names are on file and inform the Job Centre. Personnel manager Clarence Woodbury says he thinks there might be an application from a lady who was employed at Newton Abbot until the last reorganisation, when she chose to leave rather than travel to an available job at Exeter. She had been so insistent then that she could not possibly travel to Exeter, even at the railway's expense that I would not be inclined to appoint her.

Tomorrow I am supposed to have a briefing from budget clerk Ken Boobyer while on a train to Birmingham in readiness for a regional out-turn meeting. The meeting has now been put back and Ken cannot accompany me so I have to make time today for him to go through the detail. We are officially predicting a minus £30k out-turn but expect to break even and will be muddying the waters to prevent HQ seeing the full picture. The theory is that they will ask for further emergency savings before the year end. Last year we predicted a break-even and they then demanded an £80k betterment so this way we will have something up our sleeve with which to start. Ken says that the latest HQ budget run had suggested £617k would need saving across the Western Region Areas. *In retrospect this sounds rather unethical on my part but it was in response to the arguably unethical actions of the Region and the equally unethical situation where some areas just spend regardless of the budget out-turn and expect the efficient areas to share their burden.*

Friday 26th September 1986

A pleasant journey to Birmingham is spoilt as usual by following a West Midlands PTE unit in from King's Norton (*and this was well before the current 10min interval service was introduced*) arriving 1½min late. The meeting is on the 9th floor of Stanier House. How can the railway support colossal headquarters organisations like this? It would be bad enough were this the only one in Britain but there are at least four others plus the Board HQ and before we even look at Derby.

There are 26 people at the initial meeting which has been called inter-regionally to discuss how budgets can be sectorised. Any form of discussion is impossible. I had been asked to contribute something on 'if' they could be sectorised and not 'how' but a computer programme has been devised and is to be implemented. The meeting is bad-tempered. As Richard Morris, former area Manager at Paddington (*and future president of the Institute of Railway Operators*) puts it, he is fed up of kids pretending they know it all when they know nothing. Mind you, the chairman is no kid. Neither is he effective. He allows the computer boffins to chat endlessly about minor details and those with real reservations are admonished, such as the Railfreight man who was told his doubts 'were taking the subject back not forward'. When he tries to raise specific examples his arguments are dismissed because the new system 'will not be right first time', yet 15min discussions on esoteric accountancy classifications continue unrestricted.

The crowning glory is a computer demonstration which can be seen by no more than ten of the people there and makes it impossible for anyone to formulate questions. The meeting breaks up at 16.00 and I start my budget review with Bernard Norman, a gentlemanly member of the regional operating team whom I first met when he was an instructor at the Derby School of Transport. I think Bernard has his eye on the clock as he does not go through the detailed cost reduction 'scheme' sheets. I refer a couple of questions to Ken on the phone at Exeter. I give my party piece about the unnecessary cost of £100,000 through the concession of re-gradings by HQ meeting chairman and schemes being dropped at regional level. I concede that with an extra effort by all concerned we could just manage to break even and Bernard pronounces himself satisfied.

Since I have not been to Huddersfield for a few weeks, and to let Linda have some time with her parents who are visiting Dawlish, I catch a Manchester train hauled by No. 86247 and elect to cross the city for the Liverpool-Newcastle with No. 47412, both trains being 2min late.

Saturday 27th September 1984

I do not want to be getting to Dawlish at 23.00 with the pubs turning out and no taxis so I aim for 22.03, nor do I wish to risk a delay to the 15.49 Huddersfield to Stalybridge train as a missed Stockport connection would result in a diversion via London. I elect to set off an hour early which will result in spinning out the hour en route. No. 45114 takes me to Stalybridge and a surprise West Midlands Class 101 to Stockport, then an emu No. 304015 all stations to Crewe. Here I find No. 87006 on the 08.30 Inverness-Bristol to Birmingham and No. 50016 'Barham' takes it forward with a run-round at Gloucester. Arrival at Bristol Temple Meads is

3min late mainly due to waiting outside Gloucester for an up HST.

I am now out of options for making any further progress other than to wait half an hour for the 16.55 Manchester that I could have caught from Stockport and a booked connection into a Class 50 to Dawlish. *How times have changed in terms of reduced variety.*

There are a few interesting observations to be made during the wait. An HST from London arrives 9½min late on one power car with the screens predicting 20min late. The 15.40 Penzance-Milton Keynes Central (via Birmingham New Street and Rugby) is a well-filled Pullman Mk3 set. There is time to take a look at some paperwork before the HST arrives with a shattered outer-skin of a window, quite possibly one at which I might have been sitting.

There is a letter to write to Network South East West of England route manager Gavin Scott about the inconsistencies in the contract he has sent me to sign. I suppose my more compliant colleagues will just have signed theirs. There is the Exmouth line improvement scheme to progress. The County Council, as feared, have refused to spend their £20,000 on the new customer information scheme but the package they have decided to support is a substantial one – a free car park for rail users, station painting and raising Topsham platform. *The notes also say 'widening of steps on Class 142s' and I am not sure how that could be financed out of the amount.* Writing a presentation to the Bad Homburg German Exchange Committee, has to wait.

The HST makes good progress to Tiverton Jct where we are looped and instructed to pass a signal at danger. Engineering work is being done on the signal's overlap. Arrival at St. David's is 10min late and the Class 50 stopper loses 5min following the express as Exminster box has switched out for the Saturday night shift – an economy measure in action.

CHAPTER 19: MORE EXETER TO WATERLOO

Monday 29th September 1986

I have an early meeting with the guards' LDC. There are a few routine consultation items, such as the introduction of a trolley service in second class on HSTs and documentation for 'bargain first' tickets, but the main business concerns alteration of the local agreement for working multiple sets on local trains. The issue has come to light with the routine multiple working of Class 142s whereas it was relatively rare for 2xClass 118s to be rostered. If they were, an assistant fare collector would be booked for the extra set.

At present guards are locking up the second set if there is no fare collector or second guard for the extra one, usually resulting in overcrowding of the remaining set….and probably meaning the guard could not get through for fare collection. The situation is too ridiculous for words. The guards are clearly failing to distinguish between policy and restrictive practices, but presumably the local National Union of Railwaymen officials are backing this interpretation.

My approach has to be two-pronged. The agreement can only be altered by negotiation but management's right to exercise discretion, effectively to determine the relative priorities of revenue against comfort, is clearly a consultation issue. So first we consult on the background. There is no intention to withdraw assistant revenue collectors but we must recognise that when one is not available, passenger comfort must come first.

The guards' representatives are amenable and accept most of the points. Their admirable chairman Cliff Salter has a difficult job, having to be positive and yet allow his voluble secretary John Madge to voice his opposition to any change. The quieter members are Roy Hale and Bob Marles who usually assist with the discussion with a few well chosen words. Cliff says he cannot agree to my proposals because it is against the national 'pay train' agreement. I counter by saying there would not be an existing local agreement if it simply repeated the terms of a national agreement so a local agreement can be altered locally and summarise my stance by saying management reserved the right to manage and could no longer be party to an agreement which disadvantaged passengers in this way.

We therefore move on to the negotiation meeting. My draft agreement is 23 lines long instead of the existing four lines. Cliff fishes out a piece of paper with typing on it. "Mine is 26 lines long," he says, passing it across the table. I read it. It gives me everything I want and yet safeguards the rostering an assistant fare collector on booked-set workings, so I accept it. Implementation is with effect from 0001 tomorrow. Common sense at last.

There are two more items to polish off. John Madge wants a test with a portable ticket issuing machine because he thinks there is a danger of passengers being hit on the head if guards swing round and Cliff wants it minuted that guards are complaining of pains in their legs from working full turns on the 'Skipper' Class 142s.

Alan Bell is surprised at the success as he had failed to reach agreement with the LDC on the matter but it was no reflection on Alan's considerable talents of persuasion, more that the guards had taken time to consider their stance and get some feedback from their colleagues, who would, of course, no longer have to suffer abuse while they locked an empty set out of use.

Tuesday 30th September 1986

This morning I need to be at Waterloo by 10.30 for a meeting about the 1987 and 1988 timetables. The Golden Hind is in early. Driver Cross, formerly of Taunton is in charge with 'second driver' Ernie Pope. I get on board and take a pinch of Ernie's snuff. We are again early at Taunton and get underway. Ernie talks continuously. He says you can shut off at 100mph at Tiverton Parkway on the climb to Whiteball and run to Taunton without any power and braking only to stop in the platform. "You can learn the road better if you try things like that," he says. *This is almost the normal way of fuel conservation now, trains regularly coasting from Wiveliscombe to Bradford crossing but privatised managers treat it as rocket science, backed up by an unnecessary driver advisory system.*

Ernie switches to stories about stopping for hounds on the Barnstaple line. "They gave you £5 if you did that," he grins, "so we used to stop even if we just saw the dogs' tails disappearing through the hedge."

Two minutes early passing Castle Cary becomes ½min late due to a 30mph temporary speed restriction (tsr) on the Frome avoiding line. Maximum permissible speed improvements that are not yet reflected in the sectional running times allow us to pull back to ½min on the right side by Woodborough and, despite a 60mph tsr at Newbury, we are 1½min early at Southcote Jct. The Basingstoke-Reading unit that is booked in front of us clears into the station and our signal changes from double yellow to green for the through road.

Ernie returns to his reminiscences. He says that when he was a young fireman one of his drivers gave him some good advice. "You'll see a lot of drivers working," he had said, "and if you remember all their good points and forget their bad points you might make a good driver one day." Homespun philosophy not limited to a railway application, I suppose.

The Hind is now some 12min slower than it was then but now calls additionally at Reading. However, it is now rarely on time. Then, it was rarely late. The schedule has 6min of allowances on the Reading-Paddington section. There is nothing in front (*and no Heathrow Express with which to clash*) so, despite easing back to 120mph, we are 5min early at Slough. Checked into Paddington, we are routed across to Platform

11. "One more set of points and we'd be on the Underground" comments Ernie as we run in 8½min early. I reach Waterloo forecourt at 10.11 as the 06.43 Exeter-Waterloo draws in, having left St. David's 64min before the Golden Hind. *Of course the train had served many stations with which the Hind could not compete.*

The meeting is constructive, chaired by Tom Yarrow who is Gavin Scott's deputy and very sound. We will attempt to revert to the original pattern of departures at 10min past the hour from Waterloo and 20min from Exeter. It will still be tight entering the single line at Pinhoe and depend on down train punctuality but the crosses on the long double line section from Yeovil Jct to Templecombe will be optimised. I agree to re-specify the Pinhoe, Whimple and Feniton stops to match the market and the operational requirements without too much compromise. The Portsmouth through trains will run to Paignton when possible and the newspaper train will terminate at Yeovil Jct. The 19.40 and 20.58 up trains will be concentrated on one departure at 20.20, helping down train running in the late evening and will result in a proper Western Mark 2 set on the 06.43 Exeter-Waterloo instead of the scrappy Clapham Mark 1 set. We will also have a Network set at Exeter in both peaks to help out with the Skipper problems.

I have a salad in the staff canteen *(that felt like a relic of workers' playtime days)* with David Mather who has turned up from Swindon Provincial Services to utter two sentences that I could have contributed *(and this on the business-oriented railway).*

I catch the 15.10 Waterloo to Exeter. At departure time, trains are stacked up with a signalling fault so we are 5min late away. There is a 20mph tsr at Raynes Park so we lose a minute to Woking. The station work is sloppy, a mixture of disorganisation, heavy periodical traffic and invalid's attention. Salisbury is reached 6½min late, 8min late away and a similar pattern to Yeovil Jct but the driver regains some time. Yeovil is reached 8½min late and 2½min overtime is incurred. This is one of my stations and this is unacceptable working. On arrival at Exeter, I instruct the Yeovil Jct supervisor that there must be no station overtime for van traffic and, if necessary, the traffic should be tipped onto the platform instead of being neatly stacked onto a barrow.

A minute is regained by Axminster and then comes the interesting Axminster to Honiton section and the 1-in-80 climb to Honiton Tunnel. It was stated at this morning's meeting that the sectional running time was 12min 54sec. We normally take around 12min to 12min 40sec and the timetable shows 11min so we are 11½min late at Honiton but keen running, recovery time and good station work means we scrape into St. David's 5min late. Looked at another way, 11½min station overtime and tsrs of 20, 40, 20 and 70mph have been recouped with an arrival equal to the 5min level of the late start from Waterloo. *A good run and a bad run both at the same time.*

Paul Silvestri wants a word about the 1987 local timetable he is planning and how this morning's meeting affects his plans, then Drivers' LDC chairman Len Purse wants to bring my attention to the illegal parking taking place on Saturdays at Exeter Central civil engineers' yard. He volunteers with a chuckle that he should not have been there either when he noticed it.

Wednesday 1st October 1986

More Exeter-Waterloo duties today because I have arranged a meeting at Salisbury to discuss signal engineering performance. I was going to ride with Exeter driver Mick Lockyer on the 08.11 who has former Ilkley driver Tom Caslin learning the road. Tom is intending to move to Dawlish. *Tom was a real character with a tremendous sense of humour that enlivened wherever he was but he suffered a motorbike accident on his way to work and relatively quickly succumbed to a brain tumour.* The Exeter Area S&T engineer David McKeown is coming to the meeting so I elect to travel with him. Despite a problem at Crewkerne barriers that costs 6min (an S&T performance problem) and slight signals outside Salisbury we are just a few seconds late arriving.

The aim of my meeting is to identify action which will increase S&T reliability. Matters such as failure of the 'tokenless block' signalling system feature high on the list of delay causes. Tom Yarrow is there on behalf of Network SouthEast to underwrite any extra expenditure. The S&T representation is from area/regional offices at Eastleigh/Croydon and Reading/Exeter. The Western Region chief operating manager is represented and the Area Manager Salisbury is there with his operations manager, nine in total.

I want to determine action under two headings; immediate and long-term. The Southern engineers seem negative. Nothing will solve the problems short of total re-signalling *(It was about 20 years before this was done.)* In contrast, David and his regional counterpart, Sid King, have come with a shopping list of immediate improvements. Replacement of five level crossing barrier controls will help, £20k each. Did we know that the automatic warning system (aws) circuits were shared with the block circuits so an aws failure resulted in a block failure? No we certainly did not! They could be separated at 24 locations on the western half of the section for £6,000. I offer to sign the 'works order' immediately. Here lies the nub of the problem. They have to politely decline because the S&T department does not have provision to spend my money. This is plainly administrative balderdash and Tom Yarrow undertakes to try to find a way around the impasse.

We talk over the re-signalling options. Solid state interlocking looks the best bet. In a moving world of traction capabilities and permanent speed restrictions it will prevent abortive expenditure and be as flexible as conventional MAS. We are still talking in terms of possible 2+7/8 HSTs on the route and a range of options including 1+6 HSTs and 1+4 sets combining and separating at Salisbury. On a route plagued by the effects of loco failures, single power car formations are inadvisable. If 1+4s are used, the meeting hopes they arrive at Salisbury the right way round and not nose to nose. I return on the 13.10 Waterloo-Exeter with No. 50041 'Bulwark', 5min late from Salisbury with 1½min worth of tsrs. With committed driving and time made up at all stations we are waiting time at Exeter Central and on time at St. David's.

Thursday 2nd October 1986

I am expecting to meet the new post-graduate traffic management trainee whom I am to mentor this year. Brigid is 24 and full of confidence in many respects but she has no knowledge of railways, not unusual, but no knowledge whatsoever of geography, which is inexcusable.

Gavin Scott arrives at 10.40 to discuss the terms of my area contract with NSE, to which I have raised a few misgivings. Gavin is an earnest individual who betrays little sense of humour but I have confidence in his integrity. We reach an understanding to retain booking clerks at Yeovil Jct, Axminster and Honiton but he is a bit too focused on the issue of installing NSE litter bins for my liking. He also wants to build new accommodation for the Exeter civil engineer and rent out the current offices. If there was ever a case of taking one's eye off the ball with all the problems of running a reliable service to Exeter, then this item must surely be it. At 13.47 we go to look round Exeter Central before he catches the 14.17 back to Waterloo.

Brigid is given a training programme and is shown how to do a brake test by guard Andy Barriball *(the young guard who was involved in the sleeping car fire at Taunton not long before my appointment).* There is no doubt there is prejudice against women in railway operating positions but there are occasions like this when they receive more help than would be offered to a male trainee.

Friday 3rd October 1986

After visiting the panel for an hour at 07.30 this becomes a completely wasted day. Peter Griggs wants to go through all the cost centres and station staffing ready to chair the budget compilation meeting in a few weeks time. There is really not much to say after hours of number crunching and allocating staff to sectors. BRB Chairman *Bob Reid's customer focused railway was not focusing on the customers very much.*

Saturday 4th October

Today is scheduled to be the first return visit of Bulleid Pacific No. 35028 'Clan Line' to Yeovil Junction since the withdrawal of steam, on a special being sponsored by Salisbury area manager Gerry Daniels. *More failure to concentrate on the problems.* The trains are to run every Saturday and Sunday for three weeks plus a fourth Sunday. My customer services manager John Beer has more sympathy and it is indeed a central part of his duty to exploit commercial opportunities. He has organised some stalls at Yeovil Jct and a Class 142 special to the event. The Class 142 is then going to operate Yeovil Jct to Yeovil Pen Mill shuttles. I travel up on the Class 142 with one engine cutting out most of the way. It is booked non-stop from Pinhoe to Yeovil Jct but traction inspector Ted Bainborough *(who was to die of a heart attack in the 1990s while on the waiting list for a heart operation)* decided to halt the set as it approached a 20mph tsr at Crewkerne. Re-starting the engines, both cut back in and we pick up speed quickly, arriving 8½min late.

I feel obliged to attend today as my request for police attendance has been declined and then elevated by Ken Shingleton to general manager's level to talk to the British Transport Police administrative deputy chief constable. Although the crowd is better behaved, and only half the number, that I predicted the one police sergeant provided issues 36 official cautions for trespass. It strikes me that the police top brass are trying to cut back on overtime but the police themselves are trying to justify their deployment.

Everything goes well with Clan Line's first trip and there is time for me to go down to Pen Mill for half an hour. We carry 200 passengers in all at £1 a head so cover our direct costs and gain goodwill. After the steam engine is safely off our patch on its second trip, John Beer takes me to Axminster in the Yeovil Jct car to catch the 18.33 Saturdays only train to Exeter, which is the return working of an Exeter-based Regional Railways shopping service. We miss it by 5min so adjourn to the George Hotel until 19.54. There is a lively exchange with a local drunk who seems to think, for some reason that defeats me, that we are Nissan agents, before overstepping the mark and changing his mind, suggesting we are Dorothy Perkins representatives. I suggest that he gives up drinking if it makes him pick a fight and tell him to keep himself to himself. So he does, but John looks surprised at my delivery of both barrels.

LDC driver Fred Butler is in charge of the 19.54, reported 9min late off Yeovil Jct. Fred is trying hard and, despite a 70mph tsr for the condition of jointed track near Broadclyst *(where drivers were sometimes tempted to exceed the 85mph limit)* and a false start at Exeter Central, we are only 1½min late at St. David's.

*Photo: Preparations for signalling modernisation are well in hand as No. 50019 'Ramillies' enters Totnes station with the 09.33 Penzance to Newcastle on 7th October 1986.
Credit: R. W. Penny*

CHAPTER 20: STEAM SPECIALS AND UNIT SHORTAGES

Sunday 5th October 1986

Having been unable to raise a volunteer for today, I am in charge at Yeovil Jct. Arriving at St. David's for the 09.40 to Waterloo, I find Nos. 50026 'Indomitable' and 50016 'Barham' at the head of the train. Young duty manager Vernon Baseley is complaining that No. 50026 is restricted to 60mph *(a regular Laira trick often for tyre wear or dodgy fittings).* The benefit of better acceleration is useful only to 60mph and the time cost above this figure will be considerable. On top of this, it is booked to cross the steam train at Gillingham today, thereby risking a knock-on effect. Vernon says Control will not change its mind. I telephone the Control duty manager John Cheeseman, prepared to fire ammunition about being chair of the NSE Performance Group *(and I suppose prepared to adopt a Sector stance against the Region)* but I do not need to do so. John was not aware and countermands the decision. Pertinently he asks, "Can we detach it and still get away on time?" There would have been no point in having a late start that was worse than the potential time loss. Yes we can. A spare driver takes No. 50026 onto the down Waterloo line to Central, intending to loop-hop to Salisbury behind us.

The driver of the 09.40 is S. R. Rodgers (there is an S. L. Rodgers), considered 'awkward' but always fine with me after an initial moan. We have one of the new mobile phones on board so we try to phone Vernon on it before departing on time. We are cautioned from Central for a supermarket trolley dumped on the line at St. James Halt. I spot it under Bonhay Road bridge, just off the platform end at Central in fact. I jump down to clear it, having stood for just 1min but we are stopped again at Chard Jct to be cautioned over Crewkerne automatic half barriers that have been on local control. This costs us another seven minutes.

As No. 35028 arrives at Yeovil Jct at 11.15 there is still no water tanker to top it up. Fortunately there is enough in the loco tender for it to get back. Gerry Daniels has apparently failed to ensure the tanker firm is aware of the amended timings. The same goes for two coach loads of passengers left behind at Salisbury. At half-time on the steam specials I visit Yeovil Jct signalbox with signalman Maidment and signalman Tarr who is acting as handsignalman. No. 6998 'Burton Agnes Hall' is on the second trip and 15min late, thereby delaying the following 14.40 Waterloo-Exeter by 14min and the 16.05 Exeter-Waterloo by 15min crossing the down train at Chard Jct.

It is believed that Gerry Daniels has been conducting clearance tests *(perhaps more likely observing clearance restrictions)* with the Western Region loco. I feel that this and the consequential effect must be brought to the attention of the Western regional operating manager. This is rank bad operating on top of the decision to run an extra train over a single-line railway that can scarcely support the normal service.

After some paperwork, I catch the 14.10 Penzance-Waterloo up to Sherborne with driver Andy Snowdon, making up 1½min to the loco and 1min recovery time to arrive a few seconds early. Prosperous Sherborne is busy with weekenders coming and going. The 17.10 from Waterloo is 25min late and makes little back with driver Rowe. I ride with guard Barry Ruffle most of the way, assisting with doors. *24hrs extra out of the house this weekend and of course, no question of extra pay.*

<u>Monday 6th October 1986</u>

On arrival at work at 08.15 I find just six of the booked nine Skippers in action. The 07.10 from Honiton and two round trips from Newton Abbot to Paignton have had bus substitutions. Two passengers are being pacified by duty manager Colin Godbeer and I need to become involved. One is for Manchester and the other Stafford but there is no option but to wait for the next Cross Country, with refreshment vouchers and telephone facilities provided. *The bus substitutions are more than would be provided nowadays and* initiative has meant concentration on Newton Abbot to Exeter rather than Paignton-Newton Abbot by turning round down trains to form up ones from Newton Abbot. Of course, if you miss the Manchester nowadays there is another Birmingham train in half an hour with a half-hourly service forward from there.

There are thirty applications for the secretarial job to vet and whittle down. It is mainly a matter of catching up this morning, talking to the management team and sorting out some priorities. Alan Bell and Tony Crabtree are going to look after Yeovil Jct this weekend and Alan entertains us with his stories from his days as running foreman at Stratford – of how he used to fill up the sandboxes and put a trail of sand on the rail as reassurance they were working and how he would park the diesels as far away from the shed as possible on cold mornings with the cab heaters working to deter drivers from coming back to the office to fail them. It is 21.30 before the paperwork is completed.

Tuesday 7th October 1986

Karin is away sick and Julie is covering the phone. She is very well spoken and refined but is seriously challenged by putting calls through to me without cutting off the caller. She takes some persuading to type up my notes for the Bad Homburg exchange visit for this lunchtime. Is there any excuse for typing Networth SouthEast instead of Network SouthEast no matter how illegibly I have written it…unless of course it is deliberate? I sift through another eighteen secretarial applications before catching the 10.28 to Exeter Central and meet Tom Walker, ex-traffic manager at Newton Abbot. He is his usual ebullient self and is proud to announce he has recently won the 'Mr Macho' contest on holiday in the Isle of Wight. "It was because of my sense of humour," he claims.

The German visitors are extremely polite, as one has come to expect. They are also attentive and ask pertinent questions. After the buffet, I return to St. David's via Central but my intentions to go box visiting are defeated by administrative matters.

Wednesday 8th October 1986

I catch the 08.13 to Newton Abbot for a quick visit. Chief booking clerk Roy Watts is just back from holiday in St. Raphael, (initiated by the offensive calendar, I wonder?). *On reading the proofs, Linda remarks that we went to St. Raphael that year too.* I talk to supervisor Ernie Underhill about a recent event and return to Exeter on the Penzance-Paddington, where deputy civil engineer Colin Carr is on the platform and we sort out a few minor issues. Back in the office there are another eight secretarial applications. It would seem the pay and benefits package is better than most in the city.

At 10.15 I attend a Royal Train meeting. Prince Charles is spending two nights on the Heathfield branch; fairly routine stuff. I field a public complaint with which Tony Hill has been struggling for 20min, maintaining his composure in the face of some provocation. Captain Nicholl travels from Plymouth to Sherborne every Sunday evening and feels that the 18.25 departure to Waterloo should be held for connection with the 18.22 arrival from Plymouth. Eventually he accepts it will not be held and that retimings are not feasible. *Even if they were and, say, the Waterloo left at 18.30 you would find someone would want it retimed later again to accommodate a sub-standard non-connection from say Barnstaple or Exmouth.*

Roy Corlett, Liverpudlian manager of BBC Radio Devon and fellow Dawlish resident, is waiting to go to lunch at the Great Western. I return at 14.30 for a routine afternoon. The police want some advice about when the best time between 12.00 and 12.45 would be for a car journey over Silk Mills level crossing near Taunton for Princess Diana to avoid train movements. I depute signalling inspector Bill Marden to advise them. Paul Silvestri comes to talk about his latest refinements in plans for the local summer Sunday timetable. *Who was likely to make better local train service plans; Paul who lived on the area and managed the trains, or someone at Swindon?*

Thursday 9th October 1986

Only five of 9 Class 142s are working this morning *for an investment that laughingly provided 13 sets for 12 diagrams in Devon and Cornwall* but local supervisory initiative has produced a Class 31 with two stolen coaches on the Barnstaple branch and a Class 50 on the Paignton line. I meet Peter Warren, Jim Collins (area manager Plymouth) and David McKeown on the 08.01 to Bristol Parkway, changing for Swindon where we are going to have our second lecture on equal opportunities in six months. The general manager is in the chair to prove his support. I have no problem with the presenter's message, or how she says it, but she obviously and possibly correctly thinks her middle aged white male audience needs convincing - but none of my three colleagues would be in that category.

David Warne wants a few words after the meeting before we catch the punctual train back via Parkway. There is a curious message there for me to ring a Swindon number but no one there knows what it is about.

Back at Exeter, Alan Bell has been sectorising our train crew numbers with the business managers at Bristol. Brigid calls in to report on her training and Radio Devon rings to ask if we are very short of coaches for local trains. We are now down to four Class 142s, one loco hauled and a special empty unit from Laira to form the 18.17 to Honiton. We are trying to keep a lid on it and Diana Lee in the Swindon press office is telling the media that the shortage is a result of a maintenance dispute at Reading. Is this an inspirationally clever diversionary tactic or a demonstration of how little knowledge one person can have about their job?

On arrival at Dawlish, the main preoccupation is a collection of 200 Hell's Angels congregated on the station approach at Dawlish Warren. Funny that I did not notice them just now as I passed with No. 50010 'Monarch'. Leading Railman Percy Michell says it is a slight exaggeration and a call to the signalman confirms that it is, by a factor of ten. He estimates nearer to 20 of them. I ask senior railman Joe Cockram to contact the police to ensure it is not being given a higher priority than it deserves resulting in a misallocation of resources.

Friday 10th October 1986

A late start at 08.49 from Dawlish talking to Exeter driver Webb, on his way to work, about his continental rail holidays. At Exeter there is time for a brief discussion with Paul Silvestri about his latest 1987 timetable amendments before he goes over to Platform 5 to meet the Penzance-Paddington which has been reported with windscreen wiper failure and fumes in the cab. Driver Webb, whom I have just left, is booked to work the train forward. One of the keen ex-Cricklewood transferees, he is unlikely to cause unnecessary problems. I follow on the Plymouth-Leeds to Tiverton Parkway for a cup of tea. The relief senior railman is interested in the clerical vacancy at Sherborne. Takings are still steady with some evidence that the station was becoming popular for Bristol season tickets, *a trend that has continued.*

I move on to Taunton for a travel centre visit and a drive out to Silk Mill signal box in the signal lampman's van, the smell of paraffin being so strong that it might need to be classified as a fire hazard if I think about it too long. *To be pedantic I think it is correct to say the address was Silk Mills Road but the signal box was Silk Mill, often written, including by me, as Silkmill.* The signalman is Taunton LDC secretary Derek Locke, a complex individual who has wanted to see me for some time to make a few complaints. First on his list is the slowness of the passenger shunters and how some delays have not come to light. Second is how the pilot loco should come down to the Cider sidings at lunchtime instead of going to the Concrete Works. All his complaints are about people whom he represents and all are valid.

Meanwhile, the traffic working is interesting with a succession of down HSTs, a Class 47 waiting to follow and then, significantly, the pilot on the down relief on its way to the Cider traffic at 12.30!

Next I go to Taunton East Station box where signalman McDonough is on duty, another LDC man. We discuss the Cogload derailment and what might have happened. When signing the train register book I notice an engineering possession has not been taken from the correct points and has been taken remotely when it was feasible to take it from the signalbox. I take it back for the signalling inspectors to follow up. There is then a request to platform the non-stop Penzance-Newcastle *(the up main platform was out of use at this time)* as a passenger has suffered a heart attack.

Visiting the parcels office I have to tell the senior railman to turn off his radio, before taking the 13.47 to Exeter with No. 50021 'Rodney' 4½min early. Chester Long is on his way back from a Reading meeting so we converse to Exeter. From there I go to Red Cow Crossing for a chat with attendant Tony Pullen and then on to Riverside Yard. John Wills is west end chargeman and Tony Spiller is at the east end. There is some doubt whether he is going on a guards' course, which I undertake to follow up. The train preparer complains that the Severn Tunnel freight had run with just one wagon yesterday which he thinks was down to the supervisor wanting his bonus for signing on driver only turns. It will be worth asking the question.

Then it is back to the panel box via the TOPS office. The CO4 vacancy as a result of Barry's death is going to be held pending my travel centre review in case anyone in that grade is displaced. It smacks of square pegs but it will create some flexibility. All is well in the panel but a brew of tea reminds me that I have had only two sandwiches since 10.30. In the office, Brigid reports on her progress. She is concerned that someone has told her that she is 'not like a management trainee'. Considering some of the management trainees I have met recently that might not have been criticism.

There is a broken rail at Aller Jct that is being watched over the weekend. Apparently it is on the 'elbows' of the crossover between the Paignton-Newton Abbot up line and the Newton Abbot-Plymouth down line. The implication is that if it goes we will have single line working from Newton Abbot to Paignton and Totnes simultaneously. *For that, read buses if it were now.* The engineer would then put in plain line during a 3hr possession. That would leave us with single line working to Paignton and normal working to Plymouth. Arnold Knight is reluctant to put out the tsr boards, expecting us to stop and caution trains in both directions but the replacement point will not be available until Wednesday so there is no option but to erect them. I will need to check up on that.

No. 47622 is on the 17.25 to Paignton tonight but I am 5½min late home due to signals behind the 13min late Newcastle train. Paperwork at home contains five sets of notes and minutes about Exeter-Waterloo trains and I have to write a report for the Network Business Group about the line's performance but it is reassuring to note that the recent figures have risen to 85% within 5min of right time. With the few numbers of trains each day that is an average of two trains per day more than 5min late which is two too many but not unreasonable.

CHAPTER 21: DISASTER AVOIDED AT NEWTON ABBOT

Monday 13th October 1986

No. 50032 'Courageous' in NSE livery is on the 07.08 again. We are short of two Class 142s at Exeter again but Laira has sent two extra sets to Newton Abbot. *I presume these were conventional units as the notes are unclear.* One of the Laira units promptly fails with the same fault it had suffered from most of last week. I clear the desk by 08.30 and set off for the Area Business Group chaired by Regional Railways (RR) route manager David Mather.

Ken Shingleton rings to say that the general manager has just become aware of the Class 142 problem, six months after he thought it had been solved. *Perhaps I should have ensured he knew.* The discussion of unit reliability at the meeting is lively. Area maintenance engineer Tony Coles is in a corner and not being constructive. David Mather is prepared to underwrite some additional weekend shifts but Tony Coles does not take him up on the offer. *I suspect that doing so might have pinned him down to delivering his contract with RR.* It transpires that No. 142015 has been out of action for two weeks waiting to be fitted with flange greasers which no one thinks will work and are not required on most lines. The meeting squirms and wriggles along from 10.30 to 16.45 instead of being brought under control.

I have a cricket club meeting at 1930 in Starcross so I visit City Basin and Exminster signal boxes. The 10.55 from Manchester has failed at Birmingham so Bristol has rustled up a Class 118 to cover it to Plymouth. Its traincrew are working the Liverpool back, 20min late, and a Plymouth crew is working the Class 118 back to Exeter. Bristol is sending a guard to Exeter but no driver. Infinitely resourceful Exeter train crew supervisor Howard Davies cannot seem to find a driver either so it looks as if it will have to stay here overnight. What a pity. *Yes, it will make Bristol less willing to risk another dmu special but desperate situations needed desperate, if unethical, measures.*

Tuesday 14th October 1986

We are one short on Class 142s, with an extra set coming up from Plymouth. The news van for the 04.05 Exeter to Barnstaple is very late so the Bristol Class 118 is pressed into service down the branch hauling the newspaper van, which a Class 142 could not have done.

Ray Spackman and Roger Jones arrive from Swindon to discuss the devolution of more HQ responsibilities to area level, needless to say with no extra staff. The new duties would include all aspects of train crew control, Class 2 passenger train control and freight train running; most of which we do anyway *and little of which is now done at local level as each sector does its own.* Ray Spackman pauses to discuss appointing Vernon Baseley to a Swindon Control job and finally decides against it.

There is just time for a panel box visit, where some shunting moves need to be accommodated between the passenger trains, before returning to the office for the main budget compilation meeting chaired by Peter Griggs, InterCity route manager. This is a numbers exercise which produces only one new cost reduction scheme, the removal of one railman's post at Newton Abbot, plus a couple of investigations into staffing levels elsewhere. The main process involves allocating existing staff to their principal sectors and apportioning relief staff costs. *Did Bob Reid realise how much of this was going on?* Linda arrives at 17.00 to discuss the results of her Action Research charity committee work where the committee has been told that some of the funds raised are being used in vivisection to save children's suffering. That's a tough call to make.

No. 33056 'The Burma Star' *(a decoration held by my late father)* is on the 17.25. Howard Davies has decided he can save a double shunt to and from the stabling point by using it to Paignton and back. On its return the coaches go to Salisbury on the 20.58 and the loco goes to Cardiff on the 19.40 simply shunting from Platform 1 to Platform 6 at the Red Cow end of the station, instead of the booked Class 50 going from the Red Cow end of No. 1 to the shed and No. 33056 coming off the shed to the Red Cow end of Platform 6. I seriously doubt that it will keep time with eight coaches but I have to admit that it does not do much worse than the Class 50 on 9 we had most of the summer.

We have a Salisbury meeting tomorrow and John Beer rings to ask if a buffet is being provided, presumably to save him packing his sandwiches! Half an hour later, I remember that I had promised Vernon some feedback on his Swindon interview via John whom he is meeting for a drink tonight. John's call had presumably been a pretext to allow me the opportunity to give him the information. John's wife Sarah says John has just gone out so I track them down at Coolings Wine Bar to give Vernon the bad news.

Wednesday 15th October 1986

This morning I drive into Exeter for the 08.11 to Salisbury with John Beer and David Langton who is area operations manager at Plymouth. *In 2015, David was train planning officer with First TransPennine Express having just overseen the introduction of electric trains to Glasgow.* A permanent way man remarks at the top of his voice that "if they gave as much attention to getting other trains away to time as this one we'd have a better railway." It is a puzzling outburst that could be heard by passengers so I give him a ticking off. We do indeed leave to time though. I turf a spare guard out of first class and settle down for the trip. HQ operations officer Ken Shingleton joins at Sherborne and we arrive 3½min early with No. 50031 'Hood'.

Unlike some of our other business groups the Exeter-Waterloo one covers useful ground and devises an action plan for better performance. *Does the usefulness of the NSE meetings reflect the attitude of the sector director Chris Green or is it the fact that I feel that way because they seek to involve me? Either way, it comes from the top.* We finish at 16.30 and I catch No. 50031 back with a fast run including a good climb of the 1-in-80 bank from Seaton Jct, arriving at Exeter ½min early. I check on events of the day with the Exeter duty manager and find that the Bristol Class 118 has once again found useful employment during its Devon mini-break. I get the 19.01 HST to Dawlish which incurs 1½min overtime at St. David's, on enquiry due to the senior railman searching the van for a consignment of blood but actually due to an extended chat before remembering to give the right-away.

Thursday 16th October 1986

As I walk down the hill from home to Dawlish station, an HST zips through. Is it the Hind running late? It is too early for the Newcastle, due to pass the Warren at 07/45. As I approach the station another HST passes and, as I pick up the phone in the parcels office, another races past. The first was the 06.00 from Plymouth, the second the Hind and the third the Newcastle, all running late. My 2xClass 142s on the stopper have had door trouble at Newton Abbot. It transpires that the empty Laira to Totnes failed on Hemerdon with everything behind it, including the stock for the 06.40 Totnes-Exeter St. David's that forms the 08.11 from there to Waterloo.

Control has decided to run the Waterloo stock empty from Totnes to Exeter as its role has been taken by subsequent HST departures and the following Class 142s will cover the smaller stations. Enquiries reveal that the Waterloo stock has yet to pass Dainton so I reverse the order again and inform them. The Class 142s are 9min late at Dawlish with driver Rodgers whom I accompanied to Yeovil Jct last Sunday and recovers 2min to St. David's. Duty manager Gordon Hooper, the legendary Bulleid Pacific driver, has not picked up that the Class 142 is coming first so he has kept Platform 3 for the Waterloo stock and therefore not re-platformed the Bristol-

Plymouth that is 15min late and clashing with the Class 142s.

Control has refused to allow Gordon to turn round the 08.27 arrival from Salisbury as the 08.11 to Waterloo vice the missing stock from Laira which arrives immediately behind us and departs at 08.48. There is a panic over the inspection saloon for Mr Poynter and the BRB Director of Operations which is allegedly the wrong way round. It is in fact the right way round in as much it is booked to be the 'wrong way round' so it is the 'right way round' when it comes back with its occupants. Having flattened the wheels the last time the inspection saloon was used here I am considerably relieved that all is well. Operations manager Bernard Price is representing the area so I brief him about a few subjects about which they might have queries.

I have to chair a sectional council meeting concerning the withdrawal of supervisory posts at Newton Abbot and Taunton. The regional staff representatives are determined to protect these jobs as they think their loss would precipitate an avalanche of similar reductions. They have recently won a battle with the formidable Frank Markham at Bristol to retain supervisory jobs at Weston-super-Mare and Bath which are operationally less complex, so it is likely to be a tough battle.

The staff offer to forfeit two relief jobs instead of the six that are involved in the proposals. This would not be enough for my budget or business aspirations and it would cost money moving the relief staff around to cover. I reject it and there is a recess. Next they offer a reduction in grades for the retained jobs. I half-heartedly offer one middle turn job to permit a response to emergencies but they do not want to take it. They say the scheme will have to be referred to their headquarters under what they term the 'guidelines', as transferring work from supervisors to chargeman is a matter of principle.

I do not believe it is a matter of principle and inform them that I will be implementing the scheme imminently. I might have obtained agreement if I had offered a middle turn job at each location but there again they would probably have still 'disagreed' and used the two posts as a future bargaining base. Under the old, purely regional, regime I could have risked this but under the new system I will have no business backing and no budgetary provision, having to make compensating savings from somewhere less obvious than this. InterCity would have seen that I had 'under-achieved'. This way, if I do not succeed in implementing the changes on the date I stated and someone else concedes more jobs as a compromise it will not be me who has caved in. The benefit of the sector control should be that there are fewer fudged compromises but reasonable accommodations will be more difficult to reach.

Back in the office at 15.00 there is no time to do a great deal. Driver Eaglen has arrived from Leeds (*Brothers Dave and Peter both transferred but I do not say which here. I suspect it was Dave*). I mention that I know the Leeds area manager, Mike Hodson, but his name does not seem to ring a bell. The Leeds post is a huge task and Mike is away on an eight week course at the moment. The result seems to be not being known to your drivers.

Bernard Price reappears at 16.30 with Jim Collins after a successful journey on the inspection saloon. As we 'de-brief', John Beer puts his head around the door. A Penzance driver has passed Newton Abbot West's up main home signal at danger by 371 yards which is not far from the rear of a dmu standing in the platform. Signalman John Haycock has been on the ball and stopped the driver with a red handsignal displayed from the box window. The driver has been officially 'challenged' at Newton Abbot, accepted it was his fault and has been allowed to come forward to Exeter *(this would not have been the case now)* so Bernard goes out to meet him. The driver admits he has simply had a 'blank spot' having registered the distant as being on but having missed the semaphore home. We cover his return working and send him back to Cornwall as a passenger.

At the same time, the Press Office comes on to research details for a newspaper enquiry concerning a signal at Teignmouth which has been 'propped off' by a vandal. It would have prevented a 'line clear' response to being asked to 'accept' a train but, in other scenarios, it could be dangerous. Bernard helps the Press Office in suitably dressing it up for public consumption so that it is accurate but not alarmist. *There are some unresolved disasters, such as Charfield, where this could have been a factor and where two unidentified children were victims but that incident occurred in the very early hours of the morning.*

It is time to go home with No. 33062 on the S.R. Mark 1 set, 41sec late at Dawlish. Exeter supervisors tend to have more confidence in these Type 3 locos than most Type 4s. It transpires that Linda had just alighted from the dmu at Newton Abbot platform as the Penzance driver passed the signal and she thought at the time that there had been a bit of a commotion.

Friday 17th October 1986

The local is 10min late again this morning as a result of coupling difficulties at Newton Abbot. I ride with the driver in swirling mist and encounter the City Basin distant at caution. The fog then suddenly thickens to zero visibility as we approach the home signal, a situation in which detailed road knowledge suddenly becomes vital.

There are interviews for my new secretary this morning. The applicants include Janet Mardon who is signalling inspector Bill Mardon's widowed daughter-in-law. I have guaranteed her an interview out of respect for Bill but he has been told that the appointment will be made purely on merit. There have been 73 applicants and a lot of the interviewees want to be personal assistants. The safety issues in running a railway and the relatively inflexible structure preclude this. The front runners appear to be Janet and Elizabeth Petrie, wife of driver Petrie who has just transferred here from Manchester. I am not sure it would be a good idea to have a secretary related to a driver no matter how discreet she might be and she would be taking a pay cut from her previous job with Manchester's local government chief executive. On balance, I would prefer someone who sees it as a promotion rather than the opposite and Janet has a pleasant Devonian way about her that will go down well with the staff as well as on the phone so she is duly appointed purely on her own merits.

I go home at 15.50 for a meal before catching the 17.51 to Taunton. The locals are restless because I have said there is little supervisory content in their work. They think they have never been able to sit around for an hour doing nothing but I partially disprove their point by having a pleasant chat with supervisor Wally Pipe for 45min in which there is no supervisory work whatsoever.

The purpose of the visit is to address the Great Western Society at the Black Horse. 26 people turn up. My talk lasts about 30min and questions take another 1½hrs with a 20min refreshment break. I am driven back to the station for the 22.12 HST through to Dawlish, arriving 3min late at 23.03. I am determined to have some time off this weekend so I leave all my paperwork in the office. I do not think it has been further behind since I came to this job so, despite my good intentions, I suspect that I might end up drafting some consultation documents tomorrow.

CHAPTER 22: REORGANISATION MORE IMPORTANT THAN OPERATIONS?

Monday 20th October 1986

Arriving at Teignmouth at 07.55 the signalbox is closed. Fred Rooke is on duty but has not opened due to a track circuit failure which will cause trains to be cautioned. But the failure has self-rectified so I instruct Fred to open up for the two locals, otherwise the service would be wrecked with a Newton Abbot to Dawlish Warren absolute block section. It transpires that Fred's car had been causing him trouble this morning and I begin to wonder whether all this is a smokescreen and he has actually been late on duty. The newspaper empties come through with a Class 47 and the unit follows it up.

I go to Newton Abbot in the cab of the HST that forms the down school train before working an up Cross Country service. Graham Smith's driver training school is in operation with the booked driver sitting in the train. I have already said that this must not happen as the driver must remain in charge of his own train and if there is an incident the press would have a field day.

At Newton Abbot I have a chat with supervisor Harry Perrett and then catch the 08.41 to Totnes. After visiting the booking and parcels offices I go to the signalbox where 22year-old signalman McGowan is on duty. He is about to become a father for the second time and is contemplating a £200 per month mortgage *(I think mine was about £35 at the time).* In the face of pending displacement with the box closure and lacking the seniority to reach the panel box for a long time, he has plenty of confidence but I seem to be doing the worrying on his behalf. *Last I heard, in 2014 he was a signalling inspector in charge of the Panel so he was right not to worry. When a retired Bernard Price asked him what he was up to, while waiting for a railway funeral to start a few years ago, and being told he was a signalling inspector Bernard inadvertently said, "They must be desperate." But this was probably unintentionally unfair having not seen the individual for 20 years.*

I catch the 09.51 back to Teignmouth where I have left the car. The car park checks have not been done properly so I instruct the staff representative, who happens to be on duty, on what is required before driving to Dawlish Warren where signalman Bill Rowe makes me a welcome cup of tea. The Cornish Riviera is in trouble in Cornwall and the 10.45 Paignton to Manchester comes up first. I then set off for a 10min whistle stop at Tiverton Parkway. I am giving a talk to the Tiverton Rotary Club on managing a railway at local level and the new station at Tiverton Parkway which also involves a pleasant light lunch.

Back in the office there is an annoying 'personal telegram' demanding an explanation for countermanding the control order about the Waterloo empty stock yesterday morning. The term 'personal telegram' is a contradiction in terms since it is dictated to a member of staff in the cash office so I ensure my reply is also seen by the staff. I phone Don Horseman, the passenger operations officer at Swindon to tell him what I think. What would he have done if it was 07.44 and the 07.45 unit was ready to go with the train to which Control had given priority not having yet passed Dainton. In fact it did not reach Newton About until 08.06. He takes the point graciously.

The local management meeting wipes up a few points. We discuss the sectional council meeting tactics and I take home about five days of paperwork to occupy the evening.

Tuesday 21st October 1986

The local is 8min late this morning after more coupling problems, this time at St. David's on the outward run. Archie Beer is driving as far as Exeter, a former Exmouth Jct man, and we arrive 4½min late. Brigid is waiting to see me with a project on Exeter-Waterloo monitoring that I have set for her. She has taken the wrong course on a couple of issues but responds, irrationally, by saying she does not think she is committed enough to do all the hours expected of her. I point out that we are expecting only a five-day week. She thinks that it is perhaps just the change from education to work that is a bit difficult. She had better find out just what it is now because there will be a lot of unpaid overworked hours to do if she makes railway operating her career.

The drivers' LDC meeting starts at 09.00 with the aim of discussing the withdrawal of the station pilot. The LDC say they have been instructed, as late as last night, that they are not to proceed as it is an HQ sectional council matter. I call a tea break for a phone call to Personnel at Swindon. They go off to clarify matters with the sectional council chairman driver Ron Smith, a strong but pleasant driver representative. He sends the message back that he has agreed to the local discussion and I tell the LDC they can ring him directly if they want, partly to reassure myself that neither tone nor inference has been distorted in the transmission via the personnel department manager.

The scheme goes through quickly, minus two drivers, savings £16,500 (*how drivers' wages have risen since then!*). The rest of the agenda is not contentious with items featuring matters such as the ballast shoulder at Somerton being too deep to allow drivers to alight safely from their cabs to the lineside telephone, lining-out the car park, cleaning arrangements for their messroom and further, all entirely reasonable, requests on their part. As we discuss the 'dangerous' exit from their staff car park near the level crossing, it emerges that none of the four of them has yet been to the Panel box despite the 'Open Days' we have held. So we adjourn to the box to demonstrate the signalman's view of Red Cow Crossing by cctv. They are fascinated and stay for 75min.

There is time to go through a few items with the management team members and decide on a new interview list for the re-advertised area personnel manager's job. Clarence Woodbury, who is covering the job, comes in and runs through a few routine items including the appalling absence record of a leading railman at Taunton. Clarence then takes me entirely by surprise by handing me his notice to resign from 22nd November. I would have expected more warning but, having passed him over for the permanent post, could scarcely blame him. He has been losing sleep and making mistakes and he now feels it is the time to go. Hmmm, perhaps we all feel like that. *I must admit that throughout my time there I had been critical of personnel standards, their rigidity and then, perversely, their failure to apply proper procedures when called upon.*

I pack my bag with correspondence and chairman Reid's three-year objectives. These amount to a reduction in the NSE subsidy of about 8% per annum on a progressive basis, but a slightly easier target for commercial sectors, including Travellers-Fare, of a combined 2.7% return on assets instead of the previous 5%. They will also be allowed to cross-subsidise each other. *I still do not understand why this was eased at this time, presumably some politics over my head.* Eugene Heffernan phones me at home during dinner to ensure I have received the objectives' telex and heard the 6 o'clock news.

Wednesday 22nd October 1986

I am aiming to be in Newton Abbot by 09.00 this morning on the way to Torquay where an overnight area managers' meeting is to be held. I go directly to Newton Abbot East box where Dennis Aggett is the signalman. The 'booking lad' is a redundant driver who broke his service for sixteen weeks some twenty years ago. This has affected his potential pension and he has been informed that he is not allowed to pay in his missing contributions to make his service continuous. Can I help? Well, I am unable to influence a decision of the Pension Fund but I can at least check that his case has been properly made.

Down at Newton Abbot West, John Haycock demonstrates

how he stopped the up express from running into the dmu last Thursday. I suspect we are fortunate that it was John on duty that afternoon; a sprightly 44, experienced but mobile and quick-witted. *Since reading the Gerry Fiennes book, as a teenager, and his regrets about the performance of the Gidea Park signalman, whom he knew, in the rear end collision there, I have always been especially appreciative of signalmen who were alert.*

Meanwhile, back at the 'East', the patrolman has spotted cracks in the diamond crossing. When I arrive on site, permanent way engineer Ian Johnson is already there. The track rationalisation and re-signalling scheme will reach here in three months' time and Ian would like to save the £3,000 cost by substituting plain line. The Heathfield freight service can shuffle round it but there are two 'special' trains next week (and some Heathfield trains are royal specials of course). Should we run over the crack or shunt round it? I plump for the former, otherwise the planned timings will be badly affected. Then I will accept plain line from the following Sunday. Any future 'special' trains can then find somewhere else to stable overnight or be timed to do the shunting. In the meantime, all trains will be cautioned at 10mph.

At Torquay, there is just enough time to tip-off the station staff about who is going to be around at the overnight meeting before nipping down to Paignton to check on the standard of the HST having its turnround clean, then it is back to Torquay to pick up Bob Poynter.

The agenda for the meeting contains many items concerning organisational change *(not how to run a better railway every day).* There will be more local responsibility, including local train planning, and a guarantee of no further change to area boundaries for three years. *Bob Poynter has recently had an article in Modern Railways, 29 years after the meeting, saying he believes authority should be delegated to the lowest possible level but this belief did not survive Regional Railways empire building in 1986 and no one believed the three-year guarantee anyway.*

After dinner I chat with the general manager and area managers from Gloucester, Plymouth and Cardiff. I do not like being the first to leave such gatherings but at 23.20 I give up and drive home.

Thursday 23rd October 1986

More organisational change issues from 09.00 then a discussion on harmonising policy over assistant ticket examiners. There is a wrangle in process between InterCity and the Regional Operating Manager, Bob Poynter. As usual, InterCity does not know what it is talking about *but the railway was on the way to running with no regional operating manager or the like and half a dozen business managers instead.*

After the meeting breaks up I travel to Exeter with the guard, Sid Oak and assistant ticket examiner Terry Blackburn, by far the keenest and one who gets into the most trouble because he will not back off from difficulties, *I also thought that if I did his job I would regularly be in trouble.* Terry upsets a young woman who has no ticket for her Chihuahua. *These were the days when dogs had to have a ticket.* She says she has travelled twelve times before without being challenged. "Not on my train, madam," responds Terry and takes her name and address after a further refusal to pay. He then regales me with some of the more obscure misdemeanours he has caught this week, plus his success of preventing Pewsey standard class ticket-holding commuters from sitting in the first class restaurant accommodation throughout on the strength of a coffee and a round of toast.

I see everyone from the meeting onto the 13.46 to Bristol and go to the office. I ask Ken Boobyer to come in to see how we are going to cope without Clarence. He is not too perturbed and his ideas fit with mine. I get the clerical LDC in to tell them what is going to happen and there is no disagreement. I suspect there might have been, had I not told them before it happened. *Although I considered the personnel function basically weak, with one or two honourable exceptions, there was some depth available formed by those in their 50s and early 60s who had been station master's clerks in the 1950s and knew the mechanics of administration of the railway when operating was far more complex than now. The superstructure organisation was, however, less complicated.*

Next, I call in those who will benefit from the changes and those who will feel to have had their noses put out of joint but everyone seems to take it with equanimity. Then I speak to Clarence again. Would it be possible for him not to take the holiday he has booked for next week. "No," he replies but he will come in for the following last ten days. He could have taken his outstanding lieu leave and this way he will be paid for them instead. By the time he gets back from his week off the organisation will have clicked into action so I tell him I think that on balance it will be better if he finishes a week on Friday. Would he like to come out for lunch that day? The organisation moves on. The individuals change.

When I tell Bernard Price, he seems surprised at the harshness but feels it is justified in view of the short notice given. *This sounds like another bit of bravado on my part, similar to immediately releasing the former permanent incumbent to Plymouth.* Jim Collins rings from Plymouth to say that he does not think much to the performance of my management trainee who has been with him for carriage servicing at Laira. Bernard Price, a Shrewsbury boy, says, "She is a typical little Welsh girl, talkative and bouncy one minute and crying the next." Alan Bell, cockney and former Stratford Britannia driver, says, "She has too much rabbit." He says she asked Ray Thorn if he thought she would make a manager. He replied, "Yes, my love, perhaps at Woolworth's or British Home Stores." Perhaps she should not have asked such a bluff, plain speaking Devonian. I hope it is a short term crisis from which she will recover but she cannot expect to be carried around. *These remarks sound prejudicial, and probably were, but they were genuinely rooted in poor performance.*

Tony Crabtree comes in to discuss four items. He is showing a lot of progress, the analytical mind that gained him an MSc in chemical engineering proving more valuable in management than it was in supervision with the latter's requirement for immediate rather than optimum decisions. No 33023 takes the 17.25 down to Dawlish 1½min late. Perhaps I should insist on the booked Class 50 being provided, despite the awkward shunting necessary at St. David's at 19.30.

Reading my mail backlog I find a copy of a letter signed by the Bristol area manager but presumably written by his customer services manager Martin Sach, the equivalent of John Beer here. But the style is that of the redoubtable elder statesman Markham. Provincial Services Marketing has asked for the audit rolls to be scrutinised for six months. That means that every ticket needs to be checked to give them monitored figures for special promotions and it is required urgently. It would take several weeks' work for one person but we have had the foresight to have kept the required figures as we have been going along. Bristol's letter says the Provincial Services letter "must have been written either in jest or complete ignorance" and that, if this is all they can do, they, "do not justify their retention." I am on the right side of this request but it is clear that I am not the only rebel out in the areas. *History has praised the development of the business-based railway but, once again, it would be the area manager Bristol that was to be abolished and half a dozen sector marketing sections that prevailed.*

Friday 24th October 1986

Time for an easier start with a haircut from Linda's visiting hairdresser before walking down to the station for the 09.20 to Newton Abbot. It is hauled by No. 50020 'Revenge' which is not being worked hard and loses 5½min to Newton Abbot from a punctual start from Exeter. I have a chat with supervisor Ernie Underhill before catching an up Skipper, riding with LDC representative John Madge. Mike Luffman, who is secretary of the annual retired staff tea party and who has just stood down from the LDC, is the assistant fare collector. I give him our choices for the dinner that is held to thank the volunteers, of which Linda is one.

I brief John Beer on organisational changes and the chairman's objectives and we discuss charter trains from Okehampton on behalf of Transport 2000 plus ticket collecting performance on the Exmouth branch. Time runs away with me but I am travelling north today so need to catch the 14.17 Exeter-Waterloo with the aim of taking a look at performance on the line. Alf Trapnell is the driver. The rail is greasy but we reach Honiton on time to cross the late-running 11.10 Waterloo-Exeter but then find we are also being held for the down Brighton. We are 14½min late and then suffer a relaying slack that has probably set these dominoes falling by, in effect, extending the length of the single line. 17min late Crewkerne, pulled back to 14½min late at Tisbury. At least we have not been delayed at Yeovil Jct where I have given the supervisors a final verbal warning on how they must handle the van traffic. We incur overtime at Tisbury and Salisbury and follow a similar pattern of gains and losses and arrive at Waterloo 19½min late.

As I go to King's Cross I remind myself never to work in London. There is a frustrating mixture of rushing and selfish dawdling, plus charity collectors, one of whom swears at me for declining to contribute, and a drug addict outside King's Cross. I take the 18.50 to Leeds. It is announced that Huddersfield passengers should change at Wakefield but it is a sub-standard connection so not shown in the timetable. The guard also thinks there is the connection at Wakefield Westgate but six checks and a dead stand before Newark make it all theoretical anyway with Wakefield being reached 10min late with the Huddersfield train gone. We are invited to rejoin the Leeds train where it arrives 6½min late arriving which makes another substandard Huddersfield non-connection into minus 1½min. Fortunately that too is a few minutes late so I just catch it and enjoy a fast run with a Class 45 that means I arrive 50min earlier than advertised. This will happen repeatedly without being recognised as a problem.

CHAPTER 23: AUDITS AND APPRAISALS

Sunday 26th October 1986

The usual run home via Manchester with No. 45104 and the HST to Dawlish. The trains are full most of the way due to the half-term rush. We are 17min late from Birmingham, waiting connections from Liverpool according to the guard; from Scotland according to station announcements. Dawlish is reached 11min late and there has been time to write the report of the Exeter-Waterloo punctuality day monitoring.

Monday 27th October 1986

On my way to work I encounter problems at Dawlish. The down school train to Paignton is an HST on its way to the branch terminus to form the up Devonian but it has failed at Exeter. The windscreen wiper would not work so the fitter was called, but in the process of his repair the electrics caught fire. It is decided to cancel the 08.23 Exeter St. David's-Paddington relief and use it to Paignton. It follows the Bristol to Penzance which itself is 10min late and the 08.23 Exeter-Paignton follows as an empty stock for its return working. Not as puzzling an arrangement as it sounds as the HST was used for this train because the passenger load could not be accommodated on the dmu.

I cannot face the Chamber of Commerce 11.00 meeting and I would prefer a trip to Exmouth but I get stuck in the office talking to John Beer and Alan Bell, then taking the opportunity to meet driver Libby who has just transferred in from Southall who I feel could cause trouble. *How wrong I was, he settled in well.* In the end I take the 12.30 HST to Teignmouth with driver Stone, running 10min late. Passing DM 202 we are surprised to receive an automatic warning system (aws) warning. Surprising because the signal has not yet been commissioned. I phone the S&T engineer to sort it out as it is both distracting and confusing, especially in fog when the aws signal often represents a bookmark to reassure drivers that they have their bearings.

After lunch at home I catch the 14.20 Paignton-Newcastle to Exeter and chair the local management meeting. It is uneventful but Alan Bell says that he thinks a female trainee guard will fail the course as she is unable to handle buckeye couplings. Following on the management trainee issue, this could easily be construed as discrimination but it clearly was not such. The lady in question was married to an Exeter supervisor so had a few allies but she was middle-aged and buckeye couplings are heavy. One might claim that accepting her onto the course and not pre-judging the issue showed a lack of prejudice perhaps. I am comforted to be reminded that a displaced male platform staff member of slight stature had failed on the same criterion and been accommodated as an assistant ticket examiner.

At 17.30 I go to the panel signalbox and at this time of day there is time for long discussion with the signalmen, The 17.33 to Waterloo departs behind Class 33s Nos. 33101 and 33025 in multiple. At least someone is trying to maintain the timetable as Waterloo sent down only No. 33025. I then find that the second engine was provided principally because the eastbound speedometer on No. 33025 was defective and this was the most effective way of sending it home.

George Reid, the train crew supervisor, is trying to arrange for the cement train to Exeter Central to be banked by the loco off the Paignton. The booked Class 50 is working the Paignton turn today and is supposed to go light to Plymouth and work the Glasgow from there to Penzance but this week George has been double-heading the Glasgow from Exeter to assist over the banks to counteract leaf fall problems. The Glasgow has 13 coaches which can only just be fitted into Platform 4. If the loco attachment were to be done here it would have to be done either 'not within fixed signals' – i.e. with the extra loco straddling the track opposite the platform end signal – or with the rear coach left blocking the level crossing, so it is replatformed to number 5. Any loss of time will be recouped by doubling the power. *There is very little scope for local initiative nowadays and inconsistencies in the train plan recur on a daily basis.* I set off at 18.45 to winter cricket nets which are to be held occasionally this off-season.

Tuesday 28th October 1986

By coincidence, I encounter driver Stone on the 08.11 to Waterloo this morning. Whether it is the driver or loco No. 50004 'St. Vincent' that is the difference from last Friday's run, the performance is a lot sharper, standing time at most Southern stations despite slacks of 70, 20 and 60/40 approaching Axminster. Arrival at Salisbury is 2min early. The Exeter-Waterloo performance group work is rather stodgy and I suspect that the number attending might have grown too high. Despite this thought, I am disappointed to note that the area manager at Plymouth is not represented, the excuses being a Royal Train and the discovery of fraud in Truro travel centre. Salisbury is a long way from Exeter by train but there is another 2½hrs extra travelling and carriage cleaning is their only contribution, important though that is.

With 75min between the end of the meeting and the train back to Exeter I decide to risk a 2min non-connection at Westbury. It looks doubtful, especially as we start 5min late but I can always continue to Bristol for a 27min connection and save 15min on my arrival compared to time spent here. *In the modern age the 75min at Salisbury would have been used to good effect with the use of technology.* The westbound HST is 8min late at Westbury so I make the connection easily, travelling with Chester Long and his Sectional Council colleague Ivor Dingle who is also on my pay roll. I think Chester and I reach an understanding over the Sectional Council C platform staff taking on extra work from the supervisors I hope to remove. One of the supervisory representatives has spoken to Chester about refusing the transfer of work from his members, as this practice is frowned upon by the regional representatives but there is no love lost between the two. Chester knows that accepting the extra work will safeguard his staff.

There is time for a long discussion with Bernard Price about the operation of the relatively new flashing yellow signals, the misunderstanding of which on a complicated layout at Colwich has caused the head-on crash that has killed one member of staff but miraculously no passengers. I clear my in-tray, being annoyed to find a badly produced memo from Mike Stacey in Personnel, typed by Julie and checked by no one. This is wasting everyone's time and it is time to put my foot down.

Wednesday 29th October 1986

I decide not to ride with S. R. Rogers on the loco of the 08.11 to Axminster this morning, travelling with John Beer in an aging Brake Composite Compartment coach (BCK – K being the code for compartment and C in use for a mixed-class vehicle). The wrong set has found itself on the working this morning but fortunately there is a First Compartment (FK) coach on the rear where a refreshment trolley is operating. We lose 3min at Honiton crossing a 10min late down Meldon ballast empties. *The poor punctuality compared to nowadays resulted partly from Meldon stone trains and their returning empties being squeezed through. When the empties were cancelled and the loco needed to go out for the next loaded train we often ran it attached to the front of the Class 50 on a passenger train.*

Works engineer Colin Carr is on site to discuss the poor fabric of the station which dates from 1859. I offer to do an outline appraisal evaluating four options. These will be minimal repairs (essentially 'do nothing' except legal requirements) major refitting of the old building, a new office retaining the old one and a new office and demolishing the old one. Although the building is not listed, I am certain it will be as soon as it is threatened. This should leave the second option as the most likely solution.

We go in Colin's road vehicle to Honiton for a similar exercise.

The situation here though is different. NSE has announced a five-year repainting periodicity should be enough to keep the 'pre-fab' style building in operation for some time, with some beefed up security.

John has a meeting with the mayor of Honiton, a difficult individual who will not let John get a word in edgeways but also adds that he does "not like his attitude." The down train reaches Exeter 2min late behind No. 50004 'St. Vincent'. I transfer to the 12.40 to Exmouth riding in the cab. We lose a little crossing the up train at Topsham and have an extended station stop at Lympstone Commando, arriving 2½min late. Peter Legg, a former Exeter LDC member who has recently transferred to Exmouth is on the barrier. This is one of the few barrier checks retained under the 'open stations concept' which changed the emphasis from station checks to those conducted on trains. The amount of short distance travel into Exmouth would have meant that no barrier checks would have been too costly. *This has of course been completely reversed and there are few stations without barrier checks and Exmouth was obviously not the only place that should have retained them in the first place.*

Peter does not think the proposed new 06.25 to Exeter from next May to connect into the 06.00 Plymouth to Paddington will be a success but the booking clerk thinks it will. My suspicion is that Peter does not fancy the earlier start this will involve. The decline of services in east Devon has been reversed recently with a clock-face half hourly service, all trains reaching St. David's and many extended beyond there and now an earlier train so it is dispiriting to encounter opposition. The half-hourly service has increased revenue by 30% the week before last and, although it was only 10% better last week, we are again well ahead this week. I return to Exeter with driver Lear, arriving on time. The new service needs more discipline than the irregular less-than-hourly one but it seems to be falling into place nicely.

I phone Terry Gale, a Yeovil supervisor, who has apparently

made a log entry that doors should not be closed if it is considered the van is overloaded with mail or parcels *(not sure what I meant by this and what Terry meant either).* I leave him in no doubt that his attitude amounts to putting his job on the line by varying my instructions. There are then more discussion with assistants and Chris Hughes concerning the new procedures for minor repairs and new works. Clerical officer Bernard Reynolds seems snowed under by the work but he is on holiday this week. He is so conscientious he would just work through until late in the evening without any thought of overtime. *Eventually I had ever-so-nicely to order him to go home on time.* Chris and I try to sort out the mess. *Chris is now a senior manager in First Great Western.* There is just time to advise Tony Crabtree that phrases such as 'aide memoire' are better not used in the heading of letters intended for posting on the guards' notice board. My 17.25 is back to Class 33 haulage with No. 33045.

Bernard Price rings at 19.00 to say Terry Gale will be phoning me tomorrow to apologise because he now sees the error of his ways. He has phoned Bernard at 17.30 and no doubt been advised not to antagonise me further, Bernard has been out on an inspection saloon with a firm called Norsk Whittle and he is optimistic that there could be a new private siding by June. *It did not happen.*

Thursday 30th October 1986

As I cross the stream at Dawlish at 07.55, locos 33045 and 31404 appear over my shoulder hauling three empty newspaper vans. Apparently No. 31404 failed on the newspaper train and the empties are now on their way to Exeter to meet up with the other vans. We have a full service of Class 142s this morning although my train is 10min late again after coupling problems and I join the driver.

Paul Silvestri comes in to discuss alterations to the next timetable. InterCity is making what they call 'a few minor adjustments' such as extending an extra train to Penzance which they have been badgered to do since the first draft. It has taken them a long time to realise the mayhem of public reaction from Cornwall that would occur when they found out. *This was typical of the 'headquarters knows best' arrogance of InterCity at this time.*

My passenger audit starts at 10.30, chaired by Swindon passenger operations manager Don Horseman as David Warne is in charge of the Royal Train to Penzance with Prince Charles. Bernard Price and Karen Graeme are there to answer some of the more specific questions on individual incidents. Fallen leaves have again been instrumental in causing problems and the poor performance of the Class 142s are the main issues and we cannot run punctual trains without stock, but it goes well on the whole.

The meeting ends at 13.30 and I catch the 14.01 to Taunton with drivers Fred Cole and Bob Dack. Fred's bubbly personality, well known for deliberately exaggerated military exploits in every conflict since World War 2 is an 'in joke' to all members of staff and it is fascinating to see how he draws the reticent Bob out of his shell, mainly because Bob was a rare survivor from the rank of RAF rear gunner in the war. No wonder he is reticent. There is just enough time to visit the travel centre and supervisor before catching the 14.54 through to Newton Abbot. The driver reports having seen children run across the line. Because he saw them leave railway property there is no requirement to caution trains but I decide to ensure the driver of the next up train is told to proceed at caution past the location.

I catch the 16.33 up stopper with guard Brian Cocks, an affable character who manages to disarm a cheeky teenager with a good-humoured and polite put-down. As I alight at Dawlish, Tony Crabtree joins the train having completed a parcels 'teach-in' with the platform staff who also man the parcels office.

Friday 31st October 1986

At last, my local is on time with all four coaches. Riding with the driver, we receive aws warning horns at three non-operational new signals and spot a missing red aspect from one ground position light. Time to phone the S&T with a strong complaint. David Langton, area operations manager at Plymouth, phones to ask about performance last night. The down Glasgow had failed at St. Thomas. Control notified us of the wrong order of approaching trains and we ended up with the down Golden Hind blocking the station, after having hauled the Glasgow back into the station, with the Paignton – Exeter standing outside St. David's and the up Penzance-Paddington standing at City Basin with the driver for the down Golden Hind in charge. We take 16min to get a fresh crew out to the Hind to be relieved by the up driver at St. Thomas. We had decided not to transfer the Glasgow passengers to the Hind because of the difficulties in getting the largely elderly clientele over the bridge. Instead, we transferred them cross-platform from No. 4 to No. 3 into the following Newcastle, running on one power car and riskily sent forward in the falling leaf season.

Bob Poynter arrives to conduct my annual appraisal. He is surprised to have seen Nos. 37901/37902 in Riverside yard. The Ince & Elton-Truro fertilizer train had failed at Crewe just as these two locos came out of the Works. At least our new Leeds drivers know Class 37s but it would be handy if we could train more drivers on them.

The appraisal goes relatively well but I get only a 2, on a scale 1-5 and compared to a 1 last year. There are strict quotas and 80% of managers should fall in the range 3+ to 3-. I will get a 5% pay rise on the payscale (plus inflationary rises) which will take me to the top of the range but a 1 is classed as 'exceptional, a very rare achievement' and commands a 7% rise. I ask in what respects my performance has been worse this year than last year but the boss replies that I have not done worse, it is just that other managers have levelled up. I am unconvinced and wonder who might have been given a 1, assuming a quota of just one is available, this year but Bob Poynter will not respond well to being badgered.

At 13.00 I take Clarence Woodbury out to his retirement lunch, finish some paperwork and catch the 17.25 with No. 33001.

Saturday 1st November 1986

A dull Saturday afternoon allows me time to do a long letter on point-to-point timings on the Exeter-Waterloo as well as some routine stuff.

CHAPTER 24: LONG DAYS AND SHORT SHRIFT

Sunday 2nd November 1986

The weather is better but the workload is still there to be done. Part of the catching-up process involves the creation of a contingency plan for a possible sea wall collapse.

Monday 3rd November 1986

The up stopper has slipped to a stand at Torre. I liaise with Control for special stops in the 07.30 Plymouth-Paddington for Teignmouth, Dawlish and St. Thomas, the latter for passengers alighting to go to work. It transpires that the operation of single line working at Teignmouth yesterday has been subject to criticism and Bob Poynter wants a report. Bernard says that the criticism has been made with the benefit of hindsight but, looking at the detail, I think that he is, for a change, wrong this time.

I take appraisals for Tony Crabtree and John Beer and Alan Bell. Then I meet my management trainee to discuss her carriage cleaning week at Laira and Paul Silvestri about his plans for local services on summer Saturdays next year, before doing Alan Bell's appraisal. This is followed by the area meeting with a few new faces around the table. At home I do paperwork from 18.15 to 20.15 which includes a complaint from an M.P. that Bernard Price has intimidated one of his constituents who has applied for a job. What we have to put up with! I reply extremely strongly and stand back to await the fireworks.

Tuesday 4th November 1986

After calling into the office I catch the 09.07 down to Plymouth for a British Transport Police liaison meeting. After the Totnes call, the Plymouth-based guard comes to talk to me. He is transferring to Exeter from next week and discusses his interests. He is a bluff Yorkshireman and Sheffield

Wednesday supporter whom I first encountered in the brake van leaving Newton Abbot with a female member of staff sitting on his knee. One of his major activities is disabled scouting including carrying disabled children over Dartmoor. All of this shows how important, and prejudicial, first impressions can be.

The Plymouth meeting goes on until 14.15. Inspector Geoff Holmes, another Yorkshireman, is more of a policeman than a meeting chairman and he tangles with S&T engineer David McKeown who is indulging in some uncooperative spoiling tactics.

I return to Exeter on the 14.35 to Paddington with driver Whittle at the controls. It is a confident and precise effort over the banks running into Exeter 1min late after being diverted via the up loop at Dawlish Warren.

I then take the car home for a 2hr break before attending a meeting entitled 'Teignmouth into the 1990s'. The town is well served by its Chamber of Commerce chairperson Joan Johnson but badly so by local politicians who seem to think the key to progress into the 1990s lies in the arguing over decisions made in the 1970s. Some constructive points are eventually agreed and it breaks up at 21.30.

Wednesday 5th November 1986.

An early start today leaving the house at 06.30 bound for Swindon only to find the station in darkness and the relief senior railman from Newton Abbot late on duty. I use guard Graham Braund's handlamp from the front of the train to help him get it away. At Exeter the HST acquires two drivers learning the road so I ride in the train to Westbury with Dave Counter from the civil engineer's office, transferring to the cab from Westbury when the road learners have alighted. It is a routine run, on time from Westbury and on time approaching Reading until a last gasp 2min signal check as priority is given to the 06.30 Swansea-Paddington. I cross to the 09.03 to Swindon.

The meeting, concerning route speed improvements, is already underway. I contribute a presentation on the replacement of existing approach control signalling at many locations in favour of flashing yellows, but much of the discussion concerns South Wales. A stretch of 120mph between Swindon and Reading could be raised to 125mph and the general manager asks what the saving might be. Brian Gaudern, assistant regional civil engineer reaches for his calculator and I tie with him getting the correct answer - seven seconds.

After the meeting I press Bob Poynter to review my appraisal. I have since discovered that a 2+ is available this year for borderline 1 / 2 cases but he will not be moved. Perhaps he did not mean that it was a borderline decision when he told me it was and my confidence in his integrity takes a knock. *Seems I was right in saying he could not be bullied though!*

In the afternoon I lobby for the retention of the 80mph limit from Starcross to Dawlish Warren. Instead of the existing profile from Exminster to Dawlish of 90/65/80/65/75/60 the engineer wants to give us 100/75/60. The final result should ideally be 100/75/80/75/60. *The final profile was different only in a 70mph limit at Langstone Cliff instead of 75mph giving a 100/75/80/70/75/60 profile.*

There is also some pie in the sky discussion *(blue sky thinking nowadays?)*. Brian Scott thinks we could remove the 40mph restriction at Cheltenham Spa by moving the station but the costs compared to the benefits, with nearly all passenger trains booked to call there, make it not worth further consideration.

The new Totnes layout is left until the end and we agree modest speed increase and a flashing yellow entrance into the up platform which will both help train running and mitigate a signal-passed-at-danger risk at the bottom of Rattery Bank. The meeting finishes at 17.40. The train home requires either a 2hr wait at Bristol or a 2min connection there. We are 4min late in after signals on approach and our train has gone. Area civil engineer Peter Warren and I adjourn to a nearby pub *(pre-Wetherspoons)* for soup, plaice and chips. Our next train is the Manchester with a 9min connection at Exeter, fortunately on time. 50025 and 50005 are waiting on the local to Dawlish, Waterloo stock heading for Laira, and I reach Dawlish at 22.07.

Thursday 6th November 1986

A lie-in before catching the 08.49, riding with the driver. John Beer, Ken Boobyer and I prepare for the Travel Centre Review meeting. It is pretty hectic then before Ken and Chris Hughes, who has stepped up to cover Ken, and I catch the 12.57 with No. 47439 on 12 non-stop to Bristol for our budget meeting 1½min late from Exeter and 10½min early into Bristol. The meeting is lively and starts with a jibe that we are mob-handed. How dare they? - there are seven of them with every sector represented. These meetings used to have four people pre-sectorisation.

Barry Ward is very aggressive, chairing the meeting as regional chief finance officer and we struggle for answers before hitting our stride. Since our meeting with Peter Griggs, he has been unable to summon any support for the second announcer we need from about 08.30 to 18.30 for Taunton, Newton Abbot and St. David's station announcements and customer information screens to be handled from the panel signalbox. Peter says that the sole announcer will therefore announce only InterCity trains. I will not countenance this. I accept Peter is attempting to draw the others out into the open but I suspect that, if I had agreed, that is what would have happened. *I might be persuaded that these were teething problems with sectorisation but the costs of administration were escalating out of control at this stage of the process.*

Mick Donovan from NSE wants some changes made to my cost centres but I decline as it would make ground level management - which is what actually controls the cost – more difficult. Mick is normally helpful and sensible but he counters by saying we will just have to get used to such paper exercises. I treat his remarks with the scorn they deserve. There is some time available to sort out some finer business details but we miss the 16.15 so have to wait for the Glasgow which turns up 6min late behind 47140 which has replaced a failed Class 47. We have an exceptional run to Taunton with 'load 12' and then on to Exeter making up 8½min despite only 4min recovery time and having lost a minute at Taunton as the guard wandered from one end of the train to the other before giving the right-away. At Exeter we replace No. 47140 with No. 50031 'Hood', that will be able to provide heat, which takes 10min. Ken Boobyer gives me a lift to Dawlish arriving home at 19.00

Friday 7th November 1986

Arriving at work at 07.45 by car it is 08.15 before I reach the office after talking to the supervisors and Harold Luscombe about assistant ticket examiners. He thinks we have too many and I tend to agree but I would like to see how long it is before devolution means I am officially empowered to diagram them. My office is receiving a coat of paint so it is an uncomfortable existence. I do Bernard Price's appraisal in his office and visit the panel box. Bernard says he still has ambition to be operations manager at Bristol or perhaps Crewe, to get back nearer his native Shrewsbury.

Karin tells me that an engineering department staff representative has been on the phone to say that National Express adverts have appeared on hoardings on our land at New Yard (on the down side approaching the station from Taunton) and if they have not been removed this weekend he will take them down himself. Karin has told him that he will be committing an offence if he does. This one could blow up into a major public and staff relations problem with embarrassing newspaper headlines but, if the advertisements are there, no one wants them down more than I do. I nip up to the yard in the car and find two very large advertisements on Mills and Allen boards.

I get through to British Transport Advertising on the phone and discover they sub-let their sites. However, they confirm that the contract gives them the right to prevent this happening and they will be removed as soon as possible. So, if the engineer's staff representative takes them down he will do us all a favour. I ring Peter Warren to brief him on what has happened. I ask him to thank his member of staff for alerting us to the problem but to explain that he will get more co-operation by omitting the threats.

Driven from the office by the painters, I take my paperwork home at 13.00 and have caught up all but the largest issues by 17.30. It is my rules examination next Thursday so I ensure all my publications are up to date and do a spot of revision.

Saturday 8th November 1986

Linda would like to go shopping in Bath so we catch the 10.16 HST to Exeter and go forward with No. 50005 'Collingwood' on 13 bogies, arriving 9½min early. This enables us to catch the 12.05 Portsmouth train with No. 33025 'Sultan' on five instead of the 12.35 HST to Paddington. It is a superb run, 1½min early at Bath and excellent late braking for the Keynsham stop.

We return with No. 33043, 5min late into Bristol and then forward with No. 47552 on the Newcastle, punctual tonight with a less sparkling run but still 2min early at Exeter. The 17.25 stopper is a Class 142 on Saturdays full with football fans led by one of our youth training scheme (YTS) trainees who appears to recognise that his interests will be well served by keeping them quiet. At Dawlish, another YTS takes the initiative by engaging us in a few polite words of conversation; a very good sign.

CHAPTER 25: TOOTH-ACHE PROVOKES AN ASSAULT

Monday 10th November 1986

Most of the day is taken up with the next round of the area personnel manager's job interviews. The best applicant is a 27 year old Information Technology assistant at Bristol but the situation has changed since Clarence left. First, Ken Boobyer is proving resilient. I could not have promoted him over Clarence's head but I could appoint him now. Second, while Ken and Clarence could have remained in their posts and supported a young personnel manager, I could not ask Ken to do it now by himself. Regional personnel manager Ken Beresford is my 'second man' and says that an applicant from London has a reputation for causing trouble. Another from the engineer's department at Redbridge is unsuitable for an operating area. There is also a 24 year old from Aberdeen who thinks he knows it all but has a poor reference from his previous Westbury job. After some discussion, I offer Ken the job. There is the added advantage that this allows the young Chris Hughes in the technically complicated budget job the advantage of being able to consult Ken as his line manager.

After another hour preparing for the travel centre consultation I visit Phil Shepherd, who is Plant Engineer at Laira, in the orthopaedic ward at the hospital where he is having an operation on his back.

This evening we are holding a beer and skittles evening for the guards who volunteered for the carnival float last summer. Wives and girlfriends are invited too. Tony Crabtree has organised it and he and his wife Erica will be there. There is time to watch the station working and visit the panel box before going down to the Prince Albert at St. Thomas. There is a wonderful atmosphere, and everyone enjoys themselves, the total cost for a free bar for three hours being an abstinent £61.

Most of the guards come from the younger end and I can picture the steady older brigade in their youth at a similar event. Their haircuts are different but I can see them developing into the backbone of the future railway. Take Graham Braund, so enthusiastic but, I think he would agree, a bit hot-headed at times. He has just married a Sherborne girl and you can already see her steadying influence and I can see his supervisory qualities coming through. *A prediction that came true.* The party breaks up at 22.40 and I get home at 23.10.

Tuesday 11th November 1986

There is time to check strategy with John Beer ahead of our forthcoming meeting with the Dart Valley Railway and check a few more facts and figures for the travel centre review. At 11.00 Barry Cogar and Mike Henderson arrive from Buckfastleigh. *This was before the split between the Buckfastleigh and Paignton operations.* We discuss the last operating season. I reckon we just about cleared the £10,000 costs on our side of the house at Totnes, incurred principally due to paying the conductors £6,000. Barry gives the impression he is not bothered for keeping the direct link. We have made more money with the through bookings from B.R. to Kingswear. I suspect if we withdrew from the Totnes-Buckfastleigh operation any lost revenue would appear in the Paignton figures so we are not that keen. We undertake to re-examine the conducting costs, fix next year's rates and adjourn for lunch.

Barry wants to run steam specials from Kingswear to Exeter next year as we nearly managed in 1984 when we were prevented on the spurious grounds of undermining the 1985 GWR 150 celebrations. The impending abolition of the Steam Locomotives Operating Association semi-cartel will help its chances this time too. Winter Sundays are the best bet for not interfering with normal services but we will be ripping up Newton Abbot with the rationalisation and re-signalling scheme next April which would have been a good time for running. We will investigate further.

Back in the office I have eight long service awards to conduct. It is hard to maintain enthusiasm sometimes and hard to engender an atmosphere among the participants. The finish is always even more awkward with people being reluctant to be the first to leave and the risk of any hint being seen to be heavy-handed.

By 17.00 the Chamber of Commerce meeting seems even less enticing than usual so I send my apologies. Just before I leave the office, Torquay travel centre manager John Hedge rings to say there has been an unsavoury incident today and could he could he come to see me tomorrow morning? The answer is obviously 'yes'.

Wednesday 12th November 1986

I am in full flow by 08.00 but have to break off to see John Hedge at 09.15. He has no objection to John Beer being present, his direct manager and needing to be directly involved. One of the booking clerks left for a dental appointment yesterday without getting proper permission or making it clear what time he would be going. When he had returned, John asked him where he had been at which point John says the clerk had pinned him to the wall by the throat, shouting and swearing at him.

John Hedge (need to be careful here with all three participants being 'Johns') was obviously shaken. The correct action would have been to have sent the clerk home directly and reported the incident immediately but at least there were eye-witnesses. John Beer thinks we should suspend the clerk pending disciplinary action but there are complications involved in doing that. Action should have been taken yesterday, the clerk being been sent home yesterday and told to report for a fact finding interview this morning. Meanwhile, he is now at work.

I tell John Hedge to collect reports and I will ring the clerk, telling him to report to my office as soon as possible. The clerk is difficult on the phone and I have to ensure he has understood my instruction and that he intends to comply. He arrives at 11.40 and appears to have a marble in his cheek. "Can you speak up?" he asks, his hearing impaired by his toothache. He denies using foul language or employing a threatening manner. He admits there was a long argument.
"Was there any violence?"
"No."
"Did you grab Mr Hedge by the throat?
"No."
"Did you touch him at all?"
"I did get hold of his tie but not in a threatening manner?"
Then he explodes. He wants to know why he has not been given an advocate. I explain it is not necessary at a fact-finding interview.
"Don't shout at me I'm your senior," he yells.
I settle him down again and continue to question him in precise terms and he is deliberately goading me by dumb insolence, pretending not to understand the questions. I ask him to go out for a few minutes. When I call him back in I tell him that I am satisfied that a serious incident appears to have happened and he will be subject to disciplinary action. "In the meantime....." I begin and the clerk gets up, says his toothache is too bad and he is going. I suggest that it will not help his case but off he goes declaring himself sick until further notice when he gets back to Torquay.
It is the first time I have had that happen and there is nothing that can be done until he declares himself fit, is absent after the expiry of a sick note, or is off so long he is effectively in breach of contract. There might indeed have been some extenuating circumstances but he has now dealt his case considerable harm. *In retrospect I might have chosen to delay the fact finding interview until he was no longer in pain but I had not realised his problem had not been resolved by his dental visit. If he simply said that he had done everything*

through being crazed with pain I would have had to have been less strict.

Ken Shingleton (Bob Poynter's No. 2 and former divisional manager at Reading) is waiting to take me for my Rules exam. It is only 18 months late. If I had a backlog like this that was discovered at my safety audit my job would have been in danger. The delay is not Ken's fault and he is an extremely keen manager who is universally liked. I have been revising - Saturday evening, three hours on Sunday and two hours last night so I have reminded myself of the more obscure items. Ken catches me out on a couple of points but I reciprocate by correcting him on how to carry out a brake test on a partially fitted vacuum-braked freight train. 3½hours later, and after some discussion of his American holiday and my future career he pronounces me as 'without equal on the Western Region'. Then we go across to the Panel box before he joins young Exeter driver Nick Edwards on the 16.18 to Waterloo. *Nick was to go on to be national DB Schenker driver manager and Royal Train officer.*

Thursday 13th November 1986

I leave home for Newton Abbot at 06.30. The whisper is that the staff side at tomorrow's consultation will be making a big play on the inability of working Newton Abbot booking office with one clerk between 07.00 and 08.45. At 06.50 I start making a second-by-second assessment of the workload. It shows that one clerk would be occupied 79% of his or her time but this hides the fact that the 15min before the departure of the 07.30 Plymouth-Paddington, 133% of the time would have been taken up. Still, our proposals were intended to give enough elbowroom to put in a part-time clerk. The clerks I am monitoring are spinning it out a bit, even to the extent of trying to book a seat for a passenger on the 07.36 to Birmingham for her connecting train to Glasgow, which I discount from my figures as I am convinced it would not have been suggested had I not been there.

At 08.30 I leave by car for Torquay. I have a sinking feeling about the way the tooth-ache incident will be handled. The clerk has not given notice to resume duty but his 09.00 turn has not been covered even though he is not expected to turn up. John Hedge is due to arrive at 09.00 but he is not there either. There is a knock on the door and the shift leader David Tucker leans across the counter and opens the door, even though he should not have done so as it could have been a robber. It is my tooth-ache clerk preparing to take duty. If I had not been here, he would have done so. He walks over to the book where he signs on. No wonder I had misgivings about how this might have been handled. *Writing this I am not sure why I did not let John Beer deal with it but I guess it was because it was elevated directly to me and delegating it would have been seen as dodging a difficult issue.*

My mind is racing.
"How are you today?" I enquire.
"Fine," he replies.
"Fully recovered then?"
"Yes, I always come to work when I can."
"In that case I will speak to you next door," I respond.
I say that he should not have been allowed to come to work today but in the circumstances he is required to go to Exeter travel centre and work in the telephone bureau. He then says that he will go sick. I tell him that in that case he will not be paid as he has just told me he is alright. He calms down and sets off for Exeter. *I can see how I would not like to have left this to a travel centre manager or someone who had not had a case like this before. The line of approach was learnt from my Middlesbrough area manager Arnold Wain who was single-minded.*

When it is over, John Hedge arrives and he is shaking. I interview the staff who witnessed the incident including one who elected to go out onto the platform to ask the senior railman about a local train in the middle of the confrontation. Another clerk submits a report that could be construed as 50/50 responsibility.

"Yes," he confirms, "that is how it was."
I question him further and elicit that John Hedge did not swear or act in a threatening manner but the clerk did. Another witness says John was diplomatic but I doubt that equally. I drive to Teignmouth and return to Exeter by train. There is time to do some homework for the sectional council meeting that is essential to gaining the confidence of our apparent new InterCity paymaster, before ensuring the tooth-ache victim gets his disciplinary charge sheet, known throughout the railway as a Form 1. The hearing will be as soon as procedurally possible, next Tuesday. In view of the seriousness of the charge there will be a personal hearing even in the unlikely event of the clerk not asking for one. I catch the 15.26 down to Teignmouth where there are pre-resignalling track circuit disconnections in force and the box is in the hands of recent YTS trainee Matthew Kinsella and equally young Alan Rosewell acting as a 'check' for working without track circuits. When I arrive, I find a Pinhoe signalman visiting them in the box. We have not provided two signalmen to have them distracted by unofficial visitors.

I send the Pinhoe signalman on his way and send Ian for a walk before ticking off Matthew and then sympathising with him for the sudden death of his father who was head teacher at the local Roman Catholic primary school, I lost my father at 16 so I have some idea of how he might be feeling. It has hit him hard and one could argue that it is not a good idea to have him working a signalbox if distracted. I take the view that it is better on balance to have him distracted from grief by work. There is then a silence as the clock ticks away the final seconds in the life of the box which will close on Saturday.

The signalman at Newton Abbot East sends 'train out of section' without call attention which implies the young signalmen at Teignmouth have been too busy chatting to see my approach and to warn the Newton Abbot man to work 'straight up'. He is the most awkward, yet most experienced, signalman on the patch but accepts his rebuke with equanimity.

I turn my mind to the method of working and find the distant signals have been disconnected but the stop signals are working normally. I phone Bernard to ask if there is a reason for this that I cannot see *(such as a temporary special instruction of cautioning trains this way in view of the track circuit disconnections, but the signalmen did not know why)*. He goes on to the S&T to tell them to restore the distants, thereby saving up to 3min per train. Glad I visited. I get home early at 17.00 for the usual paperwork. *Hmmm, three irregularities in one visit – unauthorised visitor, bell signal problem and, distants disconnected without operating authority. This combination of inexperienced staff, complacency, low morale through impending redundancy, and management of a complex engineering scheme constitute enough factors to produce a serious incident.*

Friday 14th November 1986

I drive in for 08.00. Brian Griffiths from Personnel at Swindon has come down early for the travel centre consultation meeting but InterCity has decided not to attend. I could say chickened out because, for the most part, the proposals represent what they are prepared to underwrite. Colin Leach has come from Provincial Services and is said to be holding InterCity's cards. We discuss tactics before catching the 09.19 up to the meeting room at Exeter Central.

The Class 142 arrives from Barnstaple having hit a landslip at Copplestone. The train is examined and I climb down with the driver to inspect the mud. Alan Bell and Ian Johnson have the matter in hand, the unit has stood up well to the incident and the delay has been limited to 6min.

It is an hour before we get into the joint meeting as the staff side sort themselves out. Sectional Council A chairman would have been Barry Thorn until his sad death but today it is Brian Grey presiding today. He is still most upset about the outcome of the supervisory meeting a few weeks ago. We get the usual abuse about their perceived standard of the document and the problems they foresee but they do not require answers to any of their twenty or so questions if we will first hear their counter-submission.

They claim higher grades for the travel centre managers at Barnstaple, Yeovil and Exeter, the shift leaders at Exeter, an additional clerk at Taunton (at grade of CO3) and a regrading of a comparable existing post at Torquay to CO3. In addition they want five CO1 jobs to be regraded CO2. Is that all? Ah yes, the retention of four jobs, one each at Newton Abbot, Paignton, Torquay and Barnstaple, that we have proposed for withdrawal. *I think it is true to say if I had simply said yes to this I would have been out of the job on Monday.*

After two bites at the cherry and 5hrs of intense argument we come to some form of reluctant agreement. We concede the Barnstaple Managers job to CO4. It is already a CO4 but we had, possibly cheekily, proposed a downgrading. Yeovil goes up on comparability grounds. They have a good case for the extra job at Taunton which takes the similar Torquay job up with it in consequence. We offer a 5day x 2hr part-time post at Newton Abbot to cover the early morning situation and hold on for the rest of our savings, emerging pleased with the results.

Saturday 15th November 1986

The line is blocked between Exeter and Newton Abbot for most of the weekend for implementation of the new signalling, so I switch from budgets, customer service and consultation back to operating. *Unlike nowadays,* there are 'windows' in the possession to permit the passage of trains. There is an emergency block post at Dawlish Warren and a special instruction has been issued from Swindon to permit drivers to travel at full speed instead of a 'suitably reduced' one.

I go to Newton Abbot at 09.30 and find we are incurring some avoidable delay that could be improved by better communication with the S&T. I meet Bernard Price at Newton

Abbot West and then pull away to Teignmouth and Exeter where operations are going smoothly. The greatest disruption is caused by the 10.10 from Paddington running 30min late, demonstrating how narrow windows can have to be left wide open. I go to the panel and then see the guests for the regional operating manager's weekend at the Livermead House Hotel (not subsidised by the tax payer, I hasten to add) off on their coach. Linda and I go to the Great Western for lunch.

At 14.30 the arrangements are working well with Ray Thorn and John Phare performing their usual wonders with the bus arrangements, so I go home to change for this evening's event. I have reluctantly, and after taking wide counsel, accepted an invitation to judge the Miss Devon contest on behalf of Golden Rail for the Radio Devon Children in Need appeal at the Plaza leisure centre at St. Thomas. The B.R. rail travel arm has donated a London Weekend prize. On the way up to the event I note an empty stock train drifting past Cockwood Harbour and think no more of it, other than the fact it is definitely not travelling at full speed.

The contest is badly organised and descends into a bit of a fiasco, the hospitality is not good either, and I get home at 23.30 after performing one of the more unusual *and, from a modern standpoint, antediluvian* aspects of an area manager's duty. *Had it not been for Golden Rail's request that I represent their interests I think I would have declined as I had considerable misgivings at the time.*

CHAPTER 26: REAR END COLLISION AVERTED

Sunday 16th November 1986

Linda's birthday today and it begins with a phone call at 09.30. Bernard is ringing to tell me that we have had two trains at the same time in the emergency block section from St. Thomas to Dawlish Warren during the re-signalling work. The train I had seen when driving to Exeter was being followed by an HST dispatched in error by a relief signalman who was the handsignalman at St. Thomas - working to the instructions of the panel signalman.

The handsignalman had given unclear instructions to the driver of the stock train, who had stopped to query them at the first red signal he encountered. Even worse, it also had its tail lamp out. The panel signalman had then phoned the handsignalman to tell him what he had to say in future. The handsignalman misconstrued what had been said and relayed these remarks to the HST driver who was waiting for authority to proceed.

Bernard had been in the panel at the time and overheard the panel end of the conversation. During the next nerve-wracking ten minutes, a call was made to Dawlish Warren, where signalling inspector Derek Old was located, urging him to go out and meet the stock train to get it inside the protection of Dawlish Warren's stop signals, then to continue to display a danger handsignalman, and presumably set detonators, to the approaching HST. A degree of irony could be found in the fact that I was briefly in the precise location best to stop the HST. In the end, Inspector Old did his job and the trains in question did not even see each other, the handsignalman's ten minute torture was eventually relieved by being told there had been no collision.

I make sure Bernard arranges for the handsignalman to report for a fact-finding interview in my office at 09.00 on Monday morning and not work his relief signalman's booked shift at

Pinhoe tonight. We must also ensure that the revised method of working is emphasised to all staff involved today. I consider withdrawing the authority to run through the emergency sections at full speed but it is a published instruction in the engineering notice and tampering might create greater confusion. I will resist future similar arrangements and lobby for adherence to the Rule Book instruction. The argument that the regional authorities would use for full speed is that the Rule Book 'suitably reduced speed' is for ad hoc situations and not for planned and published possessions. On the other hand, the suitably reduced speed instruction goes some way towards counteracting errors such as those last night. Bernard assures me that he pressed for a speed restriction at the pre-planning meeting and that his opposition to the published easement is minuted.

If there had been a collision that night, I wonder what would have been made of the regional operating team wining, dining and dancing at a Torquay hotel. But, even worse, what would have happened had they then found the area manager was judging a beauty contest? I have no doubt that Alan Cook who used to organise the Torquay weekends had set the date before the engineering dates had finally been set and that I had been backed into the judging business under pressure to fulfil my liaison role with local media. Perhaps both parties should have been strong enough to cancel their commitments when they became aware of the re-signalling dates.

After visiting Phil Shepherd, who is out of hospital and should be back at work in two weeks, I go to Newton Abbot where everything is working smoothly and then go up to Exeter where there is time to talk with Bernard and visit the panel box, returning home for birthday celebrations at 18.00. *Linda comments, "Another fun birthday for me!"*

Monday 17th November 1986

I awake from an unbroken night's sleep to find the possessions have been handed back on time, work fully completed. On reaching Newton Abbot by car, the booking office clerks are, understandably, not being communicative. I catch the 07.36 to Exeter, a cautious run and 2min late after a tsr.

I explain to the experienced and normally reliable relief signalman who appears to have perpetrated the error on Saturday night that he will be allowed to continue as a relief signalman on his normal work pending disciplinary action if he recognises his mistake, accepts it and is able to maintain his professional confidence.

My new secretary, Janet Mardon makes a quiet start to her new job as a letter arrives on my desk barring recruitment into clerical grades with the exception of travel centres. Paul Silvestri finalises his local train service summer Saturday proposals and then I begin a meeting about the Class 142 position. We have Swindon operating managers David Warne and Ray Spackman, Laira depot engineer Ian Cusworth and Plymouth area operations manager David Langton. We are still regularly short, our service being delivered by 7xClass 142s instead of nine, relieved slightly by the use of the stolen Class 118.

I go down to Newton Abbot to pick up the car only to find that the Bradford-Paignton is to terminate at Newton Abbot and form the 14.35 to Paddington. It has been refused back onto the Eastern Region as it is limited to 100mph. The Newcastle-Plymouth is to terminate and return as the 14.20 Paignton-Newcastle, some 15min late from Newton Abbot with the London stock forming the Plymouth Cross Country starter. *A switch is not possible nowadays but I doubt a 100mph train would be refused in the first place.*

There is a Torbay Rotary Club meeting at the Oswald Hotel and I am giving a short talk after lunch. There are some good questions which is usually proof that it has gone well. I drive back to Teignmouth and pick up the Newcastle train which is 12min late at Exeter, more or less as expected. Had it been on time, I would have missed it. Cross Country manager Brian Johnson (a management trainee of my intake) is on the footbridge and we have an uncharacteristically tetchy discussion on the platform. The winner of the Miss Devon contest Golden Rail prize is also there and I discover that the Radio Devon fiasco has been compounded by her prize not having been handed over. Back in the office, I get onto them to sort it out. Karin is back from Waterloo where she is overjoyed at having been selected for a CO3 relief post, which is a promotion as well as a transfer to suit her domestic situation. More paperwork, including a huge pile of accounts, and then the 18.18 to Teignmouth, talking to a rail enthusiast all the way when I wanted 25min of reflection, and take the car home for 18.50.

Tuesday 19th November 1986

On arrival at work I go to see Paul Silvestri who is duty manager this morning. There are 8x142s and 1x118 in action. The Bristol-Plymouth is 11min late and has to be re-platformed to No. 4 from No. 1. I go over with parcels manager Tony Crabtree to see how the Post Office staff perform. It takes 55sec for the first datapost parcel to reach the platform barrow. Tony thinks the Exeter traffic is spread over too many vans and it might be possible to concentrate it, although this might involve somewhere else with more work. An up stopper needs to cross the bows of the Plymouth train but we save 30sec on our dwell time.

At 09.00 a Mr Day of Exmouth comes to talk about forming a Rail Users Support Group. I must admit that I find myself secretly hoping he fails, but I realise that I cannot discourage an organisation whose very title says it intends to support rail travel. At 10.00 I see Nigel Gooding to discuss his application for the management training scheme as a staff entrant. Nigel is the young man I have identified to move into management as he has the ability but also to prevent him diverting into a union career.

Next arrival is Jim Rogers to run through BRB Property Board matters throughout the area, which takes two hours. I then prepare for the toothache disciplinary hearing which will have Transport Salaried Staff Association (TSSA) assistant line secretary Peter Davis as the clerk's advocate; a strange situation as I am a TSSA member and as much one of his members as his current client.

There is little or no new evidence. The clerk admits most of what is alleged but Mr Davis tries to manipulate the facts to sound as though responsibility was 50/50. He also alleges that John Hedge has accepted an apology. I take a recess to see if this is true as it tends to undermine the disciplinary situation - in practice if not in theory – but John is at lunch. My options are either dismissal or a final warning and transfer to a CO2 in the paybills section. Letting him stay in the same office as John Hedge is not an option on safety grounds or in terms of placing the manager in an awkward situation. I consider the clerk working in paybills and the kind of provocation he might receive from a driver arriving with the wrong pay. If a driver was provoked into hitting him for saying half of what was said to John Hedge, the driver would lose his job. Then there is the onus on the head of paybills who would feel obliged to watch his step to avoid being assaulted. The clerk would have a 07.00 to 17.45 day to and from Torquay so he might claim domestic difficulties and he might always be applying for lateral moves back to Torquay. Dismissal would also show others that they could not behave like this and expect to keep their job, similar to the guard I had to dismiss for tampering with mail bags. So, dismissal it is and then explain the rights of appeal. He might just get back if he gets a soft regional appeal officer.

There is time to discuss a few things on the mind of traffic/public complaints section head Tony Hill, including the timetabling of Exeter Central stops in Waterloo-Exeter trains as 'set down only'. This would help punctuality as sometimes trains arrive there early with a path down to St. David's which has disappeared by departure time. It would also prevent the services being quoted as a connecting service into long distance trains from St. David's and the risk of poor punctuality jeopardising these journeys, admittedly at the price of not giving a connection at all, so, on balance, this will not be pursued.

I have a message to ring Councillor Mrs Rose-Mangles about Somerset County Council affairs, including the Westbury-Exeter local service she is proposing with station re-openings, at the likes of Somerton, and the Yeovil plans. At 17.10, an 'O' level student rings for information about Tiverton Parkway for a school project, before I catch the 17.25. The Newcastle does not leave until 17.26 and we follow at 17.29½, unchecked at Exminster now the re-signalling is in place.

Tuesday 19th November 1986

I am heading for Newton Abbot this morning so I go to the station for 08.30. The 06.35 Bristol-Plymouth is late again this morning and passes at 08.38, exactly the time the local dmu should have arrived. Amazingly, my train pulls in within 5min, more quickly than it could have done if it had been standing in Dawlish Warren for it to pass under the old absolute block signalling. It is exactly 2min from the mail passing the automatic signal at the west end of Dawlish platform until it turns to green again. I travel with the unit's driver to Newton Abbot where he is relieved by a Plymouth man so I then ride in the train. At Torquay, I take John Hedge for a cup of coffee to explain the action taken and to point out the error of his ways in handling the tooth-ache incident, principally that he should have ensured he was present when the clerk reported for duty last Thursday and he should have reported the apology, and particularly his acceptance of it, as soon as possible.

The local HST takes me down to Paignton with guard Brian Cocks *(who was to become chairman of the Dart Valley Buckfastleigh line in his retirement)*. After visiting the booking office where John Hedge's son is on duty, I meet the chargeman Dai Putt. He is upset that a surplus guard, who has been accommodated in a leading railman job at Paignton, has retained a rate of pay higher than Dai's own, even though Dai had been promoted from guard to chargeman some years ago. It is a complicated situation that has been exacerbated by the 1968 Pay and Efficiency national agreement which created many anomalies, but also maintained security for displaced staff such as the leading railman about whom he feels disadvantaged.

I ride back with the driver of No. 43013 *(seen in February 2015 on the Network Rail new measurement train at St. Pancras)* incurring 2½min overtime at Torquay, arriving 2min late at Dawlish with the signals suggesting we were going into the loop at the Warren. We sidle through the points and the outlet signal clears up from red to green with another green available at Starcross. Ernie Pope re-mans the train at St. David's and I go to the office to phone Derek Old in the panel box. He says that a bump had been reported by a previous train so this arrangement suitably reduced our speed over the defect until the permanent way staff arrived on site without the need to stop and caution our train. This is contrary to the rule requirement for dealing with a suspected track defect and I ensure proper arrangements are made, asking Bernard to make sure that official procedures are used in future.

It is my intention to visit Yeovil this afternoon so I take the 12.20 with loco No. 50032 'Courageous'. At Pen Mill I visit the booking office, parcels office and signalbox before going back to Yeovil Jct in the outbased 'Metro'. Terry Gale is on duty and this is the first time we have spoken since his apology over the 'leaving doors open', so the conversation has an awkward feel to it. While at Yeovil Junction signal box a Class 31 arrives via Castle Cary with an Exeter crew to shunt the engineer's siding. The 13.10 Waterloo-Exeter arrives with No. 33104 leading No. 50047 'Swiftsure' - great for acceleration and I note 94mph at Broom level crossing which is some 9mph over the permitted speed. We run into Central 2½min early, a situation where the set down arrangement would have worked. There is time to 'sign up' before going home with No. 33063 and walk up the hill home talking to driver Whittle.

Wednesday 20th November 1986

The luxury of another day free from meetings. Although there are some major projects and documents to get off the ground, the temptation to start them is resisted as time to tour the area is far more valuable. The morning starts in the cab of my normal commuter run with Nos. 142018 and 142025. As we leave Dawlish Warren loop, the exit signal is flashing from green to red and back again very quickly. We stop immediately and are cautioned past. Apparently the microprocessor has failed and we have to resort to 'through route working' with all trains via the loop until the defective 'card' is replaced at 09.10, a good response from the S&T but it is worrying that a new installation is suffering such failures.

I take the 08.31 to Tiverton Parkway where there are 50 cars in the car park, continuing an upward trend. *It would be considered to be deserted nowadays with such a number.* After being kindly given my customary cup of tea, I proceed to Taunton with Nos. 43004/43013. There is a good reception at the travel centre and another cup of tea because they have done relatively well from the consultation exercise. On the other hand, supervisor Bob Johnson who has moved to this job from Gloucester panel signal box is concerned at the prospect of potential redundancy. It is surprising that a man of his ability, experience and contacts (he knows Bernard Price very well) has not read the signs about what jobs will be available for which people, but I think I manage to put his mind at rest and he appears to be quite grateful.

A headquarters traction inspector is on board the train back to Exeter with Fred Butler so I choose to ride in the train. Fred will sort him out and, as expected, it is a restrained run with a 1min late arrival.

There is time to collect this morning's mail before taking the 11.28 to Barnstaple. Our only former Gateshead driver is in charge with driver Eaglen *(again Peter or Dave is not specified)*, a relaxed run on which driver Eaglen ensures I am seated most of the way, despite my best efforts to do my share of standing. We are 1min late into Barnstaple, chiefly as a result of a special stop at Newton St. Cyres – *not sure what the justification for that might have been.*

Richard Burningham, the 23-year-old travel centre manager, has been interviewed for a lateral move to Dartford. I tell him that would be a bad move. He has not applied for the travel centre manager at Bath, which would be a good move. His predecessor made this same transfer and I would rate Richard the better manager, certainly the one with more potential. We discuss the reasons for the 10% recent revenue rise while consuming spaghetti bolognese in town. Good salesmanship, the right level of local fares, and maximised connectional possibilities are all important and significant in view of the opening of Tiverton Parkway that critics said would shut the branch - proving my view that extra supply increases the volume of the market and all market operators are likely to take some share of the increase.

We have conceded his post back to a CO4 so Richard, young and mobile will be able to stay at Barnstaple but this means that a local clerk in his 50s will now be displaced instead, with the nearest job at Exeter, to which he does not wish to travel. So much for the TSSA looking after its members. After discussing rostering possibilities we return to the station to see George Facey in the parcels office and then Ken Ley in the signalbox before riding back to Exeter in the cab of the Class 142.

Back in the office there is a stream of visitors including Alex McNabb, the able NSE South West marketing officer, who has some proposals to integrate Exeter fully into the NSE fare structure. This would mean abolition of the low saver fare but the availability of more day returns. The Network Card would be valid from Exeter which will be a positive move though.

At 17.05 Bernard Price comes in. He has been making investigations into the 'through route' working at Dawlish Warren. At this time of year we could miss out the Warren by running main line and avoiding much delay, serving the few passengers by minibus as necessary. The balance changes in summer but Bernard thinks the S&T could provide a simple switch for the technicians to select whichever through route we need.

The headline in the Exeter Express & Echo concerns the plans to replace Red Cow Crossing with a bridge. Talks have been going on for a year now but the current plans involve an unacceptable loss of B.R. car parking. However, it would be great to avoid a cause of delay and the method of working which is as safe as reasonably possible but not completely safe. Ralph Ponsonby rings from the civil engineer's department to fix a meeting for discussion of the engineering and commercial feasibility. The paper mentions a budget of £1million but I would be surprised if three times that figure would cover it. *Still no bridge!*

Just to add a bit of variety tonight, my train is double-headed with Nos. 33206 and 33023, the former being a narrow-bodied Hastings line loco. I expect fireworks after a 5min late start following an electric train heating problem but it is the worst driving performance I have experienced on this train dropping 3½min from St. Thomas to Starcross, no more than 1min of which was due to a tsr at City Basin and arrival at Dawlish is 9½min late after gaining a minute at stations. Dave Whittle is walking up home again today having been to Severn Tunnel Jct, a trip I must sort out for myself one day.

Friday 21st November 1986

The chief job this morning is to handle three retirements. First is signalman Hughes from Eggesford, whom I have recently seen to give him his long service award. Then there is a driver who has retired early with a hearing problem, having 'shopped' himself to the doctor. He says he knew he was sailing close to the wind but he knew something had to be done when he experienced difficulty hearing the aws horn. It is worrying that the system has not been able to pick this up and has had to rely on his personal integrity.

Then comes the paybill clerk whose job might have gone to my tooth-ache clerk. He is a widower in poor health and I am afraid that a lonely old age is in prospect but he has two children living locally and his grandchildren. Clarence Woodbury also pays a visit to pick up his valedictory card.

At 12.00 Colin Carr arrives to run through the revised new works' procedures that he is giving to us with Chris Hughes and Bernard Reynolds and I think we might be making progress towards higher standards and faster response times.

It is a Huddersfield weekend again, this time in the cab of No. 43011 on the 15.38 to Paddington. We are pretty well on time despite being stopped outside Westbury and then held in the platform for a non-stop Class 33 to pass through on a Portsmouth-bound train. The departure from Reading is 2½min late with 4min recovery time to Paddington. Approaching Slough we are checked to 45mph as a Class 47 crosses to the down relief line in front of us. We are soon back into our stride and arrive precisely on time. There is time to reflect that if we had been a minute earlier from Reading we would have been stopped at Slough and probably have arrived late.

The Circle Line is in its normal state of disarray so I do not have long to wait for my 18.50 to Leeds. It is tempting to risk a Class 47 on a 19.08 Newcastle relief to Doncaster but it is tight for the last train to Huddersfield if there is any disruption. Eventual arrival in Huddersfield is with one of the re-engined Metro-Camm units with just one engine in each power car, 2min late. As I leave the station, the temperature difference from Devon is immediately apparent and there is snow on the ground.

CHAPTER 27: A SIGNAL BOX FIRE AND MICHAEL PALIN VISITS

Sunday 23rd November 1986

A routine trip home in semi-light with No. 45139 to Manchester and an HST home in darkness. There is a tiring 35min wait for boarding in Manchester. Restrictions and station overtime means we are 11min wait at Barnt Green but on time again by Cowley Bridge Jct before the 20mph tsr at City Basin renders our arrival 2½min late at Dawlish.

Monday 24th November 1986

Former Leeds driver Caslin is in Dawlish parcels office, having just moved to town. He takes my customary place in the cab to have a look at the new signals. The main task today is the disciplinary hearing for the Taunton leading railman with the shocking attendance record. He has had a reduction in grade and a suspension during my time here but there is no record of any previous trouble. Today the charge is that he has failed to attend for duty with the regularity required and has failed to reply to correspondence. Our records are not as complete as they should be but advocate panel signalman Denis Davy does not press us on individual dates and letters. Partly in response, and partly through realising that our case might not withstand a determined appeal, I decide not to further reduce him in grade or suspend him. The railway doctor has said he is not alcoholic and there is no reason why he should not attend work regularly. The main aim is to get him functioning again so opt for a severe reprimand and, crucially, a final warning. I explain that this means that if he is disciplined again on similar grounds he will be dismissed. There must be a marked and immediate improvement.

Lunch is taken at home, leaving on the 12.20 and returning on the 14.50, going straight into the management meeting. The first task is to ensure measures are in hand to get the budget back to break even and then examine the means of saving the new £48,000 imposed by the regional operating manager that must be made 'without affecting service quality'. Ha! Ha! We can scrape together a possible £35,000 but this assumes no adverse factors to eat into it. There is some interest in having a management and supervisors' Christmas celebration but Bernard and I lack enthusiasm and it is concluded there is insufficient time to start doing it now.

At 17.25 I go across to the panel box for an hour. There is 8X59, a long-welded rail train, approaching. It needs to be extended from Exeter to Newton Abbot Hackney Yard because Riverside is full with Meldon traffic in a situation where capacity has been reduced by the pilot having damaged the catch points. I ensure that it stays in Platform 4 and is not pushed out in front of the 15.45 from Paddington that is put into Platform 3. 8X59 eventually follows the 18.18 Paignton stopper. As I go out onto the platform there are three parallel freight moves; the Westbury-Exeter Central cement is pulling along Platform 1 to await its Class 50 banker, a Class 08 is coming down Platform 5 to pick up car empties from the stabling point and No. 45111 sets off from Platform 3 on 8X59. I visit the signing-on point and tidy the desk before going out to watch the unofficial attachment of the Class 50 to the Aberdeen train in Platform 5. The problem is that there is no Class 50 to be found and 5min overtime occurs looking for it before it is discovered that it has set off light as per diagram. Supervisor Gordon Hooper is rather embarrassed. I disappear to the cricket meeting at Exminster.

Tuesday 25th November 1986

Today was earmarked to accompany some American visitors from Exmouth to Exeter with East Devon tourist officers but there has been a cancellation, creating a free day. The temptation is to complete the outstanding consultation documents but the phone rings at 07.00. Odds on it will be Bernard to tell me of some operational emergency he has sorted out but thinks I need to know about before getting to work. Apparently Newton Abbot East signal box has caught fire at 04.55. Despite large flames, it has been extinguished but only after it had destroyed the back of the box, leaving a 5ft hole. As an important box in its own right itself, and now as a fringe box to the panel, its destruction would have produced chaos. The signalman on duty was the experienced relief man that had not sent train out of section on my recent visit to Teignmouth and this has 'nearly happened' three times before, some say five.

At 08.15, I set off for Aller Jct where John Congdon is on duty as always seems to be the case when I visit. Then it is off to the booking office and West box where signalman George Dennis is his usual pugnacious self. At the East box, feathers have been ruffled by the hole in the wall. Young signalman Kevin Davies *(the senior man in the panel at present)* threatens to go home if it is not repaired. I tell him not to be so touchy -the carpenter is on site - but I phone Colin Carr to ensure it will continue to get top priority. Travelling on to Dainton signal box, Totnes box, parcels office and booking office this is not so much the technique known as 'management by walking around' so much as 'management by sitting around, drinking coffee'; slightly more enjoyable and less hard work.

I drive home for lunch and catch the 14.50 to Exeter, being driven by HQ inspector Cheesley. In the office, standards seem to have been dropping with Karin perhaps seeing the finishing tape. Documents I need for tomorrow have not been brought out as requested and a letter has been detained for two weeks without being sent while waiting for an attachment. Ken Boobyer comes in to have a session about producing the consultation document with the platform staff that is necessary as a result of the supervisory reductions.

A guard, whom I do not recognise, arrives in the outer office. He is the Bristol man for the 17.25 to Paignton and says that the windows on the 17.25 Clapham Jct based Mark 1s are so dirty inside and out that if they are not cleaned by tomorrow he will refuse to take the train. Although he is right about the fact that the diagram does not put the set through the carriage washer, and we do not have one, the interiors are more dingy than dirty. He cannot be allowed to have the last word on this, especially in front of other staff and I inform him in no uncertain terms that he must leave on the understanding that he will be required to work the train tomorrow whether or not it has been cleaned to his own satisfaction. There seems to be no immediate alternative other than hand-washing at Clapham, unlikely to say the least, beyond its scheduled replacement in next summer's timetable. This is a matter now for Frank Markham, the urbane and tough area manager at Bristol. When I explain what has happened he replies, "That's easy, I'll have him seen tomorrow when he signs on and challenge him whether he intends to take the stock or not." I will tip off our supervisors about what might happen so they can have a move up their sleeve if it proves necessary.

It remains for me to go out and catch that very stock today, only to find it has disappeared. It has been pressed into service to run Exeter-Plymouth-Taunton to cover for the 06.57 Newcastle-Taunton HST that has failed at Temple Meads. After repair, the HST is being sent empty to Taunton to meet No. 33063 and its dirty coaches, with the Class 33 running round and setting off back at 17.00 from Taunton to form the 17.25 to Paignton, incurring a 4½min late start but having achieved another minor miracle of improvisation.

Wednesday 26th November 1986

I meet Jim Collins on the 08.00 to Bristol for the area manager's monthly conference, arriving 2min late after a signal stop outside Bristol but with time for a coffee and discussion of mutual problems before the meeting. We are treated to a video about the Channel Tunnel. Its presenter tells us that they are keen that visitors from the European mainland will be encouraged to venture beyond London but the line drawn on the map to show this ends at Windsor not Plymouth, Exeter, or even Bristol. He does not think that it is important exactly where it has been drawn.

After discussion of a few points that were mainly considered at the overnight Torquay meeting, Bob Poynter directs us to the question of how we are collectively going to save £500,000 in the remaining 20 weeks of the financial year. We contemplate diverse possible measures such as reducing engineering coverage at weekends and closing information offices on Sunday mornings and definitely decide to temporarily withdraw traction trainee recruitment. *Presumably to increase recruitment the following year with a budget that reflects this additional cost?*

After lunch the British Transport Police talk to us about football hooligan control. Ken Shingleton suggests a force of special constables drawn from railway ranks but the policemen immediately become defensive. Perhaps that would mean less overtime for the lads? There is then just 45min devoted to current performance. Ken decides to travel west with Jim and me on the 09.43 Newcastle-Penzance which is 3min early at Taunton and 3½min early at Exeter. I see Ken off on the 17.33 to Waterloo. Anxious not to incur displeasure through a late start the platform staff dispatch the train at 17.32.10secs. I wince, and reflect that perhaps it is time to restrain our enthusiasm for right time starts.

Thursday 27th November 1986

Having driven home last night I set off at 07.05 to drive into Exeter but, as I unlock the car I can hear the noise of a Class 50 leaving Teignmouth, three miles away and with a cliff in between. It must be 3min late and I succumb to the temptation to catch it from Dawlish. No. 50015 arrives at 07.10. Gordon Hooper meets me at Exeter to say we are short of units again so he has sent our loco-hauled 'secret set' to Barnstaple, which has worked out well because it has taken the late-arriving newspaper van with it.

At 07.45 John Beer and Ken Boobyer join me to discuss the room for negotiation this morning when implementing the travel centre consultation agreement. Brian Platt is first, representing the Paignton staff and we agree 8hr 13min days with extra occasional rest days to balance up the hours, thereby allowing the two shifts to overlap in the middle of the day and provide the necessary coverage. Brian's remit seems to be the retention of 12hrs between the first signing-on time and the last signing-off time so the staff can retain their unsocial hours percentage payment, which I am happy enough to concede as it is budgeted. Ken and Brian go off to finalise details of the rest day roster *(the kind of thing that station master's clerks used to do in the 1950s and which Ken can do easily despite being involved in purely budgets in his last job)*. John goes off to the Guildhall to do an interview with Devonair plugging Christmas shopping by rail and our special late night shopping bargain fares.

Next comes Torquay, more awkward than Paignton, and more complicated too, but no real problems. Newton Abbot is the third meeting, represented by Keith Edwards and 'another' John Beer, a relief clerk based there. They want 8hr 13min days but I do not need the same overlap as at Paignton and am offering 7hhr 24min days with one rest day per week. Their proposal requires three rest days every two weeks. If we 'fail to agree', and the matter is referred to Sectional Council, I know the region will not back me as the change from the current 7hr 42min turns to 7hr 24min will leave spare capacity in the rest day roster that will result in concession. The difference between us is therefore the 31min between 7hr 42min and 8hr 13min multiplied by three turns per day.

How long do the individual shift balances take to do per day? Keith offers an exaggerated figure, four hours per day, an hour each including the CO3 supervisor's till. Ken has worked in booking offices and even I have done individual till balances at Huddersfield and Mirfield when I was 18, unfamiliar with the process, and it never took this length of time. It is where I learnt to add up across columns accurately as, otherwise, it would never balance the vertical column and result in unpaid overtime for me until it did.

Individual balances were introduced when I decided that shared tills were resulting in excessive surpluses and losses, and usually losses. I could now withdraw this requirement and save four hours a day, according to the staff side's own estimates, minus the substitute 'periodic balance' time that would have to be done instead. This would comfortably cover the 3x31min in dispute and perhaps open up the way for further savings. This robs them of their case. Keith tries to proceed towards a 'failure to agree' but he cannot do that without stating his grounds and I have countered those arguments. *On reflection this approach was pure Arnold Wain at Middlesbrough. If they had said the daily balances took an hour my case would not have stood up.*

Keith then finds a sticking point on covering Dawlish booking office rest days from Newton Abbot saying they will feel able to cover it only within their normal working day which would have to include travelling time. I reckon we cannot roster this but we could use them as necessary on spare days and the overtime in travelling would probably be gratefully accepted. I think I can cover it from Exeter anyway, using the Newton Abbot spare days to reduce overtime and therefore earnings even further. They should take a leaf out of the Exeter Drivers' LDC and not refuse any extra workload for the staff they represent. I think they are being orchestrated by Newton Abbot chief clerk Roy Watts and the TSSA branch secretary, and will be worse off by having done so.

Meanwhile Alan Bell, in typical no-nonsense fashion has seized the initiative and organised the management and supervisors' Christmas lunch for the Three Tuns at Silverton so I offer to take Ken Boobyer and his wife, who live at Teignmouth, in our car.

Now it is time for the disciplinary hearing for the signalman who perpetrated the two-in-a-section incident between St.Thomas and Dawlish Warren. I had left the issue of the 'Form 1' charge sheet to Bernard and find it to read that the signalman 'did not comply with' three specific rules. The three rules mentioned could be subject to dispute by a skilled advocate (the clever but honourable Ken Winter will be defending him) and the charge does not mention the specific train so it could be argued that he had obeyed the rules - for the first train for instance. After some reflection, I decide to withdraw the Form 1 and re-issue it. Bernard is understandably a bit miffed but we have to get this right. Bernard has also not put on paper the conversation he overheard in the panel box or stated where and when the signalman admitted his error before being allowed to take duty at Pinhoe, as I had instructed. It will be a matter of Bernard knowing what was said where and when, but having no patience with the paperwork. However, I am taking the hearing and cannot be seen to be guessing if the advocate asks a question or tries to implicate Bernard in any confusion over the transmission of messages or the subsequent chain of events.

No. 33111 is on the train home. The awkward Bristol guard is working the train and just happens to have Exeter stalwart guard Sid Oak rostered as his assistant fare collector, a classic move by the train crew supervisors to cover any eventuality, but not needed because the Bristol guard is quite amenable to discussion and his basic point about the windows being below an acceptable standard is undeniable. I should really try to get the set platformed for some hand brush cleaning if possible.

Friday 28th November 1986

No. 50020 'Revenge' is on the 07.08 this morning and we have 9xClass 142s available for once. I sort some tricky problems out with John Beer and Tony Hill and start on some new consultation documents.

At 11.45 a Mr Belmont arrives from the S&T to confirm he cannot move two customer information screens by my required 20cm for less than £1,000. When I say I'll get the work done by a private contractor, he counters by saying that the S&T will then cease to maintain them. He then gives himself away by saying, "I've been speaking to the staff at Newton Abbot and they don't think it is necessary anyway." Even if he is right, it is not up to him to decide. When I was at Newton Abbot two weeks ago many people were enquiring about platform numbers because the screens were too high for them to notice they were there. I reckon it might be worth about £200 to have them moved. The ludicrous estimates for some engineering jobs really ought to be exposed. Area managers have long thought engineers inflated the estimates for jobs they do not want to do, much as builders and joiners do in the real world, I suppose. I show Mr Belmont the door and say I will be elevating the issues to regional level to see if it is thought the matter has been handled equably. After he has gone, Karin says he was annoying her while he was waiting to come in.

At 12.00 I take Karin out for lunch at the Great Western before she catches the 14.17 to Waterloo and a new job. John Beer and I discuss security expenditure at NSE stations and the information I need to reply to the Yeovil Rail Users' Group about the 20-year-old bus operated by Air Camelot (yes, really) that has taken over from Southern National on the Pen Mill to Yeovil Jct shuttle The new arrangement does have the advantage of charging 20p instead of 50p though. We decide to invite them and Red Bus, who operate the Sidmouth-Honiton link, to the Institute of Transport Christmas lunch. This Red Bus is not the same operator as North Devon Red Bus who, John thinks, do not merit any invitations.

John leaves the office at 16.50 to find John Hedge asking to see us. Is this more trouble? We explain the implications of the negotiation meetings yesterday and John says he thinks the Newton Abbot staff representatives were silly to refuse the Dawlish work. We also discuss the tooth-ache disciplinary case for which the appeals officer, Bernard Norman has expressed support. Bernard is another pleasant and reasonable member of the operating team at Swindon, whom I first met when he was a lecturer at Derby School of Transport, but we will see how he does at the hearing next Monday. No. 33005 tonight on the stopper with the awkward Bristol guard again, who is thawing out and stops for a 5min chat.

Saturday 29th November 1986

This afternoon I have to address the national AGM of Transport 2000 at Oldway Mansion in Torbay. The setting itself is magnificent, built in the style of a French chateau by the founder of Singer sewing machines for Isadora Duncan. The meeting is to be chaired by Michael Palin of Monty Python and Great Rail Journeys fame. The person to whom I am introduced seems serious, thoughtful and retiring, not a bit like his TV image.

He introduces the discussion in his usual easy manner and is followed by Harold Luscombe from Devon County Council. He is also an HQ inspector and speaks first on the local impact of transport policy. I follow with a thread that leads from legislation through financial limits to sectorisation and how this process manifests itself in the resultant train service. *It sounds boring even to type it and I cannot remember anything about it other than the fact that the redoubtable Mr Palin was a difficult act to follow.* Harry Blundred is next with his usual spiel on the privatisation of Devon General. Perhaps I should not have spoken so directly to the subject I was given. Harold and I stick to our 20min but Harry over-runs to 35min, thereby reducing the question time for every one before the 17.15 finish.

CHAPTER 28: A TUCC VISIT AND A POSSIBLE MOVE TO YORK REFUSED

Monday 1st December 1986

I join the driver of the local to Exeter, pleased to have been told that we actually have a spare Class 142 this morning. We would have been on time but the Bristol-Plymouth is 9min late with rolling stock technician attendance so we arrive 4min late.

There is not much time to turn round before catching the 09.38 to Feniton, making a 10min late start because the shunters have not been informed that there is a scratch set on the inward working that is going to be exchanged for the booked set which is waiting in New Yard. I rarely manage to get to Feniton and today's visit is a bit of a waste of time because Exeter relief leading railman Pengelly is on duty. My return is on the 07.00 from Waterloo running 6min late, but still in time for the railway 'volunteer first aid' AGM Christmas lunch in the Bystock Hotel near Central station.

Returning to the office at 14.15, I am met by the news that the tooth-ache appeal has been turned down and therefore the clerk remains dismissed. I notify John Hedge who seems more worried than one might have expected. Ken Shingleton rings, following up a complaint from Paddy Ashdown about diversions on the 22nd of November when one of my staff told him that they had not been told about the alterations until the previous Friday, which is plainly ridiculous.

The day finishes with the local meeting and discussion of a deteriorating budget position as a result of some yet unexplained train crew costs before taking a bag full of correspondence home.

Tuesday 2nd December 1986

After a very steady ride in with driver Clarrie Keys I decide to devote the day to getting on top of the admin work. With four hours' work last night the pile has been considerably reduced. John Beer is entangled with three LDC negotiation meetings, concerning Taunton, Barnstaple and Exeter.

Ray Bulpin from the ROM's training arm rings to say my management trainee is considering asking to transfer to the personnel training scheme. I take a break at lunchtime riding up to Central with guard Ruffel and back with driver Laskey, having purchased a new calculator, watch and stopwatch.

John is still chairing the Exeter LDC meeting when I go home with No. 33006, and he is reportedly determined to stick to 7hr 24min days instead of the 7hr 35min and occasional extra rest days enjoyed now.

Wednesday 3rd December 1986

I sit next to Ken Boobyer on my way to work, who tells me that the LDC meeting did not break up until 19.00 with 7hr 24 days in all cases bar two posts which means that I will be able to leave one CO2 relief post unfilled and therefore a saving on the budget. At 09.15 an auditor arrives to discuss a project he has been given on the revised new works procedures. The main problem is that our budget is not real money at present but a subvention of each engineer's allowance so the sooner this money becomes our own the better we can mange it.

After a succession of visitors has been in and out, the Transport Users' Consultative Committee arrives, at least a part of it; secretary and former railway engineer Ian Nalder (who should be pre-disposed to understanding railway problems but is not) Devon County Councillor Mrs-Saxon-Spence, often familiarly addressed as 'Saxon' and whom I always find prickly, and a Mr (probably actually a rank) Cummins who is a retired naval officer, brewery executive and all-round gentleman.

It is not long before Mrs Saxon-Spence and I start to argue. She seems to be in a fractious mood and takes up the case of

the last up Paignton stopper being substituted by a bus to cover pre-planned engineering work when she felt obliged to call out her husband to give her a lift. *Nowadays there are buses for a full week for engineering work because it is deemed to be cheaper than doing the jobs at night.* On the way down to Newton Abbot that day she did not have her ticket clipped and perches the evidence on the edge of my desk for inspection. I ignore it. Her 'station visit results' strike me as being carping whereas Mr Cummins has visited, if anything, slightly worse stations and gives them high praise. Mrs Saxon-Spence says, "The staff at the stations felt that....."
"I'm sorry Mrs Spence, did you say staff or customers just then?" I ask.
"Staff."
"I'm sorry, I do not wish to appear difficult, but it is my job to speak to the staff, you should be speaking to the customers," I rejoin, and Mr Cummins appears to agree with me.
After discussing how Tiverton Parkway is doing, any opportunities for running empty stock as passenger trains and the merits of how a few recent complaints have been handled, we adjourn to the Great Western for a bar snack and, on our return, show Ian Nalder how the telephone enquiry monitoring equipment works.

There is time to have a few words with John Beer about the unwelcome news that he will have to delay some recruitment to the travel centre vacancies that have been held pending finalisation of the consultation owing to budgetary constraints. It is his job to deliver high customer service standards for which I hold him accountable and now here I am telling him to save money and accept poorer standards. That seems to be his position and I can see his point. The difference is that meeting the budget is the current top priority and that customer service standards are not giving cause for concern so the balance of the argument means that improvements will have to be postponed for a while.

He can recruit his CO_2s to limit expensive rest day working and leave the CO_1s uncovered, slowing down the recruitment process by about four weeks but ensuring everyone is in place as the Easter rush builds up which, after all is the sort of traffic level on which staffing levels are based. John is not really any happier.

I catch the 15.26 to Dawlish to turn round for the Railcards Team Challenge, railway sponsored Badminton match at Torquay Leisure Centre. Vernon Baseley rings to say the BRB rolling stock control are ringing to demand the release to traffic of our secret set of Mark Is. The time has come to let them go, despite David Mather agreeing only this morning that we could retain them. Surely he has not shopped us to the BRB? We will start the process of acquiring replacements from passing Mark 1 trains, beginning with the first train to appear carrying two brake vans and therefore having one to spare. These will then not show up on TOPS as having been retained here for a long time. The BRB monitoring works gradually does not usually happen until '99 days' have expired.

Linda and I leave for Torquay at 17.50 for drinks and 'trout fingers' Trout fingers? It transpires that the event is dual sponsored between British Rail and British Trout! The badminton is of a high standard with the best British players Gillian Gilks and Steve Baddeley playing. The problem is that it goes on so long. Tony and Erica Crabtree slip away at 21.30 but we remain with our guest, the head postmaster of Torbay, until the end of play at 22.40, arriving home at 23.30.

Thursday 4th December 1986

I drive into Exeter and catch the 08.00 to Tiverton Parkway, 2min early. A cup of tea then on to Taunton, 2min early again. In the travel centre, manager Mervyn Berryman is asked to investigate the effect of the way InterCity has zoned Tiverton Parkway fares with Exeter instead of Taunton. Their lack of local knowledge leads them to think Barnstaple is 50miles from Exeter by rail where it is actually 40 or so from Taunton by road, but they charge for the 31miles to Exeter and the 50 beyond, which the market will not bear. Now, Tiverton

Parkway has been sucked into this misunderstanding. Signalman Manning is on duty at East Station box – he is hard work and never gives much away. Then it is on to Silk Mill in the van, encountering deputy general manager Brian Scott at the foot of the station approach, on his way to a CBI meeting.

My return from Silk Mill is just in time to catch the 10.45 to Newton Abbot arriving 1min early, only to find Bernard Price had joined the train at St. David's so I decide to drop back onto the 2min late 11.45 to Torquay to prevent appearing 'top heavy'. There is still an atmosphere in the travel centre. John Hedge says the tooth-ache clerk is going to an Industrial Tribunal, which does not concern me, other than the time it will entail. I have followed procedures, considered alternative courses of action and meted out a punishment that would be open to a reasonable employer.

I discover that David Tucker is being paid a CO4 rate of pay today, contrary to my instructions that this new post was not to be covered this week. It transpires that the extra hours of the new turn are not being worked but he is being paid at its higher rate. Staff representative David Liggins is informed that this will be the last day that this happens, and then tell David Tucker.

There is time for an all-day breakfast for lunch before catching the 07.00 Bradford-Paignton with Nos. 43025/43164 with just long enough to visit both boxes, the booking office and chargeman Dai Putt. Staff representative Brian Platt is on duty in the booking office and relatively happy with the negotiation results, particularly as there will be a job for Mark Hedge. This has not occurred by accident and it never ceases to amaze me how little the staff representatives think we spend ensuring there are slots for everyone if at all possible.

The running of the 14.20 back to Exeter is a model of perfection as far as Dawlish, never more than 10sec early or late before running into St. David's 2½min early. *Modern railway operators would say this time should have been* dissipated to save fuel but arriving early meant that any station incidents could be accommodated without a loss of time and when there was a public/working time differential of one or two minutes, the train could go forward correspondingly early on working times with that time in hand for contingencies such as temporary speed restrictions.

I have time to clear up for a long-promised day off tomorrow and sign off a few matters with principal assistants. John Beer has been interviewing for booking office staff and has a few lined up who will be able to reduce rest day working immediately, such as an existing booking clerk from Faversham. John is still sore about the instructions I gave him yesterday and when he says he 'could have taken the hump' I have to explain that it was not really an option.

Bob Poynter rings to ask whether I would 'wish to be considered' for regional performance manager on the Eastern Region at York, third in the hierarchy of the operating team. I decline without any further ado but it is nice to be asked. *I had entirely forgotten this until reading the diary notes now but, on reflection, I think I should have gone for this job.*

No. 33006 gets a 2min late start tonight waiting a brake test and I make a note to follow that up on Monday morning.

Friday 5th December 1986

I wake up at 09.00 and we catch the 10.05 Skipper through to Exeter Central. The train is well loaded and 1min early. After buying my new suit for Mike Hodson's wedding we catch the 13.10 Barnstaple train from Central and the 13.20 Skipper from St. David's. It looks as though it will be a perfect trip until we are stopped for two track circuit failures, costing 8min. The 13.20 was put on to compensate for the winter withdrawal of the Torbay Express and it loads quite well with 40 or so passengers, the numbers possibly exaggerated by Christmas shoppers. *A passenger complement of 40 would be considered lightly loaded on any Exeter-Paignton train nowadays.*

CHAPTER 29: TRACK CIRCUITS DON'T WORK UNDER SEA WATER

Monday 8th December 1986

My management trainee is back on the area this morning. I make time to discuss her situation and alleged preference for the personnel training scheme. She is undecided how and whether she should continue so I give her a project on freight marshalling.

At 12.00 John Beer and I are joined by the owner of Red Bus who co-ordinates his Sidmouth service with trains at Honiton and the traffic manager of Air Camelot, formerly Brutonian, which operates the Yeovil Jct to Pen Mill shuttle, for the Chartered Institute of Transport South West Section lunch. The event goes badly with a late start and slow service. The after-lunch speaker gets to his feet at 14.30 and sits down at 14.40. I have been nominated to give the vote of thanks and have to take care to ensure that it does not last longer than the talk itself.

At this afternoon's local meeting we run through the budgetary provisions again to make sure our cost-saving measures are in hand. In the afternoon, the sea wall signalling deteriorates to an unacceptable level with thirteen track circuit failures caused by short circuiting from sea water. The problem is that once the line has been examined the sea water often disappears and the track circuit works again but the next big wave occupies it once more, necessitating another examination of the line. Clearly, this is unacceptable – not only for the effect on punctuality but for the complacency that routine and repetitive examinations engenders in signalmen and train crew. Bernard Price has the matter in hand, as far as can be done, by establishing emergency block posts at Dawlish and Teignmouth. During the planning stages, we had been assured by the S&T that this would not happen and it is obvious that the problem will not be limited to just today's conditions. *It was subsequently discovered that the track circuits were shorting through the ballast, assisted by the salt.*

Tuesday 9th December 1986

At 10.15, Lesley Holland, equal opportunities manager at the BRB arrives to deliver the 'Equal Opportunities Roadshow' at Exeter Central. There are about fifty people in attendance including both engineering and operating supervisors and management. Lesley Holland talks for over an hour and probably makes the mistake of assuming she is addressing a hostile audience which is not the case, except for a few diehards. It is incumbent upon the senior managers to make supportive remarks, which is no imposition to any of us.

There is a problem in the afternoon when David Thear, deputy regional personnel manager, phones to ask the direct question whether the Taunton signalling staff to whom suspension punishments were given for the firewood sale irregularities have had their suspensions implemented. This sets me back because I thought there would be no back-check. I explain that 'unfortunately' many of them retired before it was possible to do this, with the re-signalling work and related matters. David does not twist the knife.
"You won't be the first person not to have applied suspensions," he says.
This turn of events surprises me and I do not know what to make of the issue being raised but David phones back later with a message that I interpret as saying, if not using the actual words, "forget it." *There had been a crisis when the local B.T. Police had uncovered their equivalent of the Great Train Robbery with a relief signalman persuading operating and engineering staff to claim a little-known concession of buying used sleepers for firewood, then selling it to the signalman organiser. The small print said it was 'for your own use' and selling it was therefore fraud. I was instructed to dismiss all my staff involved, as was Peter Warren the civil engineer. It was wrong to instruct us in the first place, the job would have been stopped for lack of signalling staff and what*

did the issue matter anyway? One signalman had given it to his son and that was also treated as fraud. I suggested if the firewood had been burnt at Christmas and he had been sitting in front of the fire he would have been using it. It was all that silly. In the end I ensured my disciplinary hearings followed the first of Peter's (it was after all his firewood!) and he did not dismiss his first tranche of staff. I levied a few suspensions but had deliberately not implemented them after tipping a wink to the advocates that I would not be wrecking the record of loyal staff, many of whom were about to retire after the re-signalling, over what I considered a petty matter where a reprimand would have more than sufficed….and thereby avoided appeals and more H.Q. attention. Looking at events from here, perhaps I should have dismissed someone and seen how tough H.Q would have been. In the end I dismissed the ring leader after being told it was either him or me. I told H.Q. that if I was asked at the Tribunal, and on oath, whether I had been instructed to dismiss that person I would have to answer 'Yes'.

Wednesday 10th December 1986

Time for a day out on the Waterloo line. Driver Guerin is on the 08.11 with No. 50012 'Benbow' and two former Leeds drivers who are road learning. After starting 1½min late, waiting connection out of the late Bristol-Plymouth, we arrive on time at Crewkerne. Senior railman Alan Keirl, a tremendously conscientious former Southern man is on duty but he is rather 'anti' the current establishment, in terms of the fact it is now Western, not Southern, and now Exeter area management, not Westbury. *Also, and even primarily, that it is British Rail not Southern Railway.* I have deliberately created a fuss over a conversation he has held directly with Ken Shingleton (Ops Officer at Swindon) about time-keeping that has also been raised by Paddy Ashdown and Alan fears my visit is related to this. Ken has already been magnanimous enough to apologise for his part and I can genuinely assure Alan that the matter has already been closed and my visit is entirely coincidental.

No. 50015 'Valiant' appears for my down run to Axminster, a slow run with a Salisbury driver whose performance has been so noticeably tardy in the past that his colleagues have bestowed him with the ironic nickname 'Action Man'. I find the booking clerk, who has a similar attitude to Alan Keirl but a less pleasant way of expressing it, is absent on a visit to the dentist at the busiest time of his shift and, so far as I can ascertain, without permission. *What on earth was it with booking clerks and dentists?* Senior Railman John Cornelius, only six months out of the signalbox, is doing very well indeed but I suspect his compliance with the booking clerk's absence. If it was not an emergency, he could have gone after work. The phone has been left off the hook and I end up answering enquiries after replacing it.

Because 'Action Man' was 8min late at Axminster and there is a 20mph tsr at the foot of Seaton Bank, the up train is 13min late, having effected the booked Honiton cross. The forthcoming retiming of the 09.38 to 10.20 will reduce the impact of such a tsr. No. 50041 'Bulwark' pulls the lateness back to 11min at Sherborne where the two members of staff seem in good spirits.

My 09.10 Waterloo-Exeter down train has crossed the late-running No. 50041 at Gillingham, rendering it 8min late at Sherborne. No. 50032 'Courageous' in NSE livery and blue nameplate is in charge. The run is much sharper than my last down run and time is also regained at Yeovil Jct and Axminster making it 5½min late from there and 8min late at Honiton (after the Seaton Jct tsr) where I alight. Action Man and No. 50015 are heading home to Salisbury on the next up train, the 12.20 Exeter-Waterloo running 6min late after crossing No. 50032 at Pinhoe. A less than dynamic run loses four more minutes to Yeovil Jct. If the 11.10 from Waterloo-Exeter had been on time it would have been 1min late after waiting for us but it is reported 9min late already. It runs in 5½min late, departs 4min late and is 1½min late from Axminster, a clear demonstration of the different standards between the running of the successive down trains. I find it necessary to have a word with the guard, the second one I have addressed today, to remind him of the requirement of using a green flag to re-start the train from stations. It does not take any longer than waving one's arm: it is just sloppy. Anyone can wave an arm on a station platform saying goodbye to relatives but not many of them do it while holding a green handkerchief.

After the Seaton Jct tsr we are 4min late from Honiton with 4min recovery time to Pinhoe. There is a precautionary 70mph tsr from Crannaford to Broadclyst due to the current condition of track on this historic racing ground so we pass Exmouth Jct 40sec late. The efforts of this driver and guard have given a chance of working the cumulative delay out of the system. Then the ex-Bristol trainee driver who is under instruction is late cancelling the aws horn approaching Central and ends up 2min late at Exeter Central and 1min late at St. David's. When I approach the driver he hides his head in mock shame. "Just my luck to do that with the boss on board," he says. You cannot ask for much more than that – committed driving, and an honest mistake regretted and acknowledged.

There is an opportunity to nip down to Exmouth on the 14.42, arriving at 15.04 and a longer than usual 11min turnround. Fred Batchelor is the driver, crossing Fred Cole on the up service at Topsham and running precisely on time both ways, showing that the half-hour service that I recommended and implemented can run reliably.

After clearing the desk I go across to the panel box. Ken Shingleton has passed on a complaint about one of my ATEs not enforcing first class on the Paignton branch this afternoon. I see him and the Plymouth guard on their return at 17.46. Better dealt with by me now, rather than Alan and the Plymouth train crew manager some time in the future. There seems to be some delay in despatching the Glasgow parcels with the signals off and Red Cow barriers down. The senior railman says he was checking the guard was on board and checking the doors because of the casual attitude of some of the Post Office working, both of which could have been done without incurring delay. I then go direct to Kenn School, where Linda is teaching, to watch a production of Oliver.

Thursday 11th December 1986

Most of the morning is occupied with retirements. The first is the sad case of a 58-year-old driver with a brain tumour who is going to Bristol for an operation. Next is signalman Gilham from Chard, aged 65 with 50 years of service. What changes he has seen on the Southern since 1936 and not many for the better. Third is leading railman Taylor who used to be a goods guard but developed colour blindness and was accommodated as a signal box booking 'lad' at the huge Exeter West manual box. After it closed he took a job as cleaner in the panel box, a job which he has performed with conspicuous conscientiousness.

He is a testimony not only to management's ability to look after its staff, even if it is in an institutional fashion, but also the adaptability of members of staff who are prepared to adjust in the light of adversity. Staff who are reduced in grade due to illness retain their rate of pay minus 50p, the kind of feather-bedding some would say was typical of nationalised industries but others would claim was basic humanity. Both camps might ask why bother with the 50p reduction. I do not know the history of this but I presume it started when 50p was ten shillings and a lot higher proportion of basic pay and has not been subjected to inflationary increases. Of course, such generosity has not helped in the situation the Paignton chargeman raised recently that he was being paid less than someone who had been placed into a job two steps below his substantive grade due to illness but who is to say the Paignton chargeman might not need to avail himself of the concession someday.

At 12.36 I leave for lunch at home on the 10.10 from Paddington and go on to Teignmouth for the Harbour Commissioners' meeting and the main problem of whether the Commissioners should take over the pilotage under the provisions of the new Marine Pilotage bill which sounds to me like effective privatisation of Trinity House. What do I know? There is time to look in at Teignmouth for ten minutes on my way home. Ostensibly it is a waste of time to be a Commissioner but it keeps contact with business interests in this part of the area as every one in the room is a potential rail customer if nothing else.

Friday 12th December 1986

I arrive at work at 07.45, determined to get my desk sorted out. I spent some time last night doing a statistical analysis of the announcers' workload for the future combination of the Taunton, Exeter and Newton Abbot jobs in the panel box from May.

There are many phone calls to be made including one of over an hour to Peter Griggs, the InterCity route manager, concerning the announcers, additional stops, the travel centre review and station staffing. There are major meetings to set up concerning passenger-operated lifts *(there were none in the South West and in most other locations in those days)*, the establishment of a town centre office in Yeovil where our only presence is well out of town at both existing stations, plus rebuilding and re-development of Axminster and Exeter Central. I also try to get hold of someone who might be able to progress the potential extension of Teignmouth Quay and a private siding for an operation that would be similar to the china clay working in Cornwall.

At lunchtime Ray Thorn comes in to say he is having trouble sorting out his brother's estate. The railway has said it will not be making any calls on it but the Staff Association will not commit itself. I undertake to have a quiet word with Exeter travel centre manager and staff association local chairman

Frank Lethbridge. He says that there is no intention of making any claim but it will be early in the New Year before this can be ratified.

Alan Bell arrives to discuss a new instruction to inform LDCs there will be a 24hr notice of rest day cancellation (on the Eastern this would mean the need to work a rest day but on the Western a rest day cancelled means the same). This concession is not too troublesome for weekly-rostered staff but for guards, of which we are very short, they are in effect rostered on a daily basis it will create difficulties and inefficiencies, both in terms of staff being rostered who are not needed or, conversely, avoidable cancellations. Talking to David Thear, he responds wisely by undertaking to let us 'kick for touch' for a while.

After writing a few letters and correcting the highly inaccurate minutes of the recent TUCC meeting it is time to go home. The 09.43 from Newcastle is in platform 4 and the Fridays-only Paddington-Plymouth runs past it through platform 5. The driver for the Newcastle train is on the delayed up train from Penzance causing it to leave at 17.26. My 17.25 is in Riverside with No. 33001 which leaves from the same platform as the Newcastle 6min behind it but suffering from a track circuit failure at Dawlish and arriving 10min late.

Photo: Nos. 142015 and 142026 crossing Broadsands Viaduct on 13th December 1986 with a through B.R/Paignton & Dartmouth Railway Kingswear-Exeter Christmas shopping special.
Credit: R. W. Penny

CHAPTER 30: CHRISTMAS IS COMING

Monday 15th December 1986

The week starts with a cab ride on the stopper with Fred Batchelor again. John Beer's quiz team has been knocked out of the Great Western Society competition in the first round having been unluckily drawn against last year's winners.

This is Christmas week and I want to get round the area as much as possible. The reason is obvious but I make my plans in awe of Chris Green when he was area manager at Hull in the mid-1970s who is understood to have visited all manned locations on every shift each Christmas Eve – and there were a lot of crossing keepers to be covered. The policy puts single members of staff at remote fixed locations higher in his pecking order than the mobile train crews but the latter were likely to be seen more frequently during the year and would see a supervisor every day when signing on. One suspects Mr Green had his car driven for him, did not rely on sparse train services and had less track mileage than most current areas but still.......I think he also used to organise a small token present as well and I am sure the issue of cost would not concern him or his equally maverick Doncaster divisional manager and my former mentor Cyril Bleasdale.

My itinerary looks like taking four days and is far from covering all shifts but does not use a driver much, or road for that matter, unless unavoidable. That seems to leave today technically spare but that depends on the lack of adverse events on other days. I start with the 10.32 to Tiverton Parkway and back on the 11.00, changing to the cab of the Skipper to Exmouth and back on the same one to Topsham signal box.

Ted Swift has the kettle on as usual and Exmouth Jct fails to call attention before sending 'train out of section' for my up train. It might be Christmas but this is a box visit, the train register book has to be signed and a blind eye cannot be shown to slackness. The Exmouth Jct signalman accepts his telephone admonishment then promptly offers the next down train without calling attention. This time it is an official and recordable warning. If he cannot work to full standards while management is present, standards will fall to unacceptable levels when no one is around. *The philosophy was simple but it did not create much seasonal goodwill. How many official warnings did Chris Green hand out on his Christmas Eve tours I wonder?*

I ride up with driver Cook whom I last met on the Golden Hind. *It is a moot point whether this is more or less efficient than the privatised system of keeping HST drivers on the main line, although they have recently had a bright idea to use their spare time on local work which happened in the 1980s, was abandoned on privatisation when a different company ran the locals and ignored for the first few years of First Great Western ownership of the local trains.* I pick up the car without risking being detained in the office and drive to Honiton, then back to visit Feniton followed by Pinhoe for a discussion on green politics and Exmouth Jct where 'green badge' relief signalman shows me the 1962 Exmouth line timetable.

Back in the office at 16.00, Brian Johnson, Cross Country route manager, is on the phone to respond to my request for some stops in his trains at Torre in order to maintain a service without running as many local trains and serve local hotels. I plead that they might impede his expresses if I run my stoppers but he is adamant that he will not concede any. Eventually he allows two, one each way, the down one being a new Scarborough-Paignton aimed at cleverly serving the end-of-holiday Scarborough market and the start-of-holiday Torbay one. *Perhaps Brian should have marketed a two-centre holiday, one week at Scarborough and one at Torquay – no, the second week at Torre! If I were Brian I would have taken his stance but there can be no doubt that this is an example of sectorisation increasing costs by incurring extra mileage. I can hear my detractors crying that I am failing to see the bigger picture but the bigger picture was composed of pixels such as this.*

At the local meeting the chief topic is clerical recruitment. The issue is complicated by a phone call from Martin Sach, John Beer's opposite number at Bristol, asking for my opinion about Richard Burningham, so it looks as though he might get the Bath job. We also discuss the case of a cash office clerk who has transferred in from a peripheral rail business *(specifying which one would be unfair)*. He has previously refused a travel centre job but now says he would like one. He has already handed in his notice giving various reasons, different ones to different people – to me it was to help in his wife's business. Now he wants to withdraw his notice. If we allow him to do so we risk wasting expensive training costs and if we retain him in the cash office he might well be agitating for a move at every opportunity. At present I am minded to let his notice stand.

Ken Boobyer and I travel home together. The guard accosts me with the repair book for TSO coach No. 3919. Fault: No heat. Endorsed at Clapham Jct with no date, no signature and in pencil, "Will repair when possible." This is the same part of the industry that turned out a Waterloo set from the depot recently with the first coach without heat and the last coach without lights. No. 33031 pulls into Dawlish 2min late. *Was this state of affairs the result of sectorisation or was it caused by not having discrete repair facilities? I would probably concede the latter.*

Tuesday 16th December 1986

The main event this morning is the meeting between H.Q. and Devon County Council's engineers concerning Red Cow level crossing. We want closure or full payment for the crossing attendants. They want their bridge. Engineers would, wouldn't they? Today's meeting is to decide whether any of the plans are acceptable and not discussion of financial arrangements. All the options that are tabled use part of the main, overflow or staff car parks and fail to give access to Premier Transport which is a freight customer and a Property Board tenant. When we draw lines to show the encroachment limits with which we could live, it presents major constructional difficulties and/or circuitous pedestrian routes. The earliest available budget provision would be 1996 so perhaps it is all a bit academic. *Indeed it was, and still is, even now.*

After half an hour in town buying Christmas presents I visit the Parcels Business Machine training coach. The clerk whose resignation is hanging in the balance wants to speak to me about his position. I suspect he is expecting me to talk him into staying but he does all the talking, talks himself to a standstill and remains on notice to leave.

Bernard Norman phones from Swindon about the budget cuts. I have submitted a list of measures – 'above the line' which I will do unless instructed otherwise and 'below the line' which I will not pursue unless instructed to do so. I am relieved to hear that he wants me to do all the schemes above the line and none below it.

After a bout with the paperwork I leave at 16.30 to turn round for the Christmas dinner at Silverton, picking up Ken Boobyer and his wife. After arriving at 19.00 we enjoy a pleasant and relaxed evening, refuse coffee and scrape home for midnight.

Wednesday 17th December 1986

I am doing a round of Christmas handshakes today starting in Teignmouth at 08.45. The senior railman wonders if we could do something about amending the 03.30 signing on time for attending to the newspaper train. We could, but it would mean the introduction of a self-contained part time job. I go to Torquay and stay for over an hour. There is not much Christmas cheer around and the handshakes are strained. There is an opportunity to explain the wrongful dismissal procedures to John Hedge and reassure him that the worst we can face is a compensation payment. There can be no requirement for reinstatement. He seems surprised how calm I am at the prospect of the hearing.

Paignton is next. Both boxes, relief man Jack Eveleigh at the South and young Ian Rosewell at the North. He is thinking of applying for Par before he is displaced, as a junior man, by resignalling. It would be a good move.

Totnes follows with a pause for spaghetti on toast in the café *(before it moved to the signal box).* A sign on the wall reads, verbatim, "The cups are mine the contents are yours. My beakers get carsick, trainsick etc. Besides my name is not Rothschilde or Getty so leave them where they are." The establishment is privately owned but is this really how we want our customers to be addressed on railway premises? It is run by Olive, the mum of Totnes senior railman the likeable but roguish Colin Harmes.

There is a long and miserable rain-drenched walk to Dainton signalbox from the overbridge and through the cutting, followed by Newton Abbot. Former Teignmouth signalman, young Matthew Kinsella is training on ticket examination with leading railman Pulman. Perhaps he should be training with Terry Blackburn who banks 2½ times more money than the second person in the league table, although with a corresponding complaint ratio.

Gordon Tincombe is at Newton Abbot East, his main concern being when he will be allowed to take his golden handshake. He might be going back to Australia where he was born and he remembers the bodyline cricket series at first hand. *I think I am correct in saying that out of around one hundred signalling redundancies in the course of the whole resignalling scheme all those who wanted to stay found a job and all those who took the golden handshake wanted to do so. If there are any ex-signalmen reading this who would dispute the statement, I apologise, but this was certainly the intention and largely achieved.*

I call in at Aller Jct where Phil Mann is working, a very able young relief signalman whose parents are returning from their Long Island home for Christmas and which is also his holiday destination. It is still raining hard as I drive back to Dawlish to pick up my mail which I have had sent down from Exeter. I spend an hour going through it for anything urgent and am touched to find a photograph from railway photographer David Hunt of the Royal Train for the Duchess of Kent at Honiton. *David is still regularly having his photos published and keeping me advised of developments by occasional e-mails.*

Thursday 18th December 1986

The availability of the Yeovil Mini Metro is in doubt so I decide to do today's whole journey by car from Exeter, reaching Axminster by 08.05 for a cup of tea with the clerk who was at the dentist last time I visited. *No mention in the notes of how his absence had been resolved.* The senior railman says he has something to tell me. A member of staff is allowing a young man to operate the CCTV level crossing equipment, sometimes without supervision. This is a serious allegation that could result in dismissal. The inspectors will need to check and have a quiet word even if there is no direct proof, which will probably be no more than is needed in circumstances that are a little more complicated than can be related.

At Chard Jct signalman Foster is on duty, having been made redundant at Athelney before transferring here after a brief period on platform duties at Taunton. A tough Mancunian, he has no problem with the 04.45 start of his new job every other week. My arrival at Crewkerne coincides with a routine station visit by Yeovil supervisor Terry Gale so the three members of staff available attend to the 07.00 from Waterloo which arrives 3min late and departs a triumphal 2½min late. Guard Albert Reid is taken aback. *Albert's brother George was a supervisor, later train crew manager, at Exeter. Albert went to be a driver manager with a freight company and retired in about 2013 as a train manager with First Great Western at Exeter.*

Yorkshireman Vince Dyson is working Maiden Newton box on the Castle Cary-Pen Mill-Dorchester West-Weymouth line and in his usual pugnacious mood, but only in a Yorkshire manner and one that I understand. The S&T are working so I slurp Vince's tea and move on.

Next comes Yeovil Jct station and signalbox, then the same at Pen Mill. Sherborne booking office has a visiting taxi driver who has to be ushered out as I approach, then it is a 90minute drive back to the office. John Beer and Ken advise me on when to implement the travel centre alterations, January 19th being chosen. We have heard that one of the Newton Abbot clerks who went last year in a redundancy offer to 'Over 55s' might be interested in the part time job there, which would save time and expense, but with the disadvantage of favouring convenience over Equal Opportunities' best practice.

The 17.25 tonight is a luxurious affair with Nos. 31406 and 31404 in multiple. I am not sure how we have acquired them but they provide more heat than the normal Class 33.

Friday 19th December 1986

The final pre-Christmas trips today, starting with the 09.25 to Taunton for the usual round of visits but when I reach Taunton East I am shocked, disappointed and worried to find that the last supervisory visit here was mine on the 4th of December. I ask supervisor Wally Pipe (the Taunton supervisors are primarily responsible for the box visits for an explanation and withdraw the visits book for Bernard to follow up. I intercept the pilot on its way to Fairwater Yard and visit Silk Mill returning to Exeter in the cab of the 10.10 from Paddington to Exeter with drivers Gage and Cole. It is a good atmosphere and we run into St. David's 2½min early. I mean to get the car for a Barnstaple line trip but I am delayed by 30min before getting away.

Crediton is a duty stop with a particularly difficult signalman on duty. Bill Butt is at Eggesford, over 65 and staying on until box closure. I also call in to see Harry Toulson in the station house. With heart trouble and needing a new hip, he is in a poor state and has elected to take resettlement next year. I am offered tea and mince pies laced with a dose of rum, which is probably safer than mince pies and tea dosed with the rum, before driving to Barnstaple. The staff here have too much time on their hands on the remains of the modern railway. *It is probably only now that I appreciate how close the good old days were in their minds whereas the heyday of the local branch lines seemed like ancient history to me at that time.* Morale is certainly low. The lighting in the signalbox is causing trouble, the clerks do not like their new rosters and the parcels office staff say that one man is inadequate on the Saturday morning before Christmas.

I drive back as quickly as possible, arriving at 17.05, 70min from Barnstaple and the fastest Skippers are booked in 55min. *This has deteriorated in recent years with more station stops, better frequency and no signalman key token signalling requiring a phone call instead of being handed a token but the road time has probably followed suit.* The same two 31s are in harness again tonight, 9min late following a 16min late 14.35 Fridays-only Paddington-Plymouth.

CHAPTER 31: SANTA VISITS THE EXMOUTH LINE

Sunday 21st December 1986

The guards have been organising Santa Specials on the Exmouth line. We have advised them on what can be done but they have done all the work so I will be looking in on the operation.

On arrival at Dawlish station, I find the booking office closed with senior railman Joe Cockram booking tickets from the upstairs office *(now not used, possibly on security grounds, but it seems a waste).* The relief clerk is travelling down on the 13.15 train instead of the 12.50. Joe says the clerk has missed his connection, changing slightly to it being his lift that has let him down. The clerk's face drops when he finds me waiting for him and tells me he is late because his wife is ill. Perhaps all these reasons are not necessarily mutually exclusive but just one would be more convincing. I request that he submits a report and catch my train. At Exeter, a passenger is asking for the train to be held for his son coming over the bridge but it is dispatched straight away, 1min late on public times and 1min early on working times; an awkward decision that might have been different if it had been a last service or long wait for the next. Fortunately the child gets the full brunt of the passenger's criticism.

A guard's compartment has been fitted out as a grotto and guard Phil Jeyes is acting as Santa. Phil certainly has the right profile for the role and enhances his normally droll personality to fit his more jovial role. He plays the part so well that he cannot even be tempted out of his den by the Kentucky Fried Chicken that is being passed around. The staff are volunteering, Steve Drabwell driving and the guard *(Brian Cocks, I think)* has 'deeley boppers', which extend and squeak through an extension tube from his mouth, and a monkey glove puppet.

The train is half full on the way down to Exmouth and more than full on the way back. Everyone seems to be enjoying the trip but one family fails to alight at Polsloe Bridge as they did not know how to operate the doors so I offer to drive them back in the car. I get back to Dawlish at 15.45 and decide to let the clerk off the hook. He has been at the long service awards recently and I know his wife has mobility difficulties. It must be the spirit of Santa getting to me. The clerk says he has been worrying all afternoon. He is told that I do not appreciate being told different stories and it will be disposed of by a written warning. The post will be withdrawn on winter Sundays next year.

Monday 22nd December 1986

Christmas greetings are confined nearer to home today with visits to Riverside, the station, travel centre and the panel box.

Tuesday 23rd December 1986

More visits around the station before taking the 10.43 Exeter-Glasgow relief. Well, that was the intention but passenger loadings are heavy and, the 09.25 Plymouth-Paddington is losing time on its way up. The Glasgow relief empty stock is running behind it and looks like arriving at about 10.51 with the parent train 5min behind it. If we window label and seat reserve the relief, the Glasgow will overtake it and the relief risks being behind it all the way with the parent train overcrowded and the relief empty.

I undertake to do the labelling en route so the relief with No. 47660 is in the platform for just 3min but stands outside Taunton for 7min as the London incurs 8min overtime. The supervisor has not appeared on the up side to assist or redeployed any of his down side staff so overtime is inevitable despite the best efforts of the two members of staff present. Perhaps this is poor morale with the threat to their jobs and perhaps it is not surprising that we will not be that much worse off without them.

My return is on the 10.10 Paddington which is 2min late at Exeter after a good 22min 54sec run. There is time to do a round of the office and then meet Linda on the 15.06 for the Christmas break. A bomb scare is in full swing at Bristol but we are just 3min late at Sheffield where I have my first run on a sprinter, a Class 150 to Leeds which is disappointingly noisy, rather like being transported inside a vacuum cleaner. At Wakefield I see my first Class 144 and a Metro-Camm set converted to a parcels unit before travelling to Huddersfield on a more conventional 2-car 720hp Calder Valley which is no slower and certainly no noisier than the sprinter despite the window rattle.

Wednesday 24th December 1986

A visit to my grandmother in Southport is a regular feature of our 'pre-Christmas' but one that rarely goes smoothly. Last year we came back through Liverpool at around 17.00 on Christmas Eve which we found extremely threatening on the walk from Central to Lime Street. So this year we opt for the new combination of a local Huddersfield-Manchester Victoria with a similar Manchester-Southport, and a return journey to match, a dire 2½hrs for 60miles with 25 stops. I feel unsafe with the absence of AWS on the Diggle route with the manual signalling and the unit each way, Metro-Camm 53237/53320 was not so equipped either. *My notes are unequivocal about this but I find it hard to believe that this was the situation in those days.*

Monday 29th December 1986

After the festivities I rise late for a trip out and catch the 11.12 from Huddersfield to Sheffield being delayed 10min at Penistone crossing the down train. No. 47659 is on the Newcastle-Plymouth full and standing so I alight at Derby for the following St. Pancras HST which is much quieter. It stands time for 7min at Leicester and nips up to London 9min early.

At King's Cross No. 47503 is at the head of a rake of declassified Mark 2s on a relief to Newcastle. We have a special stop at Stevenage so it runs with spirit and reaches 93mph before Hatfield. We go slow line at Huntingdon for the 15.50 King's Cross-Leeds to pass, diving out onto the main line to get into Peterborough for the 16.00 to pass. So far, so good, but we stand outside Grantham and then 5min at Newark Crossing which makes us 10min late at Doncaster. I have 19min for my Huddersfield connection at York so I should be O.K. but we grind to a halt at Moss and stand for 15min while an up oil train is examined, arriving at York 27min late having passed the outbound Liverpool at Holgate Bridge. It is not too long to wait before the 19.24 departure though, with No. 47423 and an average run 3min late at Huddersfield.

CHAPTER 32: PROBLEMS AT PARSON'S TUNNEL

Thursday 1st January 1987

I suspect today will be relatively light for travelling so we decide to return home via Stockport. The 10.55 Manchester Piccadilly to Plymouth HST is starting from Birmingham with a special 10.55 to Birmingham. There is nothing in the Bank Holiday booklet to suggest it might have no first class, but indeed it does not as a Class 304 turns up, vintage around 1959. It loses time intermediately but regains much of it at stations, arriving Birmingham New Street 4min late with the HST waiting across the platform. Mr Poynter joins at Bristol on his way to visit his parents in Exeter, where we arrive on time as usual nowadays on the NW/SW axis.

Friday 2nd January 1987

No crises at work so we have another day out. Cheltenham and London are the candidates and we decide on the 09.33 Paignton to Paddington relief running in the Exmouth dmu path. The loco is No. 50031 'Hood' on five coaches and being driven with great gusto, even after the Exeter driver change. 15min 19sec from Exeter to Whiteball is good, as is 35min 9sec from Taunton to Westbury. Loco hauled trains are limited to 95mph on the Western Region except on the main lines between Acton and Reading, in a little known sectional appendix instruction, and the driver is not taking any liberties with a maximum just short of 98mph. An early departure from Reading with the parent HST train on our tail and a 26min 13sec run gives a 12min early arrival. Amongst other activities, I visit the prototype Deltic in the Science Museum before returning on the 17.45 Paddington-Penzance 'Golden Hind'. It is a disappointing run with heavy checks from Maidenhead to Reading and Kintbury to Bedwyn. We are stopped outside Taunton with the 13.18 Fridays Only York-Plymouth ahead. It is struggling with No. 31441 in charge. The Hind overtakes it at Silk Mill loop and the relief is some 20min behind the HST at Exeter with Exeter supervisors having arranged for a Class 47 to re-engine the underpowered Class 31. The 20.10 stopper goes out in front of it after some fiddling around with the doors.

Saturday 3rd January 1987

A short shopping trip into Exeter on the Paignton-Manchester and a Skipper up the bank, returning on the 14.28 from St. David's. I am waylaid by many members of staff as well as Geoff Lendon, a rail enthusiast who has had an unsatisfactory railtour to East Grinstead of all places. Geoff is the Dawlish cricket umpire so best to keep right side of him in case he gets a twitchy forefinger when I am batting.

Monday 5th January 1987

Back to routine after such a long break with a start on the 07.08 and No. 50047 'Swiftsure'. The paper pile is not too high, probably reflecting holidays at headquarters. Mike Hodson has given us two large bean bags so Tony Crabtree's advice is taken on the best way of getting them to Dawlish by Rail Parcels. The chief operational events have featured three broken rails and, while I am discussing them with Bernard Price, there is word of another one near Dawlish that was found at 09.25. He rounds up Bill Mardon and heads for the site, arranging for single line working staff to be called out as he descends the steps.

At 10.30 trains are still at a stand with Exeter's 09.25 to Paddington halted at Parson's Tunnel. I go to see the St. David's duty manager and then head for the panel. The T.V. screens are not showing any 'minutes late' figures and the special screens are showing seat reservation instructions. I put this right and organise free hot drinks for delayed passengers. The 07.25 from Paddington does a crew change with the up London at Teignmouth before the up train is backed through the crossover at 11.03. I set up the delay predictions on the screens which are likely to be run 'wrong line' before the 08.50 Paddington is allowed down. The figures look terrible: 145min late, 130, 110, 105, 85 and the last one, the 10.45 Paignton-Manchester, 85min late again.

The up trains have to back across again at Dawlish Warren but at least they can use main line signals without as much clipping of points as before re-signalling. Bernard is on site and predicts a resumption of normal working at 12.30 but then says it is likely to be later as the welding equipment is playing up. It looks as though we will be able to run the six up trains and then three down trains before the 09.33 Penzance presents itself at Teignmouth around 12.39. The six up trains arrive at Exeter St. David's 145, 129, 109, 101, 81 and 87min late just to prove what can be done in situations where so often trains seem to be going backwards on the cctv screens. Times set up at 11.05 were still valid at 12.57. Further delay occurs to the York at Taunton while train crews are sorted out. The delay has been heavier than it might have been but the implementation of single line working 95min after the incident was reported reflected the need to run down trains and the difficulty of withdrawing trains from mid-section rather than starting from being in Teignmouth station.

In the middle of the incident there has been a call from the up side catering supervisor to say that some passengers were coming round three times for free drinks. She asks when they are going to be stopped and then relates the details of a trip she had experienced coming back from Plymouth once. I had told her I did not have time to listen and she should just get on with serving the passengers' well-justified requirements. I seek out the young catering manager who apologises and continues by saying all the right things. The arrangement went better than previously though.

At 17.20 I return a call from a lady who has insisted on speaking to me personally about being refused tickets at family railcard prices. The new Network South East posters show me with a phone in my hand saying I am on the line so I can hardly say I am unavailable! At least the time of the call shows I am around after 17.00. The passenger has lost her temporary card and cannot remember getting her permanent one. It is a complicated story but it could have been dealt with as well, indeed a good deal better, by Tony Hill or John Beer at 12.00 but the customer would not let them be involved.

Tuesday 6th January 1987

Ken Shingleton is on the phone at 08.35 to discuss yesterday's events. At 10.15 I chair a meeting with the regional telecommunications and civil engineers about replacing switchboard equipment. My objectives are to improve internal office efficiency, reduce cash office costs and improve their sub-standard accommodation. The technical departments feel there is a viable scheme and go away to investigate budgetary implications. This is followed by an hour with Alan Bell on train crew developments.

To Bernard's chagrin, Ken Shingleton has decided that he wants a report concerning yesterday's single line working *(so when I say nowadays that if single line working took longer than an hour to implement 'in my day' someone wanted to know why, it is not an exaggeration)*. Ken also wants to know more about the 13.20 from Newcastle delaying the Golden Hind, having itself been delayed by the 16.45 Paddington terminating at Newton Abbot running on one power car. Ken seems to think we should have done something differently but any such arrangements are clearly a Control function. If we start interfering they soon tell us to get their permission. I tell Ken that this is not the first time that there has been veiled criticism over not regulating the Newcastle behind the Hind (despite the former's need for Cornish connections) but there is no guideline. I add that Control should be answerable to the regional operating manager for what has happened if he is not satisfied. Ken goes very quiet and I am unable to tell whether this is because he is annoyed or accepts my point.

John Curley rings to take the Yeovil town centre travel centre site a step further and then spend over an hour with a guard to discuss his application for management training and half an hour with booking clerk Paul Scanes about his similar aspirations. The guard is a maverick applicant; it is not that we don't need mavericks but he does not have a rounded background *(I think he went away and became a driver).* Paul Scanes came close last year but fell at the final hurdle for the marketing version of the scheme that now exists. He should be a strong candidate this year but I guess I would probably back Nigel Gooding who has more edge, awkwardness if you like, than Paul. Our other potential applicant is second man Eddy whom I do not know well enough to assess just yet. Odds are none will be appointed *(but Nigel was in fact eventually selected).*

At 16.30, a Mr Laurence, on behalf of out-of-town shopping developers at Digby on the Exmouth line, comes to discuss the merits of his planning application in preparation for a forthcoming public hearing. We discuss our services and costs for a potential new station plus the strengths and weaknesses of competitive schemes. He leaves at 17.15, just as Brian Scott phones to discuss the forthcoming Paignton Dart Valley meeting on Friday leaving me with a bit of homework to do for his briefing. The 17.25 is 15min late due to a 'shortage of drivers' for shunting out the stock so I catch it by the skin of my teeth before investigating the detail.

Wednesday 7th January 1987

An early start with No. 50040 'Leviathan'. The set looks reasonable but one coach is very dirty with a toilet that seems to have been out of order for ten days. The 'Skipper' position is that we have 9 for 9 diagrams but we have one short at Exeter and one surplus at Newton Abbot so a Class 33 on two coaches has been sent to Barnstaple. The BRB stock controller has demanded that the two coaches must be attached to the 06.35 Bristol-Plymouth but this would cause overtime and put it in excess of its timing load so I have grounds for refusal. I consult the Control duty manager who agrees. *If he had not done so I would probably have phoned Ken Shingleton to point out that punctuality was being compromised, having still refused to attach them.*

I am determined to square up the paperwork this week but my efforts are interrupted by a discussion with area civil engineer Peter Warren concerning the arbitrary cuts I have imposed on his weekend work programme engine power to meet my super-imposed budget reductions. We harmonise our figures after I have exercised a little 'discretion' as instructed by Swindon. Peter remains short of one turn but squeezes a job to make ends meet. Ken Shingleton calls it 'constructive tension' but from my viewpoint it looks more like the people who do the work carrying the can. *H.Q. imposed cuts come back to bite the general manager this way if the civil engineer cannot work.* Next week our offer will be 12 three-crew turns for an aspiration of 18-22. The difference is at least £1,500 on the budget.

Next, I write Bernard's report for the single line working and save him an hour or so. I am not sure if he is glad or not, but the job is completed. He wants to take some blame for not withdrawing the HST from Parson's Tunnel earlier but he was justifiably hoping the break would be made fit for it to pass at caution.

The clerical LDC is playing awkward over signing the minutes of the travel centre review discussions. John Beer is concerned that he feels to have been 'set-up' but I see it more as the staff side wanting the minutes altered to reflect what they should have said not what was actually said. I can play awkward too though. I go to see the staff side secretary to tell him off for sending me TSSA literature in B.R. envelopes and find him making a long distance external phone call. Of course, he was going to pay and I make sure he does. Later that afternoon I have a meeting to ensure that the aspects of the review that save money are implemented immediately and the concessions that cost us money are delayed until the end of March.

While in this mood I have time to ask Swindon why an empty stock was sent from Penzance to Oxford on the same day one was sent from Old Oak Common to Penzance. I have examined the possible reasons but can see no justification. This is the same organisation that imposes budget cuts and then expects specials and short notice moves to be crewed out of thin air.

At 17.02 I meet Bernard in the corridor. We have been told that the 16.03 Paignton to Exmouth has killed someone in Parson's Tunnel. That's two incidents this week. Will there be the third to come? 17.00-18.00 is a busy time on that stretch. Alan Bell and Derek Old are on their way and Bernard and I set off for Teignmouth in case another episode of single line working is necessary. Perhaps I should stay at Exeter to ensure sensible decisions are made there but that would look like ducking out. We arrive at Teignmouth at 17.36 and find nothing has yet moved and then reach Parson's at 17.44 to discover the body of a 20yr old male being put in an ambulance on a stretcher. I avert my eyes. Alan Bell is in the cab of a Class 47 on the Glasgow parcels moving into the tunnel and normal working is resumed at 17.46. This is where multiple aspect signalling pays off and where having a capacity far higher than demanded by the timetable allows a quick recovery from disruption. There is an up train every couple of minutes until 18.10. The 17.25 stopper has been cancelled as the stock was used to cover the Cornish Riviera at 11.30 because the HST was delayed by another broken rail, this time at Gwinear Road in Cornwall, for 150min. The train had been stopped by a permanent way staff member, coming to a stand straddling the break.

Our special with the 17.25 stock was supposed to come straight back but had not done so. Plan 'B' was to work short-formed on the Exmouth branch and a single Class 142 to cover the 17.25 but the two class 142s that had been involved in the fatality had required examination at Exeter. Driver Jim Lear had continued to Exeter and been relieved there. Had I remained at Exeter I suspect I would have influenced duty manager Vernon Baseley to hold the Newcastle-Penzance at Exeter until 17.25 with Dawlish and Teignmouth extra stops.

Instead, the regulars were supplied with an 18.00 bus that would have been pushed to beat the 18.18 train – but provided extra capacity.

Back at Teignmouth station I watch the 15.45 Paddington cruise through 2min late and the up line is back to normal. We are grateful to the police for moving the body immediately. It is unusual for this to start before the railway representatives have arrived but the word is that neither the police nor the ambulance staff fancied hanging about in the tunnel. 50min from impact to normal working resumption inside a tunnel at an inaccessible location more than counterbalances our performance earlier in the week…. but there is always scope for improvement.

Thursday 8th January 1987

Another early morning, with No. 50011 'Centurion' on the 07.08. We are back to Class 142 shortages with one being covered by loco and the coaches we could not manage to attach to the 06.35 yesterday. A final onslaught on the paperwork precedes trying to get out on my rounds, making sure I write a letter of appreciation to the police for their work last night which might also go some way to smoothing future incidents. I do some preparation for tomorrow's meeting with the deputy general manager about the Paignton-Kingswear Railway. I see driver S.R. Rogers on a Class 50 for the 12.20 Exeter-Waterloo stock and tell him I have obtained him a Network South East tie as requested, if he calls into the office some time.

I arrange a meeting with Mr Boyne of Teignmouth Quay and Railfreight over the possibility of china clay returning to rail, speak to Vernon Baseley about last night's incident and career paths, and travel centre manager Frank Lethbridge over a collection point for business reservations. By 16.30 the inbox contents have moved across to the outbox and there is just one phone call to make. I have been trying to make contact with the person who is supposed to have been involved with stopping the HST near the broken rail last Monday. Bernard has been unable to find this Mr Woodhouse of 'Summerlands' in the phone book but the original document shows his name as Whitehouse. Holcombe resident Phil Shepherd says he has never heard of Summerlands but there is a Sunnylands chalet park near Smugglers' Gap. We were there last night! I drive down there and discover Mr Whitehouse is a winter resident of a holiday chalet. He returns from walking his dog looking unkempt and not wearing a coat despite the cold. I introduce myself, thank him and hand him my card. He looks 'dropped on' when I offer him a first class return ticket to anywhere in Britain.

Friday 9th January 1987

I arrive by car at 08.00. We are two Class 142s short again. The meeting with Brian Scott and the Dart Valley is to set the contribution the private railway is expected to make to the re-signalling at Paignton South. With overheads, our bill is £37,750. DVR director Mr Evans and manager Barry Cogar profess to be staggered. We talk round the problems and the options open to them and then a pie-in-the sky review of all property in the area and another multi-million pound redevelopment scheme which does not meet our 12 months timescale so we switch to discussing staged payments. In my opinion the essential matter is the avoidable cost to us by not signalling the DVR. They should then certainly be charged the whole amount plus a contribution to power supplies etc. The options of no connection, truncation at Goodrington or financing their own installation to the satisfaction of the Department of transport are unattractive ones. They retire to consult their lawyers and we will assess our final position on paper, one that appears to be fully covered by the Running Powers Agreement if the decision to re-signal is deemed reasonable.

Mr Scott takes me to lunch and grills me on relationships with the sectors, management & supervisory development and a few other matters. I see him off on the Paddington train along with chief controller Ray Spackman who has been investigating Monday's delays. I then discuss with John Beer whether we would want to run winter Sunday steam trains using Dart Valley stock. Pathing would be tight at the times we would want to run and arrangements could be disrupted by engineering work. Perhaps Paignton-Newton Abbot would be more sensible but would it be attractive enough to make money? Would it be revenue generative or abstractive? Is it worth the management time, attention and opportunity cost of not attending to something else?

With a clear desk I catch the 16.22 to Newton Abbot leaving 2min early on working times and running in 18min 44sec *(which was a good time then and is often exceeded even now)*. I chat with supervisor Ernie Underhill before catching No. 50030 'Repulse' back to Dawlish. At 17.00 Newton Abbot Platform 3 has a Class 50 on Paignton-Exeter Mark1s and Platform 4 has the same combination on a Penzance-Bristol. Mine is a school train but not too rowdy, first class containing an overflow (permitted and controlled by the ATE) due to heavy Torre-Newton Abbot loadings and arrival is ½min early.

CHAPTER 33: SNOW CHAOS AND INSUBORDINATION

Monday 12th January 1987

The weather is bitterly cold this morning. The 07.00 News is warning people not to travel in Kent due to snow. I arrive on Dawlish station to find the 07.08 to Exeter and the 07.20 Penzance train both 11min late. There have been problems at Taunton with late arrival of empty stocks from Bristol but most other trains are on time. We are short of three Skippers but that is another problem.

No. 50044 *Exeter*, inappropriately in NSE livery, is on the 07.20 now 8½min late. I ride with driver Cross to Newton Abbot as the first hint of daylight appears over Hay Tor revealing the River Teign frozen in its shallows. *The writing up of the diary has sadly coincided with the death of the genial Roy Cross, in his late 80s.* There is time for a quick tour. After supervisor Harry Perrett has the graffiti removed which I asked supervisor Underhill to clean last Friday, I catch the 08.09 to Taunton. We would have been smack on time at Taunton but there is a problem in the single up platform. A Class 33 push-pull fitted loco has been provided on Mark 1 stock vice a dmu. It cannot be coupled up so we are allowed into the otherwise disused up main platform under emergency derogation that we have, with guard John Pearman making a suitable warning announcement. *One benefit of privatisation has been the re-commissioning of both main line platforms which British Rail could not afford to do, particularly as the already sub-standard platform height was worsened by the track being raised by re-ballasting for 100mph running.*

I award supervisor Bob Johnson's First Aid long service medal and wait for the 09.46 back to Exeter for my 10.15 appointment but it is 52min late. This is not a problem as I was aware that the H.Q. team I am meeting is also on the delayed train. It has encountered snow, a hot axle-box alarm and a points' failure at Yatton. A tamper has preceded us to Exeter which cannot be relied upon to activate track circuits at Hele auto half-barriers, an arrangement that requires the next train, ours in this case, to be cautioned. We are 60min late as a result. It has been agreed to re-install treadles to prevent such delays but heels are being dragged.

My meeting is with an admin review team concerning future reorganisations and sector relationships. *Undeterred by operational problems, reorganisation seemed to be more important and a cancellation on my part would have been seen as uncooperative.* It is revealed that proposals will be published next month and there is even a rumour that it could involve the creation of extra regions. *It seemed unlikely and it was indeed unfounded.* At least it seems that there is no intention to take the Yeovil area from me.

Meanwhile, the train service has deteriorated into total disarray. 100min late from Waterloo, 85min late from Penzance, 54min late from Paddington but Devon is an island in a sea of snow. I spend much of the afternoon on the phone to engineers arranging frost precaution cover at key locations, more than the adverse weather forecast of severe frost would normally merit. Civil engineer decides to cancel squadron tamping tonight and tomorrow night which will release some of my staff too.

One of Peter's assistants, Arnold Knight comes on to talk about the arbitrary cuts I have placed on their weekend engine power. It looks as though we will get an improvement over and above our plan, partly through the adverse weather.

At 16.00, the area team meets to assess the position. It is reported that the budget outturn is now £20k better as opposed to £18k worse and the Sundays restriction might make it £30k better. We also discuss plans for summer working and consultation timescales. I was intending to go home for lunch and stay late but I go home at normal time to relax in case the weather situation deteriorates further, with a heavy snowfall, sea wall collapse or other Act of God.

The operating team is struggling but mainly processing the disruption occurring elsewhere. My train is No. 47556 on ten including two newspaper vans, required back at Waterloo for their 01.40 departure that Vernon had borrowed to accompany a passenger coach on the Barnstaple line replacing a dmu. We still have only five 142s for traffic because we have sent one to Yeovil vice our 14.17 departure, the down train having been exceptionally late, and is making its way back. Another has failed with a coolant leak, causing the cancellation of the 16.15 to Exmouth. There are two track circuit failures on the sea wall, causing my train a 7min delay.

Tuesday 13th January 1987

Arriving at Dawlish station, much muffled up against the elements, I choose to catch the 07.08 to Exeter at 07.18 rather than the 07.20 down train at 07.23. All is well until we pass Powderham and get a signal check, stopping 100 yards short of the red signal with the locomotive dead. The driver is in the engine room and emerges triumphant having reset a trip-out and we are then cautioned for the track circuit failure that has caused the stop.

With Bernard Price on leave, I settle into being Area Operations Manager instead of Area Manager and make arrangements for some YTS trainees to clean carriage windows on the platform as the freezing weather has rendered the automatic carriage washers inoperable. More liason with the engineers follows and it transpires that two of our three track circuit failures have been caused by broken rails. We can pass over these at 20mph and welding is arranged for 02.00 the following morning. The third failure has been caused by short-circuiting through frozen sea water in the ballast at Dawlish. Further investigation with H.Q. reassures me that plans for replacement of the track circuits with axle-counters (well before these were commonplace) are well advanced.

At lunchtime I retire to the panel box and wander around the station. The 14.17 is formed of a Class 33/0 on a 4TC set. Our drivers are not trained on the 4TC controls, and this is not a push-pull fitted Class 33/1 anyway, so the loco runs round to the Waterloo end. The 09.10 from Waterloo has been waylaid en route west and Salisbury has done well to find this solution.

Back in the office I square up the desk, discuss summer car parking policy with John Beer and await the arrival of the snow. The local weather forecast says we will definitely have snow by this time tomorrow. No. 50020 'Revenge' is on the 17.25

Wednesday 14th January 1987

Snow starts to fall as we leave Dawlish with the 07.08. Exeter is again short of units and things seem to be falling apart at Bristol. Much against my better judgement I catch the 08.11 to Axminster for a meeting about station improvements. People had rung up yesterday to see if the meeting was still on and I had told them it was, so I had better go. Driver Ellis is the driver who, intentionally or otherwise, seems to resent me and confines himself to minimal formalities. I really cannot be bothered to use energy handling this so ride in the train.

Axminster clerk Derek Grayer provides a welcome cup of coffee. The architect and area civil engineer turn up but the NSE and Property Board representatives fail. We make sufficient progress for me to be able to start an evaluation of a major improvement of the existing building. We go to Honiton by road, as conditions deteriorate, for a flying visit to confirm some structural alterations there and then proceed to Exeter Central where we intend to re-start the improvement scheme in the foyer that InterCity has refused to sponsor but which NSE is now keen to support. *One benefit of privatisation and a big step forward compared to the closure of booking facilities which I immediately deleted from the budget cuts when I arrived here in 1983.*

There is considerable disruption, especially to trains from the east and the first two down HSTs both need loco-assistance to proceed over the Devon Banks. Despite the excellence of our shunters, they cannot do much with equipment that is badly designed and even more badly maintained. The rolling stock technician has to be called to fix the drawbar on the first HST's front power car. He eventually gets the front flap open but then we cannot pull out the extension piece which is frozen up. A few lusty hammer blows coax it into action. The story is the same on the second set.

In the panel box there is good co-ordination between the signallers and the civil engineering staff concerning the freeing of points. We have no heaters at Exeter as statistics did not justify their provision. The density of trains means that there is little scope to reduce the number of points being worked and the need to clear platforms means we need access to both New Yard and West Yard. I make a mental note to consider using Riverside more in such situations as run round movements there do not need point detection, but the risk of derailment from points not fitting-up is greater. This is avoidable but the problem is that we would lose shunters for longer that way.

Late running is now serious and at 13.20 we receive the dire news that the 12.20 Exeter-Waterloo is a failure at Axminster with its brakes seized on. With the worsening state of the roads, and minimal maintenance staff within 80miles of the location, I have visions of a long-term blockage and a stranded train. As I start to liaise with control, Yeovil supervisor Gale (working a double shift because his relief Vic Hull, who lives at Langport, cannot get in) rings to say the 12.20's driver has freed the brakes using a crowbar. We breathe again.

By late afternoon we are really struggling. The 16.47 local to Paignton is cancelled. All moves are taking far too long. The 16.35 from Waterloo rolls in at 17.45 but it is 18.40 before we can clear it, run round, find an empty platform and send it back an hour late. Projected delays from the north are now 4hrs and Bristol seems to have ceased to function entirely.

John Beer comes out to relieve me at 20.30 and I wait for the 19.40 arrival from Barnstaple, expected at 20.45 to form the 20.10 to Dawlish. It arrives as expected but the horns on the front car are not working. The only replacement is a Class 142 on one engine, a real hostage to fortune. This is a real problem, if a silly one, but my mind goes to the three permanent ways staff who were killed at Severn Tunnel Jct in a blizzard last year. I know there are no snow clearance workers between Exeter and Newton Abbot and the points have been set for the main line at Dawlish Warren. Normally they would have been set for the platforms but winter use of the station is so low it would have been illogical to delay all trains by an extra four minutes or so on their behalf.

I suggest to the relieving driver that if he could see a way to go, I would ride in the rear power car and sound the rear horn continuously if he buzzed me on the intercom. This is entirely irregular so I will go through to Newton Abbot. Arriving safely at our destination we return immediately with railway staff on board. We have conveyed the night turn Newton Abbot East signaller to work and stop at the box to take the late turn signaller home to Exeter. I drop off at Dawlish, getting home at 22.10.

Thursday 15th January 1987

The 07.08 is miraculously on time but has to stand 15min outside St. David's with a points' failure. Driver Whittle is also going to work on this train and is remarkably philosophical about the delays he might encounter, saying he will 'take things as they come'. Tony Crabtree has relieved John Beer. There are six dmus operating but three have only one engine. One is struggling away on the Paignton shuttle and the other two are coupled to good sets making just four local trains in all. We reduce the Exmouth service to hourly, maintain the Barnstaple services and cancel the 07.52 to Penzance. A special has left Bristol for Plymouth, expected at about 08.40 and covering both the 07.52 and 08.20 departures. Worst of all, the 17.09 from yesterday evening rolls in 16hrs late! This receives extra-special media attention and I wonder why someone has not 'terminated' it en route and called this a special. Apparently six trains were lost between Bristol Parkway and Temple Meads at one time yesterday evening.

Driver Colin Pulleyblank is on his way home having signed on at 14.20 yesterday for a Paddington train via Bristol to work the 20.15 back but, by the time he reached his destination, it had already left. He got back to Chippenham at 00.50 but did not reach Bristol until 09.20. Gas supply to the point heaters is said to have failed but deeper questions need to be asked.

I go to the panel box at 10.00 and have a cup of tea with signalling inspector Bill Mardon. On the box operating floor there is a flap going on. They want to re-platform the 07.25 Paddington to Penzance into No. 3 but they cannot find Vernon Baseley to give permission despite using every means possible. A few weeks ago Paul Silvestri had pointed out that his operational planning was sometimes disrupted by ad hoc replatforming by the signalling staff without his knowledge, hence the instruction not to do so without the supervisor being told. It is suggested that I could authorise it but I decline. The suggestion misses the point entirely and my agreement would be no different from the signallers pleasing themselves. I try to phone Vernon on his normal number and he answers first time. The move to Platform 3 is set up and the station announcer, who sits at the rear of the box, is informed.

As I move forward to sign the occurrence sheets that are the modern equivalent of train register books with one at each operating position, I hear a remark made behind me from the announcer. He is an explosive character who falls out with everyone, especially station staff seeking train running information. He is also secretary of the station LDC. The remark is loud enough for all four signallers plus technicians to hear.
"*Expletive deleted* college kids who think they can run the railway and can't."

I immediately realise it would be easier for me to pretend I had not heard it and even easier to pretend it was directed purely at Vernon, who shares a mutual dislike of the announcer. On the other hand, perhaps the signallers think it is aimed at me and that I will take such insubordination this time and therefore whenever they want to chance their arm. In such circumstances, a quiet word to put him right as I would have done in private will not be satisfactory. Even if the remark had been aimed at Vernon, it was a most destructive remark when we are trying to maintain morale in difficult circumstances.

"Stop what you are doing and come with me now," I say, trying to sound icy. I lead the way through to the signalling inspector's office and request Bill Mardon to leave.

"Was that remark directed at me," I ask the announcer.

A reply saying, "Oh, certainly not!" would help. I get almost the opposite.

"At anyone who wants to pick it up," he replies. I know the announcer well enough to know he would be unlikely to back down even in the face of the possible consequences so I give him a second chance and repeat the question.

"Not entirely," he replies, retreating slightly. I push it further.

"Does that mean partially?" I query.

"If you like," he replies in a surly manner standing his ground.

"In that case I am sending you home for that remark. Report to my office at 09.00 tomorrow morning."

He says nothing, collects his things and goes.

I tell the 'back desk' (supervising) signaller Ken Snell that the announcer has been sent home and the job will be covered as soon as possible. Tony Crabtree is located, who rustles up an announcer and keeps the customer information screens going himself.

Back in the office I inform personnel manager Ken Boobyer about the events and then Ray Long, the LDC chairman. He knows already because the announcer's first stop was Ray's mail sorting office to demand that the staff should be called together to vote for an immediate strike. Ray says he told the announcer that the area manager can send people home if he thinks it necessary and will not get the staff together unless proper procedures have not been followed. I am rather surprised and extremely relieved. Whatever the circumstances, H.Q. never looks kindly on a stoppage, especially when we are trying to keep the railway functioning. After the event, the reasons never withstand scrutiny in comparison with the consequences and those in charge always think they would have handled it differently.

Accordingly, I tip off Swindon operations officer Ken Shingleton and regional personnel manager Ken Beresford. Since the announcer is a staff representative I also make a call to the National Union of Railwayman (NUR) local organiser. Next job is to gather my ammunition. Signaller Ken Snell is asked for his report to confirm the circumstances of the remark. I also review the papers on my desk concerning a complaint by travel centre staff that the announcer had been 'unhelpful and abusive' when they were seeking information during last week's Parson's Tunnel fatality. When the reports had finally been assembled for that incident, it was likely that formal discipline was going to be pursued but it stands alone and separate from today's events. I ask myself the question whether I could have handled it better and console myself that I had given him three chances to recant. Because of my personal involvement any Form 1 hearing for the insubordination would be held at Swindon and I request that this should be by a manager who is senior in grade to me. That means Ken Shingleton so that an appeal could be heard by the boss, Bob Poynter.

Back on the railway, delays are reducing and we are causing none on our patch. The supervisors can easily handle this situation but it is necessary to show the flag, and also to show that I have not been thrown by the announcing incident. There are two teams of YTS trainees cleaning windows and door handles as I have requested, under the supervision of the scheme leader Roy Slack, by coincidence, another prominent Exeter labour councillor.

I make another couple of visits to the panel box, one just

before the shift changeover. I have to make sure that Tony Crabtree is not still glued to the CIS computer when the afternoon announcer comes in as he might view his taking duty as condoning both unfair action against his colleague and management staff doing the job. This could provoke another strike call. I am just in time. On both visits the signallers are more than usually pleasant to me which, perhaps mistakenly, I take as a measure of support. Back on the station three or four platform staff broach the subject. I confine my remarks to simply confirming the fact the announcer was indeed sent home. I sense no sympathy for him and, later in the shift, even the normally agreeable afternoon announcer Larry is exceptionally helpful when I have cause to talk to him. *I still become tense even now reading this but I still think the action was correct, despite the high risk of strike disruption, and that it was a good policy to maintain the high profile after the event as I was already doing during the bad weather.*

Our main operational problem reverts to being the unit shortage. Some mainline trains are still being cancelled throughout such as the 16.05 from Bristol to Paignton. We have an 18.55 empty stock to Laira which we are going to run as a special to Plymouth at about 19.30, or whenever appropriate to cover a gap caused by likely cancellations.

I adjourn to read the announcer's personal file. The path for this discipline had been well prepared with a warning of what to expect from a further contravention of discipline after a direct confrontation with John Beer and Tony Crabtree (*by the announcer's personal reckoning, two college kids I suppose!*). Ten years ago there was another incident when he chased Henry Gawler, who is now a chargeman, down the platform and pinned him to the bookstall. In 1978 he was disciplined for foul and abusive language and then walking off the job. The papers say the hearing was taken by 'an assistant area manager'. Ray Long had defended the announcer on the grounds that foul language should be tolerated and other people who felt it necessary to address the announcer in a similar fashion had not been disciplined. The 'A.A.M.' let him off with a verbal warning *(presumably neither foul nor abusive)* which did not need a Form 1 issuing in the first place, on a defence that could have been anticipated and without mention of walking off the job. It is not surprising that the announcer still has the bit between his teeth. In the light of this research I write my report, carefully mentioning that my actions were not precipitated by the swear word and that any alternative derogatory word would have resulted in similar disciplinary action.

Two Class 50s have been assigned to the 19.30 special which is now going to run at about 20.20 as a connection out of the 20min late Golden Hind and vice the 20.10 stopper. Due to a lack of communication between the supervisor, the signaller and, most importantly, the Laira train crew, the locos have escaped light to Laira. The only other engine available is no heat No. 47331 in Railfreight livery.

Jon Morton, 31, is in charge, reputedly the fastest driver in the West. I sit in the secondman's seat and talk to him about his career. He has shown interest in the management training scheme but decided against applying. He says he will apply for a supervisory job "when the job becomes boring with complete 142 and HST operation." In the meantime he is enjoying driving too much, especially Class 50s on full power. *Jon is still driving, a formidable senior hand who is still just as keen, a part-owner of a Class 37 and now chairman of the Dart Valley Railway Trust in his spare time.* Unfortunately it is too dark for me to time his effort with this Class 47 except from Dawlish Warren to Dawlish where his 3min 12sec time would be perfectly acceptable if achieved nowadays by a sprinter. I get home at 21.00

Friday 16th January 1987

The early train is on time again despite the disruption and the unit position at Exeter is better. Paul Johns, an ex-mechanical management trainee, and a Laira fitter have been working here all night and have done an excellent job.

I collect two reports from travel centre staff concerning the abuse by the announcer during the fatality incident and prepare for the 09.00 fact-finding interview with him. Ken Boobyer will sit in as note-taker and to corroborate what happens. The announcer is not much dismayed and studiously avoids any hint of an apology. I suspect he knows it is too late for that and it would be an admission of weakness on his part. His attitude pushes me towards having to suspend him instead of what I would like - an assurance that there will be no similar outbursts if he is allowed to return to work pending his disciplinary hearing. However, it suits my purposes for him to remain at work today and resume his duties tomorrow so I content myself with warning him what might happen if indeed he does not control himself. He then says that the offensive remark was not aimed at me. I tell him that I am judging this remark in the light of his three refusals to say that yesterday and that I must view it in the context of it being made with the prospect of what was in store for him.

The announcer is sent to learn how to make permanent alterations to the CIS programme and I decide on how to frame the Form 1 charge. "that on.......you made a grossly insubordinate remark in the presence of the Area Manager (this keeps the hearing officer options open concerning the defence) and that......you made unhelpful and abusive remarks to travel centre staff....." I have decided not to disregard the fatality incident, which I could, of course, hear myself. However, I cannot issue two Forms 1 on the same day and I cannot save up the first event for a later date. Although the inclusion of the second part of the charge might result in its importance being watered down, its inclusion would mean that any punishment would have to be directly related to the performance of his announcing duties. In future, any lack of cooperation will be pounced upon and at age 59 he might currently be two steps from the sack. *I have only met the announcer once in my long retirement and I was pleased that I felt our brief chat was mutually respectful and almost cordial.*

Coincidentally, at 10.30 I start a meeting with InterCity, Investment staff, the regional signalling engineer and area maintenance engineer about station announcing after the completion of re-signalling. I have mentioned earlier InterCity Peter Griggs's decision that only InterCity trains would be announced if he was solely paying for them. I have prepared some information about the workload involved in announcing all trains at Newton Abbot, Exeter and Taunton and operating the CIS. Peter immediately agrees to 3½ posts of which he says Regional Railways has agreed to pay for one. The problem is solved. I use the remains of the meeting to gather information ready for my consultation document. We adjourn to the panel to test that announcer Ted Davy can clearly see 'Taunton' from his seat opposite 'Exminster' on the display. Then the S&T take a look at how to put cctv on the concourse to replace the old fashioned and tatty slide-board system we are using now.

Next comes a visit from the B.R fire officer Tim Goddard to look at our lifts. We want to convert the lifts to passenger use and operation but we lost the scheme and Devon County Council financial support last year after the Exeter city brigade chief refused to allow passengers to be on the footbridge between the two lifts without a staff presence. I am now trying to resurrect the plans. Tim is a former Holbeck secondman which could explain the unusual amount of common sense he displays. He absorbs the facts and will arrange a meeting with the Exeter officer, plant engineer Phil Shepherd and me. Phil advises that a hydraulic, as opposed to electrical, mechanism would help our case and Tim agrees.

Devonair rings to ask about the circumstances of the Teignmouth sea wall broken rail incident. They have picked up on a report in the weekly Teignmouth News and want an interview. I stress it was not 'nearly a derailment' but they want to know how many broken rails occur each year. To say 'one' would make it a less than routine event and I reply, "three or four a year". This is probably accurate over a long period but it is made in the knowledge that there have been five in the last month.

There is time to catch up on paperwork before meeting John Beer and Richard Burningham at 15.30. We cover what Richard has achieved since his appointment and I offer some gratuitous advice on his new appointment as travel centre manager at Bath. He has shown flair and promise which should take him far. Outside, the service is running well with the exception of the Liverpool-Plymouth 25min late with a Class 45 in charge.

CHAPTER 34: DISCIPLINARY HEARINGS AND NEWSPAPER TRAIN STAFFING

Monday 19th January 1987

The unit position is 7xClass 142s and 1xClass 118, stranded after the snow, so there are no capacity problems. It does not prevent the Express & Echo ringing about shortages on the Exmouth branch on four days out of twelve. One was the snow and another the fatality but it is still not good enough. There has been a serious incident on Saturday when the 17.45 Exmouth-Paignton ran into a concrete sleeper at Parson's Tunnel. My feeling is that this is a direct result of scaremongering in the local paper about the 'near derailment' that has given some elements of the public the idea that an accident might entertain their vacuous lives.

At 08.30 I start a disciplinary hearing with a relief leading railman from Taunton. He received a final warning three months ago from Bernard Price and has had half a dozen charges against him, mainly for absence. His advocate is Denis Davey, who clearly has no patience for such behaviour which leaves his responsible members needing to cover, so there are no mitigating grounds for any decision other than dismissal.

There is another disciplinary hearing at 09.30 for the signaller involved in the 'two-in-a-section' handsignalling incident at St. Thomas. Most unusually, Chester Long appears to defend him. He tries to blame the signaller for imparting ambiguous information to the senior relief signaller acting as handsignaller. The signaller whom Chester is seeking to blame is none other than Denis Davey who has just left my office after defending the Taunton leading railman. *I never came to grips with union internal politics.* I point out that his 'client' would not have been allowed back in the signal box if he had claimed this defence at the time of the incident as he had been allowed to resume duty on the grounds he had recognised and accepted his error. Bernard's notes imply he accepted his error but Bernard might have been trying to ensure someone who had been helpful to him in the past was not given a precautionary suspension.

Most hearings take 30-45min but this one goes backwards and forwards for nearer 90min. Eventually driver Diggle, who was on the train that was instructed to enter the occupied emergency signal section, is called as a defence witness to the fact the handsignaller was told to let Diggle's train go and properly repeated the message. The young driver comes in confidently and repeats almost the exact wording signaller Davey says he used and that Bernard Price overheard in the box. This is not what Chester had expected and he clearly looks a little put out.

I intend giving a one day suspension but Chester persuades me to reduce this to a severe reprimand on the grounds that the signaller has lost three days pay after the incident and he is to retire in May. This is probably justified on the grounds that an appeal with Chester at Swindon is likely to succeed, given the deferential attitude of some H.Q. officers and that the signaller is most unlikely to re-offend in that time. That leaves the message that it gives to other staff and any precedent it sets. His colleagues are intelligent enough to read between the lines and the circumstances are extremely rare. *On reflection I suspect I, too, was being deferential to Chester Long but I would like to think it was a concession to the imminent retirement.*

There is time to bundle my papers into my bag and catch the 12.34 to Plymouth, to reach the Institute of Transport meeting, with driver Caslin in charge. He is accompanied by a secondman on an 'M' turn which is a throwback to reducing second-manning many years ago *and from memory entailed the protection of some turns when spare secondmen or passed drivers were otherwise unused. 'Old Spanish custom' might be a less complicated explanation.*

I had spent 20min talking to former Leeds driver Tom Caslin

and his wife about their impending removal to Devon while out for a walk a week last Sunday. We are 4min late at Dawlish following a late start but on time by Hemerdon, arriving at Plymouth 1min late because of a Class 08 shunter crossing the main line at Laira Jct on a freight.

The meeting is a presentation by a representative of the Freight Transport Association on the subject of the 'The Heavy Lorry'. Although it is a low-key talk, I take up the cudgels on behalf of railways. The committee meeting that followed has to be cut short to allow chairman Martin Pearce to return to his English China Clay office at St. Austell. A further meeting is set for two weeks time.

The journey home is in the company of Phil Shepherd and former Stoke Divisional manager Trevor Anderson who now lives at Bishopsteignton and who wants to discuss the current management style and reorganisations. There is 2hrs of paperwork to be done this evening.

Tuesday 20th January 1987

It is the early train today with No. 50050 'Fearless'. The main business this morning is an LDC meeting with Newton Abbot staff to take out the night leading railman post. I counter their arguments that residual ticket-issuing duties are not covered in the proposals by conceding that the post to be removed will be the night railman's post instead.

The crunch time in the workload is at 04.25 when one member of staff goes down the Torquay branch with the newspaper train to assist with unloading while another is needed at Newton Abbot to assist with the newspaper dispatch and logging in of red star parcels. After a recess I suggest that an extra man could be provided by bringing on the 05.00 shunter at 04.15. I also hint that this would be ideal for a part-time post, which the NUR normally resists. Staff side feels it cannot disagree that this would work but decides to submit a counter proposal by offering the fact that the newspaper train does not really need a member of staff to accompany it down the branch, presumably to avoid unsocial signing on times or part time staff. I accept the offer and pocket the savings. There is more work on a Sunday morning when the volume of newspapers is larger but I remove the Sat/Sun night shift and replace it with a 3hr Sunday turn signing on at 02.45. *Under conditions at the time a 3hr turn would be paid for 8hrs whereas a turn of 3hrs 1min to 8hrs would be paid 14hrs! On reflection I suspect that the person who should go down the branch might normally have gone home early instead and possibly that they expected me to know that and expected me to bring the point up.*

A former Leeds driver comes in to say he is not settling here. His 18yr old daughter has obtained a job with the Yorkshire Post, his younger daughter is upset at the prospect of moving and his wife is resultantly upset at what has developed. He is thinking of resigning if necessary. The 'Drivers Promotion, Transfer and Redundancy' agreement is a national one with few exceptions to cater for individual difficulties but I undertake to try to find a way through. *It was certainly inflexible but designed to stop people making a career out of repetitive moving and training.*

I devote the afternoon to paperwork and dispatch the announcer's disciplinary papers to Swindon. The Exeter & Echo has managed to relegate the Skipper shortage to three column inches on P. 12. I am quoted as saying that the shortage has been caused by matters outside our control but, if anyone challenges this I can quote the snow and fatality. I opt for the 16.47 tonight which has Class 118 Nos. 51370/51412. We have deliberately timed this round trip for a Class 118 so we drop only 1½min to Dawlish, mainly due to a 40mph tsr at Exminster.

Wednesday 21st January 1987

No. 50050 'Fearless' is on the stopper again. I catch the Golden Hind to Taunton with driver Pulleyblank. My choice of train is not accidental as this is the first day of a revised manning agreement which requires the second driver to be provided from Taunton after 'travelling passenger'. Colin Pulleyblank is the driver and the second driver is sitting next to him. His response to my requirement for him to resume his seat in the train is performed with ill-grace as he trudges down the platform to standard class. This seems a little petty but it would not have been a good idea to condone an unofficial arrangement on the first day. *The altered agreement was aimed at reducing the need for a second driver to 110mph sections only.*

The weather is foggy but no problem thanks to the automatic warning system and colour light signals. Despite a 40mph tsr at the east end of Whiteball Tunnel we are 2min early at Taunton after a 1½min early start on working time. I then take the Newcastle train from Taunton, meeting Tony Crabtree for a session at Bristol with regional parcels manager Keith Joint. He wants to discuss the parcels business specification which entails detailed objectives under each aspect of his responsibility - newspapers, red star, post office etc. *Judging by the fact that traffic is no longer carried by rail (except minimal amounts of post) this seems to have been at best unsuccessful and at worst a complete waste of time.*

At 10.45 we meet John Curley, Regional Railways Weymouth route manager, to discuss the Yeovil town centre booking office. Parcels and NSE are also represented. I reckon we will save one member of staff and generate revenue. We could easily make an extra £20,000 a year in parcels revenue, which would equate to an increase of 8 large parcels a day. The issue is complicated by possible plans to concentrate train working at Yeovil Jct. As ever, the biggest problem is agreeing the split of costs between the sectors. Instead of four posts and two relief being split proportionately to the current '4 to Regional and 2 to NSE' it is altered to '2 Regional and three to NSE'; the latter sector being more dynamic and more prepared to accept the transfer of the existing travel centre manager to its paybill.

I go to catch the 13.28 to Exeter, which is the Liverpool train, but it is running an hour late. A 3-car Valleys Class 118, formerly Devon-based, Nos. 51311/51326 has been provided for a special to Exeter. Colin Pulleyblank is on the platform to work the Liverpool and believes he should work the special with the spare crew working the Liverpool, saving me some overtime along the way. Bristol supervisors want to keep their men on the unit and bring the set straight back. They have been caught out in the past by not doing so and they deserve full marks for taking the risk of sending it anyway. The unit is clearly the special so I do not take on the argument.

The set reaches 69½mph at Nailsea but drops to 67mph on the level. We are held outside Taunton with the London in front. When we drop into the platform I am surprised to be told by the guard to change trains. Supervisor Ernie Widger, a serious, conscientious and experienced man, says Control had told him to connect the special into the London and terminate it but the London has made up time and preceded. Control has now confirmed the dmu should go through so we rejoin it, having lost 7min by miscommunication with the train crew.

Maximum speed before Whiteball is about 63mph at Wellington, dropping back to a noisy and vibrating 47mph at the summit. We pick up speed downhill scraping 71mph at Tiverton Parkway and arrive in Exeter 11min late on the Liverpool's timing.

Back in the office I discuss the possible candidates for the Barnstaple Travel Centre job and suggest that budget clerk Chris Hughes should apply; another young man showing promise. Ken Shingleton rings at 17.05 to discuss very little and I jump onto the 17.25 with No. 50040 'Leviathan' on five coaches. It leaves 30sec early and gains another minute to St. Thomas, takes only 30sec for the booked 1min stop and leaves 2min early. I go to see the Bristol guard.
"My watch, which is correct to the second, shows 17.28," I tell

him as we pass the bitumen siding. "We should not leave St. Thomas until 17.29." He clearly feels challenged and gets out his own watch. It shows 17.25!

"By your watch we should just be leaving St. David's," I exclaim, trying to ignore the funny side and fervently hoping we have left no-one behind. The guard looks sheepish and says he did not think they could make up much time to St. Thomas and he had not checked. On arrival at Dawlish I am informed that the Milk Marketing Board and local farmers have been operating a road tanker in the car park every morning at 06.00 so I make a note to ensure they pay a facility charge.

Thursday 22nd January 1987

No. 50005 'Collingwood' this morning. 7xClass 142s and one Class 118. Bernard is back from leave so I fill him in on events. David Mather arrives to be updated on our local services planning. We want to talk about what we need at ground level and publicity this coming summer. David, on the other hand talks for two hours about more emergency budget cuts. He wants to reduce the travel centre coverage which we have just implemented and cut the 1987 budget we have only recently agreed. I refuse to get involved and say I will make an issue of any such proposals.

Tony Harrington, the national Godfrey Davies car hire manager arrives and takes me across the road for a ploughman's lunch to discuss the Newton Abbot agent for his 'Serviceman' product. We find a car parked in one of the Godfrey Davies reserved spaces, which is a touchy subject with them as their customers can subsequently find nowhere to park when returning cars out of hours. I discover the vehicle belongs to customer services manager John Beer so have no hesitation in putting a ticket on it!

Meanwhile John has made some progress with David Mather on publicity matters but David still wants to continue the meeting and I have virtually to throw him out at 15.00. This is not before he has explained his sector's strategy on pricing.

This involves two fare levels, one for locals with a 'Devonrail' card which will give discounts on a range of purchases and another for visitors. I think what annoys me most is the certain knowledge that if John and I had suggested precisely the same idea it would have been dismissed.

The driver's assistant who is going to apply for the management training scheme arrives for an interview but he displays a slightly annoying attitude and there is not much depth in his answers so I have difficulties in identifying the potential he is said to have shown on a recent Westbury training course.

We have had 140 applications for the new travel centre jobs at Taunton so I take a look through them, whittling them down to fewer than 20. No. 33201 takes me home using the Waterloo Mark 1 set. This is a sore point. Apparently the 09.10 from Waterloo required to have two coaches knocked out so Howard Davies sent out a 5-coach Mark 1 set, itself in poor condition, to Waterloo. Perhaps he thought it was the Waterloo eight Mk 1 set? I'll investigate that tomorrow. On top of that it seems that Paul Silvestri has sent the now 7 car set off the 09.10 up to Waterloo on the 16.18 instead of the set off the 11.10 which will result in the busy 06.40 from Salisbury to Waterloo tomorrow morning having only seven coaches. Ken Shingleton is hopping mad on the phone and I am not much less angry myself. Bernard says he will investigate tomorrow.

Friday 23rd January 1987

I start on the 08.13 to Paignton and Phil Shepherd joins at Teignmouth. The assistant fare collector seems to be thinking his duties might be better performed sitting in a first class compartment when I get on. I ride through to Paignton where Steve Drew is the chargeman and Ken Giles the booking clerk, returning to Torquay to visit the parcels office and travel centre. On reaching Newton Abbot, the 10.34 to Plymouth is 16min late due to sheep on the line at both Brent Knoll and Whiteball and then 17min late with 2x40mph tsrs from Exeter.

We have a good run to Plymouth though making up 2min recovery time and then an extra 4min on top.

The aim is to talk to Plymouth area manager Jim Collins about neighbouring matters, moan about provincial services and devise some management indices through which we can monitor the standards of Exeter-Waterloo coaching stock maintenance and cleanliness. We then go to the first aid competition in a local church where we arrive just in time for a pasty and the awards. I catch the 14.35 HST back to Dawlish, riding in the cab with Exeter driver Mick Lockyer. It is a 2+8 set with power cars 43033/43029 and quite rough. We start the customary and sloppy 1min late and work it up to 70mph, reducing to the 60mph limit through Tavistock Jct. The line limit rises to 80mph and we power up to 77mph running the whole of the 1-in 42 Hemerdon Bank in the top notch, number 5 and taking the summit at 60mph. Mick is a young, fast and thinking driver and takes 25min to Totnes, a slight loss on a tight schedule but with a poor set.

Totnes up loop has to be taken steadily. There is a controlled approach signal at the foot of Rattery bank and a 15mph entry turnout from the up main. Driver Lockyer and I have been talking about it and the proposals for flashing yellow signalling at 25/30mph into the loop. Today we are still doing 33mph as we reach the AWS ramp about 200metres from the signal as it turns from red to green. Mick must have sensed my knuckles clenching and turns, with a grin, to say, "If you are doing 35mph at the ramp and the signal does not clear you can stop in time." He has just returned from an Egyptian holiday *(an unusual destination in 1987)* so discussion alternates between pyramids and trains. We lose another 12sec to Newton Abbot but have made up time at both stations as we leave the latter station a minute late with 2min recovery time, arriving at Exeter 2min early.

As I alight, there is an announcement that passengers from the Plymouth train who are travelling to Barnstaple should hurry across the bridge. Paul Silvestri says train crew supervisor Colin Godbeer has passed a message from Control asking for the 15.34 departure to Barnstaple to be held for a participant from the ambulance competition to get back in time to have a 12hr rest period before his 05.00 shift in the morning. Control denies making any such request as does the roster section and Bernard. As far as I am concerned the ambulance competition is a day off and not subject to minimum rest periods. It transpires that the request has come from the Plymouth supervisor, and ultimately, presumably, from the Barnstaple chargeman himself. The consequence is a 2½min late start for the Barnstaple train and a minute to the following London, a minor incident in itself but a substantial breach of operating discipline and one to take up with those concerned. I discuss the interviewees for the new CO1 posts with John Beer and the errors with the Exeter -Waterloo stock yesterday with Bernard.

The 17.25 has to shunt its stock out of the yard after a cross country 17.16 departure and avoiding delay to an up parcels train. Today we are 1½min late with a five set instead of 8, losing no time to Dawlish, despite the Exminster 40mph tsr, as a result of the lighter load.

CHAPTER 35: THROUGH CREW WORKING TO WATERLOO AGREED

Monday 26th January 1987

Another fourteen hour day begins with No. 50005 'Collingwood' again on the 07.08. Operating clerk Karen has lost my graphs of Exeter-Waterloo punctuality which were to be part of a presentation. She is upset and says it will take me ages to do them again but I tell her it will take about an hour and I will do them at lunchtime. We have just 4xClass 142s this morning, supplemented by a Class 118 and two loco-hauled sets of illegally purloined vehicles – but still one short.

I go to Yeovil Jct on the 08.11 and we run on time or slightly early all the way with driver Bill Harris. *Bill was probably my keenest driver although not one of the youngsters and former Western Region trained. Reviewing the log now, it certainly looks like a model of how to keep time with Waterloo trains. He holds the fastest known Taunton-Paddington time with the Golden Hind which I timed in my retirement in 88min 9sec with, I think, three tsrs.* There is just time for a 12min visit before picking up the 07.00 Waterloo back, unusually on time. No. 50030 'Repulse' is the loco on the now filthy Clapham Jct set. We stand 5min at Honiton waiting for the 09.38 up from Exeter. It arrives with a Class 33 on five coaches. Three were detached (defective) from the 06.09 from Salisbury and then the booked Class 50 failed at 09.30. When we get away we make Exeter Central on time and arrive at St. David's 1min early.

There are a few items to take up. First is the fact that the log shows the 06.09 from Salisbury an entirely unnecessary 3min overtime booking tickets. Second, I want the 07.00 Waterloo stock to have its windows manually washed at the very least but I have to accept the supervisor and Bernard's verdict that they cannot make any impact on the grease and dirt. Karen offers to re-draw the graphs but I polish them off in 55min.

At 13.30 two officers of Devon County Council arrive to discuss their version of the West Yorkshire Rail Scheme which covers enhanced facilities for rail freight. It mainly concerns land use planning but also includes passenger and parcels facilities. It is futuristic and has yet to show results in West Yorkshire *(still has to, Wakefield Europort excepted?)* but the prospect of transport-led planning permission and influencing infrastructure investment on a tripartite basis between B.R. the local authority and a freight forwarder is a real opportunity. *The ideas have arguably more recently achieved results on say the Tesco flows from Daventry.*

There is time to consult John Beer and Tony Crabtree about the establishment of the Serviceman facilities (car repairs adjacent to rail car parks). *The idea was not fruitful, presumably due to lack of volume. 330 cars in a car park would average, 1 per day for its annual servicing if people could be persuaded to leave their local garage owner?* The local management meeting discusses clerical support to release management time for higher-grade issues but we do not make much progress, partly because Bernard Price and Alan Bell are fiercely independent and prefer to do it without any assistance, I think. Home on the 17.25 with No. 33029 and 2½hrs paperwork including reports on management trainees and to take issue with some recent personnel initiatives.

Tuesday 27th January 1987

As I arrive on Dawlish platform at 07.05 the 06.00 Plymouth-Paddington is approaching, having left Plymouth 17min late. This has rendered my Totnes starter 13min late, 10½min late at Dawlish with Nos. 50005 'Collingwood' and 50047 'Swiftsure' in multiple on eight bogies. It is a fast run; I suspect my fastest run from leaving Starcross to passing Exminster (3min 42sec), making up time at stations and arriving at St. David's 5min late.

I have a few urgent phone calls to make before a two-day area manager's conference and a day off on Friday. I speak to Bernard Norman at Swindon about obtaining severance payments for supervisors who are shortly to be surplus and have intimated they want to leave but look like not being allowed to take voluntary redundancy. This would result in the doubly unsatisfactory position of leaving them displaced and saddling me with a budget deficit. Then I contact Devon County Council for a meeting about Teignmouth Quay Company freight, which seems to be a good example of taking freight off Devon country roads in line with yesterday's meeting, and the Exmouth line package of new works where we are in danger of losing their £20,000 contribution if we do not act quickly. David Mather is to tackle the G.M. for resources today.

Bernard Price comes in to say that the Salisbury-Meldon ballast empties has failed at Crewkerne at 08.25 and the 08.11 to Waterloo is standing at Chard Jct. We have dispatched an engine from Exeter which is already 'in section' between Honiton and Chard Jct before being cautioned into the next section with the failure in it. Even so, the 07.00 Waterloo stands at Yeovil Jct from 09.30 to 10.53 and the 08.11, despite being given priority, does not leave Chard Jct until 10.30. We could have saved time by rescuing the ballast with the 08.11 loco and re-engining the 08.11 with the rescue engine after handsignalling to the front of the 08.11. The down Waterloo train recovers 10min to Exeter.

It is appropriate that we start the Exeter-Waterloo performance meeting after its arrival. Down trains are meeting their modest targets of 50% absolute right time and 70% within 5min. If there are special circumstances for such low aspirations, they lie in the fact that one failure wipes out all 'within 5min' arrivals for the whole day, requiring almost perfect running on the other six days. Up trains, on the other hand, rarely meet even these standards. We also discuss the method of dealing with defective coaches, maintenance of sets with no-heat vehicles and an arrangement to return all defective vehicles on the 18.55 empties. As an aside, we are often using the Class 37 that lays over here and which we are using for unofficial driver training on the stock train.

After the meeting, there is time to go to the panel box where I find that Alan Bell and Bill Mardon are attending a suicide at a farm crossing just west of Stoke Canon. Alan has used his best East End diplomatic skills to persuade the civil police to allow trains to run again, assisted by the new Exeter B.T. police sergeant who happens to come from York- a formidable team. Trains have been standing for just 30min. The 14.20 from Paignton is delayed 20min and the down line is running at caution, with recovery of body parts continuing, and directly over three covered pieces in the 'four foot' (between the rails). A signaller who is undertaking panel box suitability training nearly lets the up train go by mistake when authorised to let the down train go but signaller Guerin is as ever alert and prevents the error. Despite being experienced in manual boxes it is doubtful the new signaller will make the grade.

I push Ken Shingleton and Swindon personnel manager Eugene Heffernan to arrange the disciplinary hearing for the announcer. Chester Long seems to be prevaricating, possibly in the expectation that the issue will have lost some of its steam by the time he is available to act as advocate. His diary is full with sectional council and Exeter city council matters so H.Q. needs to allocate him some time away from consultation meetings. Ken agrees to give all concerned the hard word for Friday. Meanwhile I intervene between the current announcer and his CIS colleague who have just reached their preferred but erroneous spelling of 'fatality'.

Back in the office, Bob Poynter wants me to phone him, usually an ominous sign, but this time he has good news. Exeter drivers have secured three round trip turns through to Waterloo from the new timetable and we need to start driver training. Even Exmouth Jct steam drivers did not go beyond Salisbury and I have been pressing for this productivity increase for some time. The stumbling block is the need to train two links of drivers on a route that is a long way from their home depot, intensively signalled, third rail electrified most of the way and might depend on the cooperation of Salisbury drivers who are losing work.

To ensure reliable coverage, within links that include other work of course, we will need to train 24 drivers and 16 guards, who have only two turns. The standard road learning guidelines are 35 days for drivers and 15 days for guards which will be almost impossible to accommodate in the time. Such 'norms' do not officially exist as learning depends on the drivers' self assessment of their own confidence – *something which smacked of modern enablement but had evolved from the earliest days and has now been replaced, probably correctly, by examination.* The drivers want the work though so Alan is assisting them to meet the deadlines by containing the number of days. First step is to send out the brightest and best to learn the road first, sign it and set the standard for the others. Furthermore, it is not official until sectional council has been informed at a meeting arranged for 10th February. Our turns are up with the 06.43, 12.20 and 14.17, back with the 11.10, 16.42 and 19.10. Waterloo has been given the 13.10 and 15.10 down and the 17.33 and 19.47 back. Working home into Waterloo with the 19.47 at 23.00 through the London suburbs having signed on 8½hrs earlier is tough.

Stuart Palmer at Gloucester and I discuss the possibilities of some redundant Gloucester guards transferring. It failed to materialise last time and we have nine trainees on a course at present. If eight pass we will be up to establishment but if more drop out we could need them. There is time to thank the police for their help at Stoke Canon and discuss arrangements for an Arsenal-Plymouth forthcoming F.A. Cup fixture, before driving home. I notice that the exterior light is on at the disused Exminster signal box as it was last night when I went home by train. By reaching through a broken window with a block of wood I can knock the switch to 'off' and save a penny or two. I make a mental note to have the supply discontinued as I try to close the gate. The post has been knocked over and it now hangs limply whereas it was always meticulously closed when the box was operating.

Wednesday 28th January 1987

I have to attend an overnight meeting at Westonbirt near Bristol, catching the 08.00 to Bristol Parkway and transfer to the special minibus. The Fox and Hounds is comfortable and we start by discussing the recent performance in the snow and assistant fare collector policy. After lunch we have a seminar about improving supervisory performance, the keys being said to be communication (team briefing) and assessment. We watch a John Cleese film on how annual assessment really ought not to be done and have another session after dinner, finishing at 22.30. As normal, the more interesting discussions occur in the bar until after midnight talking to Ken Shingleton, Stuart Palmer, Reading area manager Nigel Fulford and David Langton who is substituting for Jim Collins from Plymouth.

Thursday 29th January 1987

As seems usual, I am syndicate chairman this morning on the communication theme and have to make a presentation with the flip chart. At least I get some congratulations. The purpose to my mind is not so much writing down a large number of impractical ideas that will accompany the flip chart notes into the wastepaper bin but to secure implementation of some existing good ideas before they too are lost. I catch the 14.25 from Bristol Parkway to York, the Leeds-York leg being a joy ride. We enter Leeds via Whitehall Jct rather than the viaduct to avoid conflicting with the late running Liverpool train and I return from York behind No. 47544. *The viaduct line was closed as being unnecessary under electrification which became one of the factors in congesting Whitehall Jct that eventually required an expensive extra double set of tracks from the station to Copley Hill.*

Friday 30th January 1987

I consign our two acquired bean bags 'to be called for' at

Dawlish for £6.01 on a staff rate. Apparently I should have had to pay 50% more for high bulk but low weight. I am Best Man at Mike Hodson's wedding tomorrow so catch a Class 45 into Leeds to pick up the Renault 21 hire car from Godfrey Davis. Taking Mike out to his Harrogate home in the fast lane of the ring road, the acceleration pedal fails with a detached cable. It is a long hike back to the station for a replacement Montego so I have a hectic time trying to catch up. *One occasion when I regret the mobile phone not having been developed.*

Saturday 31st January 1987

The wedding goes well and after seeing Mike and Susan away on honeymoon from the station we leave the car and catch another Class 45 back to Huddersfield, this time with only six coaches.

CHAPTER 36: TEIGNMOUTH QUAY PRIVATE SIDING INITIATIVE FAILS

Sunday 1st February 1987

Because our usual connection to Manchester is retimed 40min later we are given a lift to Wakefield Kirkgate to change at Sheffield and Birmingham into our usual Manchester-Dawlish. We are short of time so ditch out at Westgate aiming to get the same train at Doncaster instead of Sheffield. The trouble is that the Westgate train is diverted via Normanton and 19min late. At Doncaster, the connection has gone but the diverted Glasgow-Poole should still get us to Birmingham for the same connection….but that is retimed 40min late so we jump back on the King's Cross train….which is diverted via Hertford North. A taxi transfer with our cat in its basket after a brush with a King's Cross taxi tout catches the 18.15 from Paddington with guard Madge in charge, wearing, probably roguishly, his NSE tie. We arrive at Exeter with an incredible 36min to wait for our booked Manchester train but the 17.15 Paddington has had a power car failure so its passengers are being transferred to our 18.15 from Paddington which has been given special stops at Dawlish and Teignmouth vice the 17.15. The tide is in with waves splashing over so there is the inevitable track circuit failure but we arrive at Dawlish 31min earlier than intended.

Monday 2nd February 1987

An early start with No. 50010 'Monarch' and we go straight into interviews for a CO5 budget clerk and MS1 Information Technology assistant. We start at 07.45 with the local applicants and by the end of the day it seems that Bob Eastley is the favourite for the MS1. He has made more progress in 12 weeks looking after the responsibilities than others have made in 12 months. Chris Hughes might be better suited to the Barnstaple travel centre job and I offer the budget job to a candidate from Cardiff who wants to think about it. I give him until tomorrow. I have never applied for a job I would not take if offered. There is the usual smattering of dropouts including an applicant from Waterloo who has applied for both jobs and is said to own a small-holding at Lapford.

Bernard tells me what I missed last week. He has secured the consultation on the supervisory reductions which will be implemented this month. *I don't think I paused to consider how the reduction fitted with getting more from supervisors we were discussing at Westonbirt.* The problem is the withdrawal of redundancy payments for the three staff we will have surplus. It is not that we cannot use them but they will obviously be in danger of being demotivated and will be a charge against my budget presumably to allow some H.Q. department or other to achieve its own.

The announcer has been given a severe reprimand from Ken Shingleton. I would have given him the same but a final warning as well. *The issue was more important in principle and its example more than the severity of the offence.* Chester Long has pleaded that the second part of the charge amounted to victimisation mainly on the basis of the travel centre letter having been received before the panel box incident! *Presumably he meant nothing had been immediately done about the travel centre letter so I had tagged it on for emphasis.* I go home by car and reclaim my bean bags from Dawlish parcels office.

Tuesday 3rd February 1987

The post this morning has a letter from Europcar refunding all charges so the hassle was probably worth it I suppose - impressive public relations though. I start by driving to Teignmouth and some harsh words for the radio playing in the mess room. Phoning the office, I am told that the G.M. is on the phone to Bernard Price about a meeting he had yesterday in the House of Commons. He wants all down Paddington trains to continue using Platform 1 which will entirely undermine the re-signalling rationale, ruin platform occupation and create conflicting moves so this somewhat naïve request will not be met. What he should really be asking me for is a one page briefing note on the advantages of using Platform 4. He wants action on the lift and improved Waterloo line publicity, both of which are in hand.

I catch No. 50008 on the 09.25 to Newton Abbot and the HST to Paignton. Ernie Bittlestone is the chargeman and full of his usual moans and groans. *Nothing ever suited Ernie although this was probably because he was the product of having worked on a busy and diverse railway but, after I had left, he would cross the road to greet me.* Ernie is worried about his wife's health and, despite being a difficult member of staff to try to handle, there are some important points in what he has to say. He also chooses not to mention the fact he has been 20ft up a ladder 'boarding in' pigeon roosts – an effective and humane solution to the problem at no charge.

Returning to Teignmouth with Colin Pulleyblank and a Bristol road learner on HST power car No. 43146, he shows me two bomb craters at the side of the line outside Paignton. "Fastest run ever up the bank by the driver of the train they were aimed at," he remarks. We are on time all the way with the exception of a slight delay caused by a 20mph tsr at Hackney Yard. I take the car to check out the Church House Inn at Stokeinteignhead for lunch with Teignmouth Quay on Thursday. I call in home and catch the 13.13 back to work with driver Caslin. As we run into St. David's, signal E35 goes back to danger. I alert the driver who slams in the brake and stops just in time. The aspect immediately clears to yellow again. Investigation reveals that the reason was a mistake by the same signaller who nearly let the up train into the police working at the suicide last week. He has one week of his trial period to go and Bernard is ready to take the necessary action.

My management trainee has finally decided to resign and is in the office picking up her belongings. We have never really got on well but I feel obliged to discuss future plans but I do not think that the industry has lost much. The biggest loss has been suffered by someone who wanted the job and was not selected instead.

At 14.30 I meet the city and railway fire officers about the lifts problem. With a couple of minor adjustments, the original objections will be withdrawn and we are given provisional permission to proceed. I inform InterCity route manager Peter Griggs and then stray into discussion of the proposed 1988 timetable and making funds available for the redundant supervisors.

There are two calls from the press office concerning newspaper enquiries about Topsham up platform improvements and an incident at Red Cow crossing at the east end of St. David's station where a cyclist has been knocked off his bike by a road vehicle. The crossing attendant had closed the crossing for 30min until the cyclist was safe, causing a traffic snarl-up that spread through the city. When the press had come to see the location and interview the crossing keeper he had (wisely) told them he could not comment and to speak to Bernard Price. The reporter subsequently ventured into the office where Bernard and Alan Bell were sitting and was promptly told the Express & Echo was well known for its anti-rail bias and taking this up was another example. The news editor asks if there is a deep-rooted problem and I respond by saying not really but we look for unbiased reporting, which I define as being one that leans slightly towards my point of view. Bernard says his response was based on a ridiculous report that the crossing near Stoke Canon where the suicide had taken place was not safe. I go back to the news editor who takes the point.

Another, wider issue has emerged in the investigation. The police quote about the suicide was a little candid but the constable says it was clearly agreed he was 'off the record' but the news editor says it was taken from a B.T. Police press release that says they want to co-operate more with the press. I am the contact between the press and the railway and two voices will not work so I need to take that up immediately. *This* battle has now been well and truly lost by the railway operators as the B. T. Police have assumed responsibilities for access to accidents as the civil police do on the roads. There are also resultant press comments about the railway made by police officers who do not have an insider's professional knowledge of rail operations. No. 33114 is on the 17.25 tonight 2½min late.

Wednesday 4th February 1987

No. 50029 'Renown' this morning on the 07.08. I lay into the paper backlog straight away and emerge at 10.00. I clear my lines over the job appointments from Monday and have a long talk with H.Q. personnel manager Brian Griffiths. I tell the good news to Bob Eastley and Chris Hughes, as the Cardiff applicant has declined the budget job. *Bob never let me down in whatever task I asked him to undertake, permanently or temporarily, in admin or travel centres and was a walking testimony to the experience of staff gained in the 1950s.* Then comes the necessary but painful task of telling unsuccessful applicants the bad news. The first was a former MS1 who had moved to Devon and reduced his grade to do so but I am looking for more delivery from him in his personnel post and the second is not robust enough to cope with the demands involved with the budget post.

At 12.00 Ian Trimm from Broseley Costain Homes comes to take me to lunch at the Great Western. He is looking for facilities to distribute brochures for the new Starcross development, a starter pack, a display on the station and a possible VIP charter launch. I offer a voucher for a free weekly season ticket as part of the move-in package to promote rail travel. On my return to the office I am straight into long service awards and the usual photo sessions. Six members of Transport 2000 arrive at 15.30 to talk about local issues. There is a call from NSE to finalise the Axminster investment document and discussions over a proposal for Mike Chew from H.Q. to chair tomorrow's sectional council meeting. Nice chap as Mike is, he is a sectional council minute taker, not chairman. Home on the 17.25 with No. 50039 'Implacable'.

Thursday 5th February 1987

I drive to Newton Abbot for 08.30. A Class 50+47 combination arrives with a heavy load of china clay, the Class 50 detaching and returning to Laira. I speak to supervisor Harry Perrett and tell him that the jobs are likely to be taken out on 23rd February but at present there are no funds for redundancy payments this year and no guarantee of any next year. However, I have some hopes that some will be made available by the time of implementation. *This was thoroughly unsatisfactory and a clear example of budget pressures to reduce costs, sector agreement being obtained, consultation having been cleared and then no-one being prepared to fund the short term consequences, leaving the Area manager to clear up the mess and take the budget overspend.*

The Golden Hind has been delayed behind a failed freight at Devonport and the 07.30 Plymouth-Paddington stock has been used instead. The Penzance driver has remained at Plymouth for his down working, leaving Exeter spare driver Steve Drabwell in charge of the 08.41 to Totnes. No. 50007 'Sir Edward Elgar' (to the chagrin of those who preferred its 'Hercules' identity prior to the 1985 GW150 repaint and renaming exercise) is the loco on ten with a 7min deficit. Steve reduces this by ½min to Totnes while entertaining me with a tale of how Exeter drivers call the Abercwmboi coal train the 'apple crumble'.

There is time to visit the booking office and signal box before returning with the 09.51 HST which arrives on time, leaves ½min late and arrives at Newton Abbot 1½min late. I visit John Haycock in the West box who is eagerly anticipating a visit to the panel box where he is likely be appointed after re-signalling. I ride to Torquay with Fred Batchelor and talk to travel centre manager John Hedge who hopes to be given one of the new parcels salesmen jobs.

Andy Woolrich arrives from Railfreight to accompany me for lunch with Teignmouth Quay company secretary. The operation looks similar to the Fowey one to me with china clay being loaded at Heathfield or further afield for a run to the ship. The problem is that the current operation involves loading direct to the lorry and then direct to the ship. Worse, the rate being charged is just £1.40 per tonne which we would need to match and pay for wagon provision and movement costs. It does not look hopeful, even with any grants available to move the heavy lorries off local roads and through Teignmouth. *Perhaps I should have made a direct approach to Devon County Council at this point in view of their policy, but politics was never my strong point.* Import traffic is mainly feedstuff, most of it for local consumption but some for long distance transit. Storage space is limited on the dock so we could theoretically move even the locally-bound traffic to an inland store but it all looks doubtful.

We return to Exeter on the 14.50 from Dawlish and as I set about the paperwork Jon Morton comes to ask if he can assemble an Exeter area rail team for the T.V. quiz programme Busman's Holiday. I am all in favour and we discuss likely candidates for the team and, possibly more importantly, those who should not be selected. More variety on the 17.25 with No. 33009 tonight.

Friday 6th February 1987

Arriving at work by car I amuse myself by ticketing two cars in the 'area manager's office' spaces via Tony Hill. John Beer briefs me about a meeting he had at Somerset County Hall yesterday with councillor Mrs Rose Mangles. There is a chat with the police about communication with the press and one from the Lord Lieutenant about the Queen's visit to Taunton in May.

I gather up my papers in a rush to catch the 12.30 HST home with HST power cars Nos 43129/43139. Approaching

Exminster we get a warning horn from a temporary speed restriction 'magnet' but the warning board and termination board are lying on the ground and there is no sign of the commencement board. We reduce speed to 50mph and then accelerate. At Dawlish I phone Arnold Knight in the engineer's office. He says that the restriction is 'spate' which means normal speed has been reinstated earlier than advised. The job seems to be half done but Arnold says he will clear it up immediately. I leave a message for Alan Bell and Bernard Price and tip off control before heading home.

Before Monday morning comes I want to write a report for the Exeter-Waterloo Business Group, investment appraisals for Axminster, Honiton and Exeter Central stations and consultation documents for the centralisation of Newton Abbot, Taunton and Exeter St. David's station announcing at Exeter panel box, plus pay and display car park monitoring at Exmouth. At the very least I want to produce documents that can simply have a few engineering estimates written in the gaps. Details of present and proposed hours and duty sheets can be added later by the personnel team.

There are also some forty job applications to consider for the chief TOPS clerk and Barnstaple Travel Centre manager CO4s and the two CO3 shift leaders at Taunton travel centre. I fix some interview dates and decide that I would like the travel centre manager applicants to make a short presentation on the objectives they would set themselves and how they would achieve them. *This was at a time before such things were commonplace. My feelings, in retirement, are that it is now overdone!* For the CO3s I will want to know how they intend to improve standards by better shift leadership, in effect following on the Westonbirt ideas. This has the double aim of sorting the thorough or inspired from the lazy or boring and gets the applicant to talk from the start. Their ability to think on their feet can then be tested by question and answer. Work is uninterrupted and I am finished by 22.00 Friday.

CHAPTER 37: DISTRACTING, WASTEFUL REORGANISATION DISCUSSIONS

Monday 9th February 1987

No. 50030 'Repulse' is on the 07.08. I catch up with Dave Whittle on the walk down to the station and have an interesting chat on the way to work. The diary is blank today so I get on top of the administration and check how the agreement for Exeter-Waterloo road learning is doing. At lunchtime I visit Smith's and have a coffee with the manager Bernard Apps who wants me to allow him to sell a railway print in the travel centre for B.R. to pocket £1 for each one sold.

In the early afternoon I visit the panel to observe events. The 11.45 from Paddington is running 13min late. The 14.22 from Exeter Central to Paignton is at Central with the 'Apple Crumble' (Exmouth Jct-Abercwmboi) standing behind it. The 11.10 from Waterloo is bearing down on it with a scheduled 14.27 arrival at Central. Meanwhile the 14.17 to Waterloo is leaving Exeter St. David's platform 1. Signaller Denis Davy phones Central to tell them he wants the 14.22 unit down smack on time. The 'Crumble' follows it down with its three wagons from Exmouth Jct and No. 37699 – an indictment to the profligacy of dedicated coal trains within the Speedlink set up - re-crews in No. 1 running parallel to No. 33028 on the Newton Abbot trip for Riverside. The 11.10 from Waterloo is standing at Central but cannot leave because the 14.28 to Paignton is waiting in Platform 3 at St. David's to follow the late London HST. The Liverpool-Plymouth runs in early as soon as the down London has cleared the platform and catches-up the 14.28 unit running 10min late at Teignmouth. The Waterloo is 9min late arriving at St. David's after being on time at Central and the 14.40 to Exmouth comes out of New Yard.

I go home by car at about 18.00 after mooching around the station and communicating with the supervisors, the most pressing problem being Gordon Hooper's concerns about his uniform wearing out.

Tuesday 10th February 1987

I drive to Teignmouth for the 08.18 HST school train to Newton Abbot. We have seven Class142s and two Class 118s. The traction learning school is on board with two drivers and two inspectors and booked driver Les Stephens in the train. He should not be there and the inspectors have been clearly told what I want. Les is told to ride in the cab back from Paignton and I tick off the traction inspector at Newton Abbot. I obtain an explanation from supervisor Ernie Underhill of how we have managed to get two units on the 08.15 from Paignton and only one on the busier 07.30. Then it's to the booking office for a chat to Roy Watts and a demonstration of how long it takes to do a simple reservation on the new Apollo computer. I catch the 09.09 to Exeter, talking to an Exeter driver on his way to work.

At 10.30 InterCity sub-sector manager John Bourne and his route manager Peter Griggs arrive. John Bourne makes an arguably smarmy presentation with idiot-cards for those of lesser intelligence who inhabit area management - me and John Beer in this case. He wants to hear how well his route management is working and I pay lip service to avoid embarrassment to Peter Griggs and prevent him thinking I am being negative.

The meeting finishes as booked at 12.30 for a meeting with Post Office managers for our new regular liaison meetings, accompanied by Tony Crabtree. This is an introductory session at the Great Western hotel before meeting formally across the negotiating tables. We identify some flows which could carry more of their traffic and how it should be done, which seems to interest them.

Back in the office, I talk to Karen about monitoring lost time across the area boundary between Tavistock Jct and Totnes monitoring points and then there is a long discussion with driver's LDC secretary Len Purse, interrupted by old-hand Clarrie Keyes asking whether he can have railway issue anoraks and sunglasses. Clarrie is always smartly turned out and has a mischievous sense of humour that he cannot suppress in public or private.

Bernard Price returns from a meeting at Swindon concerning re-signalling at Maiden Newton between Yeovil Pen Mill and Dorchester West on the Weymouth branch. The cheapest solution is No Signalman Key Token (NSKT) to an unstaffed loop and then a driver-operated tokenless block system to Dorchester West. Mr Poynter (or Ken Shingleton) is said to oppose it because it would involve too many signalling systems on one short stretch which neither Bernard nor I support. We have been repetitively told these lines are at risk if we do not reduce costs so opposition to the most economic scheme needs to be credible. *I see the HQ Ops view more nowadays but that might be influenced by the fact that the lines are not presently under threat.*

John Beer comes to brief me about the points he would like made at the Exeter-Waterloo Business Group meeting tomorrow. He really wants to do an open day at Yeovil Jct on one of the steam days in June. I am sceptical that he does not realise how much work this takes, the minimal effect on the bottom line and the opportunity cost from not using the time elsewhere. We do agree that some public relations event is necessary in the vicinity though.

I just catch the 17.25 with No. 33021. Talking to Ken Boobyer on the train home, he has just returned from a full Sectional Council meeting at Swindon with Chester Long, chaired by a regional personnel manager's member of staff. Ken was disgusted at the lack of chairmanship and how staff side seemed to be running the meeting. We discuss the relief arrangements for the remaining signalboxes after May this year. It is said that Bernard Price is about to agree 9hr 45min four-day weeks at Honiton which will create more relief workload and result in more overlap than we need so I ring

Bernard from home to ensure everything is taken into account.

Wednesday 11th February 1987

The unit position remains satisfactory but I have received a highly personal public complaint from an Exmouth customer who believes the shortages are purely my personal fault. In my opinion it is libellous and I warn Swindon that I shall be replying strongly and to that effect. No. 50049 'Defiance' is on the 08.11 to Waterloo and we have a good run to Chard Jct where we lose 7min through being cautioned from the signal box. Guard Brian Cocks talks to me, and Jim Collins, presenting tickets to hear his daughter playing in a youth orchestra concert at Exeter Cathedral.

We return on the 14.37 with No. 50006 'Neptune', 1min late at Yeovil Jct. Supervisor Gale is on hand to make sure we do not incur any overtime but does not make efficient use of his time and does not put the periodical bundles out to the ground. What's more, 25 bundles are over-carried and a minute is lost putting them out at Crewkerne. No doubt another minute will be lost by the 16.18 from Exeter picking them up, and another putting them onto a barrow at Yeovil Jct. 'Spot' Roach is the guard, who could have taken them through to Exeter and left them in the van to return with the 17.33 up. 'Spot' was in trouble with me at Central yesterday for entering the station riding in the unit driving cab. I go through his actions today but seem to fail to get the point over to him.

Jim Collins confides that he is in serious trouble for not having dismissed the driver of a locomotive that collided with an HST on Largin bank in November when it was sent into the section downhill to assist from the front. *Such movements on steep down-grades were subsequently banned, but the incident looks like slipping on leaves which has subsequently been classed as sometimes being unavoidable whereas it always used to be classed as the driver's fault.* Jim has to attend for an interview with Bob Poynter and regional personnel manager Ken Beresford on Friday – high-powered stuff. *I should have suggested that if Jim had dismissed the driver one of Bob Poynter's team would have reinstated him at the appeal hearing.*

We arrive 1min early at St. David's. I try to contact Exeter City Council officers about planning conditions for out-of-town shopping and get the 17.25.

Thursday 12th February 1987

I ride on the up stopper Class 142 with the driver. Guards' LDC secretary Cliff Salter has trouble with the door interlocking and communication at Starcross and St. Thomas so we are 4min late as a result. There is not much time before catching the 09.23 to Taunton with driver Bartlett and an Exeter driver learning the load. I am going to a conference in Taunton at the County Hotel but pause to explain the arrangements for the shift leader interviews to travel centre manager Mervyn Berryman.

The conference is supposed to be about the new organisation, chaired by the able Peter Whittaker from management services at Swindon. *Sectorisation seemed to give an impetus to spending money on accommodation away from the railway.* There are three consultants and six area managers taken away from the front line. Peter is not there initially. It is all very negative, even personal, in criticising individual business managers in a way that even I might consider slightly unfair. We spend four hours going over ground which has already been covered by individual interviews. I begin to wonder if the consultants have given up on us and are just filling time for which they will be paid by the hour. Whatever the situation the adjectives being bandied about include 'obstructive, negative, incompetent and untrustworthy' – no doubt the same selection that the business managers are using about us.

When Peter Whittaker arrives at 16.00 we start to make progress. He outlines his thoughts with which I have little empathy. They appear illogical and inhibited by dogma. Peter is not usually like this and I suspect he has been given an unhelpful remit. He is recommending retention of the regions in slimmed-down form but he is not suggesting anything to co-ordinate the sectors below sector director level. The general managers could be on a similar geographical basis to now *(i.e. 1987)*, responsible to the sector directors with a deputy responsible for the sectors and an assistant responsible for safety and operations. The general manager's lines of responsibilities would be little different from mine now but he could filter stupid ideas at a higher level before time was wasted at area level.

By 20.30 Peter Whittaker seems pretty desperate. "What do you want me to tell Mr Myers *(board member)*?" he asks. I suspect he will invent something pragmatic. At 21.00 I go back to the station. The St Blazey-Severn Tunnel Jct freight has been derailed by buffer-locking of two discharged resin tanks. Bernard is in Fairwater Yard and I visit Taunton East signal box where signalman Bowker is being relieved by signalman Smith who is working his first night shift and is clearly nervous. He talks about his aspirations to move to Cornwall to remain in the signalling grades.

Back at the station I catch the 22.12 HST to Dawlish with driver E.T. Davey, a quiet but jovial man. He is being accompanied by driver Brian Long who should be travelling passenger from Westbury under the new arrangements. I let him know that I know where he should be because I want to guard against future claims that nothing changed with this easement of manning and that management was more than happy for two drivers to remain in charge while simultaneously claiming that there were no safety implications with just one driver. *Perhaps this was another example of leeway for the Long family although Brian seemed to be at arms length from its political arm.* We have a good run to Exeter arriving 3min early, despite a 40mph tsr by leaving Tiverton Parkway, 1min early on working time. Driver Hayton takes over at Exeter but loses 1min to Dawlish.

Friday 13th February 1987

We have been excused going back to Taunton today; the consultants presumably having given up the ghost. I lie in and go to work on the 10.05 Skipper. Assistant fare collector Julia Pretty is sitting in the cab next to driver Lear so I avoid a direct incident by sitting in the train. Mrs Pretty immediately sets about her proper duties so I wait until Exeter to have a quiet word with both offending parties.

Next comes paperwork, sessions with most of the team, speaking to various people about the ridiculous 'no connections' policy that has been decreed for May, and then to David Thear, assistant regional personnel manager, about the supervisory review. He has told difficult TSSA officer Ian Byiers that we will be implementing the scheme very soon. Byiers wants to know if our offer of an additional trouble-shooting supervisory job that I offered at consultation still stands. The answer is a clear 'no' because I wrote it out of the budget when they refused the offer. He cannot expect to call my bluff and then reverse his stance when I call his. I bet I know what region would do if it was their scheme though. In any case, if supervisor Widger at Taunton, who was the intended occupant of such a job, decides to opt for early retirement in the absence of redundancy pay there will not really be anyone to fill it. It is all cat and mouse. Presumably, if I had conceded it, he knows I would take it out next year anyway. It seems to be more about their image than their members' long-term benefit.

Devonair arrive to conduct a radio interview about Christopher Wall, a 12 year old from Teignmouth who has written to us asking if he can work for us for nothing. Ken Boobyer has responded by arranging for him to have a day with us and get a flag and whistle as well as a trip to the panel box. It makes the front page of the Teignmouth News! *A testimonial to how little happens down on the South Devon Coast.*

John Beer fills me in on the recruitment of the telephone

bureau CO1s he has been interviewing for the last couple of days. He says the quality has been high and advertising them externally has worked well.

I tell Janet about an incident with Nigel Fulford, area manager at Reading whose secretary received a phone call from someone who had said he was from Bart's Hospital and that one of Nigel's relatives had been involved in a serious accident. The secretary called Nigel out of a meeting only to find the caller wanted to complain about the cancellation of the 07.21 from Didcot Parkway that morning and ended with a threat that he would make Nigel's life a misery if it happened again. I think I would have taken that to the B.T. Police *but perhaps the moral of the story is to be more accessible, responsive or to be more effective by running a reliable train service.* No. 33023 on the 17.25 tonight.

CHAPTER 38: FATALITY AT WESTFORD CROSSING

Monday 16th February 1987

No. 50047 'Swiftsure' is on the 07.08 and one coach short this morning but bang on time. A Hastings Line Class 33/2 is working the two-coach secret set on the Barnstaple line but otherwise the service is as booked.

I call in at the Exeter travel centre and ask shift leader John Steer why the third window is not open at 07.35. The clerk is late on duty but allegedly 'on his way'. At 08.30 John Beer, Ken Boobyer and Bob Eastley arrive to discuss the negotiation of Exeter travel centre re-staffing. We cannot simply insist on reducing each shift by 12min but we might manage one turn one hour shorter each week to save the same rest day cover costs.

Ernie Widger comes in for coffee and to ask what the golden handshake position is at present. He is still unsure whether he wants to retire which I think means he should decline the offer. It will cost my budget if he is spare but he has such experience and is so thorough that we will be able to make good use of him.

At 09.30 I set off to the University of Exeter engineering faculty building. They have been doing a project on developing Exeter St. Thomas station and have submitted some interesting, although highly unlikely, ideas. I have to ladle on a hefty helping of realism – maintenance costs, vandalism and tight availability of capital that always has an alternative call being made on it. They wonder if B.R. has a futuristic design fund to provide a subsidy. Er, no. Still, something needs doing there and their ideas are interesting. Something could come of the retail expansion taking place in the area and the stairs need some improvement- the down side is enclosed, dank and rancid whereas the up ones are equally steep but inhospitably exposed. Sainsbury's or The Plaza leisure centre might have some money but what we need is a functional budget-conscious update. The University undertakes to organise another meeting. *A generation later, very little has been done on access. However, concrete shelters have given way to Perspex, graffiti is dealt with quickly, customer information systems have been installed and usage has increased considerably - over and above the numbers that cynics might suggest are avoiding the barrier lines at St. David's and Central.*

Back at St. David's I block in two Godfrey Davis cars occupying Area Manager's Office spaces. At 13.15 I interview Paul Lethbridge, the travel centre manager's son. He did not impress in an interview with John Beer recently but he does just enough to get the job. I tell him and his father that the arrangement is not ideal and could cause difficulties either for me or for the family. *Sounds like nepotism in an era of equal opportunities (in the sense of the best person getting the job not just a relative who knows about it but we knew that was important even back then) but equal opportunities means that I should not disqualify a person just because he does have a relative. The problem is the manager either favours his son or disadvantages him deliberately, hence the difficult situation.*

Along the corridor I bump into drivers' LDC chairman and secretary Colin Harrison and Len Purse who are discussing how to accommodate the Waterloo work in the 'links'. They are keen to get started and ensure they do not miss the timetable deadlines. At 13.42 John and I set off for the Chartered Institute of Transport meeting in the Exeter bus station offices. Ron Filer, is giving a talk on the role of the independent bus operator; appropriate because he is one himself. We have been working with him at Barnstaple and he has been offering a good service with bus/rail feeders to Bideford and Ilfracombe as well as on the Golden Rail contract. Around a third of our rail business emanates from each of these catchment areas and his buses save a £10 (or so) taxi fare, having a positive influence on modal choice in favour of rail. As usual, I am lumbered with the vote of thanks and I suspect the audience is surprised to hear how much we know about his operation. We walk back to the station for the local meeting. Alan Bell is off sick with a bad shoulder and Tony Crabtree is at Swindon. We discuss the travel centre scheme implementation and summer staffing. 2½hrs of paperwork this evening.

Tuesday 17th February 1987

The stock for the 07.08 is in poor condition today. There are sticking sliding doors, worn upholstery in one coach and a distinctly smelly toilet, the rest looking down at heel. I will have to have a word with Plymouth to catch up specially with this set for cleaning and maintenance. The dmu position is as yesterday.

I have twenty names on my list to telephone and most are out or not available. At 09.57 I catch the unit up the bank for a meeting with engineer Dave Counter and Dave Moss from the Chamber of Commerce community programme. The meeting is scheduled to start at 10.00 in the booking hall and I arrive on time to the second. The scheme in hand is to occupy the wide wasteland between the platforms with a floral display created by a job creation programme. The location is close to the track, which has to be crossed to get there, so it is important that maintenance is low. They undertake to work out the costs and possibilities. *The planters lasted about 20 years without looking exactly stunning before First Great Western eventually removed them. However, they did look better than the rough ballast left after their disappearance.*

Dave and I adjourn to the offices to work on the schemes for Central, Axminster and Honiton. He raises an unexpected charge for roof renewal which might scupper the scheme. I go to see area civil engineer Peter Warren to talk about the plans for raising Topsham platform for which the estimates now exceed the County Council contribution. Positive as ever, Peter thinks he might be able to bridge the gap with a transfer from his maintenance budget much of which will not be needed if the platform is modernised.

After being measured at Burton's for my new B.R. suit I go back to St. David's to catch up with the phone calls. Tony Crabtree arrives to discuss his observations of the newspaper traffic at Newton Abbot on Sunday morning ready for the new arrangements and to ask for advice on how best to pursue disciplinary measures against a parcels porter whom he has discovered causing delay to a consignment Tony has traced.

I go to the panel box where everything is in order and then go to see signalling inspector Derek Old to tackle him on some out-of-hours visits to signal boxes that have been missed. Back in the office the 1988 draft North East/South West timetable has arrived from route manager Brian Johnson so I go through it in some detail. It is quite imaginative and, on the whole, satisfactory. An exception is that Totnes has only two stops but there is time to hone it further. *Nowadays there is less than a handful of trains that does not stop at Totnes and it has a basic service of hourly to Birmingham, Newcastle and Edinburgh. Ridership from the South Hams catchment area has soared.*

Salisbury depot has asked for an inter-regional meeting over the Exeter-Waterloo crewing alterations which Mr Poynter is going to sort out. There is a long call from the Dawlish Gazette about repairs to Starcross breakwater and my rather robust response to the prospective Labour parliamentary candidate whose criticisms had been published in last week's edition. I leave early to take 2xClass 142s on the 16.47 to Dawlish.

Wednesday 18th February 1987

I start on the 08.13 HST to Newton Abbot. The driver training school is out on its driving tuition trip but the booked driver is in the cab this time. I pause to talk to one of the new chargemen about how the job is to be worked from next Monday when the supervisors are withdrawn. Then I talk to Don Skinner who is one of the staff who will be displaced. He is philosophical and in some ways pleased because he lives in

Exeter and will no longer have to get up at 03.00 for the 04.00 turn. The booking office is short-staffed because senior clerk Roy Watts has phoned in sick. A customer for Long Eaton needs advice whether to change at Derby or Nottingham – easy - and a released prisoner from Channing's Wood remand home wants a ticket to Guernsey via Winchester, not so easy. He has been advised to travel on the 12.20 from Exeter but has time to get there for the 09.38.

On the 09.09 up to Exeter, former Derby Research engineer Ian Duncan is travelling with his wife. He is moving to the West Country but has yet to identify a house or business he wants to buy. I sit with Laira maintenance engineer Tony Coles and talk about his workload from the May timetable, also the withdrawal of the first Class 50, No 50011 'Centurion'. At Exeter, Paul Silvestri has been complaining that the supervisory alterations are being implemented too quickly and the duty sheets are wrong. He comes in to discuss the Cross Country specification and his plans to integrate the local service with it. I take time to explain the background to the staffing scheme and how I hope any problems can be rectified without incurring delay.

I chair the drivers' LDC which goes well. I promise a light for the car park and then turn to queries about over-running diagrams as occurred to Colin Pulleyblank in the snow recently. We confirm our understanding that drivers booked to travel passenger should not normally travel in the cab and some other issues such as how turns with mileage bonus payments should be handled within their own links. I mention that I will be having the unconventional warning sign erected at the loco exit warning drivers about the potentially confusing signal that has been passed at danger four times by drivers relatively unfamiliar with the sidings. Secretary Len Purse asks for the minutes to record the LDC thanks to management for 'their hard work in securing through Waterloo work for the depot,' which I find extremely rewarding. It has suited Exeter drivers and the productivity and reliability improvements suit me. As for the hard work, there has not really been any.

Mr Poynter arrives at 16.30 to borrow my car to visit his parents overnight. He is in genial mood but less than pleased that the 06.45 from Swindon has divided climbing Rattery this morning. It has been recoupled by two H.Q. inspectors travelling in the train. It cannot have been a pleasant task with the rear portion scotched as the front portion set back. *I am not sure I would have risked it, continuous brakes or otherwise, with the spectre of the Armagh 1889 runaway in my mind.* They used the emergency coupling and fortunately the brake pipes were undamaged. More variety on the 17.25 with No 31401; a bit warmer in the train than with a Class 33.

Thursday 19th February 1987

Nos 50008 'Thunderer' and 50043 'Eagle' are in multiple this morning on the 07.08 but not without their difficulties, as there are two unexplained intermediate stops, but we are on time at Exeter. I talk to Paul Silvestri about implementation of the supervisory scheme and he confirms that he has a few concerns but they are unlikely to delay the scheme. Paul requests a negotiation meeting but I say it will be an extension of the last consultation meeting so that we can discuss more of the background but it will be followed by a short negotiation meeting on duty lists and rosters.

Mr and Mrs Poynter arrive to catch the 08.13 to Bristol but Mrs P. has forgotten her purse at her 'in-laws' in nearby Exwick. Bob catches the train and I ferry his wife back to collect her purse. At 09.00 I receive a request to phone one of the S&T managers, Eric Hobson. He is complaining that he and three fare paying passengers arrived from Taunton at 08.10, five minutes late and as soon as they reached the top of the stairs the 08.11 was flagged away. He says it should have been held. They then had to wait until all of 08.24 for the next train. I explain that the margin between the trains is only 5min and it has to be 7min to be an official connection in the first place and even that does not guarantee a hold if there is a reasonable alternative. He gets rather shirty and I retort that 'time is time' and it might be a better railway if the S&T had a similar attitude. After another 5min I tell him I have had enough and will be terminating the conversation. Up Waterloo trains will rarely be held for down Taunton trains and never in this example.

At 11.15 I go to County Hall for a meeting about the Teignmouth Docks scheme. Railway county councillor Harold Luscombe is there as chairman of the planning and transportation committee, Councillor Strudwick, Dr Newitt of Transport 2000, county surveyor Mr Hawkins and Messrs Boyne and Robinson from the Teignmouth Quay Company. Agreement is reached that the County will consider the environmental benefits and costs saved by not needing to widen roads at Bishopsteignton and the Quay Company and I will sort out traffic potential and tariffs. *A letter in the local paper when writing this blames road congestion partly on the china clay lorries, even after the taxpayer has funded road improvements to aid the haulier to offer low rates.*

There is time for a bite of lunch in Topsham and a visit to the box where the signalman has recently transferred from Pinhoe. Then I go to Exmouth in the cab with driver Cook. Peter Legg is the senior railman, having transferred from St. David's where he was LDC chairman. He says he cannot possibly manage to cover the new car park checks. I apologise for apparently over-estimating his capabilities and offer a meeting at Exmouth at which I will time myself to see if it can be done.

A customer is looking for his shellfish due at 13.25 on a Red Star transfer from Birmingham *(a bit like coals to Newcastle?)* I telephone Birmingham on his behalf and consider myself lucky to get through at the second attempt. The customer says his parcel was sent on the 09.15 train but the Birmingham staff say it was not brought to the station until 10.40. Our customer was starting to get a little bit stroppy so I try to deflate him gently.

I go back to Topsham in the cab and visit Ted Goddard in the signalbox where I am made a cup of tea. Then it is back to the office to meet a new driver who has transferred in from Ardrossan; a strange discussion ensuing, where he cannot look me in the eye at all, so I call for his papers. The latest punctuality figures are on my desk, standing at 95% of local trains within 5min of right time and 87% of Exeter-Waterloo trains by the same criterion. Just 4 out of 334 Exmouth branch trains have been more than 5min late. No. 47658 is blocking the 17.25 platform at its departure time so my local starts 8min late with No. 50046 'Ajax' on nine, recovering 2min by Dawlish.

Friday 20th February 1987

I start on the 07.20 to Newton Abbot. The train is in early for a change with No. 50008 'Thunderer' on six with driver Andy Braund so a fast run is assured, 4min 5sec to Teignmouth and 6min 24sec to Newton Abbot. A special constable rail enthusiast has read my letter in the Dawlish Gazette and wants to start a support group. I see Harry Perrett who has just two more shifts to do before taking his outstanding leave and then the golden handshake.

On visiting the booking office, a teenage girl who has been put off the train for having no ticket comes to buy a ticket from Torquay to Exeter. The 06.40 has failed at Laira so we have split 2xClass 142s to cover the shortage.

I meet Barry Cogar on the 08.05 to Tiverton Parkway and offer to buy him a coffee. The chief steward ushers us into the restaurant car and brings us a fresh pot. Barry's appetite has been suitably whetted so decides to stay there and take breakfast. We are ½min late at Parkway. I talk to senior railman Perkins and booking clerk Simon Bubb before catching the 09.48 to Taunton. Peter Warren is on board so I catch up on some engineering issues with him.

At Taunton I talk to booking clerk Ken Boobyer (as opposed to the eponymous and unrelated area personnel manager), who is a sectional council 'A' representative, about how travel centre recruitment is coming along. *I had a policy of trying not to talk to sectional council representatives about sectional council matters when they were performing normal area-based duties.* The chargeman is a little worried about the new responsibilities he will be required to undertake from next week. There is time to have a few words with the supervisor before catching the 10.45 to Exeter. A track circuit failure at Wellington costs us 7min. On arrival, driver Geyton approaches to ask me to sign his application to be a magistrate.

The Ardrossan driver's papers are on my desk. He has had a verbal reprimand, signal passed at danger and a note that he is resentful of authority. So, I had picked up the 'bad vibes'. There are also a few sarcastic letters from him about losing items of railway uniform. I speculate what has brought him to Exeter but he looks like trouble to me. Lunch is taken at the Great Western with Patrick Henchoz from the Plaza leisure centre at St. Thomas. *There are more lunches out than I remember but we were encouraged by H.Q. to participate in the local economy this way.* We reach an outline agreement that there will be a reduction in the entry fee on presentation of a valid rail ticket and co-operation over any special events.

Back in the office, I find that Bernard Price is on his way to Westford footpath crossing just west of Wellington on the climb to Whiteball. Prior to re-signalling there was some unofficial and admittedly ineffective protection afforded by being able to see Wellington's semaphore signals. Assuming some degree of signalling literacy, the system did not guarantee a train was not coming and there were certain shifts when the box was closed and the signals were off all the time. Of course, the users were likely to be local and the cautious would work on the understanding that a train was coming when the signals were off and the box was closed. The council has asked for warning lights for pedestrians but there is no standard system for this type of crossing with this usage and it has been turned down by H.Q. *In effect, if one were to be provided here it would create a precedent for many others.*

Now, a wandering dog and a person we suspect to be its owner have been hit by the 10.00 Penzance-Paddington with No. 50045 'Achilles' hauling nine coaches weighing around 300tonnes travelling probably at 85mph. A down train examines the line and discovers half a human corpse. The London-bound train is at a stand with a broken air pipe from the collision. The 10.20 Penzance to Liverpool has been put into Tiverton Jct loop to allow an assistant loco to reach the rear of the train but the police refuse to let it approach. It is fortunate that Bernard arrives there at this juncture and after fifteen minutes or so the remains have been cleared and the loco goes in to assist. It propels the failure to Taunton and runs round, ditching the Class 50. Driver Oke, 64 years of age, who was on the Class 50 opts to be relieved and driver Geyton (who has just had his magistrates form signed) in charge of the assistant loco volunteers to take the train forward. *What excellent staff this area had.* I had taken the precaution of holding an empty stock, 5Z05 with fourteen coaches and two class 50s, at Taunton, to keep options open of using an assistant engine from the front and possibly starting a train for London from Taunton. It can now come forward to Exeter where two coaches are to be detached and the rest split to form two relief trains to Paddington at 16.40 and 16.51. *Imagine that now!*

Three up trains have been delayed, the first 150min, the second 110min and another 35min. It seems a lot but no more than 15min seems to have been avoidable (from the police over-caution). Delay to down trains has been limited to around 10min each. When driver Oke gets back to Exeter I gently interview him and write his report for him from the findings so he can sign it before he goes home. I go through the incident with Ken Shingleton at Swindon. Apparently the dog and its 36-year-old owner were on the crossing, with the dog off its lead and the owner's mother following, thereby becoming an eye-witness. When the London express burst in upon the scene the dog bolted and the owner tried to catch it before both perished.

Do we visit? If so, when? Do we write? If so, do we deliver it? Will no contact be seen as not caring? Will contact be seen as an admission of responsibility? The newspapers will certainly link the accident with the refusal to provide warning lights as presumably they would not have crossed against the advice of the lights. The driver says it was sounding his horn that seemed to make the dog bolt and there is no guarantee it would not have done so if it had been off the lead but waiting for a green light.

After talking to Bernard I have half an hour in the supervisor's office. The Class 50 on the 17.33 to Waterloo fails and has to be replaced by a Class 33 incurring a 30min late start. I see John Beer who has just returned from a NSE marketing meeting in London and brief him on events before catching the 18.18 dmu which arrives at St. David's 4min late, departs 2min late and is on time at Dawlish.

The Dawlish Gazette has a front page about withdrawal of InterCity stops in the town, my letter, and an article praising a new bus service to Heathrow and London. The Mid-Devon Advertiser has a headline proclaiming "B.R. Axes Jobs" but an admittedly fair report of the supervisory withdrawals.

John Beer rings up at 19.40 to discuss how he should deal with rostering problems that have emerged for Monday before the supervisory consultation and negotiation on Wednesday. The advice given is to exercise discretion until Wednesday's business is finished.

CHAPTER 39: CONTROL LETS ME DOWN

Monday 23rd February 1987

An urgent phone call from John Beer this weekend has altered my plans for today. It seems that two consultation meetings I was expecting to chair today have not been arranged by the admin. On the other hand, John has found that the interviews for the part-time Newton Abbot booking clerk post have been organised for today but he has a prior appointment at the Tourist Board so I go to Torquay to cover the interviewing.

Linda is teaching in Torquay so she drops me off and the papers arrive by train. John Hedge and I take the interviews from 09.30. There is a retired chartered engineer and retired bank cashier. Both seem a little wooden but would obviously cope easily. There is also the wife of Dawlish middle turn leading railman the conscientious Percy Michell but she would depend on a lift from Percy. Another claims to have experience in cash handling but that was prior to 1950 and is giving contradictory answers in an effort to give the answers for which he thinks we are looking, and another withdraws. The best applicants are two ladies of around 40 who are re-entering work and Mrs Powlesland gets the vote.

I return to the office but drop off first at Newton Abbot. The supervisors are no longer in position but there are no problems. In the booking office, senior clerk Roy Watts is being negative and acts as though he does not want his newly agreed part time assistance. I have a quick run to Exeter with the 13.39 HST and discuss the training methods for part-time jobs. *Part-timers were an untried concept at that time.* Full time training works best in order to take advantage of the training courses and to start the new staffing earlier.

Miss Hisscock, from Stoke Lyne hospital, and Devonair arrive to accept the donation from the Santa Specials. Organiser Robin Waller hands over the cheque and we all put an interview on tape.

There are insufficient of us to make the local area meeting productive so we limit ourselves to the summer staffing arrangements. In discussion with the Express & Echo it has transpired that the man killed at Westford was one of the newspaper's photographers. I have therefore decided to write a letter of sympathy which the editor has offered to deliver. It also turns out that the deceased was involved in a road accident on a tandem two years ago which resulted in the death of his son.

Andy Braund arrives in his ASLEF branch secretary guise. Driver Oke, the driver and also victim of Westford, is off sick with hypertension and anxiety state and he cannot get to sleep without a visit to the pub. Neither of us think that sounds like a good idea. We make an entry in the Accident Book and I let him have a copy of the driver's report making it clear that I have composed it for British Rail and driver Oke and it is for the driver to say if he wants it handed to ASLEF. Andy adds that there have been mutterings from the acting second man on the assistant loco, driver Mudge, that he had not been properly prepared for the scene he was to encounter. I point out that the full extent of what had happened was not fully understood until 14.15 when the assistant loco was already on its way. We agree that the driver would still have gone, had he known and I undertake to make the point with the supervisors not to edit the information before sending staff to such scenes. Andy seems happy with the outcome of our discussion.

At 17.05 Mr Scott rings to ask if I would like to be seconded to London as "Personnel Advisor" to Provincial Services for a 5% rise plus London Allowance and the prospect (threat) of it becoming permanent. *The sector seemed to have plenty of money to waste on things like this but not for station announcers. Was it really worth more than area manager Exeter? Do they really think I would be tempted either by the job or the remuneration?* The job is "to make a personnel input to corporate objectives within the sector structure." Does it sound like me? I think not, or at least I would like to think not, and have no hesitation in turning it down on at least four grounds before going off to indoor net practice at 18.30.

Tuesday 24th February 1987

I drive in for the 08.00 to Bristol which is 5min early at Worle Jct after recovery time and 10min late into Bristol. I change for the single power car connection to Parkway. This stops at two signals and loses 5min on a ten minute run. In view of the trains that were lost in the snow, I consider myself lucky that the weather is good. The HST to London is full and arrives at Swindon on time where I encounter David Langton on his way to a meeting on Laira carriage cleaning numbers for May.

My appointment is about the Yeovil remodelling scheme with John Curley in the chair and struggling. There is criticism that nothing has moved forward since the last meeting and we are still at the option evaluation phase but at least InterCity is committed to the retention of the existing Yeovil Jct to Pen Mill curve for their diversions.

After lunch, I speak to Peter Griggs about the assistant fare collector numbers for next May and his draft timetable. It is a specification that is close to that which I would have produced but I will be surprised if he gets it through consultation. I can imagine Chester Long asking questions such as on how many seconds per ticket his figures have been calculated and then after an hour's argument saying the figures contravene an existing recent agreement he has reached which were based on a similar workload elsewhere.

The 14.58 from Swindon to Temple Meads is on time despite standing outside the station for 5min. No. 47657 is on my connecting 09.43 from Newcastle on which I travel with David Lane from the civil engineer's. There is time to pick up the newspapers and for John Beer to inform me about the latest Provincial Services fare nonsenses that look set to lose money on flows such as Yeovil Pen Mill to Bath and our Newton St. Cyres Beer Engine promotion. They really have no idea of the local conditions of their own business and we recently first heard of one alteration in their 'Sales News'.

Wednesday 25th February 1987

On arrival at Dawlish station ten minutes earlier than usual I find the 07.08 cancelled and that Control has not notified the Exeter supervisor until 06.50. The stock is coming up empty in front of the Golden Hind to form the 08.11 to Waterloo but the only other arrangements Control has made is a special stop in the Hind at Totnes. I phone the section controller and the 'deputy' *(i.e. the shift manager)*. They admit they have not thought of doing anything and seem to think they are excused by the fact they did not find out until 06.35 when some observant soul noted the stock had not passed Tavistock Jct as booked at 06.10. It then took 15min to tell us. I ask whether they have considered instructing Dawlish and Teignmouth to send their Exeter passengers to Newton Abbot on the 07.20 from Dawlish arriving at 07.34 for the Hind at 07.36 which is likely to be a little late from its Totnes special stop even if it is running hard. They admit they had not thought of that. "No, that proves my point that you haven't given it any thought whatsoever," I say, more than a little impatiently. I have an audience of the Dawlish senior railman Vic Tilley, some permanent way staff and the Dawlish cricket umpire Geoff Lendon.

On reaching Newton Abbot, Bob Baker is the chargeman and I am expecting a few moans about not having had a supervisor in this situation but he is simply annoyed he could do nothing to effect an improvement because of the late advice and was concerned that I might blame him. I ensure he knows how much I appreciate his attitude.

At Exeter, I sort out the precise facts with duty manager Paul Silvestri and phone Ken Shingleton and David Warne at Swindon. The controllers will already have put their point of view and I now need to demolish it. David admits we are right and I agree to send him a six-point contingency plan for any future similar occurrence, any one of the six options being capable of being adopted given sufficient notice. Laira is also to blame for making a late detachment of a coach. If it was not safety related, for instance simply heat or lights, it should have been sent. We might even have been able to detach it at Exeter and return it on the 18.55 empties as recently agreed.

I catch the 09.23 to Taunton, a fast run in 22min 55sec, having sharp words with chargeman Phil Carrick who has not troubled himself to come over to the up side. After a cup of tea in the travel centre I am picked up by Taunton teacher Stephen Barnes to chat about project work for his business studies class and take the 12.15-13.15 session. It is an interesting exercise with some good questions and, after lunch, I return to Exeter on the 14.40. Drivers' LDC secretary Len Purse is travelling passenger in the train, as emphasised at our last meeting, so I spend the journey talking to him.

Alan Bell is back from sickness and he drops in to talk about expenditure on a new heater in the train crew toilet block. It is £1,000, *presumably an internal engineer's estimate that has a column headed '£000s',* so I turn it down.

Ken Boobyer and Bernard Price brief me on their consultation meeting with the supervisors. Bernard has told them the score because they have had difficulty believing that consultation on the principle was over at the end of the Sectional Council meeting. We had no requirement to talk further if it came down to it. *Bernard never seemed to have any difficulty in laying down the law, perhaps it was a function of being older and more experienced than the staff side.* The upshot is that the scheme is now well and truly implemented.

I have a message to ring the regional operating manager's admin manager. Would I like to be considered for a 12-week secondment to a German railways exchange scheme. The only requirement is a good knowledge of German so that rules me out. In that case would I like to go to Holland for a similar arrangement for seven weeks in the autumn. That sounds more likely as there are no language requirements and I can manage O-level and tourist French if that is any use, possibly if venturing into Belgium! If I do not want to go, could I spare John Beer instead? John is not sure that he wants to go on either of the trips and he does not speak German, *although his wife Sarah is a German graduate.* No. 50028 'Tiger' is on the 17.25.

Thursday 26th February 1987

The 07.08 is on time and, on visiting the supervisor's office I find that all the locals are also punctual. The mail has a copy of a letter from the general manager to the Express & Echo in my defence against the criticism that has been printed in their letters' page. The general manager's letter is fine and there is also a letter from the Transport Users' Consultative Committee saying they do not accept the remarks either.

At 09.30 I set off for the Transport 2000 seminar on Railfreight in the South West. There are five Exeter footplate staff at the event, including county councillor Richard Westlake. The opening address is from the chairman of the Somerset planning and transportation committee followed by Mike Jones, Railfreight national business manager for petroleum *(and future Hull Trains open access instigator)*. After lunch there is an ill-directed address from an academic about European comparisons. It is all fairly woolly and mild but quite interesting. However, the attendance of 35 comprises railway staff, trade union members and politicians. Only two are from industry, one being English China Clay which is already the best rail customer down here.

I see Mike Jones off on his train and get back into the office at 16.30 to speak to Ken Shingleton about the servicing problems being experienced at Laira. *To re-iterate a point perhaps, maintenance and cleaning 50 miles away from the line of route is never going to be satisfactory. Beyond the obvious time limitations, the managers involved never see the dissatisfied customers.* According to Linda I am 'big news' in the Dawlish Gazette again this week (!). The prospective labour party candidate has demanded an apology for the alleged slur that we only hear from him in election years and he has written a rather silly off-the-point letter. My view is that I am ahead and should therefore quit but we'll see if that's how it turns out.

Friday 27th February 1987

The 07.08 is on time again and the units are O.K. The paperwork is heavy and takes me through to 09.30 when signalman Bill Rowe arrives for his retirement after 35 years ending in signal boxes at Teignmouth, Dawlish and then Dawlish Warren from 1976. His retirement at 63 is voluntary but related to the closure of manual boxes. Unusually, but most pleasantly, Mrs Rowe accompanies him as she did to the long service awards. Teignmouth box has been demolished this week.

There is more news about the Dutch Exchange. Accommodation is arranged, 6x5 day weeks with four free days within this. Linda will get two free first class tickets to visit. John Beer is now very keen indeed but I will think about it a bit longer. I ask Karen Graeme to issue another Exeter-Waterloo *(internal, local initiative)* newsletter including the 1987 new timetable features. I also ring NSE route manager Gavin Scott in an effort to prevent some fares' anomalies that are in danger of occurring due to the NSE boundary. I also want to discuss plans for the route following the Channel Tunnel opening. Could we not go 'hourly' increase the infrastructure and run fast trains every two hours and stoppers on the opposite pattern. *A generation later the Tunnel is open with little effect on rail travel in the South West but the line has its extra infrastructure and hourly train service, unfortunately with an unimaginative pattern where no trains are 'fast' although they are, as a result, evenly spaced.*

At lunchtime I go into town to get some Austrian currency using the 12.20 Waterloo and am lucky to catch an 8min late

Skipper back down in the rain. I arrange with Alan Bell that I should cover the lunch with the senior Indian railway officers' exchange since we have changed plans about visiting Huddersfield due to Linda's work pattern. At 14.40 I go over to the panel box. The spirit is quite good with some friendly banter. Everything is running well and even the Brighton arrives on time.

Saturday 28th February 1987

At 11.19 I meet the party of eighteen Indian officers, and two overseas training assistants, for their social visit to Exeter. Although not warned, I have to give a talk on Exeter and its railways. They want to look at the level crossing and the panel box so there are a lot of yellow vests to organise. We have a pleasant buffet lunch at the Great Western for over an hour. It is an interesting group, all in their early 50s, who discuss everything from British Rail to imperialism. Back in the office I spend 45min with Alan Bell over a coffee before driving home.

CHAPTER 40: NETWORK SOUTH EAST TURNS CHICKEN

Monday 2nd March 1987

I drive in for 07.40 and try to get some phone calls made but everyone seems to be out, or perhaps 'not in' for me? I do get hold of Nigel Hicks at the Property Board to put some finishing touches to the appraisal document for the Waterloo line stations.

Then comes a bombshell. Network South East has dropped through working to Waterloo because it would make some Salisbury drivers redundant and they do not want to carry them or pay them off because they will need them next year for work cascaded from Waterloo. Sounds more like having their arm twisted to me. Mr Poynter, give him his due, allegedly hit the roof when the G.M. told him.

At 12.20 I start a meeting with Mike Donovan from NSE, John Curley and the Property Board. We identify the money we expect to make from opening the Yeovil town centre office. Network agrees to sponsor the scheme and our property man goes off to search for cheap premises in a good retail location with room for parking a small coach or minibus outside.

At 13.10 we go up to Central for a quick look round to form some idea of what can be done. In 1983, takings here were only £122,000 a year and closure of the booking office was in the budget. In 1986 this had risen to £263,000, a 'real terms' doubling after fare inflation of under 20%. We expect the new office at Yeovil would yield at least 10% on takings of £600,000 at Pen Mill plus say £25,000 for having a convenient parcels office. Rental perhaps £20,000 per annum and shopfitting- say a one-off £10,000.

Tony Crabtree briefs me on last week's Post Office meeting and I then write a dozen or so letters including one to the Dawlish paper about the alleged withdrawal of InterCity stops. A Mr Greenwood has written to the newspaper saying British

Rail's request for a contribution to repainting the viaduct, in a better style than engineering requirements dictate, is like him asking for a grant to repaint his front room. I write that I do not see the connection but there again I have not seen his front room because it is not on the tourist trail. I then decide not to rise to the bait and bin the draft. Dave Whittle then arrives to say he has written to the newspaper as vice-chairman of the ASLEF branch in my support which is both unexpected and kind, to say the least.

At 17.36 I set off for Taunton behind a Class 50 on the 14.12 from Penzance. We lose 4min to a barrier failure at Hele but then make up 2min recovery time and run down Wellington bank at 92mph with the Mark 1s. A word with Phil Carrick and then into the travel centre and I return to Exeter with Driver Craggs who arrives smack on time with the 16.05 from Paddington. The HST van sliding door sticks open and we lose 2min using brute force to close it. I go home and write the presentation for a course session I have to give at Westbury tomorrow which is scheduled to take 1½hrs and takes about that long to prepare.

Tuesday 3rd March 1987

I travel in to work with the engineering safety officer on the 08.01. He's been here just under a year and his job has just been cut out, although his move from Reading has been subsidised. The 06.35 from Bristol is in platform 1 and incurs 5min overtime. I ask Howard Davies why and unusually do not get a direct answer as I rush for the Westbury train. I'll catch up on that tomorrow *(pre mobiles of course)*. There is a Berks & Hants road-learning school out so I ride in the train and straighten out the presentation I have to give.

At Westbury, Eric Thompson the Taunton permanent way renewals engineer comes up to talk about the problems he is having with uncovered ballast trains due to the guards' shortage. It is very cold but these p.way chaps do not seem to feel it as I perish for 20min before he catches the down train.

After coffee in the staff college I address my subject, "The Area Manager's Role in Sector Cost Control." I discuss my view of the sectors and run through a couple of examples involving how to assess workloads such as station staffing. I am a bit nervous about the amount of material I have to cover a 90min session but I have to rush at the end and overrun with 15min of questions.

There is time to look at the latest developments in automated route learning. You can now call up which bit you might like to revise without fast forwarding through the whole tape. *Wow, technology has accelerated since then hasn't it?* After lunch with the delegates I go for the 14.00 to Exeter but have to wait 5min for a late running Cardiff-Portsmouth to make a connection. Despite 2x40mph tsrs we are on course for a punctual Exeter arrival thanks to 4min recovery time, 2min pathing and ½min saved at Taunton. But the Red Cow barriers are up in the air so we stop for 45sec and arrive 2½min late. The signalman has forgotten to put the barriers down, the same person who has featured twice in delays recently during his training. Bernard Price goes over to see him. It is likely that the signalman who is failing to make the transition from manual signalling will fail the competency test but it might be in everyone's best interest if he voluntarily withdraws. *From this perspective, the signalman does not seem to have been receiving much guidance from his colleagues so perhaps they were making sure our decision went the way they thought it should?*

I talk to Alan Bell about the difficulty the engineers are suffering from budget-cut uncovered turns and then to Railfreight Automotive about alleviating the congestion that is occurring by loading cars to their road transporters near the box. I do not want to employ direct tactics as we might end up with our emergency vehicles deliberately blocked in, which is more of a problem than having difficulty getting out while the hauliers are present.

Bernard wants my car for an out-of-hours visit to Yeovil where he suspects the signalman is having his wife in the box and also watching television. A regular home from home, but the supervisors are supposed to stop this kind of irregularity before we even hear about it. No. 50025 'Invincible' in NSE livery on NSE stock is on the 17.25.

Wednesday 4th March 1987

This morning I opt for the 08.13 to Newton Abbot. The up stopper features a rather game leading Skipper hauling a completely dead classmate and manages to drop just 2min on its 8min late Paignton start to its 10min late Exeter St. David's arrival. I ride with driver Colin Pulleyblank on the down train and mainly talk about the person accommodated in the Newton Abbot East 'booking lad' job who has been asking some obscure questions about pensions and Colin's Newton Abbot background is able to throw some light on the problem. Spray on the line causes some slipping but we are on time.

Everything is O.K. at Newton Abbot but chief clerk Roy Watts is still beating the drum about part time staff.
"How do you know when they are competent?" he asks.
Puzzled, I reply, "Same as anyone else."
On the platform I meet former regional signalling inspector John Forrester who has an excellent reputation amongst the older Newton Abbot staff but we never really hit it off when he was at work. *I guess it was age discrimination. He thought no one my age could know his signalling rules and regulations and I thought anyone his age must be well past it.*

I go up to Exeter on the York running 10min late and brief Bernard Price for his forthcoming trip round the area with the general manager. I conduct a meeting with a Mr Hawkins from the S&T and area I.T. manager Bob Eastley about modernisation of the telephone exchange. It is an I.T. issue but Bob is of the vintage that knows exactly what goes on in the depths of the offices in which they are located. I opt for two 'Rhapsody' systems costing around £9,000 and an additional route to accommodate Yeovil locations for around £4,500 which should improve the flexibility of internal communications.

Lunch is at the Imperial with Roy Corlett of Radio Devon. I reluctantly agree to supply his travel slot with more information although I feel he has enough at present to keep his listeners and my customers informed without making it sound as if the rail service is unreliable when similar car and bus delays remain unreported. In turn, he lets me know a few details concerning the departure of BBC director-general Alisdair Milne.

Eggesford signalman Harry Toulson comes in for his retirement and I confirm I will still call in to see him when passing his home in the station house when on my travels. Next comes Irishman Jerry O'Brien from Honiton. He is naturally talkative and has always been hospitable when I have visited him so time passes quickly before Bob Poynter and Ken Beresford (regional operations and personnel managers respectively) descend on me for coffee.

We all go up to the Imperial Hotel *(now, almost needless to say, Wetherspoons)* for what is termed a 'Senior Staff Forum', essentially a two-way briefing session with the general manager, the local managers and their heads of department. There is a 30min talk from the g.m., 90min questions and a three hour buffet. Ian Johnstone brings up my budgetary restrictions on engine power for engineering work which the g.m. asks me, effectively, to defend in public. Since it is a direct result of regional policy I think this is bad form on his part. The engineers say they are unable to run scrap recovery trains which I counter by saying the scrap they are talking about has been there for two years, the restriction has been applied for three months and they know it will be relaxed at the end of the financial year in four weeks time - finishing by saying that if people want the budget delivered they will have to listen to the pips squeak. I take Bob Poynter to his parents' house and get home at 23.30.

Thursday 5th March 1987

No. 50026 'Indomitable' is on the 07.08 so I can see off the deputy g.m. on the 08.00 and then the g.m and party, including Bernard Price, for Yeovil on the 08.11. As we wait, the Exmouth leaves and then stops to pick up the conductor from the front set who is late to his train. Mr Poynter is not amused, and neither am I.

From 09.00 I am interviewing for the senior TPS clerk CO4 post vacated by the sad death of Barry Thorn. There is no real spark from my CO3 candidates who are covering the job on occasions and an applicant from Warrington is little better. However, there is a Mancunian currently working at Bristol who is much livelier and worth a risk.

We also interview three potential applicants for travel centre jobs. There will be further interviews to come so there will be no decision today. A lady from Aberystwyth for the Taunton job has the unusual hobby of porcinology but she is… bland? A man from London for the Barnstaple travel centre manager seems excellent but his withdrawal from teaching a few years ago seems veiled in a degree of mystery. Another man from Salisbury is asked for his ideas to boost travel. He thinks there is scope for increasing continental sales, walkers' trips, and advertising steam trains in a "Gricers' Gazette". London traffic? Well, he thinks that 'can be taken for granted. *This served to deepen my prejudice against Salisbury.*

There is the good news that a rival London coach service at 07.15 from Dawlish has ceased to run after just four days. We could not begin to compete with their £10 fare but even a full coach would scarcely have earned a profit on a brand new vehicle.

At 14.15 we go across the road for the newly reconstructed Post Office liaison meeting which I now chair separately with their Exeter and Newton Abbot district management. They do not seem to have much on their side of the agenda and it seems the initiatives are coming from our side concerning safety, over-carryings, the revised train service, letting part of our parcels area for cleared bags and 'junk' mail. Would they consider forwarding mail by rail from Barnstaple? Oh, yes – could we possibly use their canteen?

Back in the office Nigel Hicks wants to review some station trading possibilities including the re-instatement of a bookstall/newsagent at St. David's, surely the largest station in the country without a specialised outlet. He also has some information for me about my Waterloo line investment appraisals which have identified some retail opportunities.

No. 50010 'Monarch' is on the 17.25 – No. 50011 'Centurion' was withdrawn last week, the first to go, for cannibalisation to ensure a supply of spares. At 20.15 I phone Bernard Price to see how his day went with the g.m. I fill him in on a few events in the panel box. There have been two delays caused by another trainee signalman misrouting trains. His reliable trainer says he did not have time to intercede but he must realise that he is the one in charge and must intervene if he sees the trainee signalman making the errors. I then read the second attempt on the draft 1989 timetable that InterCity route manager Peter Griggs has prepared and which we are to discuss tomorrow at Bristol.

Friday 6th March 1987

I board the 08.00 at Exeter to find cross country route manager Brian Johnson and a henchman sitting with Jim Collins. I have met Dr John Capey, principal of Exeter College, on the platform. He is keen on railways, although more from the steam angle, so we all travel together to Bristol.

Peter Griggs and regional railways west of England manager David Mather join us and we lock ourselves into a dingy room above Platform 7 at Temple Meads. I achieve some of my objectives in altering the specification to plug mid-morning gaps at Totnes and Newton Abbot. *Presumably I was on the right lines as at least 95% of trains stop at both stations nowadays and Totnes has realised the potential we always sensed it had.* There is a long discussion about the summer Saturday service before the meeting breaks up at 15.20. I wait until 16.14 to join the northbound Newcastle HST on which Linda is travelling.

We are 5min late and run into trouble between Gloucester and Cheltenham. Arrival at Birmingham, is 16min late and very little is recovered by Sheffield so the 6min Huddersfield via Penistone connection is broken. There is a 19.15 dmu to Leeds and we are trailed round to a Derby heavyweight Lincoln-based set in a bay which promptly fails thereby jeopardising the Huddersfield connection from Wakefield. We pick up a Hull train to Doncaster with No. 31417 to connect with the 18.50 King's Cross-Harrogate for the next Wakefield-Huddersfield train at 21.10, delivering us one hour late. There was no guidance concerning what should have been done. *Services are more frequent now of course but privatisation has not delivered any better guidance during disruption, with a few honourable exceptions.*

Saturday 7th March 1987

I go down to Huddersfield station to check on any retiming for tomorrow. There is a confusing note on the departure sheet that I bring to the attention of the ticket collector. He replies by saying that if I have a complaint I should bring it to the attention of the 'Consultative people'. This is a ridiculous response and also incorrect as B.R. should be approached first. I leave in disgust and vow to let Mike Hodson know next week. We return home on Sunday on No. 45107 to Manchester and then the through HST which is ten minutes late following the late running Newcastle-Plymouth.

CHAPTER 41: A SECTOR DIRECTOR CALLS

Monday 9th March 1987

The main business of the morning is the introduction of free car parking for rail users at Dawlish and Teignmouth. In high summer rail passengers parking their cars have to pay the £1 park charge on top of the fare. In terms of the County Council transport policy it will reduce the average car journey to Exeter even more than the orbital park and ride schemes and promote High Street shopping over out-of-town shopping centres. From our point of view we will lose revenue from car parking only on the days they are full as there are few car-based commuters and even fewer car based shoppers at present. Now that there are two units more reliably on the main commuter train we are no longer likely to score an own goal by attracting extra customers who are then forced to stand. *The scheme did not last long as Regional Railways introduced target car parking earnings without any relationship to rail carryings. So much for commercial acumen and remote management.*

Joe Cockram is the staff representative from Dawlish and we also fix the summer staffing. I am reluctant to pursue pay and display because the attendant can produce a lot of extra cash by being aware of spare spaces in this long, thin former goods yard location which can cause congestion if drivers turn round instead of finding an unoccupied berth.

At 14.00 Nicholas Rogers comes from a consultancy firm to determine my opinion as an internal customer of the civil and S&T engineers and what I consider are their strengths and weaknesses, giving marks out of 5 on each heading. A waste of time and money? Perhaps but I do feel that the 'internal customer' concept helps focus everyone. He has interviewed 45 other people *(so perhaps it was a waste of money!).* He says my marking has been more structured than all the others but I bet he has said that to all the 44 other interviewees. At 16.00 we have our local management meeting and I have to push for the Paignton summer staffing to be finalised, both for setting the budget as well as the obvious need to have measures in place.

Tuesday 10th March 1987

I arrive at Dawlish at 06.37 for the HST to Exeter, on time, with driver Boston who is another one of the excellent young drivers here, after moving from Birmingham New Street. *He was subsequently one of our two transfers to the Eurostar driving establishment. I think this was the HST that formed the school train to Paignton and then the northbound Devonian.* Driver Boston has just completed the quiz programme 'Busman's Holiday' application form and has had to answer 40 questions being on his honour not to use text books. *Once more, pre-internet!*

There is just time to pick up some misplaced papers and run for the 07.00 to Paddington. John Beer is going to the NSE marketing meeting at Victoria and wants some breakfast but I prefer a cup of tea from driver Barriball's billy-can in the cab. At Taunton, the 07.25 to Glasgow is in the middle platform and is let out in front of us converting a 2min early arrival into 3min late at Cogload Jct. We are stopped for 45sec at Taunton East Station box but the Class 50 on twelve bogies then runs clear of us.

At Castle Cary (not Westbury as booked) 'B' driver Ken Croft arrives with freshly brewed tea. Ken was on the Class 52 'Westerner' that derailed and perched itself perilously on the top of the embankment at Somerton after encountering a buckled rail, back in the late 1960s I think. *He still eased over this section as did many of his colleagues but it has now worked its way out of the culture.* After the customary overtime at Castle Cary we are 5-6min late all the way to Reading after a 60tsr at Newbury and another to 20mph at Theale.

Approaching Newbury an old man is standing on a footbridge, leaning over and waving like a 9yr-old. John touches the horn and Ken waves and turns to say, "That's made his day. Just think what some people want to make them happy." We are 5½min late from Reading with 5min recovery time to come but there is a 20mph slack in force at Acton Main Line that might cost 3min *assuming it does not cause a backlog and therefore more time* but when we encounter the warning board it is showing 100mph so we skate on through and arrive a satisfying 30sec early.

I reach Waterloo at 10.00 for the meeting about the 1988 NSE timetable but I have to sit through an hour of Weymouth line arrangements first. The Exeter line is a simpler affair. The 05.48 up train becomes 05.20 with an attractive 08.36 Waterloo arrival with most trains running to the regular crossing pattern interval.

At 14.00 I transfer to a meeting being held by Salisbury area manager Gerry Daniels over his steam train programme. He is less than pleased when I tell him I shall be debiting my administrative time against the costs of the project. He says he is not doing so as he is doing it in his own time. I don't seem to have that much spare to give him. He wants the 19.10 Waterloo to Exeter to be retimed to accommodate one of his trains but that will jeopardise the Plymouth connection at St. David's so I make an effective objection to that. I cannot but see this in the context of the sales of Network Cards at Salisbury in Period 11 last year, surely Gerry's core business, which amounted to just 28. No one I speak to can believe that statistic.

I move on to see NSE investment manager John Norman to discuss my Axminster and Exeter Central submissions. He thinks my figures are more detailed than necessary but they would have barely been satisfactory in my Eastern region days in that organisation. *I am not sure whether the NSE procedures were slipshod but I prefer to think they were perhaps pleasantly less bureaucratic.*

The meeting coincides with the 16.38 departure home. This

one is booked for the Clapham Jct '7-set' and a Class 33. No. 33015's load includes TSO S 3838 which I suspect might be the oldest vehicle on B.R., at least in a regular set. We manage a maximum speed of 80mph before Farnborough before a dead stand for signals. Then we use the down side platform at Basingstoke and incur a 20mph tsr before Worting Jct. Nevertheless, we are only 1½min late at Salisbury where Exeter driver Ivor Nation takes over.

I join Ivor during the Gillingham stop for a pleasant run to Exeter with plenty of time in hand. At Yeovil Jct I refuse to take the senior railman's handsignal for the right-away as it is dark and should be a handlamp so we are 1min late as a result. I will take it up with him more directly tomorrow. After 2min recovery time we are 4min early at Honiton and wait to cross the up train before reaching St. David's 1min early.

When I go to the train crew office Supervisor Ben Griffiths is moaning about his locker having been moved onto the floor to accommodate new fire alarm equipment. After trying to listen patiently I respond that it is probably time we should review whether all the lockers should be moved out of the office anyway. Paul Silvestri talks to me about his view of the 1988 West of England timetable before I get away to end a 15hr day. *Long but not exactly arduous!*

Wednesday 11th March 1987

I catch the Golden Hind to Taunton with John Beer to conduct interviews for a travel centre shift leader and a relief shift leader. There are ten interviewees and we have already excluded the Aberystwyth porcinologist. We would strategically like to appoint a local applicant as, otherwise, a CO_2 will be displaced and have to travel to Exeter which would be bad for morale and incur expensive travelling time. We like the look of Scotsman Jim Kerr whom we have inherited at Sherborne following the transfer of the Yeovil area from Westbury. If he was to get one of the jobs the jig-saw would fall into place. We have a senior railman that could take his clerical post which would leave a vacancy for a Yeovil resident in a Taunton platform staff job to transfer nearer home. This would then create a potential job for a displaced Taunton signalman after re-signalling.

The senior applicant is a man in his 50s from Bridgwater on a lateral move but he does not seem forceful enough to complement the mild-mannered travel centre manager. Jim scores highly on that point. The regional clerical sectional council representative is in for the jobs too. He will be away a lot which means someone who is known to have a poor disciplinary record would be likely to step up, which would need preventative action. We cannot be swayed by this, or I suppose, by the representative's adamant objections to the creation of the CO1 posts in the travel centre. Can he really then supervise the organisation he has so strongly opposed? John and I recognise that his career should not be prejudiced by doing what he thinks is right for the staff but the interview exposes some technical flaws in his knowledge. All candidates were asked how they would advise me to get to Innsbruck by rail and this candidate did not even get across the channel successfully.

Interviewees have been asked to prepare a 5min presentation on what steps they would take to improve shift leadership but our sectional council man's contribution sounds like an extract from a text book and is read out word for word. Again, there is a commitment question. After the interviews have been completed we consult the travel centre manager. There are four names we would consider, Jim Kerr, Steve Woodbury (Clarence's son), the Bridgwater applicant and one other. There has been a question about an accounting irregularity concerning one candidate and an excusatory note on his file that I would not have condoned had I been aware of it. We opt for a safe pair of hands, appointing Jim to the shift job and place Steve in the relief post. *I think this interview should have been John Beer and Mervyn but the organisation when I came to Exeter travel centre managers reported directly to the area manager and I think this was a derivative of those days.*

Obviously John had to be involved but I think I should have ducked out. Perhaps the sectional council issue swayed me.

We have just missed our train back to Exeter so have to wait 45min for the next only to discover it is 25min late from Westbury, having covered the Hungerford-Bedwyn stops of a cancelled local and therefore eventually 16min late at Exeter. My Skipper is in No. 3 receiving fitters' attention so we are 4min late as I ride to Dawlish with driver Edney.

Thursday 12th March 1987

Andy Snowdon is driving the up stopper and Regional Railways director, the fiery John Edmonds is in Plymouth. *Provincial Services was renamed Regional Railways at some point during this narrative.* The Skipper count is 'plus one' for the first time ever as there are three on my train instead of the booked two. Andy looks enviously at the blue sky and the swell. He is going surfing to Sandy Bay when his shift is finished and I reflect that drivers are getting younger.

I hold a meeting at Exmouth with staff representative Peter Stockwell about management of the 'free car park for rail users' idea there. It is his first consultation meeting so he has to be guided through it and I return on the 10.00. There was supposed to be an 11.00 meeting at Lympstone with a parish councillor but he has 'flu so it has been cancelled.

Back at Exeter I use the extra time to visit the panel box. The main problem is a 6Z50 Cardiff to City Basin scrap empties *(strange reporting number as Z was supposed to be used for inter-regional specials)* which is in danger of delaying the 08.50 from Paddington. The freight is approaching Tiverton Parkway with the road set for Tiverton Jct loop as the HST passes Wellington. As well as not being a 'Z' I wonder if it is not a '6' either as it seems to be running like a 45mph Class 7 but the Tiverton Parkway stop in the HST means the freight is looped just in time.

The afternoon is routine, catching up on phone calls and paperwork and No. 33209 is on the down stopper, so we might soon collect all the Hastings-line gauge locos on this service.

Friday 13th March 1987

We have been paying special attention to carriage cleaning this week ready for sector director Edmonds to visit *(a process not dissimilar to the one that produced the record Skipper availability yesterday from Laira I presume)*. Nos. 50008 'Thunderer' and 50003 'Temeraire' are on the 07.08 and we have the extra Skipper again. Not much point moaning about the unrealistic thirteen sets for twelve diagrams then. Mr Edmonds does not arrive until 10.20 and he has been caught for speeding en route. Jim Collins has warned me he is a 'lunatic driver' and not to go in a car with him.

We set off for Exmouth on the 10.28 and return on the 11.00. I tell the sector director what we are doing on the branch very much in the way of objectives and action plan. I tell him that some of our efforts are obstructed by the marketing organisation at Swindon and he responds by saying he is not interested and David Mather the route director is the one who decides. This is the opposite of Chris Green and Cyril Bleasdale and I note the black marks *(from him to me and me to him)* for the future.

Back at Exeter we go to the stabling point for a demonstration from the 'Dragoni' mobile washing machine. Mr Edmonds suggests we take a Ford Transit van to Italy to secure spare parts. It might be a quicker job if he drives. He then makes me feel uncomfortable by insisting we wear yellow jackets for an authorised walking route which is definitely not necessary. *It arguably is now but public foot crossings for instance do not require high-viz jackets.* He departs by road at 12.15 after his demotivational visit for a 13.00 meeting at Bristol. This could prove an expensive exercise in speeding fines. "Why on earth was he travelling by road?" ask some of the staff, quite rightly.

After he has gone, I corner David Mather. Does he think our 'Trains and Boats and Trains' promotion (train to Paignton, steam hauled train to Kingswear, river trip to Totnes and train back) will improve his bottom line? Yes, he does. Mr Edmonds has said we can ignore any opposition if David wants it, including therefore the Swindon marketing team. So I make a couple of calls to the accountants to confirm the figures I am using are accurate which gives David no choice but to proceed.

I run David up to Exmouth Jct to see if the wagon shops are suitable for conversion to a servicing point for Skippers and the mooted Exeter-Waterloo super sprinters. Such investment would render the troublesome Dragoni and its Ford Transit Italian supplies shuttle redundant but I feel Exmouth Jct is too far from St. David's. We need to be within a shunt of the station not a train movement through a relatively congested area.

John Beer comes to see me about filling the Yeovil clerical jobs. One job will go to a clerk from Lymington who will leave and rejoin to get his move back to this area. The other will go to senior railman Palmer, and perhaps senior railman Perkins will then transfer to that job leaving the Taunton platform job for a signalman as planned.

Saturday 14th March 1987

Shopping this morning and checking out the possibility of lending railway tables and chairs to the local repertory company for their production of Ridley's 'Ghost Train'. Over coffee at the Pickwick in Teignmouth we have a chat with driver Mick Lockyer, his wife and in-laws. *Mick was the other driver who went to Eurostar.*

My brother Allan, who is at present train crew supervisor at Lincoln, rings to say he will arrive on the 16.05 from Paddington at 19.14 having travelled via Birmingham, Derby

St. Pancras overnight, Tilbury, Swindon, Westbury, Exeter, Yeovil Jct and Exeter again.

Arriving at Dawlish station at 19.11 I find Joe Cockram inspecting the line between the station and Kennaway tunnel following the report of a bump by the driver of a light diesel. An up HST is standing near the Clerk Tunnel and the 16.05 from Paddington is passing Exminster. I join Joe and inspect the continuous welded rail expansion breather switches closely. I can see no problems but caution the 16.05. The permanent way sub-inspector arrives 20min later and normal working is resumed some 25min subsequently.

CHAPTER 42: NEAR MISS AT HELE

Sunday 15th March 1987

After a walk to Dawlish Warren on which the highlight was No. 33044 light diesel and No. 33063 on ballast empties we take Allan to the station for the 14.59 Skipper to Newton Abbot for the up Liverpool. His journey home will be less circuitous than the outward one.

The driver of the Skipper calls me over to say there are kids on the line through the tunnels taking a short cut with the tide being in. I can see them climbing back over the railings near Kennaway Tunnel. I phone the signalbox to say that if they receive a report about the youths on the line they are now clear and ask them to phone the central B.T. Police at Bristol to ask them to look in.

We meet our neighbours who need to go to Birmingham Airport by train in May so I volunteer to get them the information, have a ten minute talk with driver Tom Caslin and his wife and then the redundant engineer's safety officer so there is not much escaping work in Dawlish.

Monday 16th March 1987

There is only one Class 142 on my 08.01 today. The 04.45 empty stock from Laira had two sets promised despite there being a spare at Exeter, with one on the 05.15 empties. It promptly failed. Result: full number of units supplied but in the wrong place and passengers standing. *It is interesting to reflect that in those days and that part of the world, standing passengers was not seen as acceptable.* I ride up with driver Fred Batchelor who tells me he nearly joined the Jersey police as a young man instead of the railway.

This morning's mail contains a letter from the driver's assistant who has applied for the management training scheme. It is a copy of a letter he has sent to the BRB Training Adviser complaining that no one will tell him how he has done in his application for management training. I am annoyed because I am his line manager and he has an appointment to see me about it on Thursday. It confirms my view that he has a narrow view and little idea of how the management process functions. *Or fails to do so?*

I dash out to catch the 09.23 to Taunton, passing driver Colin Harrison and Alan Bell on the way. The train is running in 2min early and the driver is waiting for relief. Apparently Colin is working the train and comes puffing up the platform behind me. Fortunately for him the train is delayed with a seat reservation problem of a young woman and a disabled toddler as the senior railman escorts them down the train to find suitable seats. We do not run very quickly to Taunton but make up our recovery time.

At Taunton I have a chat with Martin Baldock and note that the monitors for my train have no entry in the cctv 'minutes late' column. I have issued an instruction that as soon as we have positive information that a train is on time we should put a zero in the column. Leading railman Chard has not done so and when I go to see him he acts awkwardly. He also wants to talk about his ailments before doing anything and I tell him to obey his instructions. The train concerned is now 2min late so he inputs '02' which I then tell him to alter to '2'.

Retired Stoke divisional manager Trevor Anderson is on the train on his way to chair a 'Helping Hand Fund' meeting at Bristol and we talk for a while before joining civil engineer Peter Warren and Laira depot engineer Tony Coles. The dominant topic of conversation is sectorisation. Our meeting includes a presentation on Cross Country changes, including 'Holidaymaker Expresses', 'Holidaymaker Saver' tickets and introduction of a Cross Country Grill. In discussion, Bristol area manager introduces a new term to the conversation to cover the infighting that dominates our current existence: intersectorcide.

At 14.15 I have to meet regional personnel manager Ken Beresford who wants to discuss his plans for overhaul of the always cumbersome but now outdated and, at regional level, discredited 1956 Machinery of Consultation and Negotiation which catered for a less centralised organisation with three times the numbers of staff. Ken is recommending one local four-person local departmental committee (LDC) for all grades instead of one or two people for small stations and four-man LDC for salaried, 'conciliation' (basically platform), guards and footplate staff chaired by area managers. Matters could be referred to a four-person council and then national level. Area managers would be able to undertake 'plant bargaining' and fix grades regardless of inter-area comparisons. I suggest a way of co-opting a local member for out-station issues to combat claims of reducing the effectiveness of consultation, in effect a three-person committee with a local co-opted member, which he is happy to consider. *No doubt a waste of time in view of the interim nature of any alteration prior to privatisation.*

I just make the 15.20 HST which waits 5min overtime for connections and loses 9min to tsrs, including an emergency one. We regain 3min recovery time and ½min at Taunton but we are still in double figures of arrears at Exeter. My bag contains a complicated story about a driver who was absent claiming jury service after he had been released by the court officials and the case of a 26year-old driver's assistant, who is at home with his elderly parents, being treated for depression and refusing to go out. I catch the 17.25, surprisingly on time with No. 33044 on nine, mainly by leaving Exeter St Thomas ½min early and saving 42sec on the Warren stop.

Tuesday 17th March 1987

At least we have two units today, which is a good job because the train is much busier. Fred Batchelor is the driver again. We are 1min late waiting for the down Bristol to leave and a 'trip freight' to go up the bank before the Salisbury comes down to St. David's. John Beer and I are interviewing for travel centre shift leaders from 08.30. The first applicant is local and has to be fetched from the admin office seven minutes after his interview time. He is woolly in his answers and kindly informs us that just because he is the senior CO2 applicant he does not think he is entitled to the job. True. We go through to 10.30 with Simon Bubb from Taunton, a CO2 from Plymouth and the affable Brian Platt from Paignton.

There is then a 2½hr break to go through the parcels' business specification with area parcels manager Tony Crabtree and regional sector manager Keith Joint. It is straightforward enough, simply setting up audit arrangements and discussing the background to the businesses so we resume interviews at 14.00. *More discussing sectorisation arrangements, this time for a sector that was going to implode.*

The last applicant for the shift leader job is a CO3 from Bournemouth wanting to move back to his home county after 20yrs away. Although he has sold tickets he professes no knowledge of enquiry work and has not worked in a travel centre. *The decision to interview him would have been the need to prove that the 'senior suitable applicant' had been appointed if challenged – easy enough to do but one has to demonstrate that applicants senior to the appointee are not suitable.*

We move on to Barnstaple travel centre manager CO4 interviews. There are three interviewees from London travel centres, one a displaced CO4 who does nothing to inspire John Beer but who warms up towards the end. He says he has not tried to settle his redundancy in the London area as he wants to move away from the south east. The best applicant might well be Mr Mileham who was interviewed 'early' last week but is in danger of suffering from the syndrome of being away from the pack. The job goes to displaced Barnstaple CO3 Brian McManus whom I note as being 'content to be a man of few words'. He will be able to handle the staff there though, and John feels he can be channelled. If we move someone in, Brian's travel costs will need to be covered, he has already refused accommodation in an Exeter CO3 and I do not wish to draw further sector attention to clerical costs at the end of the branchline. Redundancy would need funding or the wage bill would need carrying all next year. Despite these considerations, he was genuinely the best man for the job.

I query the reply to a complaint which has foxed me. Scarcely surprising as Lockerbie was mentioned in the text when it should have been Dumfries. The 17.25 has 1965 green-liveried No. 33008 'Eastleigh' and guard Sid Oak who pauses for a chat with Ken Boobyer and me.

Wednesday 18th March 1987

Once again I ride in with Fred Batchelor, guessing he will be more than fed up, but it would seem rude not to after having done so twice. There has been some good work at Exeter with loco and coaches on the Barnstaple branch, the inward train running in behind our train at 08.21 with through passengers transferred briskly to the (now) leading set of my train which leaves at 08.22 to terminate at Central. The remaining set goes forward at 08.24 to Exmouth. I catch the Barnstaple unit on its way back at 08.55. Richard Westlake is spare and comes to talk to me about the Devon County Council community programme. Arrival is 3min early and I go to congratulate Brian McManus on his appointment before visiting the parcels office. Back at Exeter, Bob Eastley comes to show me the latest computer print-out for monitoring assistant fare collector revenue against 'norms'.

I go to Yeovil with No. 50045 'Achilles' behind a Salisbury driver with Guard Jock Mundell. It is a fast run with 85mph between Feniton and Honiton and 86½mph before the brakes for Axminster. There is time for a word with supervisor Terry Gale before returning on the 11.10 Waterloo with No. 50042 'Triumph' and Alf Trapnell. He already has a traction trainee with him and a former Leeds driver road learning. It is not usual for Alf to risk exceeding a limit so that means 67mph on the Crannaford 70mph tsr but an on time Central arrival. St.

David's is reached 1½min late due to a timetable clash with the 14.28 to Dawlish leaving platform 3 at the precise time the Class 50 is supposed to leave Central. A Dept. of Transport Inspectorate decision has ruled trains cannot leave Central unless the allocated St. David's platform is clear.

At 15.30 I see Nigel Gooding to coach him a little bit more for his management training interview. Then I discuss the plans of Paul Scanes now he has not been selected before a tetchy interview with the secondman applicant who is very upset with my negative reference. He says his character has been destroyed. He proves my point by complaining that he cannot apply for a Plymouth supervisory job because Mr Bell and Mr Price have not sent him a salaried staff vacancy application form. I walk into the admin office and bring him a handful. "Why couldn't you do that?" I ask him and then tell him it will be acceptable for him to submit a late application. Guard Hayes is the fourth applicant but he does not turn up.

After a long discussion with John Beer I go across to the panel box to find it in some turmoil. The driver of the 17.00 Plymouth-Paddington with Old Oak driver Quinn was approaching Hele auto-half barrier crossing under clear signals at 90mph only to encounter the rear of an articulated trailer blocking his path, the tractor unit having stopped just beyond the open side of the crossing. The HST driver slammed the brake into emergency, blared the horn and was grateful to see the trailer move clear just in time.

He must have been brave not to have dived for the engine compartment. Driver Quinn is reported as being shaken and I ask the Taunton chargeman to ensure he is able to continue. *This was before such measures became mandatory.* All trains are cautioned and the S&T technicians are sent to ensure the crossing equipment was working properly. Once a driver has passed the entry barrier on his side of the road it is incumbent on him to clear the open exit side at an AHB crossing and the equipment is not protected by signals in order to reduce barrier down time. The result is around half a minute to clear if a train strikes in. All trains are cautioned in the meantime and I ask the police to go out and try to identify the lorry driver, probably from a nearby haulage depot given the time of evening.

At 19.15 I set off to give a talk to the Exe Valley Rotary Club at Bickleigh. I arrive at 19.40 for 20.00 and find myself the first there. One member arrives and rather rudely proceeds to reel off every train he has ever caught that has been late. Proceedings are encumbered by the somewhat unnecessary arrival of a kissogram girl to celebrate the birthday of an apparently juvenile 50-year-old. Hospitality is not of the highest order and when the vice-chairman hears the title of the talk he says, "Keep it short." I respond by saying I can keep it very short indeed by standing up and sitting straight back down if he likes. I think he gets the message. It seems to go down quite well and there is some welcome cut and thrust in the questions that requires some fleetness of foot. They say it is one of the best talks they have had in a very long time but I guess that is their standard vote of thanks. I leave without really being seen off and get home at 23.35.

Thursday 19th March 1987

I take the car to Paignton for 08.55. Ernie Bittlestone is making threats concerning the withdrawal of the chargeman's supervisory pay rates on summer Saturdays which they have been allowed for a great number of years. I tell him that I'm not arguing and the consultative process will determine who is in charge of the working. I move on to Totnes and have a pleasant hour with relief clerk John Farmer and senior railman Colin Harmes and have a chance to play with the new 'parcels business machine' computer. Starting with 'a parcel has been sent from Cheltenham to Totnes, consignor and consignee both unknown' it starts a search of what is in the system and where it might be. It then prevents Colin from sending a parcel to Maidenhead on the 09.51 advising that it is held for the 13.27, arriving after close of work. This is clearly nonsense so we over-ride it, a process that should be done only for direct transits, not transfers. I ring Tony Crabtree to ask him to iron out the wrinkle.

Next call is at Torquay for half an hour with travel centre manager John Hedge before picking up Linda from her language school teaching. John Beer is on the 14.50 when I join at Dawlish. I need to alter our holiday reservations to give Linda time to recover from her sore throat and also to arrange travellers' cheques and insurance.

It is time for an update from the police on progress with last night's incident. They are following up with the transport firm by the crossing but I tell them I would like an officer present at Hele from 17.45 to 18.45 next week if the driver has not been identified by then.

Mike Hodson has rung to say that the area manager at Liverpool Street, whom we both know, has asked to come out of his job and then asks about some applicants for a vacancy at Harrogate whom I have recently interviewed. He also says the Huddersfield ticket collector has been reprimanded over last Sunday's incident and has a Form 1 outstanding over his attendance record. No. 33017 struggles manfully with a ten coach load and arrives at Dawlish ½min late, mainly through squeezing away slightly early from some stations though.

Friday 20th March 1987

I drive in for 07.40 and clear my desk ready for the holiday. Julian Crow and Ted Solomon arrive at 09.15 to discuss development plans for St. David's station. Julian was a trainee with me back in 1974 and I have not seen him since. He is now West of England InterCity terminals manager. *This was the start of a 25-year association with the Western which ended up with him receiving an O.B.E. He was always somewhat distant with me after my retirement though, perhaps because I was impatient with him in a time-serving sector job and perhaps I could not resist telling him what needed improving in the face of what I took to be a level of smug satisfaction.* Proposals for passenger operated lifts are welcome as are waiting room and car park improvements. I object to the idea of passengers leaving the open station only to have to queue in the elements at a machine that will issue a token for them to be able to operate the car park barrier. I cannot help but think that if I had proposed this they would have said I was not looking at the problem from a customer perspective, supposedly the domain of the business sectors. We walk round the station before starting the meeting with the engineers and the Property Board, closing at 12.50. I then work right up to my train time on phone calls and correspondence catching No. 33109, ten seconds early at Dawlish tonight and walk home excited at the prospect of Vienna next week.

CHAPTER 43: BY RAIL TO VIENNA

Sunday 22nd March 1987

The holiday starts with No. 47609 'Fire Fly' emerging from Kennaway Tunnel in InterCity livery, taking the cat to family lodgings in Huddersfield. We are not expecting a smooth passage through Taunton because the engineer has over-run on the down line at Wellington and on the up at Hele. The result will be bunching of trains in each direction. In the end we are 47min late at Cogload Jct and lose our path north of Bristol. *I am rather surprised that I seem to have taken this so calmly, implying this was normal.* Despite good work at Birmingham where we are quickly re-engined with No. 86403 we reach Stockport 34min late. *These were the quaint old days when electric traction was preferred under electric wires.* It is the usual unit to Stalybridge, connecting with No. 78712/78902, a single-engined dmu presumably on a 600h.p. diagram, 7min late and its internal condition deplorable.

Monday 23rd March 1987

We are due into King's Cross at 12.14 for the 13.30 from Victoria with a jetfoil connection which has a check-in time as well. *Not so much a boat train, more a jetfoil train then and I would have denied there was ever a check-in at Victoria for these services.* It is daunting to see our 10.00 train from Wakefield Westgate shown on the screens at 09.40 as 30min late that is, before it has set off. Enquiries reveal that the 09.54 arrival into Leeds is being turned straight round. *In these automated days it would have been shown as 'on time' then 'delayed'.* It appears 36½min late behind a Doncaster stopper and the Poole train. We catch up the stopper at South Elmsall and suffer 20mph temporary speed restrictions at Balderton, leaving Grantham and Tallington with a 70mph restriction at Potter's Bar. The result is a 41½min late arrival. What happened to 'rules of the route' on the Eastern? Good job I did not go for the performance job at York perhaps.

The transit to Victoria is fast and there is just a chance of a check-in before catching the Class 411 to Dover. It is windy but the dreadfully susceptible jetfoil is still running. In fact the journey is remarkably good and the harbour exit and entry are both impressive. It is raining solidly in Ostend and the quick jetfoil means three hours to spare before the sleeper so there is time for a leisurely and pleasant three-course meal on the quayside. The train is poorly patronised and we settle down at 21.30 for a night's sleep.

Tuesday 24th March 1987

We wake to orange juice, fresh rolls and cold coffee at Thalwill, just outside Zurich, where we once spent the night when crossing Europe by train. We alight at Sargans to pick up the Paris-Innsbruck which arrives 3min behind us and splits. One of the larger Swiss locos No. 11450 attaches to the rear seven vehicles for the 13min transfer to Buchs where we reverse for the first of a series of Austrian Class 1044 loco runs, on this occasion to Feldkirch. My out-of-date Cook's Continental Timetable shows a 10min connection into the 'Bodensee' and indeed it too races in behind us so we desert our comfortable Austrian compartment for a slightly less plush Austrian open coach.

The run across the Arlberg route is operationally fascinating with double-headed and banked freights using Class 1044s and Class 1020 crocodiles crossing us at the loops on the single line. There is still plenty of skiing in action at St. Anton and we reach Innsbruck ½min late on our scheduled 11.30. We alight for a walk round the medieval centre and a contrasting McDonald's re-fuelling stop before taking the 13.58 express to Zell-am-See with 2xClass 1044s on ten bogies. The adjacent Innsbruck platform holds an Italian train bound for Munich and there is my first sighting of an Austrian 'rolling road' train with lorry trailers, traction units and couchettes. The lake is still frozen at Zell-am-See, despite strong sunshine, where we book in for the evening. *EasyJet makes these journeys somewhat easier and even cheaper than the B.R. reciprocal arrangement free tickets – not to mention the days of scarce holiday it saves. If you work on the railway you learnt more about railways the way we did it then. Of course there was no internet to check train times and make advance hotel bookings.*

Wednesday 25th March 1987

Another Class 1044 takes us over the scenic route to Salzburg rather than the direct one via a slice of Germany and we reverse there for Vienna. A couple of single-line workings are in force, at least one of which seems to have been included in the schedule, and we arrive in Vienna Westbahnhof 5½min late on our scheduled 14.00. We book into a hotel that Mike Hodson has recommended and purchase 72hr public transport passes for £4.50 each. The street trams are more enticing than the underground so we use those most of the time, ending the day at dusk on the Prater Wheel.

Thursday 26th March 1987

The Schonbrunn summer palace is on our itinerary this morning – a good '3hr' location and a tour conducted in English for the price of a cup of coffee. The coffee is expensive though at £1.25 or around 18hrs of public transport freedom. On the way back to the city centre I photograph the steam locos and electric No. 1570.01 at the Technological Museum and then take in the Belvedere and Strauss memorial before returning to the hotel.

Friday 27th March 1987

The morning is occupied by queuing for, and then watching, the Lippizanner horses going through their workout. Then there is a tour of the Hofburg at lunchtime and the Opera House in the early afternoon before St. Stephen's Cathedral and then some shopping, dinner and catching the 20.50 to Ostend.

Saturday 28th March 1987

The sleeper is very comfortable and we awake passing Koblenz. Breakfast coffee is hot this time. At Koln our sleeper is converted to a compartment in 2min and we settle down for a pleasant trip through to the channel port. On arrival, the weather is quite windy but no worse than on the outward journey so we are astounded to find the jetfoil has been cancelled. Buses arrive to transfer passengers to the ship which leaves 23min late. Being poor sailors, we opt to take a cabin so we can lie down but it is not especially rough. *Nowadays we will do three consecutive days at sea on a cruise ship though.* We are further perturbed by an announcement that our scheduled 17.15 arrival will be 18.40. Cook's hints that the longer time must inexplicably be related to using the Eastern Docks instead of the Western ones. In fact the times are explained by arriving at the Western Docks at 17.35 before the ship is going to shunt to the Eastern Docks. There is still a fighting chance of the last Huddersfield train from King's Cross at 19.50 but the crew takes 25min to swing the ramp onto the car deck. We miss the 19.50 but have time for something to eat before the 20.50 with a taxi from Wakefield Westgate to Huddersfield. Despite the final problems, it has been a fascinating holiday.

CHAPTER 44: REMOTE AREA MANAGEMENT

Monday 30th March 1987

I am aiming for a 17.00 meeting in Berkeley Square for a NSE presentation so I set off on the 11.49 to Stalybridge. It arrives with 3x2car Class 150s which take about 40seconds out of a good TransPennine Swindon set to Standedge. Passing Greenfield there is a wild lurch and it seems something has tripped out as we come to an abrupt stand. We struggle to Stalybridge after a 15min delay and find the connection has, as expected, gone. I go through to Victoria and catch the 13.30 to Euston with No. 87027. The run is reminiscent of those I have just experienced on the Continent. Dead stands outside Rugby and a slow line run from Hanslope to Roade cause only a 1min later arrival.

The general manager is here this year with David Warne representing Bob Poynter. It seems it has become more important to be seen here as the sectors grow stronger. Chris Green makes his usual competent display, well illustrated by appropriately impressive figures. The marketing talk by Tony Skeggs fails to match the introductory speech in delivery but the content is interesting. We then get a pathetic 10min from Mr Warburton (*BRB operating manager*) on what production managers should concentrate upon. Southern Region general manager Gordon Pettitt gives a rather tetchy, and even unhelpful, talk on communication during which he seems disheartened. *I was probably wrong as he switched to becoming a sector director quite readily and in retirement does not seem to resent having done so, having completed a book on the Regional Railways sector.* There is time for a quick sandwich before catching the 20.15 from Paddington with Tony Coles and Peter Warren talking railways all the way home.

Tuesday 31st March 2015

I clear the paperwork backlog between 07.30 and 09.30, talk to the new CO4 TOPS clerk about his objectives and receive a briefing from Bernard Price about last week's events. At 10.30 David Mather begins his area business group meeting with Tony Coles, Peter Warren, S&T engineer David McKeown and Plymouth area manager Jim Collins. *That's quite a lot of front line production managers' time.* We are supposed to be discussing policy and not detail but David takes until 15.00 to discuss three items. However, replacement of Class 142s is one of them. David continually allows himself to be side-tracked. It takes him a further hour to wind up and half an hour to discuss the options for Paignton South signal box replacement in the station building with David and me. Paul Silvestri comes in to obtain agreement to his latest timetable specification, David gets his train at 17.30 and I drive home.

Wednesday 1st April 1987

Despite distractions I manage to reach the panel box by 11.30, visit the TOPS office and have coffee and a biscuit with signalling inspector Bill Mardon. Back in the office there is talk of a hotline conference call about the latest pay award, a 'final offer' of 4½% which the Unions are 'considering'.

I catch the 15.38 to Paddington. Fred Butler is the driver but there are two road learners on board so I ride in the train. I transfer to King's Cross for the 18.50 to Wakefield Westgate which runs punctually and connects with a 600h.p. Metro-Camm Hammerton Street set to Huddersfield.

Thursday 2nd April 1987

There is a slightly better experience with the 11.49 today and I make my connection. I get a stopping Class 304 to Crewe where former Exeter supervisor Fred Johnson is station supervisor and shows me around for 10min before I catch No. 86255 to Euston and a Class 310 back to Watford Jct. I book in at 'The Grove' management college and former wartime LMS H.Q. *(now a luxury hotel, I note on the 'Trivago' website)*

I am due to assess personnel management trainee applicants-seven women of whom four have dropped out and an extra one has appeared.

Friday 3rd April 1987

At breakfast I resume my acquaintance with Les Binns who was divisional operations manager (i.e. No.2) at Newcastle when I was area operating manager at Middlesbrough. He is now regional parcels manager at York and is here to assess operations trainee applicants. Despite now being in the parcels sector he says that sectorisation is like snakes and ladders except the operators come down the ladders and the sector snakes squirm their way up them and no one ever reaches square 100.

The day starts with observing the applicants in a group discussion about introducing flexitime in an engineering factory. As usual, one attempts to chair it, another never ceases talking, the third says little but is positive and the fourth keeps being cut off but does not finish her sentences even when no one intervenes.

I then take four interviews. Little commitment is shown to British Rail and I get the feeling these are the ones who did not have the courage to pull out *(or are using this as practice perhaps).* They have little idea what a transport undertaking requires that is different from manufacturing and have not considered the role of the trade unions or productivity issues. Last night I was speaking to an operations scheme applicant who was the opposite in every respect, so I do not believe my expectations were unreasonable. My remit is to investigate intellectual ability and creativity, another is charged with social and interpersonal skills and a third motivation and adjustment. There are also tests on verbal reasoning, numerical analysis and special problems.

When the interviews are over, the three assessors meet to discuss the results. The staff entrant comes out best but it is her second attempt and there are nagging doubts about her suitability. Two others are ruled out straight away but there is a move to award a stand-by place to the fourth. I have severe doubts about her suitability for industry and successfully oppose this – partly because I think the others have suggested this through a desire not to appear negative. *(Never bothered me too much!?)*

At the front door I find my two colleagues getting into a taxi so I reach the station just in time for the 16.15 Manchester Pullman to Stockport with No. 87007 connecting via Stalybridge with No. 47420, 2½min late into Huddersfield.

Saturday 4th April 1987

The two-week rail marathon ends with No. 45121 to Stalybridge, an HST from Stockport to Exeter St. David's that arrives 3½min late and No. 50001 'Dreadnought' on the 21.48 to Dawlish arriving 1min late. It has been a relief to have my last run with Nos.53421/53487 on the Stockport shuttle, an ex-Blackpool line set with white roof ends and the worst vibrating windows I have ever encountered. Three journeys this week has been quite enough. The HST journey is punctuated by frequent visits from a Teignmouth commuter who is returning from Birmingham this evening and former Derby Research Ian Duncan who has had no luck buying property in the West Country and is considering West Wales instead. *At the distance of 28 years I am rather mystified on how I really justified this week of semi-absence following a week on holiday except on the grounds of seeing more of our families. I think it must have been a two-week holiday minus the days back at work.*

CHAPTER 45: PRINCE CHARLES STUDIES OPERATIONS

Monday 6th April 1987

I feel to have been away from work for a full two weeks as I walk down to the station where I pick up a letter from local staff representative Joe Cockram about the implementation of free parking for rail users. No. 50044 'Exeter' in Network SE livery is on the up stopper.

After tidying up some paperwork I meet InterCity route manager Peter Griggs at 09.00. Top of my agenda is his appearance at the Dawlish Rail Users' Group formation meeting, without any reference to me, which is unacceptable. Whether InterCity like it or not I have to field local public relations issues and this cannot be done if I am not informed. *This was clearly the way the wind was blowing and the result was minimal local management after privatisation with no one attending such meetings.* Peter has some good personal news for me though. The 07.35 Plymouth to Paddington is to call at Dawlish from October so I will have a better choice of trains to work.

The next meeting is with the provincial services market research assistant to talk about the gains we might be able make from the Yeovil Jct town centre sales point, then Peter reappears with Brian Johnson, the cross country route manager, to discuss summer working for 1987 and 1988. We check the turnround times and estimate the staffing we require. Much of the afternoon is spent discussing staff matters with Ken Boobyer.

16.00 sees the local management meeting when I brief out the NSE promotional ideas. Examining the end-of-year financial position we find we have bettered budget by £30k, a small percentage of the overall expenditure - no more than two members of staff average earnings - but exactly what we had promised headquarters at the outturn reviews.

The down stopper has No. 50045 'Achilles', 10min late following the 19min late Newcastle which has No. 50028 'Tiger', looking as if it has replaced a failed Class 47 *(by its smirk presumably)* en route, and delayed further by being cautioned over Stoke Canon barriers.

Tuesday 7th April 1987

No. 50048 'Dauntless' this morning with another uninspired run and 1min late at Exeter. Ten letters written before 08.30 then on to this morning's mail. I discuss the arrangements for the forthcoming royal visit to Totnes on Thursday then visit the Travel Centre and arrange to see the three new starters. I am having a word with supervisor Vernon Baseley about his career when Bill Mardon rings. The 09.30 Paignton to Exmouth has been involved in a suicide at Powderham crossing. Traction inspector Graham Smith was on board with Fred Bachelor, an elderly, experienced driver with whom I had ridden three times last week. The 07.25 Paddington-Penzance HST has examined the line and reported it clear except for an arm and a boot between the rails of the up line. *I guess this would not be acceptable now and not really sure how much it was then but it got the job moving.* By this time I am in the panel box and I decide, with signalman Morgan, to run at caution on both lines. I keep Control in the picture and ensure the customer information screens are correct, announcing delay is 'due to a fatality at Powderham' as, strictly speaking and I have to reluctantly comply, suicide can only be determined by a coroner. We guess at a 15min delay for the London and 10min late for the Glasgow and they arrive 15min and 8min late respectively. Driver Bachelor is badly shaken and goes home with the Class 142 unit that was involved being changed and departing for Exmouth 18min late. Bernard Price rings up from the site and says trains can now run at normal speed but he might need caution again when the undertaker arrives. Back on the platform, I meet inspector Smith on his way to give a statement at the Transport Police office so I take him upstairs for a strong coffee and half an hour's chat about anything but the fatality.

The general manager arrives at 12.22 with John Bourne of InterCity, Press Officer Ron Drummond and David Mather from provincial services. *How typical this was of the sectorisation era, four people to do what two could more than easily have managed.* We are lunching at the Great Western with representatives of the local press, radio and television. The discussion is wide-ranging and I talk about the need for responsibility on their part and not scare-mongering over issues such as the Teignmouth broken rail incident.

On the way back to the office I raise the question of the breached confidentiality of my submission about relationships between the areas and the sectors. At Watford on Friday one of the consultants whom I encountered had said that he hoped I had not had any trouble "if the non-attributability had been breached." I assured him I had not but, this morning, Dave Prescott (No. 2 in provincial services at York and a management trainee of my year group) rang to discuss my opinion about property developers Cameron Hall on a retail outlet scheme in which he was involved and had mentioned that he had seen everything I had said about relationships with the sectors.

The general manager tries to soft soap me but I'm not having any of it. The issue has nothing to do with sectorisation it is purely and simply the promise of confidentiality and the subsequent breach of trust. Had I been told it was attributable I am sure I would have said just the same. Just because the G.M. says the provincial director thinks I am very sound and it has not done me any harm, I am supposed to be happy. I tell him that I have received a questionnaire from the University of Lancaster this morning on behalf of the BRB which says it is confidential but I threaten that I will be sending it back uncompleted.

Ron Drummond says he has been unable to secure a carnival float for the staff to use in this year's programme around Devon. John Beer and I try to straighten out a few more provincial services marketing nonsenses and Tony Crabtree resolves some parcels problems before going to a two-night sector conference at Stratford-on-Avon. *They seemed to have money to burn but they would soon be completely out of a business that in the last 25years has expanded considerably.* Home on the 17.25 with No. 50014 'Warspite' 1½min late.

Wednesday 8th April 1987

John Beer phones at 06.55 just before I leave home to say the engineer's TRAMM plant machine has derailed within a possession with the points unlocked and unchecked. Traffic is passing on the relief lines.

I decide to ride to Taunton in the cab of the Golden Hind with driver Cross and inspector Ted Bainborough. As we pass Tiverton Parkway I give up my seat to Ted and he whispers to the driver to ease off speed from 95mph to the regulation *(pre-resignalling)* 90mph –the handle comes back and we take the summit at 89mph.

At Taunton, I speak to the announcer and chargeman before looking in at the travel centre and briefly meeting the two new members of staff. The train onwards to Bristol is 5min late after a caution at Bradford barriers which had failed after the Hind had passed. Arrival at Temple Meads is 1min early after an exceptionally fast 29min 57sec run at an average start to stop speed of 90mph. *Still a good time, even for a Voyager now.*

I opt to change here and take the single car unit up to Parkway which is a mistake because the fairly-frequent loco-hauled relief from Temple Meads is running behind No. 47555 'The Commonwealth Spirit' so that was a missed timing opportunity. As we pass the shell of Swindon Works in the HST a Class 08 struggles past with six scrap Class 25s in tow, a sad sight.

In '125 House' I meet Bernard Norman and the BRB solicitor

to discuss the dismissal of the Torquay clerk with tooth-ache who assaulted the travel centre manager. We go through all the papers in detail and I am glad we have it so well documented. There are just a few blanks to fill in and Bernard Norman (whom I first met when he was an instructor at Derby School of Transport when I was a management trainee) gives me full backing, agreeing that the clerk will not return to B.R. employment even if he happened to win his case.

Lunch is taken in the canteen with John Mummery, David Warne and David Hounsell before catching the 13.30 back to Exeter with assistant area civil engineer Colin Carr. We are 3min early back at Exeter having discussed many 'New Works' schemes and yet another BR investigation on its organisational structure. *One might be forgiven for thinking they had nothing else better to do.*

Back in the office, Alan Bell has returned from leave and the Exeter City Council is complaining that I have given preference to a Chamber of Commerce scheme over their manpower services commission one, even though the MSC has produced nothing in 15 months. *Now unsure what this concerned though.* A Devon County Council official rings to say he is co-ordinating the Teignmouth Docks rail connection scheme and I point out we are still waiting the information they said they would provide concerning their policies and potential contribution.

Thursday 9th April

Linda and I set off at 08.15 for Totnes to receive Prince Charles on the Royal Train. Bernard Price has been handling the detailed arrangements and checking that everything is in order for the overnight stabling stop on the Heathfield branch and arrival at Totnes. When we arrive the police and their sniffer dogs are in action and, after about 20min, the VIPs start to arrive – the chairmen of Devon County Council and South Hams District Council, the chief executive of South Hams and the mayor of Totnes. The Lord Lieutenant arrives to marshal everyone in line, military fashion.

There is cause for concern because the 06.45 from Swindon is running 5min late and would check the Royal at Dainton. The Royal arrives 1min late behind No. 47628 in green livery. Prince Charles thanks me for the arrangements and, self-effacingly, expresses his hope that he has not caused any trouble. He than asks about the double shunt necessary at present to leave the Heathfield branch for the Totnes direction so I briefly refer to the re-modelling. He responds by asking which end the engine was on and I say there was one on both ends.

Everyone disperses and we drive back to Dawlish before catching the 11.15 into Exeter. At Dawlish, a woman has been causing a scene, complaining that the booking clerk would not accept that her son could buy a Young Person's Railcard. She shows me his national insurance card and a Dawlish school lunch card. *I cannot remember what the acceptable proof of age was in those days but I seem to think it was far less strict than these things are nowadays.* I authorise the issue and say I will refund the difference on the ticket that has already been bought if she sends it in.

In the meantime the clerk has allowed a lady to leave without her senior citizen's saver to Derby and given Linda this ticket instead of her privilege fare ticket to Exeter so there is some shuffling to be done to rectify the situation. We go to the Great Western for lunch and I catch the 14.11 up to Central and the 14.28 back down with No. 50009 'Conqueror', 2min late with traction inspector Graham Smith in the driver's seat.

Back in the office, we have received a Joint Inquiry report from Headquarters concerning severe delay at Ealing Broadway that was caused by a seized parking brake on an HST which I decide should be finalised with a 'letter of guidance' to the Exeter driver.

S&T engineer David McKeown and I discuss a problem of

drivers misreading the route indicator 'feather' approaching Exeter St. David's on the down main. David thinks fibre optics could be the answer. He informs me that renewal of his level crossings on the Waterloo line has been authorised which is a pleasant surprise to us both. The delay they have been causing has been highlighted through the Exeter-Waterloo performance group and seems to have prompted the decision from NSE - a *rare example of bureaucracy working as it is supposed to do.*

I write a long letter, as requested by the regional operating manager, explaining why computerisation, has not saved the number of posts expected and why it might well continue not to do so before catching No. 33062 home. The Express & Echo is carrying a report about the withdrawal of many station calls at Lympstone. This station has actually been given more stops than it had but the extra new half-hourly services off-peak do not stop there. I shall need to respond but the lunch with the media asking them to consult us before printing bad and inaccurate news has not borne fruit.

Friday 10th April 1987

I am at my desk by 07.30, putting the finishing touches to the letter to the Express & Echo's editor, then making sure that HQ public affairs, the press office and Provincial Services do not duplicate the response and even undercut it. I also get hold of the senior reporter at last week's lunch and ask him to review the accuracy of the report.

At 09.00 former Newton Abbot driver Jim Lear arrives for his retirement. He is very apologetic that his wife is not accompanying him due to a bronchitis attack. He has been deaf in one ear for 20yrs and confined to branch line duties all that time and believes it was caused by the driver on a Newton Abbot 'Castle' that he was firing sounding the whistle all the way through the Severn Tunnel which perforated an ear drum. The conversation is difficult. Jim chats away relating many interesting anecdotes but he has difficulty hearing what I say. Possibly his hearing aid is turned off. I tell him how grateful we are for his 49yrs and 8months service but when I hand him his valedictory card he looks surprised.

Peter Robinson arrives to conduct a survey on delayed wagons and status codes. I still insist on checks like the ones we regularly used to do at Tees Yard so there are very few errors and he continues by going through imminent developments to TOPS.

At 10.00 a Mr Jeffrey arrives to tell me about a sponsored charity trip he has conducted by rail; a round trip from Axminster via Glasgow, Edinburgh and London in 24hrs. He has paid us the full round trip fare but he is kind enough to hand me a pennant from Axminster Lions' Club, appropriately made out of carpet. *Not sure what the point of this was. Perhaps he was expecting a refund for the benefit of the charity or perhaps he was hoping I would give it more publicity and I cannot help but think I might not have responded in the way he had hoped.*

I catch the 10.32 to Tiverton Parkway, delayed at Hele by barrier failure. *The unreliability of all the crossings is far worse than I remember.* There is very little time before catching the 10.59 through to Newton Abbot, 4min late due to a temporary speed restriction and the barrier caution. This leaves me just 4min to join former-Leeds driver Smith on the Paignton stopper. Shunter Warren, without high visibility vest, transfers some parcels from the down London train across both sets of tracks to the up side. I tear him off a strip. The action was not only foolish and dangerous, it showed either a disregard for my presence or a worrying lack of awareness. The driver is very cautious and drops 2min to Torquay.

The purpose of the visit is to have a long chat with travel centre manager John Hedge about subjects that range from appraisals of his staff to social activities he undertakes in the community, he says, on behalf of British Rail. I reluctantly agree to defray some of his expenses but leave wondering whether I should not have taken a stricter line.

The Bradford to Paignton arrives 4min late and I take it to Paignton, having a chat with chargeman Dai Putt and others on arrival. After visiting the booking office I have a long visit to Paignton South where a promising young relief signalman Phil Mann is working. It is important that we do not demotivate people like him during the resignalling reductions. He has fallen just short of getting into the panel box and might end up in a platform post for a time. I undertake to find out some idea of his position before his displacement interview next Thursday.

I take the 14.20 back to Newton Abbot and visit a member of the booking staff who is querying his appraisal - the only one to do so. I take him out to the platform to prevent any heated words being overheard and spell out the position to him man to man. I perceive him to be negative and that we are getting plans done despite him and not through him. He says that he knows where he stands and will now willingly comply with our expectations of him. The person concerned is a Transport Salaried Staffs' Association office holder so I phone David Thear, deputy personnel manager at Swindon, and ask him to make sure that Eugene Heffernan, in his organisation, does not ring up as he did last week to ask what is being done because of a TSSA complaint.

I take a message about a blind lady on the Liverpool needing assistance and catch the HST to Exeter with another former Leeds driver Peter Eaglen, whose brother has also transferred to Exeter but has not settled. We are 1½min late with 2min recovery time. There is a 50mph tsr at Teignmouth, a caution over the hole in the sea wall and a check in from Marsh Barton but we are only ½min late. It is obviously slackly timed as I have previously pointed out to train planning at H.Q.

My return to the office is unexpected so I have time to finalise some paperwork and have 20min with Bernard Price to thank him for the Royal Train arrangements and discuss Phil Mann's position before catching the 17.25 1min late with No. 33059, a first time appearance on this duty.

At 18.50 I spend 10min trying to get through the Exeter switchboard to Phil Mann at Paignton South. I explain that he is now about five positions short of being appointed to the panel but there is the likelihood that some of the more senior signalmen might decline to be appointed to the panel and that he might be absorbed into a platform job but spend most of his time covering signalling jobs until October. Even then, five vacancies should take him to the new box. The travesty is that the appointments are on seniority providing the person is competent and that he would have made the first cut on pure ability. British Rail must take on the unions on this issue, even if some kind of buy-out is possible. *The unions feared appointment by arbitrary managers applying their own personal preferences, a bit like privatisation I suppose.*

Saturday 11th April 1987

Despite a head cold I had better show my face on NSE because it is a Network Card day - hold or buy a £10 Network Card and travel all day for £1. The summer relief trains are running additionally to help cope with the expected surge in demand, and the popularity enjoyed by the western extremities of the permitted area.

I catch the 13.13 'Skipper' to Exeter, riding with driver Smith as yesterday to Torquay, arriving at 13.33. The loco for the 13.35 up NSE train is just backing onto its train, having been late arriving. No. 50008 'Thunderer is the loco, on a set strengthened to ten for the occasion. The problem is that the guard is on the down Brighton, 50min late at Chard Jct. A spare guard is found to take our train to Central 5min late to swap there with the Brighton's guard and in the meantime I brew a cup of tea for the incoming guard that we are expecting to turn straight round. We are 21½min late. Common sense might initially have suggested we could have changed guards at Pinhoe but the 11.00 from Waterloo is 30min late so we have to wait there for 10min. In effect we have saved time overall by not stopping the down Brighton at Pinhoe for the crew change. We are retimed to be 6min later than usual so the late running is 26min late, 25min late at Yeovil Jct. The up Brighton is 17min late behind us so the 15.36 down train that I join is held until 15.43. We incur 2min overtime at Axminster detraining an invalid. Our 4min recovery time has been artificially squeezed to 3min so that makes us 5min late at Pinhoe. The 16.15 Exmouth-Paignton is given preference at Exmouth Jct. Unless it is deliberately intended to break the Torbay connection at St. David's, this is wrong and I will take it up on Monday, and we are 9½min late on our retimings. The Paignton connection is announced on our arrival, leaving Platform 3 3½min late. It is a Skipper on a Class 118 timing so we regain 3min to Dawlish so perhaps not all that wrong a decision at Exmouth Jct. The NSE additional bookings at Yeovil Jct alone amounted to 350 adults and 107 (free) children. Only 20 Network Cards have been sold but passengers had been buying them in advance ready for today.

Photo: No. 50009 'Conqueror' arrives at Sherborne with the 15.10 Waterloo-Exeter St. David's on 21st April 1987
Credit: Colin. J. Marsden

CHAPTER 46: LION EATS PIGEON

Monday 13th April 1987

I travel down from Dawlish to Newton Abbot in the cab of the 08.13. The person with whom I had trouble last week has yet to turn over the new leaf he promised. Today he is objecting to John Beer having asked him to deal with the 'culprit' on his staff who has caused a public complaint. He is taking great exception to the word which seems quite accurate in the circumstances and fully within the customer services manager's rights to use.

The current track layout is a temporary one, part way towards the revised one, so there will be pressure on platform occupation for the next three weeks until the next stage of remodelling. I catch the up London arriving at Exeter St. David's 1min early.

Mr Poynter is already there to conduct the safety audit. First, we go to the signal box to meet Bernard Price and Bernard Norman who are dealing with some of the more detailed points on our mutual behalf. The r.o.m. starts by making a point about the computerised personnel records (known as MANIS) not being up-to-date. The rules exams are accurate but some of the other details are not correct. I point out a wrong entry on my record, which is the responsibility of H.Q. This would have served to deflect most people but Mr Poynter does not let me win and says it is unwise to make a point like that so early in the audit. He is partially joking, I think, and enjoying the sport. We go through our treatment of mishaps, signal box visit records and terminals' safety records such as dangerous goods vehicles' certificate of closure and readiness in the working manual pink pages. Tees Yard experience comes in useful again. We also cover depot safety and the amount of work over a line that is reasonable to retain route knowledge in a drivers' work 'link' before catching the 13.20 to Newton Abbot.

After taking a walk round the layout, we visit Newton Abbot West with signalman Brian Warren who is in slightly less than awkward mood, I am pleased to say. As the boss leaves I mention to the signalman that Phil Wain on the morning shift has forgotten to sign off- just to prove I have noticed when signing the train register book. He knew. I'll take it up with the normally reliable Phil later.

We are waiting on platform 4 for the 14.20 Paignton to Newcastle when Bernard Price rings to say that another hole is developing in the sea wall. We pass the 11.45 from Paddington on the down line and negotiate the stretch safely ourselves. *The engineers were set to deal with it but I do not think I am exaggerating to suggest no trains would have run for quite some time nowadays.*

Back in the office we have our 16.00 local management meeting, The agenda is light. We are £500 overspent in the first week of the new budget week despite having deliberately postponed recruitment of the 5xCO1 posts in Exeter travel centre, equal to another £500. There could be many explanations that are not immediately evident, from the transition from one budget to the other perhaps, but it will need watching if there is some inherent inaccuracy in our figures.

There is a 'round robin' from the Yeovil staff asking to be told what the general manager was looking at when he visited last week. *The diary does not say what he was looking at and what was done in reply. The general manager does not need to be looking at anything specific of course but I guess from this distance in time he was familiarising himself with the infrastructure with the discussion going on about running the Weymouth line into Yeovil Jct. The spirit of Beeching was obviously still stalking the messrooms twenty years on and frightening the staff.*

I have also received a letter from supervisor Ernie Underhill, the displaced Newton Abbot supervisor who has been accommodated at Exeter for his final year of service. I am able to reassure him that supervisor Colin Godbeer has requested resettlement and is now considering his position. If Colin elects not to retire, Ernie will be used as a supernumerary for a year (saving me a lot of overtime payments no doubt) but it is likely that he will be given Colin's rest day relief job. I take the car home, intending to drive in to catch the 08.11 in the morning.

Tuesday 14th April 1987

Breakfast goes by the board whilst we attend to a sodden carpet caused by a leaking radiator before I drive into Exeter by 08.05 for the 08.11 to Crewkerne. The loco is No. 50050 'Fearless' on eight MkIIs with driver Jon Morton, so a recognised fast combination. The 08.15 arrival is not a booked connection and it is approaching platform 4 so we leave 20sec early to prevent being late with passengers (mainly B.R. civil engineering staff) transferring. We make good time and stand waiting our departure time at many stations, crossing a Meldon ballast empties at Honiton.

The time from leaving Axminster to passing Chard Jct is just 5min 30sec and we arrive on time at Crewkerne. I have half an hour with Alan Keirl between brisk business at the booking office window. The 07.00 from Waterloo is 17min late but makes up 1min to Axminster. There is time to talk to booking clerk Derek Grayer and senior railman John Cornelius. John has been displaced from his signalling job and hopes to be made permanent in this post after his displacement interview on Thursday.

The up train is now inevitably late; 13½min. The crew is determined to make up time and the train reaches Sherborne 9½min late. Of course, the 09.10 from Waterloo is waiting for this train at Gillingham which will make the 12.20 up from St. David's 8min late from Pinhoe.

My train encounters another Meldon on the reversible at

Yeovil Jct. The ballast empties' driver comes into the office to ask why he has not been given a run. I explain that he was 20min late at Templecombe and would have delayed the up express between Honiton and Pinhoe. He gets away at 12.02 and I go across to Pen Mill in the out-stationed Metro for a talk with travel centre manager John Dubbin but, on my return, find that the ballast has exceeded its running time to Honiton and the up train is 17min late as a result. *Delays on this route are usually in multiples of 20min or so, resulting from the length of the single line sections.*

Despite all this, Jon Morton is making better progress with the 11.10 from Waterloo but has no option other than to wait at Yeovil Jct for the 12.20 up hauled by No. 47658, having replaced a presumably defective No. 50049 'Defiance' off the 07.00 from Waterloo. We set off 6½min late and regain 1½min to Chard Jct. Passing Broom crossing at 90mph we have a bird strike – the last of a pigeon flock and a clean hit to the drivers' side marker light. The unfortunate bird comes right through into the headcode box over our heads and showers us in feathers. Our loco is No. 50027 'Lion'. Lion eats pigeon? On investigation at Axminster, we discover that the Perspex is complete and can be refitted at Exeter so I pass a note to the platform staff at Honiton so that Exeter can be prepared. With the benefit of 4min recovery time we are 20sec late at Exeter Central but the timetable glitch of the 14.28 in the way surfaces again and we are 1min late into St. David's.

Parcels manager Tony Crabtree tells me that the lifts are out of action at Newton Abbot and he needs to incur extra overtime costs to drag brutes round via the barrow crossing from 14.00 to 22.30. I accept that Newton Abbot station staffing is now tight but this seems excessive. I agree to four hours cover up to 18.00 tomorrow and Thursday to ensure some coverage can be arranged in advance but that Tony will check the situation tomorrow. Next week we have a supervisor there for the multiple aspect signalling (mas) work so there will be a road vehicle there that might help. Lateral thinking. *From this distance, I am not sure just how I expected this to work.*

Oblique thinking perhaps.

I get hold of the electrical engineer in charge of the lifts, Phil Shepherd, to emphasise the importance of the lift repairs but Phil is a step ahead. The defective motor will be removed by 11.00 tomorrow and sent to a contractor for repair and return by Thursday morning. Tony is impressed and so am I. Let's hope it works.

John Beer briefs me about the provincial services marketing meeting yesterday and Bernard Price tells me what has happened at today's signalmen's displacement interviews. Then the new railway employment inspector, Mr Lewis, comes to introduce himself.

There is an unpleasant public complaint in the inbox, copy to the Daily Mail, TUCC etc. The writer has been excessed by one of my assistant ticket examiners (not Terry Blackburn thank goodness) and had his family railcard confiscated. He was travelling without being accompanied by a child, in contravention of the conditions. He told the ATE that his son was looking for the buffet car but in his letter he says his son was trainspotting from the front coach. When the ATE told him that his son did not appear to be on the train, the writer did not seem worried. Eventually the writer phoned his wife and...surprise! His son had decided, immediately before departure, not to travel, alighted and gone home to mum. Now the writer is creating a smokescreen and making all kind of threats. Even his family railcard photo looks threatening! We resolve to take a firm line – a diplomatic letter but to treat it as an attempt to defraud and refer it to the B.T. Police – just what we would have done had there been no threatening letter.

At home, Phil Shepherd phones at 21.15 to ask what time the down Sleepers pass Dawlish in the new timetable. His filming interests have involved him in the BBC shooting of a John le Carré spy film and he has promised to find out for the producer.

Wednesday 15th April 1987

The second Skipper failed before leaving the depot this morning so there is only one on the 07.30 but it is school holidays so it does not cause too much difficulty.

The main job of the day is to chair the Sectional Council meeting concerning the combination of Taunton, Exeter and Newton Abbot station announcing into Exeter panel box. The S&T representative arrives at 10.00 and it is 11.50 before we go into the meeting after the internal staff side discussions have been concluded. Any pressure I might have put on myself to make a concession in order that earlier-than - scheduled budget savings can be made is removed when the S&T state they cannot do the telecoms work before mid-August. The main issue is likely to be the fact that my proposals involve part time staffing to which the trade union remains opposed.

Staff side chairman Chester Long takes us through the usual rigmarole of easy questions; how the system will work, who will do what, where the equipment will go etc. He says that the principle of part-time staffing is unacceptable to him as it will be at a future meeting on assistant ticket examiners. His proposal is for my part time announcers to be full time from 07.00 to 21.00. This means three staff will be on duty from 13.00 to 15.00 which is not justified by any construal of the workload involved. For that matter, neither are two for most of the time. Chester argues that a shift changeover period is required - more so than panel signalmen, who do not have one? I refuse to accept this and Chester would like to do nothing more than to create such a precedent. Chester says my proposals cater for a changeover period, which they do not.

I have personally conducted a survey of the announcements to be made at all three stations in 5min blocks throughout the day and the consequential CIS screen work so I can say with confidence that my proposals amount to the need for only a part time job, albeit a 6hr one. We recess to discuss Chester's proposition further. Chris Hughes has been taking the minutes so I ask him for his opinion. He circles around the direct question for a while but no more so than I might have done at his age. He then reads the situation wrongly as he thinks I am ready to concede an extra half-post. After twiddling our thumbs for the ten minutes that might be deemed acceptable to give full consideration to the counter-proposal we go back into the meeting and decline the idea. Chester invokes the regional guidelines that management's proposals hinge on a point of principle. I normally counter these statements by saying I deem consultation to have taken place and giving an implementation date for the scheme, which usually causes whichever Sectional Council is involved to go spluttering back to H.Q. trying to wring some concession from the personnel people there, usually unsuccessfully if I have conducted the consultation in accordance with recognised procedures. I tell the S&T to proceed on their current timescale as it will probably take that length of time for Swindon to sort anything out so we will lose nothing. If we were not to insist on part-time announcing this time we will never break the mould. The Union is of course frightened that part-time staff tend to resist unionisation.

The afternoon is spent clearing up paperwork. Nigel Fulford phones to discuss his six-month secondment from Area Manager Reading to Inter-City. I give what advice I can but I know I will never hear from him again in this fashion once he is sectorised and he will never return to area management. *Proved to be true.* Phil Shepherd rings to say it will be Saturday lunchtime before we get the Newton Abbot lifts back in order. I suppose it was too much for which to hope. It's my birthday today so I suppose Brunswick green No. 50007 'Sir Edward Elgar' on the 17.25 is appropriate even if the NSE stock is less so.

Thursday 16th April 1987

Just one Skipper on my train this morning with only seven in service, soon falling to five which includes one with a plank of wood across the gangway connection and another with no safety cover over the door buttons and requiring an additional guard travelling with the set to protect them. Adrian Featherstone is the deputy manager at Laira so I ring to put some pressure on for an improvement.

Bernard Price and Ken Boobyer are continuing with the signalmen's displacement interviews. Only two of the 52 discussions are described as being awkward. We have been assisted by the resignation of two signalmen at Honiton, which is unaffected by the resignalling. One has left to join the Post Office and one has had his wife leave him with three children making a shift signalling job impractical and probably unremunerative I suppose. This leaves two slots for Taunton displaced staff as it is not too far cross-country to Honiton.

At 10.30 I leave the office to catch the 10.43 relief train to Taunton with No. 47453 on five coaches. I whip up custom by asking announcer Larry to broadcast that the parent Glasgow train is full and standing and that passengers without seat reservations are advised to catch the 10.43 additional train. *There were no complications with sectorised or advance specific-service tickets in those days.* We are checked at Silk Mill but the signalman says the barriers were down in good time. In the travel centre I speak to the two new clerks and listen to them in action on telephone enquiries. Both are doing well.

Back on the platform I see one of the Dawlish Action Group members, Mr Connell, who is interested in obtaining a charter price for a train to York. I inspect the emergency 'red' engineering notice case in the signing-on point and make a few notes on the shortcomings. Essentially the red notice case should contain emergency speed restrictions. It should not contain any extraneous material and expired notices should be removed immediately.

I catch the 12.02 to Exeter and then the 12.50 to Totnes being checked at Aller Jct and stopped at Dainton by a light diesel to Plymouth. On enquiry with Nigel Turner in Totnes box it transpires that this was the loco for the 14.15 up mail from Plymouth and was given priority on control instructions. This was a marginal decision but not one to contest.

After a long talk to booking clerk Mike Shord I catch an HST back to Exeter in the cab with newly appointed driver Colin Wreford who performs well. The transit of the temporary layout at Newton Abbot is performed confidently and a temporary 10mph turnout to platform 3 is scrupulously observed. We are one minute early arriving.

I go straight to the panel box. Things are quiet and No. 33107 is being dropped onto the front of the Class 50 on the 16.18 to Waterloo to balance it back to the Southern and save a path over the single line. There is then the unpleasant task of calling in Nigel Gooding to tell him he has not been selected for the management training scheme but he takes it very well, thereby making my job somewhat easier.

Back in the office, I piece together the dismal story of a test load of ball clay from Heathfield to Warrington. The Tavistock Jct-based trip did not pick it up, mainly due to the restriction of the temporary layout and it arrived at Riverside too late to make its forward connection due to a misunderstanding. It is a nice change to be involved in freight, mainly because Bernard is tied up with the interviews, but this is to say the least unimpressive.

I have half an hour with Alan Bell about the difficulties we are likely to encounter in next Wednesday's consultation meeting about assistant ticket examiner posts. Part-time working will again be the focus. InterCity has not produced any robust figures and has achieved its projected savings by guessing the workload. I suspect Sectional Council staff side will pulverise them. The savings they are tabling have already been negated by Network and Provincial sectorising the remainder instead of integrating the diagrams - both with each other and also spare time in other sectors' guards' diagrams. *And we are led to believe that the business-led railway was the way to efficiency.*

Friday 17th April 1987

Good Friday and Linda is language school teaching from 10.00 to 12.45 so I spend an hour catching up on action over notes I have accumulated in my pocket book and preparing a sea wall contingency plan for the new timetable, using only the up reversible line. Looking at the public timetable, I discover a large number of errors. It seems that the new organisation cannot even do the basics such as putting together the services it has to offer. Some columns show two trains, lines of print are missing. Trains that run overnight from Sunday to Monday – in one case arriving at Exeter at 10.24 – do not appear in the Mon-Fri pages.

Photo: No. 142019 at Yeoford with the 11.20 Exeter St. David's to Barnstaple on 18th April 1987.
Credit: Colin J. Marsden

Photo: British Telecommunications liveried set P460 (Power cars 51302/51317) passes Newton St. Cyres with the 10.10 from Barnstaple on 18th April 1987. Credit: Colin J. Marsden

CHAPTER 47: A LESSON FROM PARLIAMENT

Wednesday 22nd April 1987

After an unusual Easter with no train travel and just a couple of trips to the beach, watching a few loco-hauled reliefs, I have managed a slight tan. Highlight from the picnics was No. 50007 'Sir Edward Elgar' accelerating alongside the promenade on a long-welded rail train recovering from being checked by the 14.20 Paignton.

Back at Dawlish station on the Wednesday morning, I find No. 50050 'Fearless' on the 07.08. In the office I have a new framed photo to put on the wall, now withdrawn No. 50011 'Centurion' on the Old Oak newspaper empty vans at Teignmouth in 1983. It is No. 373 in a limited edition of a mere thousand.

I catch the Golden Hind with driver Dingle to Taunton, four minutes overtime at Exeter (2min early to 2min late on a 2min allowance) due to second driver Bob Dack having failed for duty and the supervisor using the 08.11 to Waterloo driver to cover him. I must check that driver Dack was properly notified of his turn because this is not typical. *Driver Dack had been a rear gunner in the RAF and I was told this week that he held the DFC.*

We get a signal check to 70mph at Silk Mill because the barriers have not been lowered in time. Apparently the closed circuit television camera is being moved today and the panel signalmen are not allowing enough time to get the 'crossing clear' assurance from the temporary keeper.

Calling in at the travel centre I see that they answered 670 calls yesterday. I let the 07.00 Plymouth cross country HST go because my Bristol meeting is not until 10.00 so wait for the 08.40 Taunton-Bristol stopper which has No. 45140 with BG/BSK/SK substituting for a dmu. We are full and standing from Weston-super-Mare but have no difficulty keeping time.

Ken Shingleton chairs an uninspiring meeting about performance challenges in the new timetable but there is precious little new in the way of ideas in the three-hour discussion. As usual, I beat the drum about unrealistic sectional running times and the way time is kept by borrowing unused recovery time. *It is still no better and I'm still complaining about it.*

I catch the 09.20 from Liverpool back to Exeter, 13½min late from Bristol and 8½min from Taunton. Then comes the caution for the work at Silk Mill and a barrier failure at Victory so 19min late at Tiverton Parkway and 16min late at Exeter.

The desk is full but there are no crises. The Sectional Council staff side took all day assessing the ATE proposals and, as I predicted, it looks to be heading for trouble. The staff know far more about the workload on each train than the Sectors, particularly InterCity. The proposals are less well-founded than any I have seen even worse than the recent travel centre scheme which was similarly concocted.

I have a long talk with Alan Bell and tell him about the intention for St. Blazey to work the Heathfield branch – another sector based idea, to use a freight depot for all freight work. I guess that means that they will be doing all the Royal Train work on the Heathfield branch, which should be interesting after catering for unproductive travelling time from Cornwall, or will we need to maintain route knowledge by special turns instead of in the normal course of booked work?

I get away to catch the 17.25 with No. 50003 'Temeraire. Supervisor Paul Silvestri points out that the 16.35 from Waterloo is 50min late. *I think he might have been trying to avoid being caught between irate passengers and an irate area manager who was on the way home for his evening meal.* It does not take a genius to hold all connections or break all connections. There is an art to managing them effectively and balancing passenger requirements with punctuality; time-keeping being a passenger requirement in its own right of course. There is also pressure from the rom to break connections and from the sectors not to hold connections from other sectors. In the guidelines I have issued this would classify as a 'running in' connection - basically that it is held if the passengers can see the connection they had missed but it also needs managing in terms of announcements and a 'sweeper' to chivvy the stragglers and inform dispatch staff everyone has transferred. So, if the Waterloo appears from the tunnel by 17.25, we make a running in connection and, if it does not, the 17.25 goes. In the end it arrives at St. David's at 17.25½ and the connection leaves at 17.29½, reasserting my position with staff who believe in permitting long 'holds' that a running-in connection is, in effect, a 5min holding margin – not that I admit that to H.Q. operators. No. 50003 'Temeraire' is known to be a good loco and gets to Dawlish 3min late after some smart station work to match.

Thursday 23rd April 1987

Another bright, sunny day as No. 50031 'Hood' pulls in on the 07.08. John Beer has a large backlog to discuss with me and I catch the 09.31 to Bristol for another Royal Train meeting. It is an uneventful run to Bristol, except for the Silk Mill barrier work again.

The meeting is fairly straightforward. The train will arrive on the down side at Taunton, loco to run round and empty stock to be worked away to Bristol. The Queen's car will have to cross Silk Mill twice, risking delay to trains if we are not careful. The Police will liaise by radio with Bernard Price to find the least disruptive solution. The afternoon departure is from Bridgwater, so Bristol area manager Frank Markham is involved. We will run round the empty stock from Bristol at Taunton with the aim of delivering it to Bridgwater at 15.55 for a 16.00 departure. The snag is that if the Queen arrives back early there will be no train for her to board and Bridgwater's facilities are worse than rudimentary so we manage to sell the run round to be done at Bridgwater so it can be positioned at short notice.

Bernard and I return on the punctual 11.57. I rashly undertake to assess the carriage cleaning workloads for overnight and turnround cleans at the likes of Paignton on Bernard's behalf. It is one area where I have more experience than Bernard and I am familiar with adapting staff numbers to 'standard minutes' work study values.

Tony Crabtree comes in to discuss parcels matters and as a side-issue we decide to set up a video library of B.R. material, including route learning footage, for staff to borrow or watch in any spare time such as a layover between trains. *I cannot recall this quirky but progressive idea went any further though.* I want to get away early to turn round for a National Youth Orchestra concert in Exeter Cathedral, to which guard Brian Cocks *(later supervisor and then chairman of the South Devon Railway)* had invited us and in which his daughter Ellie was playing. So I get home a shade after 16.00, do some paperwork and set off at 18.45.

Friday 24th April 1987

The 08.01 is 12min late with door problems. The leading set has just one pair working manually, with the guard positioned at them. After some urgent paperwork I catch the 10.20 back to Dawlish with the yellow telecomm unit working the train and riding with a young 'passed man' driver. The train is quite busy with 38 joining at Exeter St. Thomas but conductor John Pearman is slow on the buzzer and with lost time running we are 4½min late at Dawlish.

I pick up the car and leave some paperwork for later, having a quick coffee before driving to Teignmouth. At present there is a late night full turn on duty, mainly to deal with the newspaper traffic but I intend to alter this to a desperately unsociable 03.30 part time turn. *Linking the hours of duty to the demonstrable workload and having part time turns is one way to increase productivity.* The staff representative is Les Comer and I ask him to make sure there is a proper notice out to show the temporary resignalling train alterations for next week.

By 12.15 I am in Torquay. Travel centre manager John Hedge and I are going for lunch at the Livermead with the new Torbay Conference Centre manager Bob Tolley. We cover some useful ground on joint promotions as we will be looking to his clients to justify the winter extension of through trains to Paignton, both Cross Country and from Paddington trains for 1987 and 1988.

Basil in the parcels office is a true character and gives life to the otherwise probably quiet confines of the Torquay parcels office. His very presence contributes a great deal to retaining customers. *Apologies for not remembering Basil's surname but every one always called him just 'Basil' - so it has not stuck.*

My next job is to visit Westford crossing near Wellington where we had the recent horrific fatality and where we are under pressure to provide enhanced safety measures. It is about an hour's drive. Bernard Norman, from the ROM's office at Swindon, is already there when I arrive and we time a few trains over the crossing. Visibility is only about six seconds and the horn is heard 2-6secs before that, although the zinging of the rails is an even bigger give away.

At 17.00 we assemble in the town council's office. The Department of Transport agreed standard is that warning lights should be provided for pedestrians if the number of pedestrians multiplied by the number of trains reaches 24 in any 15min period. The maximum score on our records is 15. If we provide warning lights here we will be creating an expensive precedent for many other locations. A few councillors make play on the recent tragedy. A friend of the railway, Mrs Rose Mangles, is there from Somerset County Council and is sympathetic to both standpoints but is unable to contribute anything from her already stretched budget. There are 34 crossings in her county whose local government representatives will be watching what she does here and that is before she supports any road pedestrian crossing facilities.

Sir Edward Du Cann M.P. is there and deftly guides people towards compromise, away from a potential stand-off. There is an allegation that 1-2% of train drivers are not sounding their horns and I promise action if supplied with times and dates. I would see it as a case for formal discipline if the same driver's name appears a second time after a first letter of warning.

Our estimate for the work is a staggering £30,000 which I find an embarrassment. Several councillors are rightly scornful but the amount includes £12,000 of allocated (and spurious) overheads applied to 'private party' work. This seems to me like something that would benefit the railway and should not be entirely treated as private party. I lean over to prompt Bernard to offer up some of this and he replies, "Later." After 5min of further discussion Sir Edward, seated some 10ft away, interjects. "I detected a conversation between Mr Heaton and Mr Norman a few minutes ago – perhaps they have something they could offer us?" Thirty years in Parliament has taught him the tricks of negotiation. We agree to firm up estimates and offer to fund a proportion in the form of the overheads in three weeks or so. This way the public will get its safeguard, the council will be seen to have done something and the railway will not have spent any money that would not otherwise have been spent- just a theoretical 'opportunity cost' of the work that might have been done in a back office on an alternative scheme. Everyone seems relatively happy. After the meeting Sir Edward thanks us and I tell him I have learnt not to disclose my hand in the presence of an experienced parliamentarian. He laughs and pats my elbow in an avuncular fashion.

On the way home I call in at Tiverton Parkway for ten minutes to talk to Ted Studley, who is moving back to Taunton in the latest shake-up, and get home at 19.40.

Saturday 25th April 1987

On a shopping expedition to Teignmouth I call in at the station to inspect the car park checking record and tell Les Comer that I have decided to propose an 03.45 turn to replace the 23.30 existing duty. I also chat with John Farmer, who is covering the booking office on the clerical relief roster, about the implementation of the new APTIS booking computers, to which he is looking forward.

From 13.00 I relax in the garden with the sun shining – the ideal setting to work out the carriage cleaning establishment and to write the consultation document, finishing at 18.30 with two posts saved, on paper at least.

Photo: No. 47631 accelerates a Paddington-Plymouth relief train from its Exeter St. David's stop on 26th April 1987. Credit: D. W. V. Hunt

Photo: An engineering train in the hands of No. 33006 at Aller Jct on 26th April 1987
Credit: D. W. V. Hunt

CHAPTER 48: NEWTON ABBOT'S TURN FOR RESIGNALLING

Monday 27TH April 1987

There is time to sort out the desk before an 09.00 meeting with the 'Board's Barrister', his clerk, and Bernard Norman on behalf of the regional operating manager. Today is the Industrial Tribunal for the Torquay booking clerk with a toothache problem who attacked the travel centre manager, John Hedge, last November. The barrister ensures that I would have chosen dismissal even if I was not concerned that I might have been sending out a message that other supervisors could be assaulted without the assailants losing their jobs. I am confident this is the case because the 'message' issue would have been a consequence of a decision not to dismiss - not a primary reason for dismissal. However, it is a purely hypothetical. We have followed all the procedures and our paperwork is faultless.

The tribunal starts on time and I am first in the witness box. The evidential process is inefficient. I am asked a couple of questions followed by 5min or so of evidence being read. It goes on like that for just over an hour. The clerk's representative is Ian Byiers of the Transport Salaried Staffs' Association with whom we share a mutual dislike of each other. He asks why I had not dismissed a certain Exeter shunter for thumping the Exeter duty station manager. I explain that it was a scuffle over who should have possession of the telephone receiver. There had also been a few preliminaries such as the supervisor having told the shunter to get his dirty boots off the carpet but Byiers does not take me there. Bernard Norman, who took the appeal, gets away with 15min and we wait 20min for the verdict which is unanimously in our favour as 'an action within the ambit of a reasonable employer.' However, we are left with the impression that the panel thinks it was severe, which is possibly where the 'message to others' came into play in my deliberations. If the case had been in a fruit shop in Dawlish the employee would probably have been summarily dismissed without any procedures and probably still failed to win his case. On the other hand, if I had exercised summary dismissal, I would have been wrong because the circumstances were insufficiently extreme, especially in a large organisation with room to move people out of harm's way. The result would probably have been a recommendation for reinstatement and British Rail (and therefore the taxpayer) paying compensation in lieu of re-employment.

After seeing everyone off on their way, I go across to the Panel Box. Things are quiet but, on signing the occurrence sheets, I notice that an engineering possession has been accepted back to traffic status from a different 'person in charge' from the one who took it. The surrender of the possession should not have been accepted without suitable relief arrangements having been recorded. On investigation, signalling inspector Bill Mardon finds that the top-class and reliable signalman who gave permission for the possession had inadvertently written down the wrong name- a genuine, if important, slip of the pen. That does not excuse the error of the similarly reliable signalman who accepted it back to traffic. Disciplinary 'Forms 1' would have been justified but Bernard Price suggests that letters of warning would suffice and I accept his judgement. *I might not have done so had it been an actual unrecorded change of personnel rather than the wrong name having been written down.*

We hold the local management meeting and discuss coverage of the forthcoming new timetable and the steam specials in June. The new budget position that had looked worrying last time has self rectified because the inexperienced budget clerk had not spread an item to best effect and left it in one lump sum to be regained in the last accounting period of the budget year.

I catch the 16.47 to Dawlish, 5min late following the late-running 14.15 from Paddington, then drive Linda to Torre before undertaking some out-of-hours visits. First on the list, in view of this morning's events, is Torquay travel centre where the atmosphere is in marked contrast to the unseasonably-hot weather. Next is Paignton where I can talk to booking clerk Brian Platt and platform staff chargeman Putt and Steve Drew. Young former YTS trainee Ian Rosewell, who has been helping keep the boxes open, is in Paignton North box, about to be displaced by closure but not unhappy at being accommodated on St. David's platform.

Moving on to Newton Abbot, supervisor Bob Johnson is the 'responsible officer' for pilot working on and off the branch during re-signalling disconnections. *The railway would have been closed in such circumstances nowadays of course.* A 'check' signalman is on duty to keep an eye on events as all track circuits have been disconnected. Newton Abbot West Jct is exempted from full train booking when only one man is on duty so I ask for the register to be re-instated with the check signalman being available to help, as an extra precaution. I phone operations manager Bernard Price to let him know.

Half a mile down the line Bob Baker is clipping points under instruction from the box so I wander down to have a word with him for around 15min before picking up Linda from Torre at 20.45.

Tuesday 28th April 1987

After driving into Exeter, I catch the 08.11 to Salisbury for the line of route performance group meeting. Alf Trapnell is driving and delay is just 1min at Salisbury. The meeting is relatively routine but extended by the arrival of Swindon operations officer Ken Shingleton who has a special interest in events having been born and brought up at Milborne Port. The punctuality figures at Exeter two weeks ago showed 98% within 5min; one substantially late train in five days and something to show for our inter-departmental efforts. *Pity we could not achieve this consistently though.*

I return on the 11.10 from Waterloo which is 3min late at Exeter St. David's. The Dawlish Rail Action Group wants to know if they can hand me a petition on my way to work on Thursday with press in attendance. I say 'certainly not'. They can come to my office and do it properly. At 16.00 it is the railway pensioners' party in central Exeter with over 200 present again and following the usual formula of reminiscences and a meal served by volunteers from active staff and 'partners', including Linda. *Linda says one of the reasons she went was to improve my image – and 'because they were lovely people'.* We get home at 19.30.

Wednesday 29th April 1987

There are track circuit failures at Starcross so we are 8min late this morning, with both the Hind and the Newcastle 15min late. I catch the Newcastle which makes up 10min to Bristol. It is an exhausting journey accompanied by the 'consultant' doing his Phd on the relationship between sector managers and area managers, covering the same ground as before.

We are holding informal talks between personnel manager David Thear and NUR and ASLEF over removing or reducing the need for conducting Dart Valley Trains that use the main line at Totnes. We have a 30min discussion and there is no movement on the unions' side but David says seeds have been sown. I stay for a discussion concerning what could be done at the 'double driver over 100mph' points such as Bath if no second driver is available. Management is starting to try to wriggle out of what it considers to be a restrictive practice and not a safety issue. ASLEF treats it as a safety matter but we think of it more as employment protection. *One might argue that Southall might have been prevented if the unions had maintained this arrangement in the long term but the Southall circumstances were avoidable in other ways.* Management feels it is reasonable for the train to go forward at 100mph if a second driver is unavailable but the ASLEF representatives insist that the existing agreement says two drivers are necessary where trains are 'scheduled' to exceed 100mph, as they would remain even if actually running at only 100mph. *Perhaps a good example of a hidebound nationalised industry.*

I return to Exeter on the 12.30, riding with Exeter Jack Davy in the cab of No. 50012 'Benbow' on the Liverpool-Plymouth. We are 9min late but cannot make much over 90mph with 'load twelve' on the level. Two minutes are made up by the loco to Taunton, plus 1min recovery time, but there is a 40mph tsr at Wellington near the foot of the 1-in-80mph climb to Whiteball. Jack obviously uses full power plus the booster but speed is down to 30mph at the tunnel. Still, we make up another minute to Exeter with the aid of 3min recovery time.

Alan Bell comes in to discuss a disciplinary hearing for a driver charged with being absent from duty- the one who was been on jury service for a fortnight and was released early. He thought that meant he was not required to attend work for his remaining 'jury' days. John Beer comes in. He has accepted an invitation to the opening of the Riviera Centre at Torquay but it is an evening dress event and he wants to know if B.R. will pay for his suit hire. I think not, mainly because I have accepted only one such invitation, the Exeter Mayor's Banquet for a railway mayor, which was a direct requirement of my job and I did not put suit hire on my expenses.

An Express and Echo correspondent asks 30min of questions about a TUCC report for tomorrow's paper and I discover today's example of nonsense from Regional Railways. Swindon-based route manage David Mather has unilaterally withdrawn his support for our cheap Friday night Barnstaple shopper ticket for no stated reason and is not available to discuss it. It is a perfect illustration of filling spare capacity with no abstraction. One might argue people might do their shopping more cheaply by waiting until Friday evening instead of travelling at a higher price during the day but that is a rather far-fetched possibility.

Thursday 30th April 1987

After dropping off our car for servicing in Teignmouth, I catch the 07.02 which is punctual with No. 50044 'Exeter' in charge. At 09.00 the management team gathers to watch a video about how to conduct appraisals and the spirit in which they should be received. *It strikes me now as propaganda and an example of how there was money for all kinds of projects despite pressure on the Areas to razor costs, many of which have since been written back in – for instance the 2016 expense of Exeter St. David's platform staffing must be double that of 1987 at constant prices, although traffic volume has increased since then of course.*

Don Horseman arrives at 10.00 to perform the passenger audit. We discuss connectional margins, a list of delays, follow up a few control log items and carriage cleaning. There is little if any criticism.

Between 12.00 and 14.00 I make inroads on the paperwork. The Exeter Express and Echo arrives, with a reasonably fair account of yesterday's interview, then Bernard Apps comes to discuss the details for the merchandising of the prints I have agreed to help market via booking offices.

We finish just in time for the long service awards which include ones for Ivor Stephen and Pat Crook from Barnstaple, Newton Abbot signalman Derek Aggett who transfers to the panel box on Monday, Ted Studley from Tiverton Parkway and Ted Davey from the platform at St. David's. It is a light-hearted affair and finishes with photographs. It ends in time for me to catch the 15.26 to Teignmouth, ½min late, where I talk to senior railman Les Comer about painting out some graffiti in the booking hall and ensure all is ready for the bus substitution at the weekend for Newton Abbot resignalling. I pick up the car from the garage and have a welcome 16.15 finish, discovering that I am on the front page of the local paper over the presentation of the petition arranged for next Tuesday.

Friday 1st May 1987

Linda is called out to lecture English as a Foreign Language at South Devon Technical College so I have to stay behind to look after a decorator, catching the 10.06, retimed 10.11. I am intending to spend most of the day on paperwork and checking the resignalling arrangements are in place but the day slips away after making phone calls and talking to Bernard Price and Ken Boobyer. The 17.25 has No. 47540 at the head making a record run from Starcross to Dawlish Warren. There is still a large pile of correspondence to fit in this weekend around visits to the resignalling.

Saturday 2nd May 1987

Newton Abbot resignalling weekend. Trains are terminating at Teignmouth on the down and Totnes on the up. *Even the simplest relaying at the time of writing sees no trains at all from Exeter to Plymouth.* On arrival at Teignmouth at 09.30 I discover there has been some unhelpful late running from Plymouth that has disrupted a few of the plans. There are windows in the possession to run a few of the busier up trains in the morning and down trains in the evening —*despite there being no signals to speak of.* In the middle of the day, we have to pass the 10.50 Paddington with thirteen coaches through to Penzance.

It turns out there has been a points' failure at Plymouth and track circuit problems at Marley so the 10.11 turns up at 10.50 with a stopper behind it. On the down, an HST is terminating at Teignmouth to form the 11.03 to Paddington as the Cornish Riviera and another is coming down to go back as the 11.10 to Manchester, getting away 11 and 16min late respectively.

I drive to Totnes to visit the box. Colin Harmes is in charge of the station, displaying his usual energy. As I arrive at 11.59, the 11.49 arrival from the west (Class 50-hauled Brighton set composed of Network South East Mark 1s) has been run round, propelled towards Dainton and is running back through the up main before setting back into the down platform. Ernie Underhill is supervising operations from the box so I have a heart-to-heart conversation with him. He is still undecided whether to take the Exeter job as he thinks it might be beyond him but I feel it is just a matter of self confidence rather than ability. *I always found Ernie a mild-mannered individual who did jobs quietly and it was typical that he should doubt his own capabilities, in marked contrast to those who had self-confidence and were blind to their deficiencies.*

Five bus-loads of passengers arrive for the train, with No. 50008 'Thunderer' on the 12.25 which gets away 13min late. News from Teignmouth is that the 13-coach 10.50 has arrived full and standing but has suffered a 10min delay while the points are being clipped and scotched at Newton Abbot, so that is a black mark. I drive back to Newton Abbot to check on what is happening then go home for lunch and the Rugby League Cup Final.

I set off again at 17.15 for Teignmouth. Bernard Price is preparing to go home and, in contrast to this morning, operations are working smoothly. I decide to give Totnes a miss and visit Newton Abbot East box instead. They are well-prepared for the 15.45 from Paddington which is the first train to run through the gap in evening engineering possessions. I then transfer to the West Box which is already in an advanced state of demolition with signalling being performed in a small temporary structure. There is some late running coming towards us but events are going well.

The second train through the gap is No. 47662 on the Newcastle, booked to terminate at Exeter and come forward to Newton as a stopper. Exeter driver Norman Helliwell, formerly at Huddersfield and Leeds, drops his window to remark how well Halifax performed in the Final this afternoon. I look in at Teignmouth where Ray Thorn and Wally Pipe are getting ready to go home so I decide to do likewise, getting in at 20.00 and doing some paperwork until 22.15, with three large bundles still to tackle. All covered by the basic salary payment of course - no unsocial hours, overtime or on call additions.

Photo: The sad sight of Newton Abbot West Jct signal box in the last throes of its existence.
Credit: R. W. Penny

Conclusion

It is fitting that the first year's account should conclude with the transition from manual signalling at the historic old boxes at Newton Abbot which had seen such long service through the thirties, the war, busy 1950s summer Saturdays, 1960s rationalisation and now investment for a new era. As for the area manager, he was conducting his usual battle between controlling operations, finance and keeping headquarters at bay. However, on reflection, the culprits did not usually include operational headquarters where there was generally support as exemplified with the train planning and operation this weekend and the absence of external interference to getting the job done.

By the same author:

Fassifern. *A novel simultaneously set in Jacobite and Victorian times. The duplicity experienced in the Second Jacobite Rebellion still has repercussions for those on board a Highland Railway ship that is captured over two hundred years later.*

IMAGES OF Exeter St. David's: 1st and 2nd MAY 1987

Photo: Two Tyseley sets having arrived at Exeter St. David's with a special from the Midlands
Credit: D. W. V. Hunt

Photo: Arriving at Exeter early to avoid the engineering work. Nos. 37175 and 37697 wait the road into Riverside Yard with the St. Blazey-Cliffe Vale china clay train on 1st May 1987
Credit: C. M. Parsons, D. H. Mitchell Collection

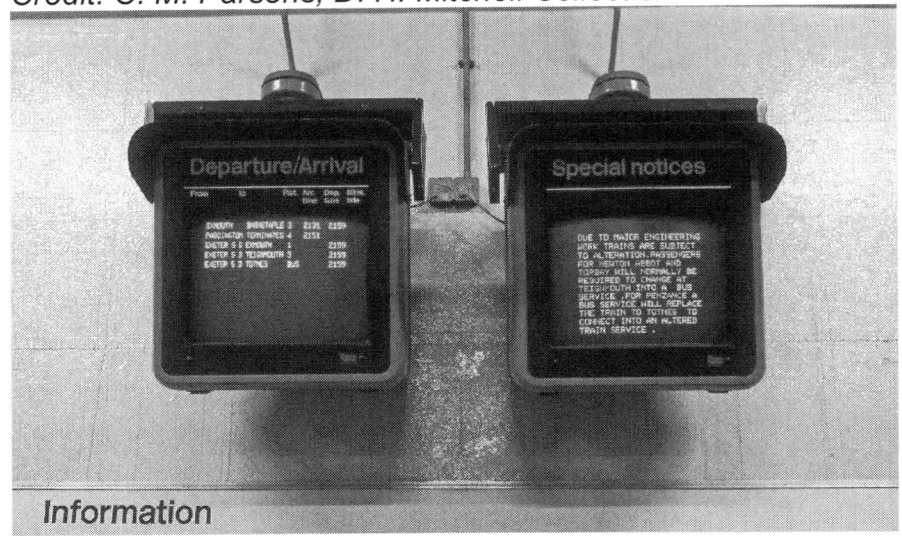

Information

Photos:
 Above. Four simultaneous departures advertised in the special working – three 'Skippers' and one rail replacement bus. Credit: D. W. V.Hunt

Below. The 21.59 to Barnstaple and Paignton on the left and the 21.59 to Exmouth on the right.
Credit: D. W. V.Hunt

Appendix 1: Lines of and around the Exeter Area of British Rail 1986-1990

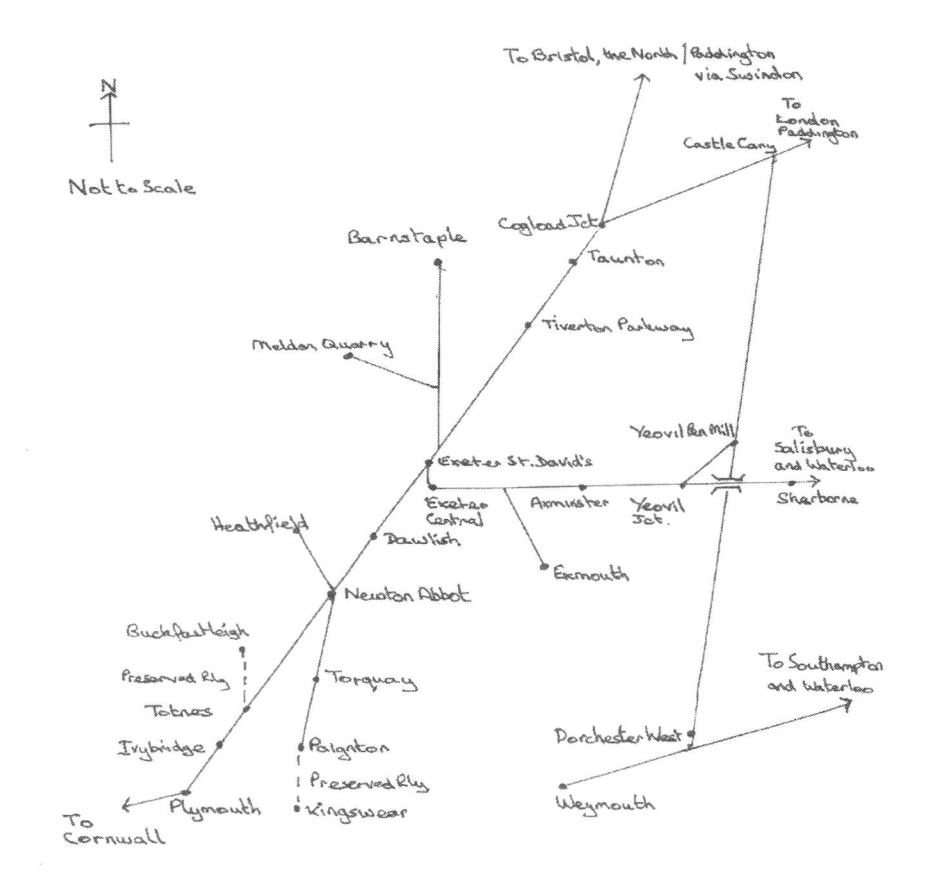

Printed in Great Britain
by Amazon